INSIDERS' GUIDE® TO THE
OREGON COAST

Help Us Keep This Guide Up to Date

Every effort has been made by the authors and editors to make this guide as accurate and useful as possible. However, many things can change after a guide is published—establishments close, phone numbers change, hiking trails are rerouted, facilities come under new management, etc.

We would love to hear from you concerning your experiences with this guide and how you feel it could be made better and be kept up to date. While we may not be able to respond to all comments and suggestions, we'll take them to heart and we'll also make certain to share them with the authors. Please send your comments and suggestions to the following address:

The Globe Pequot Press
Reader Response/Editorial Department
P.O. Box 480
Guilford, CT 06437

Or you may e-mail us at:

editorial@GlobePequot.com

Thanks for your input, and happy travels!

INSIDERS' GUIDE® SERIES

Insiders' Guide® to the Oregon Coast

SECOND EDITION

Lizann Dunegan, Rachel Dresbeck, and Dave Johnson

Guilford, Connecticut

An imprint of The Globe Pequot Press

The prices and rates in this guidebook were confirmed at press time. We recommend, however, that you call establishments before traveling to obtain current information.

Cover photo by Mark Windom, Index Stock; back cover photos © 2003 www.clipart.com
Maps created by XNR Productions Inc. © The Globe Pequot Press

ISSN 1545-1402
ISBN 0-7627-2843-4

Manufactured in the United States of America
Second Edition/Second Printing

Contents

Acknowledgments xxi

How to Use This Book 1

Area Overview 3

History of the Oregon Coast 12

Getting Here, Getting Around 20

Hotels and Motels 25

Bed-and-Breakfast Inns 40

Camping 62

Restaurants 72

Nightlife 84

Shopping 91

Attractions 105

The Arts 120

Kidstuff 137

Annual Events and Festivals 147

The Great Outdoors 154

Sports and Activities 180

Golf 207

Day Trips 214

Relocation 226

Media 256

Index 264

About the Authors 282

Directory of Maps

North Coast vii

Central Coast viii

South Coast ix

Astoria x

Gearhart and Seaside xi

Cannon Beach xii

Tillamook xiii

Lincoln City xiv

Newport xv

Florence xvi

Coos Bay xvii

Bandon xviii

Brookings xix

NORTH COAST

CENTRAL COAST

SOUTH COAST

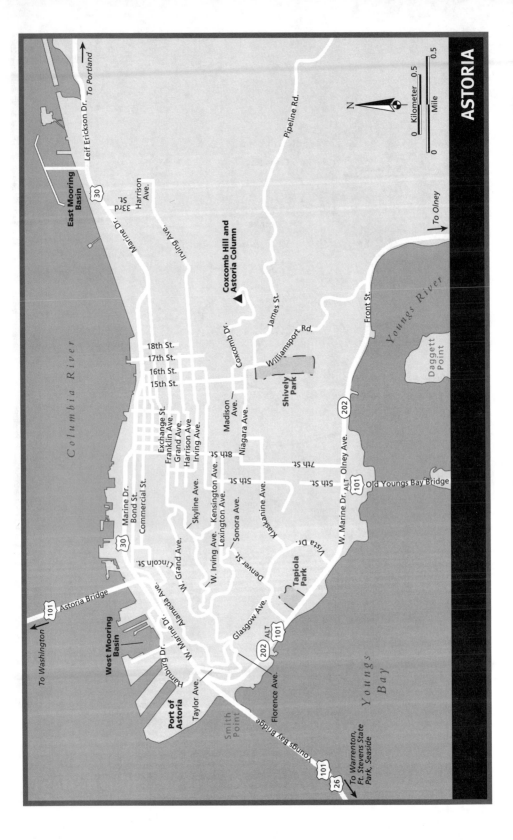

ASTORIA

N

0 Kilometer 0.5
0 Mile 0.5

Columbia River

To Washington
101 Astoria Bridge

To Portland
Leif Erickson Dr.

East Mooring Basin

30

Harrison Ave.

Irving Ave.

Marine Dr.

33rd St.

West Mooring Basin

Port of Astoria

30

Marine Dr.
Bond St.
Commercial St.

Lincoln St.

W. Grand Ave.

Skyline Ave.

W. Irving Ave.
Kensington Ave.
Lexington Ave.

Sonora Ave.

Denver St.

Hamburg Dr.

W. Marine Dr.
Alameda Ave.

Taylor Ave.

Smith Point

Youngs Bay Bridge

To Warrenton,
Ft. Stevens State
Park, Seaside

26

101

Glasgow Ave.

Florence Ave.

202 ALT
101

Tapiola Park

Vista Dr.

Kikanine Ave.

W. Marine Dr. ALT

Olney Ave.

7th St.

5th St.

8th St.

4th St.

Niagara Ave.

Madison Ave.

Exchange St.
Franklin Ave.
Grand Ave.
Harrison Ave.
Irving Ave.

18th St.
17th St.
16th St.
15th St.

Coxcomb Dr.

Coxcomb Hill and Astoria Column

James St.

Williamsport Rd.

Shively Park

Pipeline Rd.

202

Front St.

Youngs River

Daggett Point

To Olney

Old Youngs Bay Bridge
101

Youngs Bay

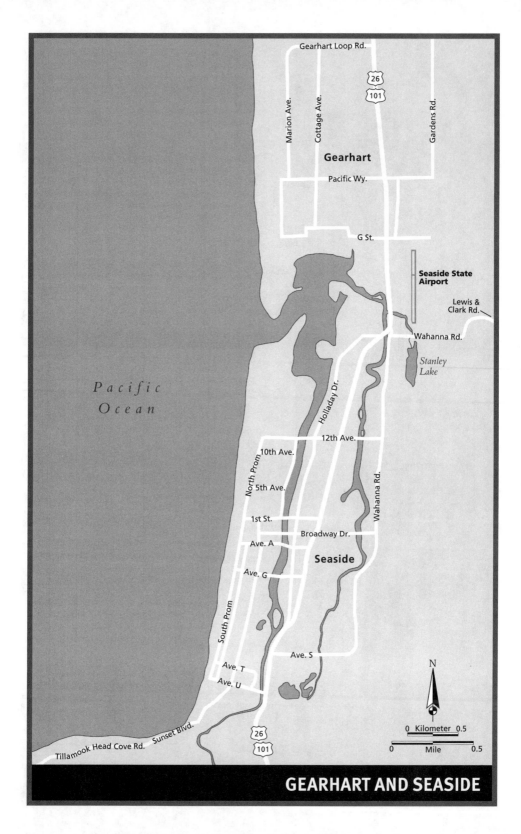

Gearhart Loop Rd.

26
101

Gardens Rd.

Marion Ave.

Cottage Ave.

Gearhart

Pacific Wy.

G St.

Seaside State Airport

Lewis & Clark Rd.

Wahanna Rd.

Stanley Lake

Pacific Ocean

Holladay Dr.

12th Ave.

10th Ave.

North Prom

5th Ave.

Wahanna Rd.

1st St.

Broadway Dr.

Ave. A

Seaside

Ave. G

South Prom

Ave. S

N

Ave. T

Ave. U

0   Kilometer   0.5

Sunset Blvd.

0   0.5
     Mile

Tillamook Head Cove Rd.

26
101

GEARHART AND SEASIDE

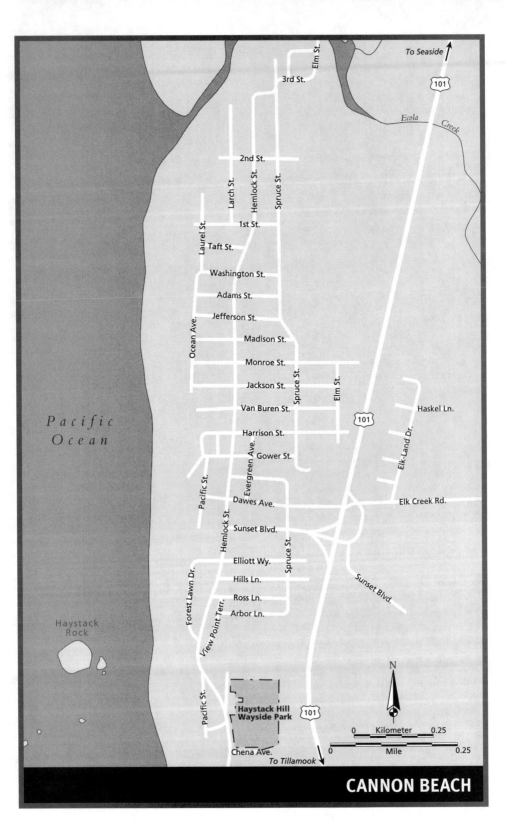

To Seaside

{101}

Ecola Creek

3rd St.

Elm St.

2nd St.

Larch St.

Hemlock St.

Spruce St.

1st St.

Laurel St.

Taft St.

Washington St.

Adams St.

Jefferson St.

Ocean Ave.

Madison St.

Monroe St.

Spruce St.

Jackson St.

Elm St.

Pacific
Ocean

Van Buren St.

Harrison St.

Haskel Ln.

Elk-Land Dr.

Evergreen Ave.

Gower St.

{101}

Pacific St.

Dawes Ave.

Elk Creek Rd.

Hemlock St.

Sunset Blvd.

Spruce St.

Elliott Wy.

Sunset Blvd.

Forest Lawn Dr.

Hills Ln.

Ross Ln.

Arbor Ln.

Haystack
Rock

View Point Terr.

N

Pacific St.

Haystack Hill
Wayside Park

{101}

Kilometer
0   0.25

Mile
0   0.25

Chena Ave.

To Tillamook

CANNON BEACH

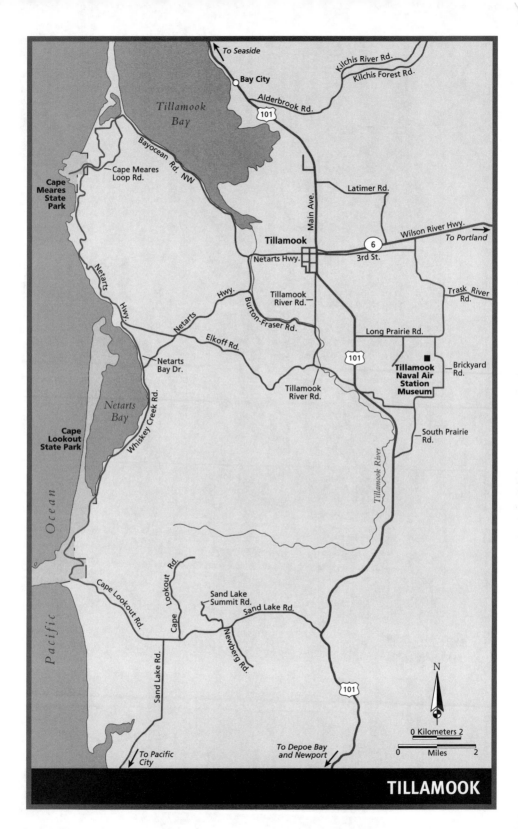

To Seaside

Kilchis River Rd.
Kilchis Forest Rd.

Bay City

Alderbrook Rd.

101

Tillamook Bay

Bayocean Rd. NW

Cape Meares Loop Rd.

Cape Meares State Park

Latimer Rd.

Main Ave.

Wilson River Hwy.
To Portland

Tillamook

6

3rd St.

Netarts Hwy.

Netarts Hwy.

Trask River Rd.

Hwy.

Tillamook River Rd.

Burton-Fraser Rd.

Netarts

Long Prairie Rd.

101

Elkoff Rd.

Netarts Bay Dr.

Tillamook Naval Air Station Museum

Brickyard Rd.

Tillamook River Rd.

South Prairie Rd.

Netarts Bay

Cape Lookout State Park

Whiskey Creek Rd.

Tillamook River

Ocean

Lookout Rd.

Sand Lake Summit Rd.

Sand Lake Rd.

Cape Lookout Rd.

Cape

Newberg Rd.

Pacific

Sand Lake Rd.

101

N

To Pacific City

To Depoe Bay and Newport

0 Kilometers 2

0 Miles 2

TILLAMOOK

FLORENCE

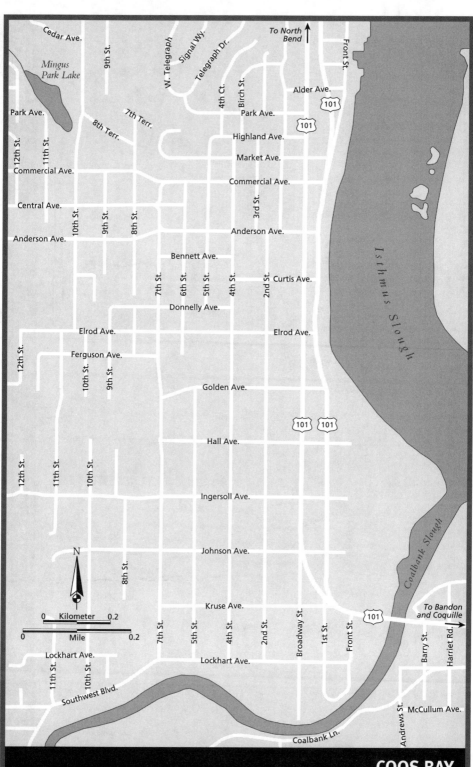

COOS BAY

BANDON

Coquille River

Boat Basin

Ferry Creek

Gross Creek

Riverside Dr.

To Coos Bay

101

To Port Orford
and Gold Beach

101

Jetty Rd.

Ocean Dr.

Streets (top section):
1st St.
Division St.
1st St.
Caroline St.
2nd St.
3rd St.
4th St.
5th St.
6th St.
9th St.
10th St.
11th St.
12th St.

Avenues (top section):
Harlem Ave.
June Ave.
Indiana Ave.
Harlem Ave.
Grand Ave.
Fillmore Ave.
Elmira Ave.
Delaware Ave.
Chicago Ave.
Baltimore Ave.
Alabama Ave.
Oregon Ave.
Allegheny Ave.
June Ave.

Streets (lower section):
1st St.
2nd St.
3rd St.
4th St.
8th St.
9th St.
7th St.
8th St.
9th St.
8th Ct.
9th St.
10th St.
11th St.
12th St.
1st St.
2nd St.

Avenues (lower section):
Chicago Ave.
Baltimore Ave.
Alabama Ave.
Bandon Ave.
Cleveland Ave.
Douglas Ave.
Edison Ave.
Franklin Ave.
Garfield Ave.
Bluff Ave.
Harrison Ave.
Franklin Ave.
Harrison Ave.
Jackson Ave.

N

Kilometer   0   0.2   0.2
Mile   0   0.2

BROOKINGS

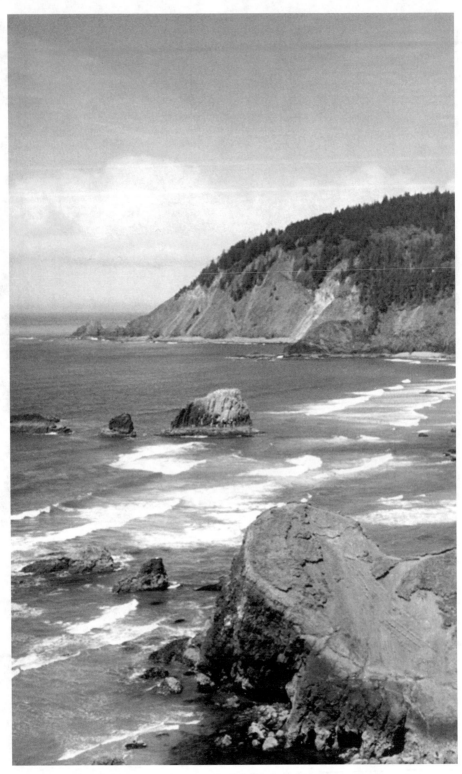

The rugged beauty of Ecola State Park is a popular spot for photographers. PHOTO: LIZANN DUNEGAN

Acknowledgments

The pleasure of writing is never more apparent than when you have the opportunity to talk with people who love where they live and are enthusiastic to share their experiences and knowledge. In my research for this book, I talked to hundreds of Insiders who were happy to spend time with me and tell me about their own unique part of the Oregon Coast. I'd like to especially thank Guy Ditorrici, Director of the Central Oregon Coast Association, for adding me to his distribution list and for helping me to get in touch with all of the chambers of commerce along the Oregon Coast. I would also like to express my appreciation to the staff at the chambers of commerce and visitor centers in each coastal community who took the time to talk with me and to send me research material. I'd also like to thank Karen Runkel of the Oregon Tourism Commission who was instrumental in sending me information about the Oregon Coast. She always answered my questions and was willing to provide me with materials I needed under tight deadlines.

I want to thank my partner Ken Skeen who was always there to support me and give me advice when I was working under tight deadlines and burning the midnight oil at my computer. He has always supported me in all my writing endeavors and is always happy to accompany me on research trips. Special thanks also to my family and friends who put up with my frequent absences from social activities as I stayed at home holed up in my office or was out of town on research trips.

In researching and writing this book, I have been very fortunate to get a closer look at the Oregon Coast—its scenic beaches, its forests and mountains, and its diverse communities and friendly people. Thank you for selecting the *Insiders' Guide to the Oregon Coast*. It is my sincere wish that as you read and use this book you, too, will enjoy its scenic beauty, diverse communities, and extraordinary people.

—Lizann Dunegan

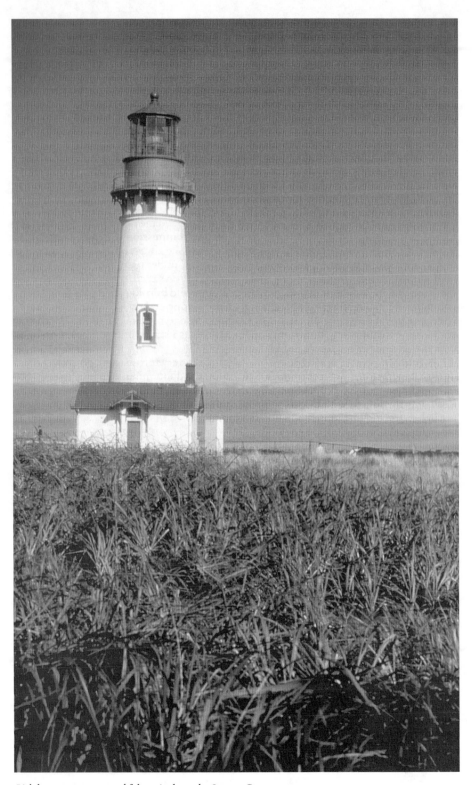

Lighthouses are ever-watchful sentinels on the Oregon Coast. PHOTO: LIZANN DUNEGAN

How to Use This Book

The Oregon Coast, like all shorelines, is a place defined by change. The beach never looks the same from one day to the next. The sands shift and scatter; driftwood sets sail to explore new coves; the tide brings new treasures and wreckage twice each day, and then takes them away again. The Coast is thrilling because it is beautiful and fruitful and barren and deadly. Modern existence, which is all abstraction and hurry, presents us with few chances to behold the course of life in its entirety, but here we see it every day. The forces of change work constantly everywhere, but here we see them hourly.

In such a landscape it is useful to have a companion who is familiar with the terrain, someone who can show you where to go, what to do, and what is different about the shoreline of Oregon. This book is designed to help you navigate the Oregon Coast so you can see for yourself what all the fuss is about.

This guide is organized both thematically and geographically in order to help you get the most out of your visit. In the thematic chapters, we explain general information about activities of interest for visitors and locals alike. We'll tell you about the pleasures of nature and of civilization, the beaches and the golf courses, the fishing and the festivals. We'll also tell you about what to expect if you decide to move to the Oregon Coast, how to find the radio station that carries what you want to hear, and short trips you can take to sample the pleasures of inland Oregon. Most of the information within each chapter follows a north-to-south pattern.

The first three chapters—Area Overview, History of the Oregon Coast, and Getting Here, Getting Around—are designed to help you get to the Coast and to orient you to the basic layout of this long, narrow region and the means of negotiating it. These chapters will let you know what to expect in terms of road conditions and weather, geography and industry.

Rugged, rocky shoreline along the Central Oregon Coast. PHOTO: LIZANN DUNEGAN

When you want to know how, or at least where, to spend you nights, the next three chapters on hotels and motels, bed-and-breakfasts, and camping will be useful. Ideas on where to eat, go out on the town, and shop are listed in the next three chapters.

The next several chapters feature the stimuli for most visits to the Oregon Coast—its beauty and all the industry and recreation that has sprung up because of it. These are the chapters to read when you want to know how to spend your days on the Coast; you'll find detailed listings on kid-friendly destinations, annual events and festivals, art galleries and theaters, must-see attractions, parks to visit, and detailed listings on a wealth of activities you can participate in.

The final three chapters return to a thematic organization—they cover day trips, relocation, and media. Just over the mountains a variety of activities beckon the adventuresome, from cave exploration and winetasting to big-city shopping in Portland. The Day Trips chapter tells you how to get there. And if, upon coming back, you decide that you never want to leave the Coast again (it has been known to happen), the next chapter, Relocation, will tell you how to find a place to settle to suit your manner of living. And the final chapter, Media, will give relocators and anyone else the news about the news.

Naturally, we think of our book as only a place to start, ever bearing in mind that the forces of change that work on the shoreline also apply to businesses, attractions, recreation, and highways. Let us know if you find changes that ought to be reported in future editions. All true Insiders explore for themselves. If, as you travel, you find you have something to tell us, you can write us at The Globe Pequot Press, Reader Response/Editorial Department, P.O. Box 480, Guilford, CT 06437, or e-mail us at editorial@Globe Pequot.com.

Area Overview

The gorgeous Oregon Coast is a mix of basalt headlands, more than a dozen rivers flowing to the Pacific, a number of estuarine sanctuaries, and some of the world's largest continuous sand dunes, backed by a cordillera of low-slung mountains that rose to heights of 2,000 to 5,500 feet above sea level between 20 and 50 million years ago.

About 25 million years ago, the Oregon Coast began to rise from the sea as sediment deposit, and ever since that geologic action, the Pacific Ocean floor has been sliding under the shoreline, causing it to rise a minute amount every year. Every 300 to 400 years a major earthquake along with a tsunami, or huge tidal wave, strikes the Oregon Coast, further shaping its landscape. The last recorded quake of this magnitude was in the early 1700s, but since that cataclysm there was a 10-foot wave that smashed into the Oregon Coast on March 27 and 28, 1964, as a result of an earthquake in Alaska.

In this extraordinary region, roughly equidistant from the equator and the North Pole, the weather is typified by wet winters and reasonably dry summers with mild temperatures year-round.

One recent meteorological event uncovered a few marvels on the Oregon Coast. In 1998, winter storms churned up sturdy tidal activity that abraded roughly 10 feet of sand from Moolack Beach near Newport, revealing semipetrified stumps and root systems of a 4,000-year-old forest. The surprise surfacing of these remnants of ancient trees was not only a treat for geologists but also a telling metaphor for fans of the Beaver State's 362-mile stretch of sand dunes, headlands, beaches, fishing villages, bays, streams, and inlets.

For visitors to the Oregon Coast, there is always more to discover: adventures just around the next windswept promontory, intriguing salty critters lurking in tide pools, or tasty hot clam chowder awaiting worn-out, hungry beachcombers. Travelers can leisurely cruise down U.S. Highway 101 or use Interstate 5 and one of nine routes over the coastal range to get to specific destinations. They can find that slice of shoreline just right for kiteflying or a take a weeklong respite at one of the state's many coastal campgrounds; they can tour the haunted lighthouses at Tillamook, Heceta Head, or Yaquina Bay; or watch from a storm-thrashed bluff near Bandon as gray whales head home to Alaska.

Thanks to Oregon governor Oswald West, who declared the state's beaches public property in 1913 as a way of designating the beaches and headlands as transportation routes, and a legislature that confirmed that decision in the 1960s, the Oregon coastline is not wall-to-wall condos and posh resorts reserved for Club Med types. There are plenty of amenities, yet the abundance of salt air, sand dunes, and not-so-gentle breezes retain the area's wildness.

To introduce you to this linear wonder of a tourist destination for all ages and income brackets, here's an introductory profile that will help you decide where to go and what to do, as well as deliver some history and cultural clues. We'll start a verbal motorcade at the Astoria Bridge across the Columbia River from Washington and meander down U.S. 101 past some incredible viewpoints, along sinuous stretches of shops, restaurants, museums, and novelty spots to Brookings at the gateway to California.

Astoria

Completed in 1966, Astoria Bridge, which carries U.S. 101 over the Columbia River, brings you to the west end of the downtown waterfront of one of the oldest American cities west of the Missouri River. Near the newly renovated waterfront, this All-American burg sprawls up high hills with dozens of charming Victorian homes, bed-and-breakfasts, and hotels.

But don't expect to find the locals overly sentimental about their town. A popular bumper sticker—"We Ain't Quaint"—expresses their sense of pride and a refusal to get too cute.

Named after fur-trader mogul John Jacob Astor, who claimed the stretch of habitable beach in 1811 with the landing of his vessel, the *Tonquin*, Astoria was the shipping point for Astor's thousands of beaver and otter pelts from the Pacific Northwest. His claim gave the United States a shaky sovereignty over the North Pacific realm. After a territorial squabble that ensued during the War of 1812, the town was temporarily named Fort George under British rule, and then returned to the United States in 1818. It then settled down into serving as a major pioneer destination.

Starting in 1866 as gold miners in Oregon and California eagerly gobbled canned salmon, a surge of salmon fishing and canning at the mouth of the Columbia turned Astoria into Oregon's second-largest city. Using small fishing boats and huge drift nets hauled ashore by teams of horses, Astorians caught, processed, and sold the tasty chinooks to diners worldwide. But that changed after World War II as fishing, lumber, and exports waned. Now, tourism beckons as the newest industry for this cheerful little town that gets more than its share of rain.

Astoria points of interest include the Columbia River Maritime Museum with its maritime artifacts; the Flavel House, a well-preserved mansion built by Oregon's first steamship captain; and the Astoria Column, a tall structure on top of Coxcomb Hill east of town. On the outside of this 125-foot tower modeled on Trajan's Column in Rome is a spiral of graphics celebrating the vivid history of Oregon including the arrival of the Lewis and Clark Expedition in 1805.

Seaside

Seaside, just north of Tillamook Head, is a lively tourist town hosting thousands of visitors from the north Willamette Valley every year, including a traditional migration of college and high school students during spring break. Established in the 1870s as a resort and as a way to sell railroad tickets, Seaside still has lots of fun for everyone. In 1873, Seaside constructed a turn-around officially designated as the end of the Lewis and Clark Trail that remains the symbolic center of Oregon's oldest coastal resort (the explorers journeyed down the coast to seek salt).

Cannon Beach

Cannon Beach, christened after a cannon that washed ashore from a fighting vessel in 1846, is a more sophisticated coastal village with dozens of art galleries on Hemlock Street—a long, thin strip of town tightly pressed between the beach and the cliffs where U.S. 101 sits. You might even miss it if you're not careful, yet few people do. You'll often find Cannon Beach stuffed to the gills with folks and their cars. On a fair-weather weekend, you may not really be "getting away from it all," as it—the traffic jams and the throngs—may have come right along with you. In the warmer seasons, the outdoor cafes and bar patios lend this town a European flavor you can't normally find in Oregon. It's at once rustic, metropolitan, and trendy, and firmly entrenched in small-town America. There are myriad colorful and unusual shops up and down this striking little town, everything from wildly decorated kite shops and galleries to unusual specialty stores and a hopping arts and theater scene. And the vast majority of the buildings here are built in a charming, rustic kind of architecture usually composed of sturdy, dark, and unadorned wood, which obviously is made to take the weather around here.

Cannon Beach is also known for its natural wonders. Haystack Rock—the

Haystack Rock is a local landmark in the community of Cannon Beach. PHOTO: LIZANN DUNEGAN

monolithic sea stack on the beach—is the biggest natural wonder around here, measuring in as the tallest one in the world. At lower tides, the base of it is accessible and parts of this are endlessly fun to climb around or on for viewing the tide pools. You're not allowed to climb on all of it, however, because much of it is a wildlife refuge. Ecola State Park is another notable site along Cannon Beach, as is Indian Beach on the park's north end. Spectacular views of Cannon Beach, Tillamook Head Lighthouse, and a nice mix of cliffs and sandy and rocky beaches create a tempting expedition package. The trails going through Tillamook Head (and which lead to Seaside) begin just above Indian Beach.

According to local legend, a Spanish pirate ship ran aground near Neahkanie Mountain, just south of Cannon Beach, prompting its captain to bury a shipment of gold and beeswax there. For hundreds of years, many people have tried to find it without luck. While chances of finding this hidden wealth are slim, a visual treasure awaits those who venture to the top of the mountain.

Tillamook

A chain of fishing villages and resort communities—Manzanita, Nehalem, Rockaway Beach, and Garibaldi—leads to Tillamook, known for scrumptious cheese and ice cream produced at the Tillamook Cheese Factory and huge blimp hangars used in the 1993 *Teen-Age Mutant Ninja Turtles* movie. The blimp hangars are reportedly the largest wooden buildings in the world.

East of Tillamook, in August 1933, a 290,000-acre forest fire known as The Tillamook Burn wiped out a half a billion feet of timber. Now almost fully reforested, the area is a tribute to tree planting by volunteers.

South of Tillamook and north of Neskowin on U.S. 101, the Three Capes Loop takes travelers on a 35-mile jaunt worth the detour. The first promontory, Cape Meares, has a state park, wildlife refuge, and a contorted spruce called the Octopus Tree. Cape Lookout is just that. Take a 2.5-mile hike out to the far edge of this 500-foot cliff for a spectacular view and an excellent whale-watching perch.

The third cape is Kiwanda, a low, sandy peninsula that is a favorite launch for hang gliders. Below this sandstone escarpment is a beach where fishermen launch dories into the pounding surf.

Neskowin

Back on U.S. 101, the next stop is Neskowin, a pleasant little resort with horseback riding, beachcombing, and, if you're in the mood, a stroll out to Proposal Rock. Two miles south of Neskowin, 1,800-foot Cascade Head offers more ambitious hikers a trek through a rain forest to grassy slopes overlooking a glittering sea.

Lincoln City

Next down the highway is Lincoln City, a long stretch of salty-dog boutiques, each with a flock of ceramic seagulls rivaling plastic flamingos in Florida. A recommended stop: the Otis Cafe on Oregon Highway 18 north of town. This Oregon institution serves outrageous hash browns and molasses bread. Another marvel is the 440-foot D River, listed in the *Guiness Book of World Records* as the world's shortest river.

Depoe Bay

Depoe Bay, a fishing town turned tourist stop, has its own spectacle worth a look—the Spouting Horns—50-foot geysers that shoot through a sea cave at high tide. Along this slice of the Oregon Coast there are also lots of great waysides, beaches, and parks with colorful names like Otter Crest, Cape Foulweather, and Devils Punchbowl.

Newport

After braving brisk northerly winds, gleaning wet sand for agates, and watching sea anemones wave back at you, stop by the Oregon Coast Aquarium in Newport, one of the nation's top ten aquariums. Although the world-famous orca, Keiko, who starred in *Free Willie,* has literally flown the coop (airlifted to Iceland), Newport, a fishing village and resort town on Oregon's Central Coast, still has a lot to offer.

Newport has two distinct districts shaped by its vivid history—a bayfront with working docks, pubs, chowder palaces, and gift shops; and Nye Beach, once a fashionable vacation spot that still charms visitors with nostalgic hotels, cafes, bookshops, and cozy gift emporiums.

It started in the 1890s when the "summer people" began to flock to Newport from the Willamette Valley simmering with stifling heat. The only way to get there in those days was on a train that left Corvallis, Oregon, to traverse the Coast Range to Yaquina City, a roughhewn harbor 5 miles up the Yaquina River from Newport. Families toting rattan picnic baskets and steamer trunks full of woolen bathing suits then boarded ferryboats that transported them down to the bayfront. At this point, some folks would climb aboard wagons that would deliver them to hotels and others hoofed it from the bay to Fall Street, a wood-planked route that descended its muddy way down to the beach. This treacherous avenue was appended in 1893 with more streets between Front Street (for a while the Roosevelt Highway, a precursor to U.S. 101) and the beach.

Finally in awesome sight and surfy splash of the Pacific, the summer people had the option of staying in posh hotel rooms, renting rustic cottages, or pitching tents on designated parcels of flat sand. Local vendors rented these canvas summer homes, cast-iron stoves, pots and pans, and utensils for those who vacationed throughout the summer. Husbands and fathers,

Newport's Yaquina Bay is home to a large commercial fishing fleet. PHOTO: LIZANN DUNEGAN

forest (*wald*) with the English word *port*. Today, Waldport has an interpretive center with a history of its charming old bridge, which was replaced by a streamlined new span.

Yachats

Yachats (that's ya-HOTS), a curve of homes and shops along the base of Cape Perpetua, is a singularly lively town and is worth a stop. Once a Native American reservation, the village evolved into a tourist stop with its first streets paved with shells from the middens left by the Native Americans forced out of their homes. Now, lots of retirees live here, as well as artists and writers seeking sanctuary for their craft. Just south is a drive up to the top of Cape Perpetua for a fantastic view of the ocean and often, particularly December through May, of the gray whales that cavort as they migrate south to Baja and north to Alaska.

The next spectacular view is the lighthouse at Heceta. According to an account in Mike Helms' *Oregon Ghosts and Monsters,* it is inhabited by a ghost named Rue—an elderly lady in pioneer garb who floats a few inches above the floor, screams in the night, and rattles dishes. Some say she is the wife of an early lighthouse keeper whose child died and was buried nearby. There are no tours of Heceta Lighthouse.

Not as spooky, but just as noisy, are the Sea Lion Caves 10 miles north of Florence on U.S. 101, where you can take an elevator down into the caves to observe these sleek beasts lolling on a slick rock while taking a break or raising a resounding ruckus. See the Attractions chapter for more information.

taking advantage of three-day excursion discounts, would work during the week and then join their families on weekends.

Oysterville

Located 1 mile above Yaquina City on the south bank of the Yaquina River, which reaches the sea just south of Newport, is the town site of Oysterville. It was here that a huge cache of these bivalves was discovered in 1861. For many years these oysters were shipped to San Francisco, New York, and other major global cities until they were virtually fished out. Yet, today, the oyster culture is back and doing well.

Waldport

South of this oyster cache, gold miners found lots of gold dust in the beach sand from 1879 to 1880. The town established nearby combined the German word for

Florence

Florence is located south of Yachats and just north of the Oregon Dunes National Recreation Area on U.S. Highway 101. With a population of more than 6,000, the town is a mix of old and new. Commercial buildings and bland malls line U.S. 101 but the real character of Florence can be found in Old Town located along the Siuslaw River. Unique shops, very good seafood restaurants, and coffee houses fill this section of town. If you want to learn more about the history of this area, visit the Siuslaw Pioneer Museum (85294 South Highway 101; 503–997–7884). It provides an inside look at the life of the Siuslaw tribe that lived along the river and contains interesting facts about the area's pioneer past.

Oregon Dunes National Recreation Area

After a wander through Old Town Florence near the mouth of the Siuslaw River, head on to the Oregon Dunes National Recreation Area, the largest ocean-fronted dune area in the world, with 32,150 acres of dunes and just over 38 miles of ocean beachfront. Some of the dunes reach heights of 300 feet. The headquarters for the Oregon Dunes National Recreation Area is located in Reedsport at the north end of town on U.S. 101. Writer Frank Herbert reported that, after a visit to this 47-mile Sahara, he was inspired to pen his classic science fiction novel, *Dune*.

Reedsport

Although Reedsport is trying to encourage tourism, it has a way to go. A good start is the newly designed USDA Forest Service Interpretive Center located across U.S. 101 at its junction with Oregon Highway 38 in North Reedsport. The center focuses on interpreting the geology, ecology, and cultural history of the nearby sand dunes. Four miles west of Reedsport, Winchester Bay harbors the largest sport charter fishing fleet on the Oregon Coast. Twenty miles south of this marina, the highway rises dramatically as the elegant span of McCullough Bridge crosses Coos Bay, the deepest harbor between San Francisco and Puget Sound. It was here that lumber baron Asa Simpson established what would eventually be the largest lumber port in the world. Follow signs to three must-visit sites: Sunset Bay State Park, a protected swimming and picnic spot; Shore Acres State Park, a surprisingly exquisite mix of English and Asian gardens built by Simpson; and rugged Cape Arago State Park, with its wind-bent shore pines and colonies of sea lions.

Coos Bay

Another good hiking opportunity is Millicoma Marsh. As any hiker who has conquered the icy flanks of a glacier to return with the graceful memory of a single mountain lily is quite aware, it is often a modest wonder that makes a journey worth the while. A short distance from Coos Bay is a near-perfect example called Millicoma Marsh.

Located at the south end of Coos Bay (the bay not the timber town), the marsh is the wet tip of a broad peninsula between Isthmus Slough, with its logbooms and cattails, and Coos River, a unassuming stream draining dozen of creeks out of the southern Coast Range. It's also home to

Insiders' Tip

Oregon's beaches owe much of their character to two governors: Oswald West and Tom McCall. Oswald West managed to pass legislation in 1913 that designated the entire wet sand shoreline of the Oregon Coast a public thoroughfare. In 1967, when a motel owner challenged the law, Tom McCall persuaded the legislature to strengthen the law to include the dry sand, too. That's why Oregon's beaches remain unspoiled.

osprey, kites, egrets, herons, ducks, geese, and bashful coots.

A mile-and-a-half hike through their marshy turf takes off from the sports field of Millicoma Middle School, between the scoreboard and a roofed picnic site. A raised trail, often choked into a tight path by blackberry vines, loops out into the marsh past meadows and ponds to the edge of the bay and back to the sports field across a shell midden that was once an outdoor kitchen for local Native Americans.

Not only a stroll for avid bird-watchers, this easily accessible, lightly thronged walk is an excellent opportunity for anyone of any age to spend time in a natural setting. There are sheltered benches and interpretive plaques and, at an obvious intersection, a side trail that continues east to an observation deck. Watch out for banana and chocolate slugs. You don't want to serve up a banana split with your boot.

Down on the northern edge of Oregon's banana belt (Coos Bay to Port Orford), after a windy summer slides into traditionally sloppy September, days actually get warmer, and the sun busts up clouds to command a bright blue sky and the wind gentles down to a sweet breeze.

A jaunt along the Coast before the onslaught of relentlessly overcast days has other advantages: There are fewer folks to elbow through to get to the sites and sounds; RV caravans have dwindled; baggy shorts, dangling Leicas, and pastel flip-flops are in short supply; and scenic-knockout picnic spots are both available and bountiful.

Bandon

Twenty-five miles south of Coos Bay, Bandon sits on the southern bank of the Coquille River. Easily the liveliest spot on the South Coast year-round, Bandon is particularly engaging during its autumnal days when brisk seaside siroccos lighten up for a while.

A historic resort town that survived devastating fires in 1914 and 1936 to emerge phoenixlike with flashy new feathers, Bandon has Old Town, a picturesque boat basin, a famous cheese plant, a cranberry sweet shop, and a historical museum that tells the remarkable tale of this fishing village that was enticing tourists as early as the 1920s.

A jaunt to this charming little burg at the mouth of the Coquille River should start with a visit to the lighthouse on the north jetty. This 47-foot austere Italianate tower no longer beams its warning seaward but remains as Bandon's official icon. A drive through Bullards Beach State Park just north of the bridge across the Coquille leads to the lighthouse. It's open only during summer but worth a visit to wander about its base at any time of year to get a splashy feel for the rough history of timber schooners, stern-wheelers, and fishing boats that challenged the most dangerous bar on the Oregon Coast.

After a vigorous stroll on Bullards Beach or across the river to the sand reaches south of the Coquille (check out Elephant Rock, Face Rock, and a host of sea pinnacles and offshore islands), you can take your fresh hunger down to the docks along First Street. Here, you can rent a crab pot from Bandon Bait and Tackle and catch your own dinner complete with pincers or have the best fish and chips in the county casually served at the Bandon Fish Market. A quick note: Some would argue that the Sea Basket in Charleston edges the market in this regard. Maybe you should conduct your own survey.

After lunch it's fun to walk along the bouncing docks in Bandon's boat basin, where a small fishing fleet sustains a local maritime tradition. Between the docks and a bluff are dozens of crafts and gift shops, chic boutiques, bookstores and a half-dozen robust eateries. Of particular note are the Bandon Card and Gift Shoppe, a rambunctiously visual treat at 265 2nd Street and The Cobbler's Bench in the old Masonic Hall at 110 2nd Street, in which a real cobbler repairs footwear on antique equipment. A renovated Old Town, combined with postcard-perfect beaches nearby, makes Bandon a premier destination.

Oregon's South Coast in autumn is a little-known place and time. The stormy weather of September and most of October eases for a while and honest-to-raingod balmy days bring coastfolk a short break before the gray settles in for the winter. This second summer also offers travelers a chance to savor an off-season, low-key adventure they needn't share with mobs of tourists jamming the salty boulevards.

Langlois to the Elk River

One good bet is the reasonably untrammeled, often stunning terrain of North Curry County. After U.S. 101 leaves Coos County a few miles north of Langlois, there is a shift in the flavor of the territory. It's a bit more mystic, perceptibly more distant from the "Valley" and its throb and clamor of civilized pursuits. The little town of Langlois (Francophiles forget the correct pronunciation—it's Lang-LOYSE) has minimal amenities but a couple of neat antiques stores.

Perhaps of more interest is Floras Creek, a fairy-tale stream tumbling down from the Coast Range. According to folklore and enthused newspaper accounts, a blustery storm in 1893 toppled an oak tree on a Floras Creek farm to reveal an ancient wall that was obviously not the work of indigenous peoples or Europeans. Amateur archeologists and historians ventured a guess that the discovery was a remnant of the Lost City of Quivira sought in vain by the conquistadors. Uh, maybe it's the air down there.

After Floras Creek, the road swoops down into a lowland with a village in the middle aptly called Denmark. A glance to the west to catch a distant view of the Pacific explains why Scandinavian settlers felt at home.

Don't expect a lot of roadside attractions along the stretch between Langlois and Port Orford. You'll not find a single T-shirt or homey painting on a crosscut saw for sale. But there are reasons to turn off U.S. 101. A good choice is the Sixes River, easily recognized by a sign and a grocery store that's been around for awhile. As you start upstream you'll pass the ghostly remains of the town of Sixes. This small town was once the hangout for miners and loggers with a post office, store, blacksmith shop, and hotel. The Sixes River is obviously a hot spot for trout and salmon fisherfolk. As opposed to the Elk and Chetco Rivers, the fish spawning up the Sixes are prized natives, not hatchery stock. The locals celebrate their stream's celebrity status. You'll drive by mailboxes in the shape of a lunging chinook and other domestic pescatory motifs.

For a few miles the Sixes runs wide and gravelly with evidence of old and more recent mining claims seen on ledges and bars. Four miles upriver you'll come to Edson Creek Boat Launch and County Park. This Curry County facility is tucked in a narrow, pleasant meadow along the banks of Edson Creek. Lots of grass and tables with grills make it a great picnic spot.

Eleven miles from U.S. 101, where the north and south forks of the Sixes join, the Bureau of Land Management operates the Sixes River Campground. Twenty-two units are spread out in a forested area with lots of room for campers.

Beyond the forks, the river gets wilder as the road climbs into a bedrock canyon. Unless you are a reckless adventurer with an all-road rig, this is a good place to turn around and head back.

The next turn is another river road up the celebrated Elk River. A designated Wild and Scenic River, the Elk flows into the ocean just south of the Sixes. Seven miles upstream, a fish hatchery open to the public gives stoppers-by a chance to learn how steelhead and salmon are raised for release in local rivers—315,000 fall chinook are planted in the Elk River. Then you'll climb into one of the most scenic river canyons in the Pacific Northwest. Fir and hemlock line the riverbank, cedar and madrone rise along hillsides, and, for a short while, a lovely arbor of white alders frames the road. And down in the green, white, and blue splash and flow, there are gravel bars of speckled granite, carved channels of striated white quartz, moss-thick boulders with bracken, licorice, and maidenhair fern.

Sunshine Bar at 12 miles up, and Butler Bar 3 miles farther, are agreeable little campsites, but the gem in this setting is Laird Lake Campground 10 miles beyond Butler Bar. Not as developed as the other two, Laird Lake has two wood-sorrel-carpeted campsites installed along a jump-across creek.

After a meander up the Elk or Sixes River, it's just about 7 miles south on U.S. 101 to Port Orford, where visitors can enjoy the sight of fishing boats lifted to a dock or lowered into the sea with cranes. Beyond this historic fishing village, Humbug Mountain rises 1,756 feet right out of the ocean! A winding trail leads to the top and a view of this magical seascape. On the route out to Blanco just north of Port Orford there's a right turn that will take you down to the Hughes House, a Victorian home built in 1898 for rancher and county commissioner Patrick Hughes. It's open as a museum from May 1 to September 30, but it's worth a sidetrip for a quick look even if it's closed. While you're down on the coastal flat, reconnect with the Sixes River in a picnic area between the Hughes House and the river's last mile to the sea.

A nighttime tour of the lantern room in the 1870 Cape Blanco Lighthouse offers visitors a chance to climb 67 steps back into history. The guided tour starts in Port Orford where lighthouse buffs are shuttled out to Cape Blanco, a 186-foot headland that is reportedly the most westerly point in the contiguous United States.

Here, at the tip of this rugged promontory, visitors will enter the oldest and highest lighthouse in continuous use in Oregon. Rather than a brisk walk-through, the visit is a two-and-a-half hour program of living history with a costumed tourguide playing the role of the lighthouse keeper and his wife telling stories of local historical context.

The evening visit is available throughout the year unless gusts (ever present even during second summer) start blowing over 70 miles per hour. There's a free daytime tour of the lighthouse that doesn't include a hike up to the lantern room.

After trekking up a couple of rivers and beachcombing along the Coast that Sir Francis Drake dubbed New Albion, it might be time to get a bite or shop a bit in Port Orford or "Port Awford" as the long-time locals say. This seaport offers visitors the historic and, to some, the disconcerting sight of offshore Battle Rock upon which explorers held off attacks by irate Native Americans. Another scene to check out is the dock where fishing boats are lifted or lowered into the sea with cranes. The eateries in this colorful little seaburg have names like The Truculent Oyster, Peg Leg Saloon, and Whale Cove. Grab some rations and grog, matey!

Gold Beach and Brookings

Gold Beach, the next village south of Port Orford, serves as the outfitting center for jet boaters and hikers heading up the Rogue River. Then south of Gold Beach, Brookings is the jumpoff for the Chetco River and the remote, virtually unexplored Kalmiopsis Wilderness. The last good camping spot before the border is Harris Beach State Park just north of Brookings.

History of the Oregon Coast

The history of the Oregon Coast is one of mystery, adventure, discovery, perseverance, intolerance, and economic prosperity. Before we start the parade of gold-hungry buccaneers, courageous explorers, and stalwart pioneers, here's a quick look at the land.

Largely made up of headlands, cliffs of black basaltic rock, long stretches of beach, and towering cones of sand dunes, the coastline was the ending spot of long masses of lava flowing westward from earthquakes and volcanoes. A good example is Tillamook Head, the final point of a 400-long flow of lava coming all the way from Idaho about 15 million years ago.

Since then, erosion and storms have whittled away at the coast, but essentially it's the same as it has been for a million years—a special, wondrous strip where the massive Pacific Ocean meets the final northwest edge of the country.

Pre-European History

Before the European explorers arrived on the Oregon Coast in the mid-16th century, the Native American population numbered roughly 45,000. As with all the aboriginal peoples of North and South America, the Oregon tribes are assumed to have arrived from the far eastern plains of Siberia 8,000 to 10,000 years ago, following game animals as they crossed the frozen Bering Straits.

Their population shrank at the beginning of the 19th century: Smallpox and other diseases, combined with conflicts generated by the incursion of farmers, miners, and other settlers, decimated the tribes. Below we give a quick sketch of tribes that once roamed along the coast.

Salish

The Salish are a large tribal group that occupied a coastal zone stretching from the Strait of Georgia in British Columbia to the Puget Sound area of Washington state. Their territories skirted the proud, ferocious Chinook at the mouth of the Columbia River, but then continued along the coast as far south as the Siletz River in Oregon. The tribe lived in wood-plank houses with intricate wood carvings, including totem poles, and subsisted primarily on fresh, dried, or jerked salmon. Known for its generous ritual of distributing wealth at "potlatches," the Salish held parties at which they celebrated their wealth by giving much of it away.

Tillamook

The Tillamook, Nehalem, and Nestucca, living along the Salmon and Nehalem rivers, were numbered at over 2,000 by Lewis and Clark during their visit in 1805. By 1970, this clan grouping had been reduced to 139.

Siletz

The southernmost Salish tribe once lived on the river that bears its name. There are still a few Siletz on the Siletz Reservation upriver in the rural portion of Lincoln County. The Siletz still sell canned salmon and Native American memorabilia in shops along the Coast.

Alsean/Yakonan/Siuslaw

The Alsean on the Alsea River at present-day Waldport, the Yakonan on the Yaquina River near Newport, the Siuslaw on the Siuslaw River near Florence, and the Lower Umpqua on the lower Umpqua River near Reedsport are all linguistically related river-estuarine tribes. These native hunters and gatherers gleaned shellfish and seined for salmon; hunted seals and elk; and gathered and traded for dentalia shells—a collectively recognized coin of the realm stretching from the far north to mid-California.

It was estimated in 1780 that these tribes numbered 5,000. After the arrival of land-hungry Europeans and the frictions that sparked the hostilities of the 1850s, most of these tribespeople were relocated to the Siletz Reservation on that part known as the Southern or Alsea Reservation. Currently, the combination of these tribal clans, with the exception of the Siuslaw, is the Confederated Siletz Tribe.

In 1916 a small number of surviving Siuslaws joined the Hanis and Miluk Coos to form an extension of the Coos.

Kusan Tribe

Two tribes that coexisted along the coast between the Coos and Coquille Rivers are the Hanis and Kusan. The northern division were the Hanis, or Coos proper, who lived around the bay and river that bear their name. The southern division were the Miluk on the lower Coquille near its estuary. The two tribes, numbering roughly 2,000 in 1780, harvested crabs, clams, and mussels from the sea and journeyed upriver to hunt the animal that is now known as Roosevelt elk.

After being moved to the Yachats agency of the Siletz Reservation and eventually returning to Coos Bay to reclaim their identity, the Coos, now about 300 strong, are currently working toward economic independence via a proposed gambling casino and other projects.

Coquille

This string of clans that for centuries camped along southern Oregon's Coquille River has historically been plagued by hostile neighbors and racist newcomers. Now, vigilant stewards of our diminishing wild forests are concerned that the "Kokwell" won't appropriately care for their ancestral forest.

This tale, a good example of how history has treated these migrants from Siberia, begins when these particular nomads arrived in the 800,000-acre territory fed by the west-flowing river that now bears their name. Here, they lived peacefully as gatherers of an estuarine bounty, as hunters who trapped elk in deep pits in mountain meadows, as fisherfolk who caught slippery salmon in willow weirs and who smoked lamprey eels over alder fires, and as harvesters who dug and toasted white camas bulbs.

To celebrate their harvests, they danced with woodpecker and puffin beaks clacking around their ankles. To spruce up, they plucked whiskers out of their cheeks with clamshells. To supplement their diet in spare times, they spiced their meager meals with skunk cabbage leaves. When someone passed on, they solemnly placed dentalia shells in the mouth of the dead for spending money in the hereafter.

The *Mishi Kwut inetunne* camped along the four forks of the upper Coquille and spoke an Athapascan tongue similar to Navajo and Aztec. Downriver, the Na-So-Mah and other Penutian speakers such as the Miluk or Lower Coos, shared their native voice with the Hopi and Zuni. In time, clans on both the lower and upper river were lumped together as the Coquilles by late-coming, note-taking Euro-Americans.

The tribal families along the Coquille River were first mentioned by Hudson's Bay Company trapper Alexander McLeod, who ambled by in 1826. He concluded that the locals were honest, if canny, traders. The Coquilles then got a taste of Anglo arrogance on July 3, 1828, when explorer Jedediah Smith and his party tore down riverside homes near the mouth of the Coquille, lashing the stolen planks into rafts to cross the river.

After gold was discovered in 1852 at Whiskey Creek, 10 miles north of the Coquille, tension between downriver Coquilles and oft-drunken miners escalated. In January 1854, a gang of 40 miners went .50-caliber ballistic, killing 16 and wounding dozens more. Then a year after this massacre, a few Coquille warriors participated in the 1855–56 Rogue River Indian War, storming out of the upper Coquille to burn cabins and cause retributive mayhem. By 1856, all but a handful of Coquille were either killed off, had intermarried, or traveled a trail of tears to Fort Umpqua or Yaquina Bay.

Those who were left were astonished when Grandmother Rock, a huge pillar jutting up from a bluff overlooking the Pacific near Bandon, was blown up in 1881 and its blue schist debris used to build a jetty, which was completed in 1900. The destruction of this sacred pillar, once used for shamanic ceremonies, was a formidable symbol of the disintegration of the Coquille, but it took an official act on August 13, 1956, to conclude over a century of insults suffered by the tribe.

On that date, the Termination Act, signed by President Eisenhower, announced that the Coquilles and 42 other bands of Native Americans west of the Cascades no longer existed. After a long struggle that lasted into the politically charged '80s, the 600-strong tribe was reinstated in 1989. Part of the agreement was the submission of an economic self-sufficiency plan. The Coquille purchased a huge plywood mill along U.S. 101 and turned it into the Mill Casino, a popular haunt for locals as well as tourists. With timberland returned to the tribe by the Bureau of Land Management, an assisted living facility, and other holdings, the tribe has dramatically bolstered its fiscal health.

Pirates and Explorers

Although many think that the first explorers along the Oregon Coast were Europeans who made the arduous trip around the tip of Tierra del Fuego, there are records of earlier explorations. A fifth-century Chinese journal gives an account of a Buddhist priest's travels to a strange land he called Fu-Sang. The details of Hwui Shan's travelog suggest that he sailed down the west coast of America, and legends among the Native Americans describe boats that might have been classic Chinese junks.

Definitely on record are the adventures of Sir Francis Drake. In 1579, this legendary English explorer and buccaneer sailed his *Golden Hind* up the Pacific coastline past the promontories at Cape Blanco and Cape Arago to be the first European to venture north of California. It is unknown and fiercely debated where he actually set foot. What is known is that he named the region New Albion because of the similarity of the headlands at Cape Blanco to the White Cliffs of Dover in his homeland.

What lured him up the coastline was not only the thrill of discovery but the opportunities to raid the Spanish vessels laden with gold from the looting of the Aztec and Incan territories. After maurauding his way north, Drake decided to search out a passage that would bring him safely east to England. This hope was virtually universal among nations that wanted the riches of the far Orient delivered as quickly as possible to their national coffers. The search for the Northwest Passage would dominate exploration of the North Pacific for centuries. But Drake had challenges, among them the "vile, thicke, and stinking fogges," and was forced to eventually give up his quest and sail west past Asia and Africa and back home to London.

In 1592, in response to the smashing success of the English pirate, the Spanish commissioned Greek captain Juan de Fuca to head north up the coast in search of new claims and more gold. De Fuca returned jubilantly, claiming that he had discovered the Northwest Passage. Although he was as wrong as all the other searchers for the elusive shortcut home, he did get a great stretch of water named after him (the Strait of Juan de Fuca in Washington).

Another Spanish sea captain, Sebastian Viscaino returned from his exploration with the news that the Oregon shoreline was empty of navigable harbors or usable inlets.

But that grim news didn't stop the explorers and seekers of wealth. New players on the scene were the Russian fur traders who ventured across the Bering Strait and down Alaska to northern California in the mid-1700s. Now the natives were bartering with, selling furs to, and pestering the English, Spanish, and Russians, who all claimed the new land for their own. With the high prices paid for fur pelts, there was a frenzy of trade: 200,000 pelts were delivered to China and Europe before the sea otters were virtually eliminated along the Oregon Coast.

In 1776 English Captain James Cook, a hero for his circumnavigation of the globe (1769–71), was appointed commander of an expedition to explore the Northwest coast in search of the Northwest Passage. His motivation was heightened by a promised reward of 20,000 pounds if he discovered that route. Leaving England with two vessels, the *Discovery* and *Resolution*, Cook ventured along the Oregon Coast. The first prominent headland Cook sighted was Cape Foulweather, just north of Yaquina Bay. Reversing his course, he sighted another headland just south of Coos Bay, which he named Cape Gregory, later given the name Cape Arago. Eventually Cook traveled to Hawaii where he was slain by natives.

By 1776, when Americans declared their independence from England, the Spanish had established a permanent settlement at San Francisco Bay. A year earlier, the Spanish sea captains Bruno de Heceta, Juan Perez, and Juan Francisco de la Bodega y Quadra sailed north from San Blas, stopped briefly near the California-Oregon border, and then made it as far north as Vancouver Island. Heceta Head, the scenic headland north of Florence, was named after Heceta.

English Captain John Meares discovered Cape Lookout and Tillamook Bay in 1778, dubbing it "Quicksand Bay." Meares sailed past the Columbia River but failed to identify it as a major river.

In 1788 Robert Gray's ship, *Lady Washington*, sailed up the Oregon Coast anchoring in Tillamook Bay, where he traded and quarreled with local Native Americans. The first known contact with South Coast Indians came three years later in 1791, when Captain James Baker's *Jenny* arrived at Winchester Bay at the mouth of the Umpqua River.

In 1792 English Captain George Vancouver, commanding the warships *Discov-*ery and *Chatham,* sailed up the Northwest coast, claiming all of it for England. On April 24, 1792, he anchored his ships just south of Cape Blanco at present-day Port Orford, naming the spot after a colleague, George, the Earl of Orford. Perhaps the most significant discovery on the part of the British was the crossing of the Columbia River bar by Captain Gray's *Columbia Redivivia* on May 11, 1792. Gray journeyed about 14 miles upriver, planting the U.S. flag and claiming the grand River of the West for the United States.

So it was a high time for adventure, trade, piracy, and discovery along the West Coast. All of this set the stage for the grandest tale of all—the overland trek of the Corps of Discovery led by Meriwether Lewis and William Clark. After visionary President Thomas Jefferson acquired the massive territory west of the Mississippi River in the Louisiana Purchase, he commissioned his young secretary, Lewis, to assemble a team to map out what Jefferson hoped would be a trade route from St. Louis, Missouri, to the Pacific. He was wrong, but the maps drawn, specimens taken, native tribespeople interviewed, and the brave endurance of the Lewis and Clark band made remarkable history. Leaving Missouri in 1803, they journeyed across the northern plains, across the Rocky Mountains, and down the Snake and Columbia Rivers to that day, November 7, 1805, when Clark wrote in his journal: "Great joy in camp we are in View of the Ocian, this great Pacific Octean which we been So long anxious to See. And the roreing or noise made by the waves brakeing on the rockey Shores (as I suppose) may be heard distinctly" Actually, it wasn't really the Pacific but the lower Columbia's estuary. After eight more days of floating westward, they climbed Cape Disappointment to see the sparkling Pacific. The lads wintered near Astoria, hiked down the coast to gather salt and a few chunks of blubber from a beached 100-foot whale, and then, grousing about grey clouds and constant drizzle as do all Pacific Northwesterners, they reversed their journey and headed home to a tumultuous welcome.

One last historic narrative is well known on the southern Oregon Coast—

the Skirmish at Battle Rock. In 1851, Captain William Tichenor decided to establish a seaport in the tranquil cove that is now Port Orford. Tichenor's plan was to construct a headquarters for the shipment of huge masses of gold yet to be gleaned from northwest gold rush sites. He hired a crew to camp on a large rock in the center of the cove, left supplies and a four-pound cannon for defense, and said he would be back in two weeks with more supplies. The 400-foot-long promontory was quickly assaulted, and 17 natives died in the conflict, mostly from cannon fire. The Europeans managed to escape the rock and straggle north to the nearest settlement.

We can only imagine the ghostly shapes of the ancient sailing ships wending up the coast to unknown territory; we can only surmise how it felt to find a "New England," a land rich with furs to take home to Russia, and more riches for the royal court of Spain. But driving past Port Orford on U.S. 101, it's hard to miss Battle Rock, with its sparse growth of wind-battered spruce and fir trees and the echo of that four-pound cannon.

European Settlement

After the close of the buccaneering and exploring era, settlers flocked to the Oregon Coast to search for gold in the black sand of the beaches, to establish commercial fishing plants, to mine for coal and ship lumber down to booming San Francisco, and to begin constructing a chain of resort/destination villages that now dot the Coast. Here are a few short tales of towns settled by those who pioneered the Coast, endured howling winds, thunderous rainstorms, and lonely isolation.

Lakeport

Let's start with a grandiose mistake. At the turn of the 20th century, a group of investors attempted to create a resort town south of Bandon. Their plan was to build a town called Lakeport around a man-made lake fed by local streams. A canal would be dug a few miles to the ocean. Boats would sail up the canal laden with rich tourists

thus creating "The Venus of the West." The lake was dug, a hotel built, and then, as the canal was about to be dug as well, an embarrassed engineer informed the investors that their property was below sea level. So much for the scheme of Lakeport.

Newport's Fashionable Seasons

A brief history of the settling of Newport is a capsule sampling of how villages along the Oregon Coast grew from rough camps into present-day tourist meccas—all without canals that would send the Pacific cascading into their shops, hotels, and restaurants.

Those were stylish days at the beach as Newport turned from the quaint 1800s to the faster-paced 20th century. A remarkable moment captured by local merchant and photographer A. L. Thomas shows a crowd of vacationers and locals in their fashionable best, promenading along the jellyfish-sprinkled plaza beneath the bluffs at Nye Beach. Instead of contemporary down vests and padded parkas, the women wear long dark skirts, white puff-sleeved blouses, and Sunday gone-to-meetin' hats while they hold parasols against the high sun. The men stand about in impeccable bowler hats and three-piece suits. Down closer to the surf, not-so-stiff youngsters cavort in saltwater-soggy, neck-to-ankle swimming togs.

In 1904 Thomas published *Glimpses of the Sea Shore at Newport, Ore.* The selection of photos included his famous shot of "Jumpoff Joe," a huge sandstone arch north of Nye Beach that has since washed away. As these alluring photos and word of Newport's tourist amenities spread throughout the country, more facilities and activities emerged at this booming resort. Along with horse rides north to visit Yaquina Head Lighthouse and meanders to browse curio shops for agate-adorned lamps and shell-speckled crockery, to sample cookies at Polly Anna Bake Shop or taffy at the Cozy Corner Confectionery, there was the inevitable visit to The Natatorium.

"The Nat," as it was fondly nicknamed, was a large wooden building that held a swimming pool of salt water and a dance floor. Built in 1912, this recreational wonder was also the site of a miniature golf course, roller skating, movies, boxing matches, and concerts by those big bands that motored between engagements in snub-nosed busses.

The Nat burned to the ground in 1921, but was quickly rebuilt to once again become the center of the Nye Beach social scene. It was torn down in 1967, and little evidence of The Nat remains—only photos, fond memories, and fragments of its foundation in a vacant lot behind the Yaquina Art Center, once a clothes-changing station for swimmers.

Another long-gone amenity was Dr. Minthorn's Hot Sea Baths, a three-story building just south of The Nat. In the late 1890s and early 1900s, hot seawater was piped into porcelain tubs for folks seeking a soothing way to recuperate from various ailments. A popular feature of this sanitorium was a veranda enclosed in glass where a bather could enjoy the sun and avoid the wind.

The most notable remnant of Nye Beach's heyday is the Sylvia Beach Hotel, a charmingly renovated historic landmark built between 1910 and 1913. Originally named The New Cliffhouse, it became the Hotel Gilmore in 1921 when Peter and Cecile Gilmore traded their chicken ranch for the hostelry. It later fell into disrepair until it was reopened in 1987 by Sally Ford and Goody Cable. The two owners renamed the hotel in honor of Sylvia Beach, who operated the Shakespeare & Co. Bookstore in Paris during the 1920s and '30s. Now a resting and reading retreat for book lovers, it offers 20 guest rooms, all named after and decorated in honor of various scribblers. Lodgers can stay in the Agatha Christie, Robert Louis Stevenson, Jane Austen, or Mark Twain Rooms. Or if one is bold, there's the Edgar Allan Poe Room, a gothic little chamber with an ornament a bit more foreboding than a dangling participle (see the Accommodations chapter).

Seaside

Railroad mogul Ben Holladay built this first coastal tourist mecca, an attraction for tourists since the early 1870s. His key service was a train that ran from Portland to Seaside. Since then, the town has continued to flourish as a tourist haven, particularly during spring break, when thousands of college and high school students come to visit and blow off some steam.

Lily Bulbs

A special industry, the growing and shipping of lily bulbs in the Chetco Valley, took off during World War II when the Japanese bulb growers stopped exporting their products to the United States. Now only 10 farms exist but they produce 95 percent of the Easter lily bulbs for the world market.

Fire Bombs

In World War II, the Japanese also had an influence on the Oregon Coast when their planes dropped incendiary bombs on Coast Range forests—reportedly the first bombs of any sort dropped on the American mainland. The plan was to start huge forest fires, thus distracting the western coastal defenses so that the Japanese could attack. The problem was that the bombs landed in forests soaking wet from constant torrential downpours. The fires were extinguished by this inclement weather.

Hume's Salmon Canneries

Robert D. Hume, deservedly know as the "Salmon King," started the first West Coast salmon-canning plant on the Sacramento River in 1864. He then built another cannery at Astoria and in 1876 started a salmon cannery on the south bank of the Rogue River at Gold Beach. The cannery at Gold Beach turned out three-quarters of a million cans annually between 1880 and 1900.

Bandon

Founded by Irish baron George Bennett, who named it after his home in Ireland, Bandon soon became an important port on the South Coast with exports of lumber, fish, woolen goods, and dairy products.

After the completion of a jetty in 1912, the maritime traffic across the wicked Coquille River Bar was safer and increased dramatically. The town also grew into a rip-snorting resort burg with horseracing, a swimming natatorium, gambling parlors, and a number of dance halls. But a fire in 1914 along the waterfront, and another in 1936 throughout the town caused by the spread of flames by oily grease, made headlines throughout the nation. Now, rebuilt and prospering, Bandon is a popular stopping point for many travelers. The sea stacks and other scenic off-shore rocks, long driftwood-littered beaches, and numerous restaurants and shops have returned this town to the days when it was *the place* to head for to cool off when the hot days of the Willamette Valley became unbearable.

Contemporary Days

In recent years the history of the Oregon Coast has been relatively calm compared to its tempestuous older days but there are a few notable events worth mentioning.

The Bonfire of the Sentries

Portland-based freelance writer and environmental activist Phillip Johnson created an answer to his frustrations with hit-and-miss efforts to protect the Oregon Coast. His vision was an unbroken chain of dedicated guardians keeping watch over the state's shoreline.

In 1992, The Oregon Shores Conservation Coalition (OSCC), founded in 1971 in support of Governor Tom McCall's beach bill, was suffering setbacks due in part to underfunding and not enough help to cover meetings and hearings and crucial circumstances affecting the environmental health of the Coast.

Then, while looking out to sea from a bluff overlooking the Pacific, an idea occurred to Johnson, a history graduate with a degree in medieval European studies. During medieval times, sentinels stood by woodpiles spaced along coastal headlands. If attackers came by sea, the guards would set bonfires to alert the locals. Johnson imagined a similar network of citizen experts, a cadre of Paul Reveres in windbreakers from the Astoria Bridge to the California line—one person taking responsibility for each of Oregon's coastal miles.

He launched his idea in November 1993 with a small grant from the McKenzie River Gathering, a statewide funding organization that provides seed money for projects and programs. The Coast was divided into 311 segments based on accessibility and topography such as river mouths and jutting capes. More than 170 miles are now cared for but more remain. For more information on CoastWatch, write Phillip Johnson at 605 Southeast 37th Avenue, Portland, OR 97214 or call (503) 238–4450.

The Debacle of the *New Carissa*

Perhaps if someone had been keeping a closer watch on the Oregon Coast, the debacle of the *New Carissa* might have been avoided. On Feb. 4, 1999, this small wood-chip carrier beached on a shoal off the entrance to Coos Bay Harbor. After attempts to burn the 440,000 gallons of fuel oil in its hold, the ship broke in two and leaked an estimated 70,000 gallons of oil. A concerted effort by the U.S. Coast Guard and salvagers allowed for cleanup of oil balls, and the Coast Guard towed the 440-foot bow section off the beach with intent to sink it by U.S. Navy torpedo. But the towline broke and the bow drifted to land just north of Waldport. Eventually, tugboats towed the bow out to sea where it was sunk by a torpedo from a Navy submarine, U.S.S. *Bermerton,* 300 miles offshore on March 11. The stern, still stuck in the sand, is an object of fierce debate. The governor demanded that it be removed from his state's beach. A number of locals advocated for a museum/tourist spot. As the debate rages on, the *New Carissa* sits offshore awaiting its fate.

The Exploding Whale

Whales have always drifted in from the briny depths to beach as confused yet alive creatures or dead masses of blubber. For Native Americans, a beached whale was cause for great celebration—a grand example of their motto that when "the tide comes in, the table is set." For contemporary Euro-Americans, it was a different matter in November 1970. After a whale had washed up on a beach near Florence and was beginning to perfume the air, the Oregon Highway Department decided to clean it up by blowing it up with half a ton of dynamite. The plan was to break the carcass into little bits that would be nibbles for gulls, crabs, and other scavengers. But the plan went awry when the dynamite exploded the whale into huge chunks that rained down upon the startled crowd and smashed a nearby car.

Two Unsolved Mysteries

Port Orford Meteorite

Geologist Dr. John Evans was a wandering scientist/adventurer who collected hundreds of rock samples in his rambles about the Sierra Nevada, Rockies, Cascade, and Coast Range mountains during the late 1900s. After Evans returned to the East Coast, one of his specimens turned out to be a chunk of pallasite, a rare type of meteorite known as stony-iron. Although he did note that the irregular-shaped mass weighing an estimated 11 tons was found 40 miles from Port Orford, its precise location was not in his notes. Since the discovery of the meteorite fragment and Dr. Evan's sparse notes, the Port Orford Meteorite Society has led hundreds of attempts to find the meteorite, but its location remains a mystery.

The Beeswax Shipwreck of Neahkahnie Mountain

Neahkahnie Mountain, a 1,600-foot cape rising just north of Nehalem Bay, is the site of two of the most intriguing legends in Oregon history. When the first Europeans settled in the Nehalem country, they were amazed by a plenitude of wax on the beach. Tons of it! Some of the chunks weighed 200 pounds, others were candle-size. Skeptics claimed that the substance was natural paraffin produced by coal or petroleum. Then cakes of wax were found stamped with the letters HIS, the sacred monogram of the Catholic Church. The local natives told a story of a beeswax ship wrecked by a storm. The survivors had been accepted into the tribe; some behaved so obnoxiously that they were killed, and others were adopted and produced fair-haired progeny.

Spanish shipping records give credence to the tale. One of their beeswax ships bound from Mexico to Manila in 1772 disappeared. So did the caravel *San Jose*, en route from La Paz to San Diego in 1769. It seems likely that one of their vessels, bound for distant Spanish missions, ended up illuminating the cedar huts of the Clatsop Nation.

Getting Here, Getting Around

Bordered by the Coast Range mountains to the east and besieged by the Pacific Ocean to the west, the Oregon Coast requires some effort to get to and some effort to travel once you're here. Of course, the remoteness of the Coast is mostly a boon. The natural landscape is varied and dramatic and relatively unspoiled. The human landscape has also benefited from being remote. It hasn't completely succumbed to the modern project of making every town look exactly alike.

Traveling the Coast may bring some surprises. Parts of the road fall into the sea, sometimes closing it. Curvy two-lane highways make high speeds dangerous. Bends in the road may reveal views so amazing that they demand you pull over to look at them. The lesson here: Don't be in a big hurry.

By Car

Roads

U.S. Highway 101

U.S. Highway 101 runs the entire 400-mile length of the Oregon Coast, from California in the south to the Columbia River and Washington State in the north. The central artery of the Coast, it provides the main north-south route for tourists and residents alike, so it is heavily traveled. Sometimes the volume of traffic will astonish even the seasoned native. U.S. 101 follows the shore, usually within sight of the ocean. Driving along U.S. 101 you will see spectacular beaches, lush forests and lonely meadows, mysterious dunes and flourishing farms, and bustling tourist towns and fishing villages. Most exhilarating are Pacific vistas as the road clings to the rocky side of a bluff with the ocean crashing into the shore hundreds of feet below.

U.S. 101 is susceptible to landslides and therefore road closures, making life difficult for both natives and tourists, who may have to travel miles and miles out of their way. This is one high-maintenance road. However, because of this susceptibility, it is also maintained very well by the hosts of engineers who are constantly evaluating its condition. You would be wise to call the Oregon Department of Transportation's road condition report at (800) 977-6368 or visit www.tripcheck.com, before going anywhere along U.S. 101 and also for mountain pass information.

This highway has plenty of roadside services, but sometimes it's a long way between them, so keep an eye on the gas gauge. You should also be aware that U.S. 101 is called "Highway 101" by most locals, though for the sake of consistency with road maps we have retained the technical name here. The highway also often changes names when it reaches a town, as in Brookings, where it is called "Chetco Avenue," or Gold Beach, where it is called "Ellensburg." But U.S. 101 is still clearly marked, even if the street signs say something unfamiliar.

U.S. Highway 30

Following the Columbia River, this busy highway is the most direct route from Portland to Astoria. It is also the most direct route from Washington State. If you are coming from, say, Seattle, take I-5 south to Longview, Washington; from there, cross the Columbia River into Oregon over the Lewis & Clark Bridge, which will deposit you onto Oregon soil and U.S. Highway 30 at the little town of Rainier. Follow the road west toward Astoria.

Coast Range Roads

Most east-west roads to the Oregon Coast cross the Coast Range mountains, some following rivers for nearly their entire length. Some roads have significant changes in elevation and others have only modest elevation changes. Whether or not there are major changes in elevation, all the roads demand alert driving, since you will find dips, curves, deer, and little towns, and since you will be sharing the roads with trucks. U.S. Highway 26 is the way of choice for weekending Portlanders, who share the road with farm and logging trucks. The road stretches from Portland to a convenient location on U.S. 101 between Cannon Beach and Seaside. In the winter, chains or other traction devices may be required. Oregon Highway 6 follows the Wilson River from west of Portland to Tillamook. A road of gentle curves, it can be a slow, if pleasant alternative to busy U.S. 26, though the eastern end of it is more developed every minute. Oregon Highway 22 leads from Hebo to Salem; it crosses Oregon Highway 18, which leads from McMinnville to Otis, just north of Lincoln City. Locals say to beware of casino traffic on OR 18. U.S. Highway 20 accompanies the Yaquina River from Corvallis to Newport, a good and very pretty road—though it can be pokey in places. Another pretty highway, Oregon Highway 34, follows the Alsea River from Corvallis to Waldport. Eugene residents take busy Oregon Highway 126 through timber towns to Florence and the sand dunes. Oregon Highway 38 is a pleasant road leading from Drain to Reedsport along the Umpqua River. It's the most direct east-west route to the South Coast. Oregon Highway 42 leads from the Umpqua Valley near Roseburg to Coos Bay through the aptly named town of Remote. You may see other east-west roads marked on your map that appear to lead to the Coast. Don't count on their being paved.

U.S. Highway 199

This road, nicknamed the "Redwood Highway," lies between Grants Pass and Crescent City, California. South Coast residents traveling home from Ashland and Medford use it, detouring into California for nearly 60 miles. They also sometimes use U.S. Highway 199 to connect them to Interstate 5 in Grants Pass when they want to go to Portland and beyond, on the theory that driving the length of Oregon on I–5 will be faster than driving the length of Oregon on U.S. 101. The road winds from Grants Pass to Crescent City with gentle curves and wide lanes, through the lonely mountain country where the Siskiyous meet the Coast Range. While most of the route is easily traveled, the western end of the road is very slow as it accompanies the Smith River and twists through the beautiful redwood groves of Jedediah Smith State Park, before it spills abruptly into

Insiders' Tip

The Oregon Department of Transportation (ODOT) has two excellent resources to alert you to road conditions on the Coast and elsewhere in the state. You can call (800) 977-6368 to check the latest road information, and you can visit their Web site at www.tripcheck.com for a comprehensive guide to roadwork, traffic delays, road closures, and other helpful information. You will be able to see for yourself through cameras keeping watch at Port Orford and Yaquina Bay.

coastal California farmland. A 20-minute drive north puts you in Brookings. Note that when you reach the California border, not far past the town of O'Brien, there will be a State of California agricultural inspection, so eat up all the homegrown produce before then.

Renting a Car

It is not easy to rent a car on the Oregon Coast. Hertz has an outlet in Astoria at (503) 325-7700. Enterprise also has rentals in Astoria at (707) 464-4228. You can also rent a car at the Crescent City airport, Jack MacNamara Field, if you're flying to the South Coast. If you're coming from far away and you want to drive while you're here, your best bet might be to fly into Portland International Airport and rent a car there.

By Bus

Greyhound Lines
(800) 229-9424
www.greyhound.com

The Greyhound bus travels along U.S. 101. Coastal Greyhound bus service is arranged by independent agents rather than official Greyhound ones, but many of the agents can give you tickets, a place for regularly scheduled stops, access to transfer routes, and package express delivery. Sometimes the agents are within restaurants, travel agencies, convenience stores, or other businesses. Other stops along the route might be signs posted on the highway, with no ticketing or other services; for these you need to make arrangements with Greyhound.

Raz Transportation Company
11655 Southwest Pacific Highway, Portland
(503) 684-3322, (888) 684-3322
www.raztrans.com

Raz Transportation offers group bus tours and charter services from Portland. With a variety of equipment, they can help you arrange bus transportation to the Coast for small groups or large ones. They include ADA-compliant equipment and video capability among their assets and will work with customers who want luxury accommodations as well as more budget-minded ones. Raz Transportation also offers regularly scheduled one-day tours of the North and Central Coasts leaving from Portland. The North Coast tour takes you through Seaside, Cannon Beach, and Tillamook, and, depending on the tour, may also include a visit to Fort Clatsop or Astoria or both; the Central Coast tour takes you to Newport and Depoe Bay.

Municipal Buses

Public transportation on the Oregon Coast is not particularly plentiful, but some cities have bus service. Astoria maintains a city bus system that you can take all around the area for as little as 50 cents.

Schedules may be found at the Chamber of Commerce Welcome Center, 111 West Marine Drive. Bus service runs from 5:30 A.M. to 7:00 P.M. Monday through Saturday. The Astoria bus will also take you to Fred Meyer in Warrenton, to the KOA/Fort Stevens campground in Hammond, and all the way to Seaside and Cannon Beach down U.S. 101. For more information call (503) 861-7433 or (800) 776-6406. Cannon Beach also has some bus service: A free shuttle runs daily from the north end of town at Les Shirley Park to the south end of town at Tolovana Park. Hours are 10:00 A.M. to 6:00 P.M. in the winter, with extended hours in the summer. The shuttle provides a bike rack and access for wheelchairs; call the City of Cannon Beach at (503) 436-1581 for more information. Lincoln County has a transit system with a combination of scheduled stops and demand stops. Call (541) 265-4900 or (541) 574-1292, or fax (541) 574-1296, for more information.

Shuttle Service

Caravan Airport Transportation
(541) 994-9645, (888) 743-3847

You can get to the Central Coast from Portland International Airport (PDX) by taking the Caravan Airport shuttle. It leaves each day from Portland International at 2:00 P.M. The cost is $39 per person each way. You'll find the shuttle at the airport outside the baggage claim area by the information booth; call to make a reservation or for more information.

By Airplane

North Coast

Portland International Airport
7000 Northeast Airport Way, Portland
(503) 944-7000, (877) 547-8411

The largest, most convenient airport to the northern Oregon Coast is Portland Inter-

Municipal Airports

Those flying their own planes can use several Web sites for information on municipal and other public airstrips. The Oregon Department of Transportation has a rundown of Oregon airports on its Web site at www.tripcheck.com The most comprehensive Web guide to Oregon airports is provided by the Oregon Pilots Association, at www.oregonpilot.org, which delivers information about runways, services, amenities, fuel prices, and anything else you may need to know. They'll even tell you which airports have flocks of birds that might pose a danger. For the most up-to-date information, however, all sites recommend you call the airfields.

Astoria, (503) 325-4521
Seaside Municipal, (503) 738-5112
Nehalem Bay, (503) 378-4880
Tillamook, (503) 842-2413
Siletz Bay, (503) 378-4880
Florence, (541) 997-8237
North Bend, (541) 756-8531
Gold Beach Municipal, (541) 247-6269
Brookings, (541) 247-7011

A cyclist taking a break on one of the many scenic waysides along U.S. 101. PHOTO: LIZANN DUNEGAN

national Airport, PDX. You can rent a car there, and take U.S. 26 or 30 to the North Coast. You can also take Caravan Airport Transportation to Lincoln City, or hire a charter service to fly you anywhere on the coast. Many airlines fly into PDX. Call your travel agent.

Central Coast

Newport Municipal Airport
135 Southeast 84th Street, South Beach
(541) 867–7422

The Port of Newport is very proud of its instrument landing system, which is designed to help pilots manage their planes even when visibility conditions are poor. Newport and areas nearby are have the rarity of being served by regular flights: Harbor Air, which has special connections to Horizon and Alaska Airlines, connects to PDX five times daily (in the summer, anyway).

South Coast

North Bend Municipal Airport
(541) 756–8531

Commercial air service connecting to Portland may also be found at the North Bend Municipal Airport. Horizon Air has four flights daily. They can be reached at (800) 547-9308 or visit horizonair.alaskaair.com.

Hotels and Motels

This chapter lists hotels and motels on the entire Oregon Coast organized by region—North, Central, and South—and then by city from north to south. These accommodations range from simple to extravagant. You'll find anything from a deluxe suite with an ocean view to a simple bungalow that is perfect for families. We've included price codes that will give you an idea of what you can expect to pay for two people for one night during the summer season. Winter season rates are usually discounted along the Oregon Coast. Hotels and motels accept all or most major credit cards unless otherwise noted. Some counties tax hotel rooms.

Price Code

$	$60 and less
$$	$61 to $100
$$$	$101 to $150
$$$$	more than $150

North Coast

The greatest concentrations of hotels and other accommodations in the North Coast are in the Seaside and Cannon Beach areas, and there are many to choose from. We figure you won't need any help spotting the national and regional chains, especially the ones that sprawl over half the beach. Occasionally we have included the familiar names if they are especially good in that area, but we've concentrated on accommodations that offer something different. Perhaps it's a guest cottage a little way up a river or a lodge renowned for its service and luxury. Maybe it's a large resort perfect for family vacations or old-fashioned beach cottages where you can practice living simply. But all the listings here offer something special.

Astoria

Crest Motel $$
5366 Leif Erikson Drive, Astoria
(503) 325-3141
www.crest-motel.com

The Crest Motel sits on two-and-a-half manicured acres above the city; its views of the Columbia River are magnificent, and its location, away from downtown, makes it a relatively quiet place to stay. It's also pleasant, with patio chairs outside in the back overlooking the river and a covered Jacuzzi among its many amenities. Other amenities include a continental breakfast, coin laundry facilities, phones, and cable television. One building is dedicated to those who don't smoke. It's okay to bring the dog.

Rosebriar Hotel $$–$$$
636 14th Street, Astoria
(800) 487-0224
www.astoria-usa.com/rosebriar

This building with 11 units used to house a convent; it's a historic landmark estate sitting on the hill above downtown Astoria with excellent views of the city and the Columbia River. The common rooms are lovely, with lots of intact moulding and a nice fireplace, with newspapers and coffee just waiting to be consumed by guests. The hotel also boasts an elaborate Captain's Suite with a fireplace, soaking tub, wet bar, kitchenette, and panoramic views of the Columbia River. A restaurant serves dinner to guests, and banquets and catering can be arranged. Don't let all the antiques worry you—the Rosebriar is modern enough to have phones and televisions and spas all in good working order. Complimentary continental breakfasts are served.

Gearhart

Gearhart by the Sea $$$$
1157 North Marion Avenue, Gearhart
(503) 738-8331, (800) 547-0115
www.gearhartresort.com

This large resort in Gearhart surprisingly does not hog the landscape. It's a four-building condominium complex. The central building is Gearhart House; just north of that is Pacific View. Just west, a little closer to the ocean, are Pacific Palisades and Pacific Terraces. And, in spite of the profusion of buildings, all the units have some kind of ocean view. Because the units are individually owned, they are all furnished differently and some of them are lush; moreover, the size and layout of the units are different. However, all units have a fully outfitted kitchen, fireplace (wood delivered daily), dining room, living room, and bathroom off each bedroom. (You can rent one- or two-bedroom units.) What's more, there are two indoor pools (the one for those staying at Gearhart House has a Jacuzzi). A golf course is on-site. Banquet and conference facilities are available, and there is a restaurant on the premises. As is common on the North Coast, a deposit is required, and rates are based on a two-night stay. While it seems pricey, because they are condos the rent can be distributed among more people. Pets are allowed in some units. A pet fee is charged.

Gearhart Ocean Inn $$
67 North Cottage, Gearhart
(503) 738-7373, (800) 352-8034
www.gearhartoceaninn.com

The Gearhart Ocean Inn is a wonderful place to stay; here you can both eat your cake and have it, too. Close to the shopping malls and tourist fun of Seaside and the golf course and beach fun of Gearhart, the Gearhart Ocean Inn is a quaint cottage-style motel restored to its old-fashioned charm. Spotless and tidy, the rooms are furnished with willow and wicker; the backyard has both horseshoes and croquet, as well as a barbecue. The modern touches include phones, televisions, and a few VCRs. Kitchens and separate bedrooms in most units, laundry

facilities, and rooms dedicated to the pets make this a good family place. Children younger than 2 stay free (cribs are free, too); children younger than 12 are $5.00 per child per night. Other people and pets are $10 each per night. No smoking here, please, and you'll need to send a deposit. (Refunds will be made no later than seven days before your reservation date, and you'll be charged a $10 processing fee.) Ask about specials and packages—there are some good ones.

Seaside

Edgewater Inn $$$
341 South Prom, Seaside
(503) 738-4142, (800) 822-3170

The Edgewater, owned by the same folks as the Inn at the Shore, is in the thick of things. Step out the front door, walk down the path, and you are in the middle of the Prom, the beloved walkway that fronts the beach at Seaside. A brief walk to the north will put you in the middle of the tourist district; one straight ahead will put you on the beach. But the Edgewater itself manages to convey a get-away-from-it-all feel. Maybe because it's a small hotel of 14 rooms that dares you to relax. All the rooms come with a Jacuzzi tub, a fireplace, a full kitchen, television and VCR, sleeping room for four, and great views. There are also a few cottages; these have the same furnishings. Extra people are $10 apiece per night.

Gilbert Inn and Vacation Rentals $$$–$$$$
341 Beach Drive, Seaside
(503) 717-1070
www.gilbertinn.com

This lovely old house was built in the early 1890s by a French liquor store operator/real estate magnate from Astoria and its old-fashioned appeal is well-preserved. It can be classified as a bed-and-breakfast, but we've included it here because, with 10 rooms, it's a little larger than many bed-and-breakfast inns, and it also has two cute cottages that you may rent.

The rooms at the inn are charming, furnished with wicker and antiques, with fir ceilings and walls in many of the rooms. One room has a turret. A stone fireplace in the sitting room provides a natural gathering place, and the pink dining room casts a cheerful glow over your morning coffee. The location is also excellent: It's one block from the beach and close to, but just south of, the main street in Seaside. No pets here, not even in the yard; older children are welcome. The cottages come equipped with an outfitted kitchen with a dishwasher and microwave, a patio, a garden, and two bedrooms (and a full bath too). A television and VCR are there for you to use. The cottages are not as fetching as the inn itself, but they are homey and comfortable. If you plan to stay more than seven days, you can use the washer and dryer. The inn has a two-night minimum on weekends and a three-night minimum on some holidays.

Inn at the Shore $$$-$$$$
2275 South Prom, Seaside
(503) 738-3113, (800) 713-9914
www.innattheshore.com

The Inn at the Shore is, we admit, a rather large hotel on the beach. But unlike most of the hotels in Seaside, it is at the quieter south end of the beach near Tillamook Head, away from the arcades and candy stores. You can still stroll up the Prom to get your saltwater taffy and ride the bumper cars, but at the end of the day, you can stroll back and watch a beautiful sunset from a peaceful bit of sand. Eighteen suites provide all the usual amenities and then some. In many of the suites, you'll find gas fireplaces, kitchenettes, wet bars, and balconies; in all of them, you'll find televisions and VCRs. Cribs are available for the wee ones; the Inn at the Shore is wheelchair accessible; no smoking, please.

Cannon Beach

Argonauta Inn/The Waves Motel $$$-$$$$
188 West 2nd Street, Cannon Beach
(503) 436-2205, (800) 822-2468

Just five units, the Argonauta Inn is an oasis amid a downtown Cannon Beach that can get pretty feverish on a summer afternoon. Each of these lovely, well-furnished units comes with fireplace and kitchen. The units, which are separate buildings,

range in size. The largest, Beach House, is good for the family reunion—it can sleep 10, and a large stone fireplace provides incentive to get people off the beach for dinner. The usual modern amenities apply—phones, televisions—and a spa pool is also available. Pets are not allowed at this inn.

Cannon Beach Hotel $$-$$$
1116 South Hemlock Street, Cannon Beach
(503) 436-1392, (800) 238-4107
www.cannonbeachhotel.com

A small, European-style hotel, the Cannon Beach has a long history of providing comfort to the weary. It was built as a loggers' boarding house, but in 1992 it was thoroughly remodeled and has graduated from its humble origins to become a delightful and cozy hotel and bistro. There are just nine rooms, one of which is a suite; they are custom-furnished; each has a private bath. Some rooms also have fireplaces and spa tubs. (All the rooms have television and VCR, of course). Breakfast is delivered to your door each morning, and room service, which is relatively rare on the Oregon Coast, is available from the restaurant. The lobby is worth mentioning too—it's a welcoming room with a fireplace, a nice place to curl up with a cup of tea to read the paper. Please don't smoke here, and leave the cats and dogs at home, but bring the children if they can behave themselves. You may want to check out the establishments affiliated with the Cannon Beach Hotel, the Courtyard and the Hearthstone, which are also very nice.

McBee Motel $$
539 South Hemlock Street, Cannon Beach
(503) 436-2569

Nothing could be as inviting as the 12 cottages of the McBee Motel. And not only are they charming, but they are relatively inexpensive, especially when you consider the immaculate, stylishly old-fashioned decorations and furnishings. Some of the cottages have fireplaces and kitchens. Pets are allowed, if they're good and if they pay.

Schooner's Cove Inn $$$
188 North Larch Street, Cannon Beach
(503) 436-2300, (800) 843-0128
www.schoonerscove.com

The Schooner's Cove is one of a number of Cannon Beach hotels that manage to be at once upscale and down home. Here, you can relax on the front lawn of the cedar-shake hotel while you use the barbecue and watch the beachcombers, or, if you don't feel like cooking, watch them from the spa, which faces the ocean, instead. The 30 rooms each have deck, fireplace, and view. The suites have kitchens, too. There is good coffee, laundry facilities for everyone, but no smoking or pets.

The Sea Sprite $$$$
280 Nebesna Street, Cannon Beach
(503) 436–2266, (866) 828–2266

The Sea Sprite is actually just south of Cannon Beach, and it's hard to find anything other than the word "cute" to describe it. It has just six units, but each of them looks out to the ocean and has a deck and porch from which you can admire the view or grill your dinner. You'll also find cable TV and VCR, CD player, telephone, and microwave to satisfy any urges to use electricity. If you'd rather curl up in front of the fire, though, you can do that too. If you get extra grubby, don't worry: The Sea Sprite has washers and dryers. Please leave the smokes and pets at home.

The Stephanie Inn $$$$
2740 South Pacific, Cannon Beach
(503) 436–2221, (800) 633–3466
www.stephanie-inn.com

Luscious and quiet, the Stephanie is a truly sophisticated New England-style country inn. There are 50 rooms, each with a fireplace and air-conditioning to make sure you're comfortable. And rooms come with Jacuzzis and cozy terry robes. A breakfast buffet and newspapers are available each day; a masseuse is on-site. Every afternoon, wine is served in the Chart Room. In short, you are pampered in every way. Perhaps the most remarkable feature of the Stephanie is its sense of privacy. It doesn't leap out at you when you're walking on the beach ("They don't wreck the beach with floodlights," said one neighbor), and when you're back inside, the inn feels unhurried and quiet.

Tolovana Park

Tolovana Inn $$$$
3400 South Hemlock Street, Tolovana Park
(503) 436–2211, (800) 333–8890
www.tolovanainn.com

Okay, so the Tolovana Inn is a big hotel on the beach (about 3 miles south of Cannon Beach), but it's an institution that still provides luxury and service, the kind that makes life easy on you. Several nearby restaurants will deliver. If you don't want to amble down to Cannon Beach yourself, you can take the free city shuttle, which stops right at the inn. You'll also have privileges at the Cannon Beach Athletic Club. The rooms are very nice, in that big-hotel way. Besides televisions, VCRs, gas fireplaces, and kitchens, the Tolovana Inn also has an on-site masseuse, free morning coffee and newspapers, and conference facilities, including a room with a 48-inch television screen so you can show home videos to all the relatives at the family reunion. They might flee to the indoor pool or the game room, however, and who could blame them? For once, the dog can come. Nonsmoking rooms are available. You'll also need to send a deposit.

Nehalem

Nehalem River Inn Lodge, Restaurant & Wine Cellar $$$
34910 Oregon Highway 53, Nehalem
(503) 355–2301, (800) 368–6499
www.river-inn.com

The Nehalem River Inn is an attractive lodge that is a mile and a half east of U.S. Highway 101. The lodge is on the Nehalem River; it's small and lush and rustic, with pleasant views of the Nehalem River. (Some views are close-ups: You can soak in a hot tub on the river.) The lodge consists of three rooms, a cottage, and a spacious suite. The three rooms have private bathrooms and big windows. And there is satellite television. The small cottage with a kitchenette, a fridge, a microwave, and a coffeepot. The suite has a cozy living room and kitchenette. For entertainment, you'll find a fireplace and a two-person spa, as well as a television with VCR. But you're really going to want to hang out on the lawn or in the excellent restaurant where they serve locally produced cuisine and their own wines.

Wheeler

Maggie's Guestrooms $$
47 Gregory Street, Wheeler
(503) 368–6881
www.stayatmaggies.com

Not all great stays on the Oregon Coast are right on the ocean. Maggie's Guestrooms is a wholly different experience from the usual standardized hotel routine. For one thing, it is a tiny establishment of just three rooms, and each has a theme. The room with the queen bed is the Travel Room; the room with a full-size bed is the Art Room; and the room with two twin beds is the Music Room. The small-is-beautiful ambiance fits in with the mission at Maggie's: to help those seeking a calmer life, especially women. Owner Peg Miller gave up the frantic pace of her own life when she moved from Chicago to Oregon. She bought a building in the charming village of Wheeler in 1999 and hung out her shingle in January 2000, where she now provides respite for other refugees from frenzy. Her rooms are on the second floor of a two-story 1930s building (it was the original post office); they all have private baths. You'll receive a yummy continental breakfast and you can walk across the street to the renowned Treasure Cafe. If you have too much at breakfast, work it off in the pool and health club run by the North County Recreation District. Maggie's also sponsors writers' retreats and workshops and local arts events. If you stay over the weekend, you'll catch the Friday night salon, which enables guests to meet one another and to find out what else is happening in and around Wheeler. These little personal touches make Maggie's Guestrooms more relaxing—and encouraging—than a grand ocean resort. A two-night minimum stay is required for most summer weekends and holidays. Well-behaved pets may stay with approval from the owner of the inn.

Pacific City

Inn at Cape Kiwanda $$$–$$$$
33105 Cape Kiwanda Drive, Pacific City
(888) 965–7001
www.innatcapekiwanda.com

A 35-room inn in the unhurried community of Pacific City, the Inn at Cape Kiwanda

Gaze at the pounding surf from your room at the Inn at Cape Kiwanda in Pacific City. PHOTO: LIZANN DUNEGAN

is a great place for a family vacation—all rooms have a gas fireplace and ocean views—or a business retreat—all the rooms have data ports and you can make use of a large ocean-view meeting room. You can use it, that is, if you can tear your employees away from the day spa, book and gift stores, galleries, or dory charter service downstairs. If you can't, walk across the street to the Pelican Pub & Brewery and take the rest of the day off. Some rooms have Jacuzzis from which you can peacefully view the ocean. The inn is nonsmoking and pets are allowed in selected rooms for a fee. A two-night minimum stay is required on weekends in July and August and all legal holidays.

Neskowin

Pacific Sands Resort $$–$$$
48250 Breakers Boulevard, Neskowin
(503) 392-3101
www.oregoncoast.com/pacificsands
While the Pacific Sands looks unprepossessing, its location on a quiet stretch of beach in the little community of Neskowin is reason enough to stay there. Pacific Sands is a condo-style resort close to golf courses, the casino at Lincoln City (it's just shy of being on the Central Coast), hiking, and, of course, the beautiful beach right there out the front door. The resort has 12 one- and two-bedroom units, many of which face the ocean, and all units have fireplace, living room, kitchen, and patio or deck from which you can enjoy the view. All of this comes at very reasonable prices: Even in the summer months, you can find units for less than $100. Pacific Sands asks for a deposit of the first night's rent and a seven day's notice to get it back. All rooms are nonsmoking and pets are not allowed.

Central Coast

There are so many hotels on the Central Coast that anyone could become bewildered driving along U.S. 101. What we do is turn off U.S. 101. Many of the hotels listed below are off the beaten path. Hotels on this area of the Coast tend to be clustered in Lincoln City and Newport.

Lincoln City

The O'dysius $$$$
120 Northwest Inlet Court, Lincoln City
(800) 869-8069
http://odysius.com
Lincoln City presents mile after mile of beach motels. Fortunately, the O'dysius is here to break up the monotony. This swank 30-room hotel on a rare peaceful stretch of beach by the D River is devoted to making your stay at Lincoln City as luxurious as possible. The interior of the building is lovely, with lacquered wainscoting, a slate entry hall, and a stone fireplace in the library. The furniture is custom-made, and the beds smothered in down comforters and pillows; you'll find whirlpool tubs and ocean views in all the rooms. Rooms also feature telephones and data ports. The hotel has many other nice little touches: wine in the evening, slippers at your bedside, shuttle service to the casino in Lincoln City, sheltered parking, and indoor corridors to keep you dry during winter storms. Some rooms are accessible by wheelchair. While this is an expensive hotel, the O'dysius offers senior discounts, seasonal rates, and corporate packages, so ask about them. Small, well-behaved pets are welcome, and so are children if they're older than 12. It's so nice here you won't want to leave. The hotel is completely nonsmoking.

Gleneden Beach

Westin Salishan $$$$
7760 U.S. Highway 101 N., Gleneden Beach
(541) 764-2371, (888) SALISHAN (725-4742)
www.salishan.com
Salishan, as it's known to locals, is one of the oldest resorts on the Coast and one of the most beloved. A thousand acres, 205 units, a championship golf course, several kinds of pools, activities for the children, wine tasting for the adults, shopping, tennis, and the beach—these are only a few of the reasons that people return often. Fireplaces and balconies come with all the

rooms, which are decorated according to Northwest principles of place (lots of stone and wood). Rooms are spacious. Cable TV and movies are available, of course. In other words, this is an outstanding destination resort that should not be missed, especially if you're a golfer. (See the Golf and Shopping chapters for more information.)

Otter Rock

Inn at Otter Crest $$–$$$$
301 Otter Crest Loop, Otter Rock
(541) 765–2111, (800) 452–2101
www.innatottercrest.com

A large resort just to the north of Newport, the Inn at Otter Crest offers tennis, basketball, and an oceanside pool and many other activities for the person who is trying to find something to do beside tide pools. The Inn at Otter Crest sprawls over 35 acres of forest, beach, and meadow. Its grounds are lovely; its rooms are too. Rooms feature large windows and decks; many rooms have a fireplace and kitchen. Pets are not allowed.

Newport

Nye Beach Hotel and Cafe $$$
219 Northwest Cliff, Newport
(541) 265–3334

The brightly painted Nye Beach hotel has added a Jimmy Buffet flavor to the ambiance of Nye Beach. The 18 rooms all have gas fireplaces and balconies and the decorations are spare but pleasant. Nice touches include willow love seats. One room is wheelchair accessible.

Some rooms have spa tubs; some have ocean views. All the rooms have cable TV, refrigerator, and phone. Pooch can stay only on the ground floor; he'll be charged $5.00 for each night he stays. Light a fire, curl up in one of the imported beds under a down comforter, and watch the storms outside.

The Sylvia Beach Hotel $$$–$$$$
267 Northwest Cliff, Newport
(888) 795–8422
www.sylviabeachhotel.com

Insiders' Tip
If you're traveling with your pet, always call ahead to verify the current pet policy.

In a world where every hotel seems to have the same decorator, the Sylvia Beach Hotel provides a valuable public service by its relief from monotony. This 20-room hotel set 45 feet above Nye Beach opened in 1988 and is dedicated to book lovers everywhere: It's named after the prescient and heroic Sylvia Beach, owner of the Parisian bookstore Shakespeare & Company, publisher of Ulysses, and book supplier to Ernest Hemingway. And books are the focus here: Not only is each room dedicated to a favorite author, but there are no in-room televisions, radios, or telephones to distract you from reading them. A fabulous reading room has amazing views of the Yaquina Head Lighthouse and the ocean if you can be bothered to look up from the books, puzzles, board games, or drinks that are offered. Rooms are charmingly appointed according to literary reputation and style. In the Hemingway Room, for instance, hunting trophies hang over the bed to guard you while you sleep; in the Edgar Allan Poe Room, it's a mechanized pendulum that keeps you company. You'll find three classes of room: "novels," "best-sellers," and "classics." "Classics" are the most expensive—oceanfront suites with fireplaces and decks; "best-sellers" are oceanview rooms that fall in the middle price range; and "novels" cost the least. They are without ocean views, though they do have patios.

Whatever your literary diet, the room comes with breakfast, served family style in the Tables of Content restaurant. Dinners are served too, if you make reservation (dinners are available to people who are staying elsewhere). They can be lively and long, since sharing tables with strangers seems to bring out everyone's most outrageous stories. The loyalty and admiration inspired by this unusual hotel is evident when you read through the journal-guest books in each room. Whether it's the quiet rooms, the stimulating dinner conversation, the immersion in literature, or the proximity of the beautiful beach, many people find their thinking improves upon staying here. Pets are not allowed at this Coast retreat.

The Viking's Cottages and Condos $$–$$$
729 Northwest Coast Street, Newport
(541) 265–2477, (800) 480–2477
www.vikingsoregoncoast.com

The Viking's Cottages and Condos offer two different Nye Beach experiences. The Cottages are decorated in the shabby chic beach house style you remember from childhood, with wood paneling and white trim, lace curtains and painted wood furniture. They are unstuffy and old-fashioned, built in 1925, though terribly clean, of course; they are also modern enough to make the television watchers in the family happy. Only two of the cottages have telephones, and the bathrooms have only showers, no tubs. But there are decks, stairs to the beach, fully equipped kitchens, and great views. And they are very reasonably priced for the area—many cottages cost less than $100 per night, while the larger ones, which may sleep six or eight people, run for less than $200 (sometimes much less). The 36 condos, on the other hand, are contemporary; they are privately owned and rented out to you. The oceanfront condos have, in addition to patios or balconies, a spa and pool, cable TV, fully equipped kitchens, and some fireplaces. If you need a telephone, though, make sure you ask for one ahead of time. Not surprisingly, the condos run a little more, but there are still bargains to be had. Expect to pay about $150 for a one-bedroom suite, a little over $100 for a studio. The large suites run over $200 for the night. Weekly rates for cottages and condos are available. Pets are welcome in the cottages but not the condos.

Waldport

Cape Cod Cottages $$
4150 Southwest Pacific Coast Highway (U.S. 101), Waldport
(541) 563–2106

The Cape Cod Cottages, built in 1938, are the perfect retreat for those who like to comb the beach without having to fight the crowds for sand dollars. Situated on a beautiful 6 miles of beach between Yachats and Waldport, the 10 rooms of this sweet and economical establishment are clean, comfortable and low key. They come outfitted with decks, kitchens, fireplaces, telephones, and cable TV; there are also nonsmoking and wheelchair-accessible rooms. There's also a four-bedroom beach house if you want to bring some friends with you (they'll cost an extra $10 each). It sleeps a total of eight. No pets, though.

Edgewater Cottages $$
3978 Southwest Pacific Coast Highway (U.S. 101), Waldport
(541) 563–2240
www.edgewatercottages.com

Each of the seven units of these charming cottages right next to the beach has a fireplace, a deck, and a view; it's hard to say which is the most attractive feature. The stretch of beach on which the cottages rest is one of the most beautiful beaches anywhere, so plan to stay awhile—and you can do it because each cottage also has an equipment-stocked kitchen. They're Fido-friendly here, as long as the dog is good and you pay the $10 per night fee, and the place is also a favorite of families with children, in spite of, or maybe because of the fact that there are no phones. Just calm down and enjoy the beach instead. The Edgewater Cottages are wildly popular; call early for reservations and ask about the minimum stay requirements. Credit cards are not accepted.

Yachats

Adobe Resort $$–$$$
1551 U.S. Highway 101, Yachats
(541) 547–3141
www.adoberesort.com

The Adobe is a resort right in the middle of Yachats, which means that a fine basalt beach is right there before you and you're still close to restaurants and shopping. The older section, with great views and fireplaces, allows pets for a $5.00 fee. The newer sections won't allow pets, but they do offer some in-room Jacuzzis, patios or porches, wet bars, and even kitchenettes to make up for it. Non-smoking and wheelchair-accessible rooms are both available (there's an elevator too). The rooms here all come with phone, hair dryer, cable TV, coffeemaker, and refrigerator; the resort complex offers a Jacuzzi and sauna, as well as an exercise room, for everyone to use. A full-service restaurant serves breakfast, lunch, and dinner, as well as a Sunday champagne brunch. (There's a lounge with stunning views, too, for the grown-ups). Ask about packages—a number of extended-stay deals, some of which include various combinations of meals, can net you a bargain.

The Fireside Motel $$–$$$
1881 U.S. Highway 101 N., Yachats
(541) 547–3636, (800) 336–3573
www.overleaflodge.com/fireside

The Fireside is run by the same people as the Overleaf Lodge (see the listing in this chapter). This is an unpretentious motel that offers great value. Two buildings hold 43 rooms; the rooms of the West Building face the ocean and all have remarkable views. These rooms also have balconies, and some rooms here have gas fireplaces. In the North Building, there are still some rooms with views, but from some you can't see the water. There is, however, a largish suite in this building; it has both a kitchen and a view. Wherever your room is, it will have cable TV, a coffeemaker, a direct-dial phone, and a refrigerator. There are wheelchair-accessible rooms, and some rooms in each building are dedicated to smokers and pets.

Ocean Haven $$
94770 U.S. Highway 101, Yachats
(541) 547–3583
www.oceanhaven.com

The ambiance of the Ocean Haven is very Oregon. This eight-unit motel is stunningly set just south of Yachats near beach trails and tide pools. The owners want you to experience the beach as it is meant to be, so no pets are allowed since they discourage the native eagles, elk, otters, and their compatriots. It's not sumptuous; instead,

it's comfortable and beachy, attracting artists and writers who like its dramatic location and quiet atmosphere (no television, no telephones in the rooms). No smoking, either; a one night's 50 percent deposit is required.

The Oregon House $$–$$$
94288 U.S. Highway 101 S., Yachats
(541) 547–3329
www.oregonhouse.com

The Oregon House is an interesting hotel a little south of Yachats. Reservations are recommended here, and they have a strict deposit policy (one night or 50 percent) and a rather complicated refund policy. Once you're here, you may have to stay at least two nights, and sometimes three if it's a holiday. Pets and smoking are unwelcome, and children may stay only in some units. But once you get past all that, the Oregon House is a splendid place to stay. A stream winds its way through the property and its wooded trails, and there are little bridges to cross it. A trail leads to the beach—it is illuminated at night. There are five buildings and ten units, all of which are distinctive, have been carefully remodeled, and have interesting histories behind them. Most rooms include fireplaces and kitchens, two rooms have Jacuzzis, and most have ocean views.

Overleaf Lodge $$$–$$$$
2055 U.S. Highway 101 N., Yachats
(800) 338–0507
www.overleaflodge.com

A modern resort, the Overleaf Lodge's motto, "Natural Beauty, Civilized Pleasures," couldn't be more apt. First of all, the Overleaf is just north of Yachats, so you can take advantage of the many recreational activities in the area, from beachcombing to hiking. Every room faces the ocean and many rooms have balconies from which to enjoy the views. The civilized pleasures include an exercise room, robes, fireplaces in some rooms, and an on-site masseuse (call ahead for an appointment; she charges about $50 per hour). You'll also find television and VCR, hair dryer, microwave, refrigerator, and coffeemaker in all the rooms. Continental breakfasts are provided in the lobby before you head out to walk on the beach. Rates are, as usual, based on double occupancy; extra folk are $8.00 apiece. Keep the cigarettes and furry friends at home. The Overleaf provides some wheelchair-accessible rooms.

Shamrock Lodgettes Resort and Spa $$–$$$
105 U.S. Highway 101 S., Yachats
(541) 547–3312, (800) 845–5028
www.shamrocklodgettes.com

The Shamrock's log cabins exude summer-camp charm, and taking a stroll down the big lawn that leads to the beach will revive buried feelings of pleasure at the thought that you don't have to go home because you're going to sleep right there. Only this time, you'll skip the s'mores and enjoy a massage or relax in the spa. The cabins all have stone fireplaces and kitchenettes. There are also motel rooms; these too have fireplaces, and some are suites with Jacuzzis. All rooms, no matter where they are, have phone, cable TV, daily paper delivery, and amazing views. Pets are welcome in the cabins only (for a small fee). All units are nonsmoking.

Yachats Inn $$–$$$
331 South Coast Highway 101 (U.S. 101), Yachats
(541) 547–3456
www.yachatsinn.com

A cute older motel with a brand-new addition and a Japanese teahouse for meetings, the Yachats Inn has managed to preserve its quaint hometown air while still bringing modern convenience to its rooms. And the view from most rooms is timeless—crashing surf and painfully beautiful beaches. There are two buildings. The original building, built in 1948, has both suites and singles. All rooms have electric heat and if yours is a room with a fireplace or wood stove, your wood will be restocked. Some rooms have sun porches. If you're bored, you can watch cable TV. The new section is built in contemporary Northwest beach-house style, with shingled siding and white trim. The new suites sleep up to four persons and are outfitted with full kitchen and a dining room. There are also gas fireplaces, bathtubs, telephones, two televisions and VCRs, and decks. The Teahouse is a handsome building with a vaulted ceiling, a wood stove, a kitchen, and a large (2,000-square-foot), glass-enclosed deck for a meeting or other event; it can be rented by the day or by the hour. Pets can stay in the older section for $5.00 per night; children under 3 stay for free; and extra people in a room stay for $5.00 per night per person.

Ziggurat $$$
95330 U.S. Highway 101 S., Yachats
(541) 547–3925
www.newport.com/ziggurat

The Ziggurat is an unusual lodging near Yachats. Covered in weathered cedar shake, it was built in the tall beach grass according to the principles of pre-Egyptian pyramids (ziggurat is the Sumerian word for pyramid); hence there are no square rooms here and each room is remarkably private. The first floor has two suites, the Southeast Suite and the West Suite.

The Ziggurat values privacy—within the suites bedrooms can be closed off; and decks, patios, alcoves, and rooms all have spaces to curl up in and ponder your manuscript without fear of being interrupted. They ask that your children be at least 14 if they're coming with you The Southeast Suite has a queen-size bed in an enclosed alcove, some ocean view, and its own sauna, and there's a twin bed for the 14-year-old. The West Suite has a glass-block shower (round) and an impressive 27-foot wall of glass that you can stare out of from your hand-carved bed. When you weary of all the privacy, or if you can tear yourself out of bed, a library on the first floor, with books and games, as well as a minikitchen for making and storing snacks, will provide some entertainment. And then, too, there are two decks enclosed in glass to keep you out of the freezing breezes. You can stay at the Ziggurat in two modes: It can provide you with bed-and-breakfast service, but you can also inquire about extended stays. These will allow you laundry and some kitchen privileges (but you'll have to make your own bed and breakfast) and give you as much privacy as you need to finish your treatise. In any case, you'll have to stay at least two nights and give five days' notice if you want a refund of your deposit. Note well: Don't bring pets or smoking implements; and don't bring the plastic either. They don't take credit cards—just cash, personal checks, and traveler's checks.

Florence

River House Motel $$–$$$
1202 Bay Street, Florence
(888) 824–2750
www.riverhousemotel.com

The River House is not luxurious, but it is clean, quiet, and really friendly (they have cookies and coffee in the lobby for those who wander in), and sometimes that's what you need the most. The River House is tucked under the bridge spanning the Siuslaw River in Florence; it's just to the west of Old Town. There are phones and TVs and the basic amenities. Pets must stay home, however. They also have an alluring spa.

The Landmark Inn $$
1551 4th Street, Florence
(541) 997–9030, (800) 822–7811
http://presys.com/~landmarkinn

The recently opened Landmark Inn is a charming, small hotel conveniently set within walking distance of the new Florence Events Center and the notably shoppable Old Town district. Not only will you find lovely views of the mountains, sand dunes, and Siuslaw River, but you will enjoy them from nicely decorated rooms, 10 in all, some suites with sitting rooms and kitchens. Guests may use a traditional Finnish cedar sauna that sits in a tiny pine grove away from the main building. The Landmark Inn was built in 1998 on top of a knoll above Old Town. Beware the steeply graded driveway, especially going down. The pavement bears the scars of hasty motorists who scraped the bottoms of their vehicles. And you can smoke outdoors only.

Reedsport

Best Western Salbasgeon Inn $$
1400 U.S. Highway 101, Reedsport
(541) 271–4831
www.bestwesternoregon.com

This may be the spot to rest your head after a long day of exploring the dunes. The Salbasgeon has 56 spic-and-span rooms, some of which have coffeemaker, refrigerator, microwave, fireplace, and whirlpool, and all of which have free movies on cable. You'll also be able to help yourself to a continental breakfast and swim in the pool. Pets are allowed in some rooms for a little extra, and some rooms are wheelchair accessible.

South Coast

The South Coast features proportionally more destination resort hotels than other areas of the Coast. Places like Gold Beach are remote enough that once you get there, you want to stay awhile. Hotels are primarily clustered in Bandon, Gold Beach, and Brookings.

Coos Bay

Edgewater Inn on the Pacific Coast $$
275 East Johnson Avenue, Coos Bay
(541) 267–0423, (800) 233–0423
www.edgewater-inns.com

Usefully set just east of U.S. 101, the Edgewater boasts that it's the only waterfront motel in Coos Bay; it even has its own fishing dock. The 82 units of this hotel include many with spa tubs, kitchenettes, and balconies overlooking the bay. They'll provide you with a continental breakfast and VCR; you can also take advantage of their exercise room or the indoor pool to rejuvenate your road-weary bones. Because it's just off the highway, the Edgewater is a little more quite than some of the motels right on the U.S. 101 strip, but you can still walk to the Coos Bay waterfront or poke around downtown.

Bandon

Bandon Dunes $$$$
57744 Round Lake Drive, Bandon
(888) 345–6008
www.bandondunesgolf.com

The top-notch Bandon Dunes Golf Course opened in May 1999, instantly hailed as

Insiders' Tip

If you're looking for a place with more room in Bandon, check out the vacation rentals at Coquille Point. Each rental unit is equipped with three bedrooms, three bathrooms, a fully stocked kitchen, a fireplace, and great ocean views. Depending on the time of year, these rentals are $185 to $225 per night. Call the Table Rock Motel at (800) 457-9141 for more information or visit www.tablerockmotel.com/vacation-rentals-coquille-point.htm.

one of the most impressive golf courses in the U.S. Once you're there, you might not want to leave; fortunately there are accommodations for you. The elegant Lodge at Bandon Dunes not only provides a wonderful full-service restaurant, a lounge, and a golf shop, but it also has 19 single rooms with private baths and queen-size beds and two suites with master bedrooms and card rooms (or sitting rooms, if you prefer). The suites will cost you $700 to $900 per night for one person plus a little more for additional guests, and the single rooms run from $150 to $270 for one person, per night. If you're exhausted from all that golf, you can soak in a hot tub, or if you want to keep the edge over your partner, you can work out in the exercise room. You can also stay in one of the Lily Pond Cottages, which run about $260 per night. If you stay at the lodge, your greens fees will be reduced, and if you go during the winter, you can take advantage of the off-season rates. Shuttle

service is available between Bandon Dunes and the North Bend Airport. See the Golf chapter for more information.

Best Western Inn at Face Rock $$$
3225 Beach Loop Road, Bandon
(541) 347-9441, (800) 638-3092 (reservations)
www.facerock.net

Magnificent views of the ocean, Face Rock, and the Coquille River Lighthouse make this 55-room resort a great place to bring the family for a stay at Bandon. In addition to the beach access—which even includes its own beach house—the Inn at Face Rock is right next to a pleasant 9-hole golf course (see the Golf chapter for more information). Many of the suites have fireplaces, king- and queen-size beds, kitchenettes, and private patios. You'll find coffeemakers, microwaves, and refrigerators in other rooms. There is also a banquet room, a heated outdoor spa, and an indoor pool for the use of guests. Some good bargains may be had: There are discounts for groups and packages, and best of all, during the winter season, prices for many of the rooms drop. A lot.

Table Rock Motel $$
840 Beach Loop Road, Bandon
(541) 347-2700, (800) 457-9141
www.tablerockmotel.com

What this little motel lacks in luxury, it makes up for in its dramatic setting. Next to a wildlife sanctuary and overlooking Table Rock, Face Rock, and the other formations off the Bandon shore, the Table Rock Motel offers some rooms with kitchenettes, coffeemakers, radios, and refrigerators. All units have cable TV, though you probably will be too busy exploring to turn it on.

Queen Anne Vacation Suites and Table Rock Vacation Suites $$$$
1260 Beach Loop Road, 835 & 845 Beach Loop Road, Bandon
(541) 347-2700, (800) 457-9141
www.tablerockmotel.com/vacation-rentals-queen-anne.htm

Brought to you by the people at the Table Rock Motel (see the previous listing), these newly built or recently remodeled lodgings are a restful and economical alternative to motel living. Three three-bedroom suites accommodate up to six people, and up to four people can stay in the two-bedroom suite. Beds are queen-size; all bedrooms have private bathrooms; and all suites provide fully equipped kitchens, laundry areas, and cable TV and VCRs. Rent the places by the week: Not only will you save money but you'll need at least that long to explore the wildlife reserve, play on the beach, golf, windsurf, and see the whales. Keep the pets at home and the cigs in the car.

Sunset Oceanfront Accommodations $$$
1865 Beach Loop Road, Bandon
(541) 347-2453, (800) 842-2407
www.sunsetmotel.com
Straddling Beach Loop Road and making the most of its breathtaking location, the Sunset provides a full array of services, including a restaurant and lounge. Some rooms have kitchens and fireplaces; some are right on the ocean; some rooms are designated for pets. You can sleep in standard or queen-size beds, and you can choose from among economy rooms or full suites. Cable TV and laundry facilities are available. And there are wheelchair-accessible rooms. If you stay in the units across the road, you can find some excellent bargains. It goes without saying that it's easy to get to the beach—just walk down the stairs. The Sunset offers beach house rentals in addition to its motel services.

Windermere on the Beach Motel $$-$$$
3250 Beach Loop Road, Bandon
(541) 347-3710
www.windermerebythesea.com
This appealing 17-unit motel is right across from a golf course, right on the beach, and just right for families. Beautiful ocean vistas are visible from all the rooms. All units have cable TV, but there are no phones in the rooms. You'll find a variety of bed sizes from doubles to kings. A number of the rooms have kitchens and sleeping lofts, making them ideal for longer visits. Its moderate prices ($89 for a queen-size bed and kitchen unit) can make the Windermere a good value for

the vacationing family, but leave the family dog at home—they don't take pets.

Port Orford

Castaway-by-the-Sea $$
545 West 5th Street, Port Orford
(541) 332-4502
www.castawaybythesea.com
Port Orford is the westernmost point in the lower 48 states, and this friendly motel might be the westernmost building. The Castaway overlooks historic Port Orford, and the ocean beyond from every room, and offers both suites and rooms with sun porches and decks from which you can enjoy the view. Amenities include beach access, easy walking distance to town, cable TV, and nonsmoking rooms. Extra people cost $10.00, but up to two well-behaved pets can stay for only $5.00 per pet per night. The off-season rates are remarkably low.

Gold Beach

Gold Beach Resort $$$
29232 South Ellensburg Avenue (U.S. Highway 101), Gold Beach
(541) 247-7066, (800) 541-0947
www.gbresort.com
The Gold Beach resort is a nice motel in a location from which you can take equal advantage of the river recreation on the Rogue River or the ocean recreation of the Pacific. It's also a good place to hold a reunion, wedding, or business meeting because the resort has convention facilities for up to 250 people. The Gold Beach Resort offers 39 rooms, all of which face the water. Each room also has a small refrigerator, a coffeemaker, a television with VCR, and—just in case you actually are in a wedding or at a business meeting—a hair dryer, iron, and ironing board. Some rooms are accessible with wheelchairs. Staying in one of five condominiums is another way to enjoy the resort: Each condo comes equipped with full kitchen and fireplace, and some have washers and dryers. These units will accommodate from four to seven people.

Whatever kind of room you are staying in, don't let the pets in, but you are welcome to munch from the continental breakfast buffet, swim in the indoor pool or spa, and stare at the beach from your balcony.

Ireland's Rustic Lodges $$
29330 Ellensburg Avenue (U.S. Highway 101), Gold Beach
(541) 247–7718
www.irelandsrusticlodges.com

Rustic indeed, these little cottages just ooze down-home charm. Each cottage has an open fireplace stocked with wood (but don't try to cook over it). There are 40 rooms in all, some of them ordinary hotel rooms; try for a cabin. The grounds have a pretty garden and, of course, the beach right there in front of you. The owners really like deposits; otherwise they might give away your cabin. Pets and extra people cost more, and no smoking here, either. If you're worried that your taste for rusticity will evaporate after dark, rest assured that you can still watch cable TV.

Jot's Resort on the Rogue River $$$
94630 Wedderburn Loop, Gold Beach
(541) 247–6676, (800) 367–5687
www.jotsresort.com

Jot's Resort benefits from its location right under the Rogue River Bridge and has installed its own marina and tackle shop from which you can charter boats and hire fishing guides. It's a rather large resort by Coast standards, with 140 rooms of varying sizes and degrees of luxury. Jot's features a heated indoor pool, a spa and sauna, and an exercise room for you to relax in. Children under 10 stay free; pets are welcome for a $10 fee. You'll also be able to eat at the restaurant if you had a bad day fishing. Best of all, the ocean is still right there around the corner.

Tu Tu' Tun Lodge $$$$
96550 North Bank Rogue, Gold Beach
(541) 247–6664, (800) 864–6357
www.tututun.com

Named after the Tuntuni Indians who used to live here, the small and beautiful Tu Tu' Tun Lodge is 7 miles east of the ocean on the Rogue River. This wonderful place is both intimate and refined. Sixteen rooms in a two-story building make up the bulk of the rooms; these have king- or queen-size beds, private patios or balconies, and some of them have fireplaces and outdoor soaking tubs. There are also two suites in the lodge and two houses. The Garden House, overlooking the apple orchard, is a three-bedroom cottage that can sleep up to six; it has an attractive stone fireplace and a full kitchen. The River House, a contemporary building that features a large cedar-vaulted living room, has two bedrooms, two bathrooms, a full kitchen, and an outdoor Jacuzzi. (It's available only from July to October.) If you stay in a suite, you'll have a kitchen in addition to an expansive living room and a view of the river. One suite has two queen-size beds; the other has, in addition, a twin sleeper in the living room. All rooms have telephones, satellite television, and refrigerators to store your catch.

The center of activity is the main lodge—that's where you'll find a cozy bar, a library, and a large stone fireplace that demands you linger in front of it. The dining room, which serves elegant, delicious, family-style meals is also housed in the main lodge. The dining room is closed in the off-season, though you'll be served a continental breakfast; otherwise, during the high season, meals are prix fixe and include breakfast, hors d' oeuvre, and dinner. (If you want to eat here and you're not staying at the lodge, you may do so by reservation only.) To work off all the calories from dinner, the lodge has on its grounds a lap pool, river paths, and hiking trails. You can also play a round of horseshoes, practice your putting on a four-hole golf course, or live out your Minnesota Fats fantasies at the antique pool table. Or explore the Rogue's white water and wild scenery by taking one of the boats that stop at the dock. But the biggest draw is the fishing: Many people use the Tu Tu' Tun as a kind of luxurious fishing camp. The lodge will provide you with the latest news on salmon and steelhead runs and other important information. The Tu Tu' Tun bases its rates on double occupancy; extra people are $10 each. They require a deposit of one night's lodging, and if you change your mind about staying here, although we can't see how that would happen, you must tell them two weeks before the date of your reservation in order to get it back. And you can only smoke outside on the terrace. Leave the pooch at home.

Brookings

Best Western Beachfront Inn $$
16008 Boat Basin Road, Brookings
(541) 469–7779, (800) 468–4801 (reservations)
www.bestwesternoregon.com

Every one of the 102 rooms at the Beachfront Inn has a small, private balcony overlooking the ocean, which may be within 50 feet of you. The Beachfront has the closest rooms to the ocean of any other motel on the Oregon Coast to the ocean. Other attractive things about its location include walking distance to the marina and the new shopping district at the Port of Brookings and the fact that it's across the street from the only restaurant in town with views of the water. But the location is not the Beachfront's only charm: These immaculate rooms and suites are comfortable and loaded with amenities. In addition to phones, refrigerators, microwaves, the Beachfront features rooms with Jacuzzis that look out upon the ocean. There are also several one-bedroom suites with kitchens and sitting rooms. Smoking is permitted in one building and pets are too, for a $5.00 fee per pet. (Extra people are $5.00, too.) If you want to have a meeting, a room that can hold up to 50 people is available. There's a sunny outdoor pool if you get tired of the beach. A number of rooms are accessible to those in wheelchairs, and there are four rooms with roll-in showers.

Chetco River Inn $$$
21202 High Prairie Road, Brookings
(541) 670–1645, (800) 327–2688
www.chetcoriverinn.com

This small retreat 18 miles up the Chetco River allows you to really get away from it all—you're even off the power grid (the inn is run with solar power and propane gas)! But don't let that worry you: It's as comfortable and modern as anything. The Chetco River Inn is a fishing lodge, and they'll hook you up with guides for drift boat or ocean fishing, but it is also urbanely furnished with marble floors, leather furniture, and oriental rugs; down comforters keep you cozy at night. The five rooms range from about $125 to $145 each night for two people, and that includes a big country breakfast. You can also arrange to have lunches and dinners made. Children are welcome if they're 12 or over (they'll be staying in their own room), but Rover has to stay home. The Chetco River Inn asks that you send a deposit of one night's lodging, which can be refunded up to seven days before your scheduled stay. Your deposit and reservations may all be handled conveniently on the Internet (or by phone). They accept checks here. Smoking outside only, please.

Bed-and-Breakfast Inns

In this chapter you'll find bed-and-breakfast inns that range from turn-of-the-century houses filled with beautiful antiques to contemporary inns. The possibilities are endless—you can stay in a chateau in a private suite or you can stay in a stateroom aboard a paddleboat. You'll have the luxury of enjoying the privacy of your own room as well as have the opportunity to visit with other guests and exchange stories with the innkeepers. The innkeepers we interviewed were happy to share their stories with us as well as their love of what they do. Their common goal is to make you feel at home and give you a chance to relax and enjoy the scenic beauty of the magnificent coast.

When you stay in a bed-and-breakfast, you'll always receive a home-cooked breakfast made from fresh local ingredients, which usually includes a main entree such as fresh crab omelets, applesauce pancakes, or fluffy French toast, accompanied by homemade breads and jam, fresh fruit, and gourmet coffee, juice, or tea. Some innkeepers serve you breakfast in your room and some in the dining area at a specified time in the morning. It's always a good idea to find out when and where breakfast is served so you don't miss out!

We've organized the bed-and-breakfasts by region—North, Central, and South—and then by city from north to south. In each of the listings you'll find the name and address, price code, phone, Web site, restrictions, a detailed description of the bed-and-breakfast itself—including what's for breakfast—and other things to see and do in the area. If a bed-and-breakfast doesn't accept major credit cards, we've indicated that. Keep in mind that most bed-and-breakfasts do not allow smoking or pets and many allow children only with prior approval.

Whichever bed-and-breakfast you stay at, we know you will enjoy good company, breathtaking views of the scenic Coast, and a hearty homemade breakfast that will make you want to come back again and again.

Price Code

Our price code chart reflects the average cost of overnight accommodations for two people during peak season that generally runs from May through October (not including local lodging tax). Here's the breakdown:

$ .... $65 and less
$$ .... $66 to $95
$$$ .... $96 to $150
$$$$ .... more than $150

North Coast

Hammond

Officers' Inn Bed and Breakfast   **$$–$$$**
540 Russell Place, Hammond
(800) 377–2524
www.officersinn.net

The Officer's Inn Bed and Breakfast is an 8,000-square-foot inn that was built in 1905 to house Army officers and the communications center for Fort Stevens. Jerry and Cindy Deford are the innkeepers of this historic house, which is owned by the Oregon State Parks and Recreation Department. The inn is decorated with Victorian elegance and offers eight guest rooms—two of which are family suites.

The General's Room is a large romantic room filled with Victorian decor with a vineyard motif and has a comfy king-size bed and private shower.

The Colonel's Room is light and bright and is decorated with wicker furniture and a white picket fence–style king-size bed and has a private shower.

The Major's Room is a corner room and is furnished with a pretty queen-size brass bed and has a separate bathroom with a tub and shower. Fluffy terry cloth robes are provided.

The N.C.O. Quarters is a family-style suite that has its own private bathroom and shower and is furnished with a queen-size bed for mom and dad and two twin beds for the kids.

The Admiral's Room is decorated with a crystal chandelier and Victorian decor and has a king-size bed and a private bathroom and shower.

The Captain's Room features a hand-painted king-size bed and jewel-tone decor, is filled with antiques and a delightful armoire, and has a private bathroom and shower.

The Commander's Room is a quiet corner room that is furnished with an antique brass bed with floral country decor and has a separate bathroom with a tub and shower. Fluffy terry cloth robes are provided.

The Bachelor's Quarters is located on the third floor of the house and is set up to be used as a family suite but it can also be used as a romantic hideaway. This attic room features a queen-size bed, two twin-size beds, and a vintage claw-foot tub where you can take a relaxing bath. Scented soaps and suds are provided to make your stay in this room that much more special.

When we asked Cindy about additional amenities available to guests at the Officer's Inn she replied, "Every evening we offer 'evening tea' with home-baked goodies, coffee, tea, hot cider, and so on. We also have a small TV/VCR guests may check out (for free) and a small video library. One of our parlors is designated as 'the library' and has a small but growing collection of books and magazines for guests to enjoy. We also have a microwave, refrigerator, and outdoor barbecue available for guests." If you love to play games, you'll find many favorites such as chess, backgammon, cribbage, Pictionary, and Monopoly.

In the morning you'll be served a candlelight breakfast in one of the two formal dining rooms. "Breakfast always includes fresh fruit and a hearty main course," said Cindy. "Specialties include home-baked breads, smoked salmon benedict, and whole-grain pancakes just to name a few.

Dietary preferences are accommodated."

For things to see and do in the area, you can visit Fort Stevens State Park (you can bicycle to the park from the inn) and Fort Clatsop. The immediate vicinity also offers endless outdoor activities including fishing, crabbing, clamming, windsurfing, kayaking, hiking, and beachcombing. If you are looking for activities more on the civilized side of things, try antiques shopping, visiting one of Astoria's many museums, or checking out some of the local restaurants (Cindy recommends Buoy Nine, located only a mile from the inn) or attending a play.

Restrictions: No smoking (except outside on the porch). No pets. This B&B welcomes families with children.

Astoria

Astoria Inn $$
3391 Irving Avenue, Astoria
(800) 718–8153
www.moriah.com/astoriainn

The Astoria Inn is a friendly Victorian farmhouse-style inn that was purchased by host Mickey Cox in 1994. The house is surrounded by a pretty yard in a quiet residential area and has four guest rooms with private baths. The Cape Lookout room is located on the second floor and is furnished with 1860s antiques, a queen-size bed, a private bath with shower, and magnificent views of the Columbia River; the Cape Meares room is located on the second floor and has a queen-size bed, private bath with shower, and nice forest views; the Cape Virginia Room is located on the second floor, is decorated with Victorian furnishings, and has a queen-size bed, private bath with shower, and a pretty forest view; the Fort Stevens Room is located on the first floor, is decorated with Victorian furnishings, and has a queen-size bed and private bath with shower.

Additional amenities you'll find at this inn are a television and VCR in the communal front room, a cozy sitting room furnished with antiques and collectibles, and a veranda where you can watch the ships pass by on the Columbia River.

You'll also be served a complimentary

breakfast that includes fresh fruit, breakfast meats, egg entree, and coffee, tea, and juice.

Astoria is full of shops, museums, and galleries that you can explore, and Fort Stevens and Fort Clatsop are within a half-hour's drive of this inn.

Restrictions: No smoking. No pets. No children.

Benjamin Young Inn Bed and Breakfast
$$–$$$
3652 Duane Street, Astoria
(800) 201–1286
www.benjaminyounginn.com

The Benjamin Young Inn Bed and Breakfast was built in 1888 and is located in a quiet residential district in Astoria. This bed-and-breakfast is an outstanding example of Queen Anne architecture and is elegant yet unpretentious. The interior of the house has high ceilings with ornate moldings, stained glass windows, and comfortable furnishings in five guest rooms, each with style and personality.

The Fireplace Suite, located on the ground floor, can accommodate up to seven people, has a large jetted tub, a king-size bed, and a second bedroom. The Honeymoon Suite is decorated in a bridal theme and has a fancy canopy bed decorated with delicate lace. The room is also decorated with other wedding memorabilia and has the wedding certificate of the original owners of the house dating back to 1873 on the wall.

The Lady Ann Room is a large, elegant suite located on the second floor that is furnished with a queen-size bed, loveseat, and two large comfortable chairs and has outstanding views of the Columbia River and this estate's gardens. This suite also boasts a private bath with European tub and shower.

The Dorothy Room is also located on the second floor and is a sun-filled room offering partial views of the Columbia River. This room is furnished with a queen-size bed, a twin-size bed, sofa, rocking chair, and a private bath.

The Rose Room is a cozy room on the second floor that features outstanding views of the Columbia River, a queen-size bed, and a private bath and shower.

Additional amenities you'll enjoy at this romantic getaway include Columbia River views, river and ocean access, wood-burning fireplace, a piano, a historic carriage house, off-street parking, bicycle storage for cyclists, homemade cookies, and a comfortable front porch.

A complimentary breakfast is served in the dining room overlooking the river between 8:00 and 10:00 A.M. Breakfast is an "event" at this inn, and the table is graced with china, silver, and crystal. Breakfast entrees include quiche with bacon, omelets, crepes, turkey, sun-dried tomato sausages, freshly baked muffins and breads, cranberry scones, a variety of fresh fruits, orange juice, and freshly brewed coffee.

With such close proximity to downtown Astoria, there are dozens of activities and exploring options for you. You can visit the Flavel House, Astoria Column, and the Maritime Museum or travel west and visit Fort Stevens State Park or Fort Clatsop.

Restrictions: No smoking. No pets.

Clementine's Bed and Breakfast $–$$$
847 Exchange Street, Astoria
(800) 521–6801
www.clementines-bb.com

Clementine's Bed and Breakfast is an 1888 Victorian house that was fully restored in 1994. This elegant bed-and-breakfast features five guest rooms decorated Victorian-style with queen-size beds and private baths and showers, with one room that is wheelchair accessible. In addition, two large suites suitable for families with children are available. These suites have a TV,

Insiders' Tip
Always call ahead to verify your reservation and to find out what the check-in time is for the bed-and-breakfast or inn you are staying at.

fireplace, and full kitchen. Additional amenities include beautiful flower gardens with more than 2,000 spring bulbs and an herb garden and a living room where you can enjoy beverages and snacks in the evening, browse the reading library, play games, or listen to music.

You'll enjoy a gourmet breakfast in the dining room, or, if you prefer, it can be served in your room.

Astoria is full of things to see and do. Clementine's has kayaks available for your use, and hiking and biking are also popular activities around Astoria. You can explore the museums and shops in Astoria, rent a fishing charter, or go play on nearby beaches. Pets are welcome in the two suites.

Restrictions: No smoking.

Franklin Street Station Bed and Breakfast $$-$$$
1140 Franklin Street, Astoria
(503) 325-4314, (800) 448-1098
www.franklin-st-station-bb.com

Sharon Middleton and Rebecca Greenway are the mother and daughter team who are your hosts at the Franklin Street Station Bed and Breakfast. Shipbuilder Ferdinand Fisher built this grand Victorian house in the early 1900s. The inn is filled with old-world craftsmanship and antique furnishings that make you take a step back in time. A grandfather clock and an old-fashioned settee are some of the lovely antiques you'll find on the main floor.

The house has six guest rooms that are decorated with pretty pastel floral wallpaper. Each room has its own special mix of the following amenities: TV/VCR, antique queen bed, private minibalcony, wet bar, claw-foot tub, and magnificent Columbia River views.

A home-baked breakfast is served to you in your room at 8:00 or 9:00 A.M. or in the dining area at 7:30, 8:30, or 9:30 A.M. Crepes, Belgium waffles, quiche, and fresh Oregon fruit are just a few of the delicious entrees you'll be served at breakfast.

If you are looking for things to see and do in the area, the inn is within walking distance of downtown Astoria that is filled with fun shops, museums, and restaurants. You are also a short drive away from

Fort Stevens State Park and Fort Clatsop.
Restrictions: No smoking. No pets.

Grandview Bed and Breakfast $-$$$$
1574 Grand Avenue, Astoria
(800) 488-3250
www.pacifier.com/~grndview

The Grandview Bed and Breakfast is a turn-of-the-century Victorian house that features inset balconies, bay windows, a tower, and open staircase. This grand home is located on the Historic Homes Walking Tour and is close to museums and shops. When you visit this bed-and-breakfast, you'll have your choice of 14 guest rooms, some with private bath and some two-bedroom suites. Rooms are stocked with books and games.

For breakfast you'll enjoy fresh fruit, homemade muffins, lox and bagels, coffee, tea, and juice.

Restrictions: No smoking. No pets. No alcohol.

Seaside

Summer House Bed and Breakfast $-$$$
1221 North Franklin, Seaside
(800) 745-2378
www.summerhouse-seaside.com

Jack and Lesle Palmeri are the owners and innkeepers at the 4,000-square-foot Summer House, which was built in 1910 and is nestled in a residential neighborhood located near The Prom (Promenade)—a mile-and-a-half-long walkway that parallels the wide, sandy beach in Seaside. Lesle describes their house as "a special home adorned with treasures from a lifetime of travels. The house is a typical beach house style and the rooms are decorated in bright and cheery pastels. We have seven guest rooms, each with its own private bath, and a small television. The first guest room is called The Taj. It has a queen-size bed and decorations that my father brought home from India. The second guest room has a queen-size bed and contains my grandmother's furniture and her collection of porcelain dolls. Next is the Whispering Seas Room. This room has a queen-size bed and is decorated with seashells and driftwood and other items you would find you'll find are books, games, and musical instruments.

A full complimentary breakfast is served as part of your stay, which includes your choice of fresh fruits, homemade bread, a main dish, coffee, tea, and juice.

Sightseeing, shopping, beachcombing, and sandcastle building are fun activities that are just a short walk from the Summer House.

Restrictions: No smoking. No pets. No children under age 3.

Arch Cape

St. Bernard's Bed and Breakfast $$$–$$$$
3 East Ocean Road, Arch Cape
(800) 436–2848
www.st-bernards.com

St. Bernard's is a magnificent European-style chateau that has gorgeous ocean views and is filled with beautiful antiques and original works of art. The interior of the inn is reminiscent of a French country home with its rich, terra-cotta tile floor, rough plaster walls, and natural cedar windows. The inn has seven large rooms and suites, which all have a gas fireplace, telephone, cable TV, VCR, refrigerator, and private bath with tile shower.

The premier suite of this bed-and-breakfast is the Provence, which is filled with antique pine furniture and has a sitting room leading to a private patio, a queen-size bed, and an inviting Jacuzzi tub. Fluffy robes are provided for guests and a video and reading library is also available.

Your stay includes a multicourse breakfast and an afternoon social hour.

While you are visiting this plush bed-and-breakfast, you can keep yourself busy during the day by sightseeing in Cannon Beach or visiting one of the many state parks in this area, which include Ecola, Arcadia Beach, and Hug Point, all of which are located to the north, and Oswald West State Park, located south off U.S. 101.

Restrictions: No smoking. No pets. Children 12 and older are welcome.

on the beach. Upstairs at the end of the hallway is the Sunrise Room. This formal, pampering room has a king-size bed and a cozy fireplace and has a large bathroom with a small refrigerator. This room has high cathedral ceilings and a nice view of the Coast Range. The Garden Room has a king-size four-poster bed, a small sitting area, and a romantic fireplace. It is decorated with an abundance of flowers and looks out over a small garden of its own. The Jungle Room is a favorite of small children and the Aztec Room can sleep a family of four."

Another element that will make your stay at this bed-and-breakfast a romantic one is to request a gift basket for your partner. Gift baskets can include flowers, cheese and crackers, cookies and fruit, and a nice bottle of wine or sparkling cider. Or, they can include balloons or bubble bath. The Palmers can make you a gift basket that fits into your budget by request. All they ask is that you give them a budget and a basic idea of what you want, and they will do the rest. Additional amenities

Manzanita

The Arbors Bed and Breakfast $$$
78 Idaho Avenue, Manzanita
(503) 368–7566

The Arbors is a 1922 two-story cottage that is surrounded by pretty gardens and has two guest rooms with private baths. Additional amenities at this bed-and-breakfast include delicious homemade cookies and a selection of hot drinks. Breakfast is served family style and includes a fruit plate with a hot breakfast entree and freshly baked scones, biscuits, and muffins served with jam and your choice of coffee, juice, or tea.

If you are looking for things to do, you are within walking distance of a long, flat, sandy beach, you can hike up to the top of Neakahnie Mountain, or you can check out the surfers at Short Sands Beach located in Oswald West State Park just south of Manzanita. Nehalem Bay State Park located north of Manzanita has uncrowded hiking and biking trails that are also sure to please.

Restrictions: No smoking. No pets. Children over age 8 are welcome.

Oceanside

Sea Rose–A Bed and Breakfast $$$
1685 Maxwell Mountain Road, Oceanside
(503) 842–6126

Judy Gregoire and Puddin the cat are your hosts at the Sea Rose, a three-story, 1938 Cape Cod–style house that has easy beach access and a spectacular ocean view. This cozy bed-and-breakfast features the Antoinette Room and the Nicole Room.

The Antoinette Room is furnished with a comfy queen-size bed, antique table and chairs, cozy rockers, a private deck with an ocean view, and a private bath with a claw-foot tub.

The Nicole Room is decorated with white wicker furniture, an oak writing desk, and a queen-size bed and has a private bath with a claw-foot tub.

Additional treats and comforts you'll find in the common area are shelves filled with interesting book titles, a piano, refrigerator and freezer, and your choice of coffee, tea, popcorn, and yummy Tillamook ice cream.

Breakfast is served in the dining room or on the deck. A typical breakfast includes a fresh citrus bowl made up of grapefruit, oranges, and kiwis; shrimp quiche; broiled tomatoes; and heart-shaped baking powder biscuits served with homemade blackberry jam. Other choices include homemade muffins, apple pancakes served with sage and rosemary sausage, cinnamon bread, and hot rolls.

While you are in this area, you can visit Cape Meares and the Cape Meares lighthouse, Cape Lookout, and Cape Kiwanda.

Restrictions: No smoking. No pets. Children over 14 are welcome.

Pacific City

Eagle's View Bed and Breakfast $$$
37975 Brooten Road, Pacific City
(888) 846–3292
www.eaglesviewbb.com

This country-style bed-and-breakfast is located on a hillside with views of the Nestucca Bay and Nestucca River and is surrounded by four acres of coastal landscape filled with cultivated gardens mixed in with a natural landscape. Trails lead you through the grounds and give you a chance to take in some of the outstanding views of the river and bay.

The inn is light and bright and decorated with country pine furnishings. The architecture includes high ceilings and natural woodwork. Five guest rooms are available and they all have a private bath, satellite TV and VCR, and a CD player. In addition, three rooms have Jacuzzi tubs and all rooms are wheelchair accessible. The rooms are decorated with handmade quilts and dolls and feature antique wardrobes and armoires. The inn features a Great Room where guests can relax by a warm pellet stove and sip hot chocolate and eat homemade cookies. Expansive decks also surround the bed-and-breakfast and you can take a relaxing soak in the outdoor five-person hot tub.

Your homemade breakfast includes a hot beverage, fruit, granola, fresh muffins, and a main entree. A typical breakfast entree is smoked salmon with cream cheese or green onions and scrambled eggs served with freshly baked croissants.

If you feel like exploring, you can visit Cape Kiwanda Beach, Cape Meares State Park and Lighthouse, and Cape Lookout State Park. Both of these state parks are located on the Three Capes Scenic Highway.

Restrictions: No smoking. No pets. Children 12 and older are welcome.

Central Coast

Depoe Bay

Channel House Bed and Breakfast $$–$$$$
35 Ellingson Street, Depoe Bay
(800) 447–2140
www.channelhouse.com

The Channel House is a contemporary bed-and-breakfast perched above the rocky shore of beautiful Depoe Bay. This bed-and-breakfast features three rooms and nine suites. The oceanfront suites have magnificent views of Depoe Bay and offer a separate sleeping and sitting area, a queen-size bed, a wet bar, coffeemaker, gas fireplace, private bath, and a private deck with an outdoor whirlpool tub. Oceanfront rooms are equipped with a queen-size bed, private bath, and private deck with whirlpool tub. In addition, all rooms contain plush robes, a television with HBO, and a refrigerator.

A hearty continental breakfast is served in the oceanside serving room and includes freshly baked breads and pastries, an assortment of fresh fruits, yogurt, cereal, coffee, tea, and a variety of juices.

Be sure to explore the charming shops in Depoe Bay, and if you are looking for more adventure, try a deep-sea fishing or whale-watching trip from one of the local outfitters in Depoe Bay.

Restrictions: No smoking. No pets. No children.

Newport

Green Gables Bed and Breakfast & Bookstore
$$–$$$
156 Southwest Coast Street, Newport
(800) 515–9065, (541) 574–0986
www.greengablesbb.com

Nestled in the friendly community of Nye Beach, The Green Gables Bed and Breakfast is a charming Victorian-style home adjacent to a 4-mile stretch of wide sandy beach. Green Gables was built in 1981 and an extra wing was added in 1996. It has two guest rooms. The Turret Suite is a bright, open room bathed with light that streams in from the bay and turret windows surrounding the queen-size bed. A French door leads to a balcony where you can gaze at the Pacific Ocean. An adjoining room provides a writing desk where you can sit and write letters to friends and comfortable chairs where you can lounge and enjoy a good novel. This suite also features a large, relaxing, two-person whirlpool tub.

The Gables Room, located on the top floor of the house, is filled with charming nooks and crannies, an antique secretary's desk, cozy chairs, and a queen-size bed. In addition, a relaxing two-person whirlpool tub is available in the large, private bathroom located down a flight of stairs. Each room also comes equipped with the following amenities: cable TV; VCR; refrigerator; microwave; soft, fluffy robes; hot pot with teas and hot chocolate; and a radio. The common area of the house has a warm and cozy wood stove, piano, and video library.

If you love to read, then you'll also want to visit the bookstore located in the bottom level of the house that specializes in women's mysteries and quality children's books.

Insiders' Tip

If you want to have a get-together with your family or friends, some bed-and-breakfasts and inns will rent their whole facility to you and your group for a discounted price.

When you stay at Green Gables, you can choose the type of meal you'd like and when you would like it served. You can also opt to eat in bed, on the porch, or out on the deck. Specialties are fluffy French toast, applesauce pancakes, apple/pear compote, lox and bagels, muffins, scones, steak and eggs, frittatas, omelets, and eggs benedict.

There are endless opportunities for fun nearby. This B&B is only 1 block from the ocean and beach and a short walk to shopping and restaurants. Other activities that may interest you include hiking, fishing, whale watching, kayaking, canoeing, or visiting the Oregon Coast Aquarium.

Restrictions: No smoking. Children 16 and older are welcome. Pets are not allowed.

Oar House Bed and Breakfast $$$
520 Southwest 2nd Street, Newport
(800) 252–2358
www.oarhouse-bed-breakfast.com

Jan LeBrun is the owner and innkeeper of the Oar House Bed and Breakfast. When we asked Jan how she decided to open a bed-and-breakfast she replied, "two of my children settled in Oregon after graduating from college and I wanted to be closer to them. Also, I had always had a yen to live near the ocean, and the older I got the more I hated the heat and humidity of Dallas. One day I was standing in a bookstore thumbing through a book titled *The 100 Best Businesses for Women* and innkeeping was listed. I just said to myself, 'I can do that!' After running a household and raising three children, innkeeping looked like a cup of tea to me. I have now been an innkeeper for almost seven years."

The Oar House was built in 1900 and has a colorful history. The 5,600-square-foot, L-shaped, Craftsman-style house was built by a Mr. Bradshaw, who salvaged wood from a wooden lumber schooner that washed ashore. With such a large house, Mrs. Bradshaw decided to open a boarding house, where she accommodated up to 30 boarders. After its use as a boarding house, it became known as the Nye Beach bordello. According to stories of longtime residents, the ghost of a woman who died in the bordello still inhabits the house—but by all means don't let this piece

of history scare you away. Carol and Dan Sutherland purchased the house in 1980 and renovated the house by adding a lighthouse tower and widow's walk and other nautical decorating touches. Carol opened the house as a bed-and-breakfast in 1987 and closed the business in 1991. Jan purchased the property in 1991 and has been running the B&B ever since.

The house has five guest rooms that each has their own unique character.

The Chart Room is decorated with a queen sleigh bed, comfy overstuffed chairs, a reading library, and an ocean view over the rooftops. This room has a private bath, which is located across the hall and features a Jacuzzi tub for two.

The Starboard Cabin has a reading library, a comfy queen-size bed, and a private bath with a Jacuzzi tub for two, and has views of the ocean and Yaquina Head lighthouse.

The Deckside Berth is furnished with antique pine tables, an iron scroll queen-size bed, two chairs, and a private bath with an oversized shower. The Crow's Nest is located on the third floor and features a dormer, gables, and slanted ceilings. The room is furnished with a queen-size bed, and a chaise and chair that face toward the ocean. This room has a private bath and a large soaking tub.

The Captain's Quarters features an English cottage-style queen bed, a secretary's desk and chair, and an ocean view. In addition, this room has a sitting room and a private bath with a shower, bidet, and walk-in closet.

Additional amenities you'll appreciate at this bed-and-breakfast include a sitting room area that has a fireplace and 30-channel stereo, the adjacent living room area that has cable TV, and a bar area with a refrigerator that is stocked with soft drinks. Hot water is also available if you would like to make a hot beverage.

Your visit wouldn't be complete without visiting the cupola, which offers 360-degree views of the ocean, Yaquina Head, and the Coast Range.

You'll enjoy a gourmet breakfast served in the new morning room area at your own table between 8:00 and 9:00 A.M. Breakfast includes ground gourmet coffee, a variety of teas, homemade bread, orange juice, and a hot breakfast entree served with a variety of smoked chicken sausages and muffins made with fresh, locally grown blueberries.

Newport has many activities that will suit just about anyone—including beachcombing, hiking, cycling, fishing, crabbing, clamming, kiteflying, and whale watching. If you want to explore some of Newport's historic areas, you can walk through the romantic Nye Beach area (where the Oar House is located) or check out Newport's bayfront that is home to Newport's largest fishing fleet. The Oregon Coast Aquarium, the Hatfield Marine Science Center, and the Yaquina Head Outstanding Natural Area are all wonderful places to visit for nature lovers and for those wanting to find out more about the coastal ecosystem.

Restrictions: No smoking. No pets. No children.

South Beach

Solace By the Sea Bed and Breakfast
$$$–$$$$
9602 South Coast Highway 101, South Beach
(888) 4 SOLACE (476–5223)
www.solacebythesea.com

The Solace by the Sea is a three-story cedar-sided contemporary beach home, which has beach access. Your hosts at this bed-and-breakfast are Todd and Lisa Whear, their son Max, and Bailey, a fun-loving yellow lab. Lisa describes Todd as the "resident massage therapist" and herself as the one who "performs magic in the kitchen." Together they make every effort to make your stay as relaxing and enjoyable as possible. You can have your pick of one of three guest rooms that all have down feather beds, private baths, and gorgeous ocean views. Additional comforts you'll find are fluffy robes, a reading library and sitting room, TV/VCR, and complimentary coffee, tea, and cold soda. If you want to have a soothing massage, Todd can give you an hour of therapeutic full-body massage for $60.00. You can also rent beach bikes for $20.00 per day, mountain bikes for $30.00 per day, kayaks for $40.00 to $75.00 per day, and crab rings for $5.00 per day. Custom guided kayak and mountain bike tours can also be arranged for you.

Breakfast is a fun, four-course affair that begins with fresh ground coffee, gourmet tea, and fruit juices. This is followed by fresh-baked breads such as muffins, scones, or other pastries accompanied with a fresh fruit plate. The main entree is made with fresh herbs and garnishes from the garden.

Restrictions: No smoking. No children. Pets are accepted but they must stay in outdoor kennel. Pet charge is $10.00 per night.

Newport Belle Bed and Breakfast $$$
P.O. Box 685, South Beach 97366
(800) 348–1922
www.newportbelle.com

If you want to stay in a different type of bed-and-breakfast you'll have to reserve a stateroom at the *Newport Belle*—a replica of a sternwheeler riverboat that is docked in Newport's Newport Marina. This 97-foot boat includes 3,100 square feet of living space on three different decks. This unique bed-and-breakfast features turn-of-the-century charm with modern conveniences.

Sherry Porter, the owner and innkeeper of the *Newport Belle*, told us the story of how she found this unique boat: "I sold my kitchen supply stores in Billings, Montana, to move back to Oregon and buy a bed-and-breakfast on the Oregon Coast. I heard about 'a boat in Bandon' and so I drove down to see it—having no intention of buying a boat. Well, once I was on the vessel, I was hooked. I fell in love with it, bought it, and had it moved to Winchester Bay. After two years of having the business in that location (since May of 1996), I contacted Don Mann at the Port of Newport and inquired about possibly moving the boat to Newport. In December of 1998 there was the calm weather window that was required for the boat to be towed up the Coast to Newport and she arrived here on December 23. After extensive dock renovation and utilities installed on the dock, I opened for business on H Dock in the Newport Marina at South Beach on March 19, 1999."

Just like Sherry, once you step aboard the boat you'll also be "hooked." Aboard this boat you can have your pick of five large staterooms. All rooms have a private

The Newport Belle *is a unique bed-and-breakfast destination in Newport's Yaquina Harbor.* PHOTO: LIZANN DUNEGAN

bath and shower. From every room you'll have a wonderful view of the hustle and bustle of the Newport Marina and of the Yaquina Bay Bridge.

You can enjoy stunning sunsets from the open afterdeck or curl up by the cozy wood stove in the main saloon where you can read, play games, or visit with other guests. Breakfast is served between 8:00 and 9:30 A.M. and starts with homemade granola served with fresh milk and raw sugar and is accompanied by your choice of fresh muffins, croissants, and a large fruit tray. Next you'll be served a delicious Mexican casserole entree (see recipe in this chapter's Close-Up) and homemade French bread with an artichoke and garlic spread and sausage links on the side.

There are many attractions in the near vicinity of the *Newport Belle* including the Oregon Coast Aquarium, the Hatfield Marine Science Center, the historic Newport bayfront, Yaquina Outstanding Natural Area, Yaquina Bay State Park, and the Newport Performing Arts Center.

Restrictions: No smoking. No pets or children. Soft-soled shoes are requested and appropriate for both the boat and the dock.

Yachats

Burd's Nest Inn Bed and Breakfast $$–$$$
664 Yachats River Road, Yachats
(541) 547–3683

The Burd's Nest Inn is owned and run by Joni and Burd Bicksler and it can be easily recognized by its bright, multicolored tile roof. The roof is an eye-catcher due to its 26,000 pounds of tiles that are proudly displayed in 10 different colors! This bed-and-breakfast features over 5,000 square feet of space and is nestled on a tree-covered hillside above the Pacific Ocean and the Yachats River estuary. The house is decorated in a country Spanish motif and is furnished with willow stick furniture mixed with an eclectic assortment of antique toys, stuffed animals, handcrafted items, birds, and birdhouses.

This inn features three colorful guest rooms. The Robin's Nest is furnished with a king-size bed, has French doors opening to a balcony with a panoramic view of the Pacific Ocean and the mountains, and a private bath with a yellow Mexican tile shower. The Swallow's Nest is decorated in a 1930s motif and has the same amenities as the Robin's Nest except it has a claw-foot tub and a ring shower. The Eagle's Nest is decorated in a patriotic theme and includes all of the amenities of the other rooms except it has a decorative brass tub. Soft, fluffy robes, hair dryers, and curling irons are provided.

Breakfast is served between 9:00 and 9:30 A.M. and hot drinks are available before that time for early risers. Breakfast usually begins with homemade oat bran muffins and a delicious fruit smoothie. The next course includes anything from veggie quiche with salsa to French toast stuffed with cream cheese (see recipes in this chapter's Close-Up). To top it off, you can have your choice of coffee, juice, or tea.

From the bed-and-breakfast you can walk to the beach or town. While in town you can check out the quaint shops, eat a gourmet meal, or visit the Little Log Church by the Sea museum. Other attractions in the area include Cape Perpetua, Devil's Churn, Strawberry Hill, Heceta Head Lighthouse, and Sea Lion Caves.

Restrictions: No smoking. No pets. No children.

Heceta Head Lighthouse Bed and Breakfast $$-$$$
92072 U.S. Highway 101 S., Yachats
(541) 547-3696
www.hecetalighthouse.com

The Heceta Head Lighthouse Bed and Breakfast is a Queen Ann–style house surrounded by a white picket fence that was built in the late 1800s and is situated next to Heceta Head Lighthouse—thought to be one of the most scenic spots on the Oregon Coast. This fully restored inn has five guest rooms decorated with period furnishings. The Mariner's Room has a mesmerizing ocean view, a queen-size bed, antique furnishings, and a private bath. The Lightkeeper's Room has an exclusive view of Heceta Head Lighthouse and the ocean and is furnished with a queen-size bed. This room has a shared bath. Victoria's Room is decorated with a four-poster queen-size bed, a trundle bed, and a private bath. The romantic Queen Anne room has a four-poster bed and a Victorian Chaise lounge. The Cape Cove Room is filled with antique furniture and has

views of the historic Cape Creek Bridge. A full seven-course gourmet breakfast is served in the morning.

While you are visiting you can explore the lighthouse and beach, the Sea Lion Caves, and Cape Perpetua.

Restrictions: No smoking or pets.

The Kittiwake Bed and Breakfast $$$$
95368 U.S. Highway 101, Yachats
(541) 547-4470
www.kittiwakebandb.com

The Kittiwake is a contemporary bed-and-breakfast built on 2.5 acres that have been carefully cultivated to build suitable habitat for the endangered silverspot butterfly. Some areas have been left natural to encourage elk and deer to graze on the property. The house sits atop a 20-foot bluff overlooking the Pacific and is only 100 feet from the ocean. The interior colors and furniture of this quiet getaway are earth tones accentuated with bright colors that make it feel warm, snug, and inviting.

The Kittiwake has three ocean-facing guestrooms that are outfitted with queen-size beds, private baths, and entrances to a deck.

Room 1 is the largest and is decorated with rattan furniture and Caribbean pastel colors and is a favorite of longer-staying guests due to its large size.

Room 2 is furnished with a cherry sleigh bed, writing desk, and whirlpool bath for two.

Room 3, faces north and west and has window seats with a panoramic ocean view. This room is furnished with a queen-size bow bed and chest and table that are made of rock maple. This room also features a two-person whirlpool tub that has an ocean view to the northwest.

Other amenities you'll find at this bed-and-breakfast include a guest lounge with overstuffed furniture and window seats, magazines, and a small collection of eclectic hardback titles; a coffee bar with mugs and stemware; a guests' refrigerator; rain gear; and colorful kites.

A full breakfast is served in your room on individual trays at 8:30 A.M. A typical homemade breakfast includes grapefruit or fresh mixed fruit; muffins or bagels;

smoked ham, smoked turkey, sturgeon, bacon, or sausage and apples; a German breakfast entree; a beverage of choice; and a scrumptious dessert. You may opt to eat your breakfast indoors or on the lower deck, where each room has a designated seating area. If you are an early riser, fresh hot coffee, tea, and cocoa are always available.

Wildlife watching is a popular activity at this bed-and-breakfast. Early risers may see elk and deer grazing on the property and eagles soaring on the air currents above the beach, as well as a variety of shorebirds. In addition, whales and seals are seen throughout the year, and if you love to look at tide pools, head to the beach where you can see a rich variety of tide pool creatures.

Other activities that you'll enjoy in this area include dune buggy rides in the Oregon Dunes National Recreational Area south of Florence; horseback riding on the beach (C & M stables is 12 miles south of the Kittiwake); and Sea Lion Caves located 8 miles south of the Kittiwake. The Kittiwake is also within proximity of dozens of state parks and designated natural areas including Heceta Head Lighthouse, Devil's Elbow State Park, Carl G. Washburn State Park, and Cape Perpetua.

Restrictions: No smoking. No pets. No children. The owners request that you do not burn candles or incense in your room and also ask that you do not wear waffle-soled shoes or hiking boots in the house.

Florence

Edwin K Bed and Breakfast $$–$$$$
1155 Bay Street, Florence
(800) 8–EDWIN–K (833–9465)
www.edwink.com

You'll enjoy your stay at this two-story 1914 Craftsman-style bed-and-breakfast. Inez and Victor West own this B&B, which has been fully restored to its original grandeur and is filled with period antiques. You'll have your choice of six large rooms with a private bath, or you can stay in a 1,000-square-foot bedroom suite that has cooking facilities and can accommodate up to six people.

For breakfast you'll enjoy your choice of freshly baked breads, muffins, or delicious apricot and white chocolate scones, egg or cheese soufflé, a fresh fruit plate, ham and sausage, Marionberry compote, coffee, tea, and orange juice.

Activities abound in the Florence area. You can explore Old Town Florence, walk the beach, hit a few rounds of golf, or try your hand at fishing and crabbing.

Restrictions: No smoking. No pets. Children over age 12 are welcome.

The Johnson House Bed and Breakfast $$$
216 Maple Street, Florence
(541) 997–8000

This beautiful Victorian bed-and-breakfast was built in 1892 and contains period furnishings throughout. Impressive gardens surround the house featuring a variety of fragrant herbs and perennials. Six guest rooms are available and three of these rooms have private baths. Personal touches you'll find at this bed-and-breakfast

Insiders' Tip

A nifty way to take in the historic charm of the Nye Beach area in Newport is to dress in period costumes of the Victorian era, the '30s or the '40s and then take in some of the nightlife in that beach zone that is full of nostalgia and historical buildings. Attend a concert or play at the Newport Performing Arts Center and then retire to the Sylvia Beach Hotel for a lovely dinner and stay in a period room named after and designed around a famous author.

What's for Breakfast?

Wondering what some of the secret ingredients are in the gourmet breakfast entrees you ate at your last bed-and-breakfast getaway? Be sure to read some of these recipes sent to us by innkeepers up and down the Coast.

Benjamin Young Inn Scones

3 cups flour
1 tablespoon baking powder
½ teaspoon salt
½ cup sugar
¾ cup butter
1 cup buttermilk
½ cup dried cranberries, raisins, or currants

Combine dry ingredients. Cut in butter. Add the buttermilk and mix well. Add cranberries and mix slightly. Turn the dough onto a floured board and knead just until the dough holds together. Pat the dough until it is about ¾ inch thick. Cut out the individual scones with a biscuit cutter. Place the scones on an ungreased cookie sheet. Bake at 425 degrees for 15 to 20 minutes until the scones are golden brown. Serve hot with lemon curd, Devonshire cream, or butter and jam. Makes approximately 15 scones.

Crustless Quiche (from Nel Ward, Green Gables Bed and Breakfast & Bookstore)

⅓ lb. cooked potatoes or frozen tater tots or taters
½ lb. grated Jarlsberg cheese
2 tablespoons flour
1 cup milk
½ cup sour cream
5 eggs
1 teaspoon tarragon
Optional: chopped vegetables, cooked shrimp, ham, or fried bacon

Preheat oven to 325 degrees. Spray a 9-inch round ceramic pan with oil. Put chunks of potatoes in the ceramic pan. Cook frozen potatoes in the microwave on high for two minutes. Put any optional ingredients on the potatoes after they are thawed. Mix flour with cheese and sprinkle over potatoes. Lightly beat eggs with milk, cream, and tarragon; pour over potato/cheese mixture. Bake for 40 minutes or until quiche is firm inside.

French Toast (from Nel Ward, Green Gables Bed and Breakfast & Bookstore)

16 thinly sliced pieces of bread (challah or walnut bread works well)
1½ cups ricotta cheese
2 teaspoons vanilla
3 teaspoons sugar
7 eggs

3 tablespoon brown sugar
2 teaspoons vanilla
3 tablespoons butter
1 tablespoon olive oil

Mix cheese, vanilla, and sugar. Spread ricotta cheese mixture on eight pieces of bread and cover with the remaining eight pieces of bread, making eight sandwiches. Cut each sandwich in half. Mix eggs, brown sugar, and vanilla with an electric mixer. Dip each half sandwich in the egg/brown sugar/vanilla mixture and fry on each side in butter and olive oil until both sides are brown. Optional: Pecans or walnuts may be added to the ricotta cheese mixture for variety. Makes 4 servings.

Applesauce Pancakes (from Nel Ward, Green Gables Bed and Breakfast & Bookstore)

1½ cups oatmeal
1½ cups flour
3 tablespoons brown sugar
1½ teaspoons baking powder
1½ teaspoons baking soda
1½ cups buttermilk
6 eggs
4 tablespoons butter, melted
1 cup applesauce

Pour the buttermilk over the oatmeal and let it soak for an hour to as long as overnight in the refrigerator. Combine the dry ingredients. Mix together the buttermilk/oatmeal mixture, eggs, butter, and applesauce. Add this mixture to the dry ingredients, stirring to form a smooth batter. Spoon the batter into a hot oiled skillet. When they are brown, flip the pancakes over. Makes about 6 servings.

B & B Oat Bran Muffins (from Joni Bicksler, Burd's Nest Inn)

4 cups bran flakes
1¼ cups raisins
3 cups flour
2 cups oat bran
5 teaspoons baking soda
2 cups brown sugar
2 teaspoons cinnamon
4 eggs
1 quart buttermilk
¾ cup oil
⅓ cup frozen apple juice concentrate

Mix dry ingredients together in a large bowl. Mix liquids and fold into dry mix. Store in refrigerator overnight before baking. Pour into buttered muffin pan. Bake at 350 degrees for 20 minutes.

Note: Covered dough can remain in the refrigerator for up to 30 days; bake as needed. Baked muffins also freeze well. Yield 48 muffins.

Stuffed French Toast (from Joni Bicksler, Burd's Nest Inn)

8-10 pieces of bread
8 ounces cream cheese
2 cups milk
8 eggs
⅓ cup maple syrup
Fresh fruit
Confectioners sugar

The night before, grease a 14"x10"x2" casserole pan. Take the crust off 8 to 10 pieces of bread and press into the pan. Cut up 8 ounces of cream cheese. Place pieces on top of bread slices. In a separate bowl, mix 2 cups milk with 8 eggs and ⅓ cup maple syrup. Pour over the top of the bread and cream cheese. Cover and leave overnight on the kitchen counter. Note: In warm climates, refrigerate overnight.

In the morning, preheat oven to 375 degrees and bake for 45 minutes. Let cool for 15 minutes before serving. Divide into 8 pieces and top with fresh fruit such as bananas, raisins, or berries. Pour hot maple syrup over fruit and toast and sprinkle with confectioner's sugar.

Burd's Nest Inn Fruit Smoothie (from Joni Bicksler, Burd's Nest Inn)

2 bananas, peeled
1 orange, peeled
½ apple, peeled
2½ cups pineapple juice

Mix ingredients in a blender. Add ice cubes to fill container. Blend until smooth. Pour into tall, slim glasses. Garnish with fresh fruit and serve.

Granola (from Sherry Porter, Newport Belle Bed and Breakfast)

5 cups rolled oats
8 cups crisp rice cereal
1 cup wheat germ
½ cup sunflower seeds

Mix together and pour over the dry ingredients:
¾ cup water
¾ cup oil
¾ cup brown sugar
1 teaspoon salt
2 tablespoon vanilla
1 cup honey

Combine and place on a large cookie sheet, bake 1 to 1½ hours stirring every 15 minutes. After the mixture cools add 1½ cups raisins. Bake at 250 degrees for 1 to 1½ hours.

Sherry's Mexican Casserole (from Sherry Porter of the *Newport Belle* Bed and Breakfast)

Prepare this recipe the night before and refrigerate until ready to bake.

8 slices of heavy bread, cut or pressed to fit heavy pan
1 tablespoon crushed oregano leaves

1 teaspoon garlic salt
1 4-ounce can chopped green chilies
3 cups shredded sharp cheddar cheese
3 cups shredded Jack cheese
7 eggs
2 cups water
¾ cup dry milk
1 avocado
¾ cup sour cream

In a 9 x 13-inch greased pan layer the first six ingredients in the order listed. Place eggs, water, and dry milk in a blender, blend very briefly and pour over the cheese. Chill overnight. Bake in a 325 degree oven for 50 minutes or until barely set. Top each serving with a slice of avocado and a dollop of sour cream. Serves 8 to 10.

Clementine's Greatest Pancakes (from Judith Taylor, Clementine's Bed and Breakfast)

4 large eggs, beaten
4 cups buttermilk
1⅓ cups cornmeal
1⅓ cups all-purpose flour
1½ cups quick oats
4 teaspoons baking powder
2 teaspoons baking soda
2 teaspoons. salt
1 tablespoon sugar
1 cup oil

Combine eggs, buttermilk, and oil. Combine cornmeal, flour, oats, baking powder, baking soda, salt, and sugar in a separate bowl and mix until well blended. Add wet ingredients to dry just until mixed. Cook over a hot buttered griddle until bubbles appear, then flip and cook one minute more. The batter will hold up well in the refrigerator for three days.

Variations: Add blueberries, raspberries, or chocolate chips, or add 1 cup mashed banana or pumpkin in place of ½ cup oil with appropriate spices.

include comfy robes, a fully stocked reading library, current periodicals and newspapers, a pretty sitting room, and extravagant bedding and linens.

When you wake up in the morning, you can look forward to a breakfast that includes a main entree of soufflés, omelets, or frittatas made with fresh herbs from the garden and fresh crab in season or Swedish waffles and maple syrup. Accompanying your entree are freshly baked muffins, croissants, and scones; fresh fruit; ground gourmet coffee; and orange juice.

Restrictions: No smoking. No pets. Children 12 and older are welcome.

South Coast

Coos Bay

This Olde House $$–$$$$
202 Alder Avenue, Coos Bay
(541) 267–5224
www.bnbweb.com/thisoldehouse.html

Sally White is your host at This Olde House, an elegant home built in 1893 that is decorated with beautiful inlaid wood floors, crystal chandeliers, and antique furnishings. The inn has four guest rooms that are furnished with king- and queen-size beds, televisions, private baths, and fluffy robes. With your stay, you'll also receive complimentary wine. If you stay three nights at the bed-and-breakfast you'll receive a complimentary gourmet dinner prepared by Sally, who specializes in Japanese cuisine. Breakfast is served with homemade blackberry syrup.

While you are in this area, be sure to visit Sunset Beach and Shore Acres State Parks and the Coos Art Museum.

Restrictions: No smoking. No pets. No small children.

The Old Tower House Bed and Breakfast
$$-$$$
476 Newmark Avenue, Coos Bay
(541) 888-6058
www.oldtowerhouse.com

The Old Tower House Bed and Breakfast was built in 1872 and is located in the historic Empire District of Coos Bay. This charming old-world house has a large main parlor with a bright sunroom where many guests like to relax and read. The main house has three rooms, the King's Room, the Blue Room, and the Rose Room, designed to fit a variety of tastes.

The King's Room features a large king-size brass bed covered with a decorative antique quilt, an Oriental rug, a wicker rocker, and pedestal sink.

The Blue Room is filled with antique furnishings, two comfortable twin beds, a delightful Persian rug, a blue-tiled washstand from Scotland, and a pedestal sink, and you can enjoy outstanding views of the bay through a gothic-style window.

The Rose Room features a 150-year-old Barley Twist double bed, vintage linens, a handmade fishnet canopy, rose floral wallpaper, vintage antiques, and a pedestal sink.

If you want more privacy, you may want to consider staying in The Carriage House suite. This loft suite comes equipped with a large sitting room, complete kitchen, hand-painted queen-size bed, TV and VCR, and an old-fashioned claw-foot tub. If this doesn't quite suit your taste, you may want to stay in the Ivy Cottage, which is a reflection of a quaint English garden cottage and is decorated with ivy wallpaper and a floral bath. This cottage comes equipped with a sitting room with TV, microwave, coffeemaker, refrigerator, a comfortable bedroom, and a claw-foot tub.

Before you head out for the day, you'll enjoy a full complimentary breakfast that is served in the sunroom on damask table linens. If you looking for things to see and do in the area, you can spend the day fishing, crabbing, or digging for clams; or you may also just want to relax in the garden and gazebo located on the Old Tower House grounds.

Restrictions: No pets. No smoking. Children 10 years and older are welcome.

Bandon

Bailey's Cedar House Bed and Breakfast
$-$$
Box 58739, Seven Devils Road, Bandon
(541) 347-3356

This friendly bed-and-breakfast was built in 1993 in a quiet, country, wooded setting and has two guest rooms. The first room is a cozy suite with a private entrance, sitting room, kitchen, private bath, television, and queen bed. The second guest room has a private entrance, queen bed, television, and private bath. A soothing hot tub is available outside.

A full breakfast is served, which includes omelets made with local seafood, scones, homemade jams, fresh fruit, juice, and coffee.

This bed-and-breakfast is only a short 10- to 15-minute drive from Bandon's Old Town, which is filled with shops, galleries, restaurants, and a busy marina. If you love to play golf, be sure to check out the world-class Bandon Dunes golf course.

Restrictions: No smoking or pets.

Beach Street Bed and Breakfast $$$-$$$$
200 Beach Street, Bandon
(888) 335-1076
www.beachstreet.com

Ray Caswell and Sharon Mclean own the Beach Street Bed and Breakfast, which was built in 1996 and rests atop an

80,000-year-old sand dune. Sharon says that she and Ray met while putting on an amateur theater production in Bandon and that "we put our heads and money together and Beach Street is the result."

Ray personally designed and built the bed-and-breakfast, which features three guest rooms that are all individually decorated. All of the rooms have an ocean view and private bath. To add a romantic touch to your stay, you'll find that all rooms have thick, fluffy towels, candles, and bubble bath. And if you're looking for an even more intimate atmosphere, be sure to request one of the two rooms that have a fireplace.

Guests can sit and enjoy a crackling fire in the Great Room where you can also visit with other guests, listen to music, or play games. Expansive decks surround the house and offer great views of Cape Blanco continuing north to Cape Arago.

A typical breakfast menu includes egg casserole, quiche, fresh fruit salad, fresh muffins, bacon, sausage, hash browns, and scrambled eggs. Breakfast is usually served buffet style in the dining room. However, Sharon adds, "When there are fewer guests, I'm happy to prepare anything to order—eggs benedict to breakfast burritos." She also adds, "Vegetarian and special diets can be provided on request."

When we asked Sharon about things to see and do in and around Bandon, she replied, "Bandon has lots of activities; the beach is famous for its magnificent views—we are only a short walk from the beach. There is a horse stable across the street, and we are only 10 minutes away from the world-class Bandon Dunes golf course. The Bandon Marsh has added a thousand more acres and bird- and wildlife-watching in this area is breathtaking. In the spring and fall we have gray whales migrating and you can see them spouting from our deck. There are charter boats available for fishing and you can go crabbing off Webber pier. River or ocean kayaking can also be scheduled. Old Town has several excellent galleries, restaurants, and unique shops that are also fun to explore."

Restrictions: No smoking. No pets. Children 10 and older are welcome.

Lighthouse Bed and Breakfast $$$–$$$$
50 Jetty Road SW, Bandon
(541) 347–9316
www.lighthouselodging.com

This contemporary bed-and-breakfast is located on the beach directly across from the historic Bandon Lighthouse. The house has five guest rooms and panoramic views of the ocean and Coquille River estuary.

The Gray Whale Room is at the top of the inn and has a dramatic view of the Coquille River and the lighthouse. This grand room features a California king-size bed, private bath with shower, TV, wood-burning stove, and a whirlpool tub for two.

The Greenhouse Room is the most romantic room at the bed-and-breakfast, furnished with a king-size bed, private bath and shower, fireplace, whirlpool tub for two, TV, and a river view.

The Deck Room has a private deck with a river view, a queen-size bed, and a private bath and shower. Karen's Room has an ocean and lighthouse view, queen-size bed, and a private bathroom across the hall.

In the evening you can relax and sip on complimentary wine in the Great Room and watch TV or listen to the stereo and visit with other guests. In the morning you are served a hearty breakfast of muffins, fresh fruit, egg dishes, French toast, ham or bacon, juice, coffee, or tea.

The Bandon area is filled with fun activities. You can stroll through the antiques shops and art galleries located in downtown Bandon; visit the Bandon Cheese Factory; try out clamming, fishing, or crabbing; or go whale, seal, and bird-watching.

Restrictions: No smoking. No pets. Children 12 and older are welcome. Please let owners know you will be bringing your children.

Langlois

Floras Lake House by the Sea $$$
92870 Boice Cope Road, Langlois
(541) 348–2573
www.floraslake.com

Floras Lake House by the Sea is a contemporary bed-and-breakfast built in 1991. This B&B features four guest rooms that all have views of Floras Lake and the ocean, vaulted wood ceilings, private baths, and deck entrances. In addition, two rooms have cozy fireplaces.

A buffet-style breakfast is served in the living/dining room area between 8:30 and 10:00 A.M. Breakfast includes English muffins, bagels, fresh fruit, yogurt, homemade granola, and a hot breakfast entree. Hot entrees can include fluffy French toast, buttermilk pancakes, quiche, or homemade sticky buns.

There are dozens of activities you can participate in close by. You can walk on the beach that is just a few minutes from the bed-and-breakfast or take a windsurfing lesson from Floras Lake Windsurfing School (run by the owners of the bed-and-breakfast, Liz and Will Brady). You can also explore nearby Cape Blanco and the Cape Blanco Lighthouse or try out your golf swing at Bandon Dunes golf course.

Restrictions: No smoking or pets.

Port Orford

Home by the Sea Bed and Breakfast $$$
444 Jackson Street, Port Orford
(541) 332–2855
www.homebythesea.com

Brenda and Alan Mitchell, owners of Home by the Sea, have lived and worked in Port Orford for more than 30 years. Home by the Sea is a contemporary home that was designed and built by Alan and Brenda. Two guest rooms are available on the second floor and each has its own private bath.

The Blue suite is furnished with a decorative myrtlewood queen-size bed and has an attached bath; and the Coral Room has a queen-size bed with a myrtlewood headboard and a detached bath located across a short hallway.

Additional amenities you'll enjoy at this comfortable bed-and-breakfast include a great ocean view, direct beach access, cable TV, laundry facilities, Web-based e-mail, and complimentary shuttle service for those who are backpacking the Oregon Coast Trail or who want to go to the Cape Blanco Lighthouse and other nearby beaches.

Breakfast includes whole wheat and honey waffles served with Misty Meadows loganberry syrup, Black Forest smoked sausage, fresh fruit, orange juice, and your choice of tea or coffee.

If you want to get out and about to explore the Port Orford area, you should try walking to the beach and hunting for agates and watching for whales. You can ask for the complimentary shuttle to visit Cape Blanco Lighthouse. You can also tour a myrtlewood factory or go out for a romantic dinner.

Restrictions: No smoking or pets. Children are welcome.

Gold Beach

Endicott Gardens Bed and Breakfast $$
95768 Jerry's Flat Road, Gold Beach
(541) 247–6513, (866) 212–1220
www.endicottgardens.com

Endicott Gardens Bed and Breakfast is a contemporary bed-and-breakfast that is surrounded by a variety of fruit trees, beautiful flowers, shrubs, and exotic plants. This home features four guest rooms. Each room has a private bath and two rooms have private decks with views of the surrounding mountains and forest.

Breakfast includes fresh fruits from the garden, freshly baked breads, a main entree, and coffee, juice, or tea.

There are a variety of activities in the Gold Beach area—jet boat tours up the Rogue River, fishing, golfing, horseback riding, beachcombing, and hiking.

Restrictions: No smoking. No pets. Children are welcome with prior arrangement.

Inn at Nesika Beach $$$
33026 Nesika Road, Gold Beach
(541) 247–6434
www.goldbeachlodging.com

The Inn at Nesika Beach is a stylish, newly built Victorian-style inn located on a bluff overlooking the Pacific Ocean. Ann Arsenault is the owner/innkeeper of this inviting inn, which is filled with antiques and other unique decorations. The inn features four rooms with soft feather beds, cozy comforters, fluffy robes, and private baths with whirlpool tubs. In addition, three of these rooms have fireplaces and two rooms have private decks with wonderful ocean views. The Fireside room is a communal area that is a great place to read, play music, sit by the fire, storm watch, and visit with other guests.

Your complimentary breakfast is served in the dining room facing the ocean and features fresh homemade breads, seasonal fruits, and a variety of breakfast entrees such as apple French toast, soufflés, fluffy pancakes, and breakfast meats. Your meal is also accompanied by your choice of fresh, hot coffee, tea, or cocoa.

World-class trout, salmon, and steelhead fishing can be found on the nearby Rogue River and you can brush up on your golf game at Cedar Bend Golf Course, located north of the inn. Credit cards are not accepted at the inn.

Restrictions: No smoking. No pets. Children 13 and older are welcome.

Brookings

Lowden's Beachfront Bed and Breakfast $$
14626 Wollam Road, Brookings
(800) 453–4768
www.beachfrontbb.com

Gary and Barbara Lowden are the innkeepers at this contemporary bed-and-breakfast located on the ocean where the Winchuck River empties into the Pacific. This B&B offers two guest suites that include a queen-size bed; private shower and bath; a living room furnished with a sofa, dining chairs, and a gourmet cart with dishes; and a microwave, refrigerator, coffeemaker, toaster, cable TV, and VCR. A complimentary fruit basket is provided and the refrigerator is stocked with juice, half-and-half, and distilled water. You'll also have your choice of all the coffee, tea, popcorn, and hot chocolate you want. A continental breakfast is served to you in the evening so you can enjoy it in the morning when it is convenient for you.

There are many activities in the Brookings area. The Winchuck River is a good place to kayak and raft, and the waves at

Insiders' Tip

When you are calling to make your reservation at a bed-and-breakfast, be sure to ask the innkeepers about things to see and do in the area you are visiting so you have time to plan your trip and make additional reservations if necessary. Also, if you have any special dietary needs, mention them when you make your reservation.

the mouth of the river provide some fun boogie boarding and surfing. Wildlife watching is also a fun outdoor activity here—you'll be able to see seabirds, seals, otters, and whales.

Restrictions: No smoking or pets.

Brookings South Coast Inn $$–$$$
516 Redwood Street, Brookings
(800) 525–9273
www.southcoastinn.com

Ken Raith and Keith Pepper are the innkeepers at the South Coast Inn bed-and-breakfast. Built in 1917, this 4,000-square-foot Craftsman-style inn features four guest rooms with private bath, television, VCR, and video library. Two rooms have an ocean view. One room also has a private kitchenette and garden. The inn also boasts a large reading parlor with an original stone fireplace and a vintage grand piano. Breakfast includes hot coffee and an entree such as Norwegian waffles with homemade jam.

Brookings is full of outdoor activities that will fill your days with fun. Hiking, boating, camping, fishing, mountain biking, golfing, and shopping are some of the offerings here.

Vacation Rentals

Renting a house at the beach is a fine way to enjoy the Oregon Coast, and many rental companies are available to help you find one. They'll set you up in anything from a rustic cabin to a luxurious house or condominium. Most companies listed below handle a range of properties within their communities and in surrounding areas. They will also let you know about local regulations for renters. Be aware that you may pay for cleaning fees and taxes if you rent a house.

Cannon Beach Vacation Rental Homes, Cannon Beach, (877) 386–3402, www.cbpm.com

Northwind Property Management, Cannon Beach, (800) 488–3301

Pat Ordway Vacation Rentals, Cannon Beach, (503) 738–0837, (800) 473–1143

Castle Rock Vacation Rentals, Arch Cape, (503) 436–3600, http://castlerockvr.com

Sunset Vacation Rentals, Manzanita, (800) 883–7784, www.ssvr.com

Manzanita Rental Company, Manzanita, (800) 579–9801, http://manzanitarentals.com

Edgewater Vacation Rentals, Netarts, (503) 842–1300, (888) 425–1050, www.oregon coastvacrentals.com

Grey Fox Vacation Homes & Property Management, Pacific City, (503) 965–4700

Kiwanda Coastal Properties Vacation Rental, Pacific City, (888) 684–3732, www.kiwandacoastalproperties.com

Sea View Vacation Rentals, Pacific City, (503) 965–7888, (888) 701–1023, www.seaview 4u.com

All Seasons Vacation Rentals, Lincoln City, (541) 996–3549, (800) 362–5229

Pacific Retreats Vacation Home Rentals, Lincoln City, (800) 473–4833, www.pacificretreats.com

Beachcombers Haven Vacation Rentals, Gleneden Beach, (541) 764–2252, (800) 428–5533, www.beachcombershaven.com

Fairhaven Vacation Rentals, Newport, (541) 574–0951, (888) 523–4179, www.fairhaven vacationrentals.com

Ocean Odyssey Vacation Rentals, Yachats and Waldport, (541) 547–3637, (800) 800–1915, www.ocean-odyssey.com

Dolphin Property Management, Florence, (541) 997–7368

Moonlight Bay Vacation Rentals, Charleston, (541) 888–5166, (800) 962–2815

Exclusive Property Management, Bandon, (541) 347–3790, www.bandonexclusive vacationrentals.com

Arcadia on the Coast, Gold Beach, (888) 227–1963, www.southcoastvacationrentals.com

Clear Sky Rentals, Gold Beach, (800) 219–8500

Practical and Professional Property Management, Brookings, (541) 469–6456, www.pppms.com

Restrictions: No smoking or pets. Children age 12 and older are welcome.

Pacific View Bed and Breakfast $$
18814 Montbretia Lane, Brookings
(800) 461–4830
www.pacificviewbb.com

Ursula and Mac Mackey are your hosts at their bed-and-breakfast, which is located in a quiet country setting overlooking the ocean. They have a suite available with a private entrance, private bath, and a sunroom overlooking the ocean. You'll also enjoy a wonderful ocean view from your room.

In the morning, you'll be served a home-cooked breakfast that includes fresh fruit, freshly baked breads, and a main entree such as quiche Lorraine and chicken and apple sausages. Fresh juice and coffee are also served.

Ursula and Mac are local experts on things to see and do in the Brookings area. You can take a hike on the Oregon Coast Trail, which is within walking distance, take a jet boat ride on the Rogue River, visit a grove of redwood trees, or play on the beach.

Restrictions: No smoking. No pets. No children.

Sea Dreamer Inn Bed and Breakfast $$
15167 McVay Lane, Brookings
(800) 408–4367
www.seadreamerinn.com

Built in 1912, the Sea Dreamer Inn Bed and Breakfast is a country Victorian-style home located on spacious grounds and has an outstanding view of southern Oregon's famous lily fields and the Pacific Ocean. Penny Wallace and Don Roy are the owners of this friendly B&B and their philosophy is "to make our home, your home." When you visit this B&B you will truly feel at home in one of its four guest rooms.

The Beachcomber room has an ocean view, library filled with books, comfortable double bed, and private bath. The Siren Song room comes equipped with a double bed and shared bath. The Port St. George room boasts a library, queen-size bed, semiprivate bath, and ocean view. The Quarterdeck room is simply furnished with a double bed, treetop view, and semiprivate bath.

A fireplace, piano, and library filled with interesting books are all additional amenities that you'll find at this cozy inn.

The complimentary breakfast is usually served between 7:30 and 10:00 A.M. The menu is always changing and ranges from empañadas and quiche to egg and vegetarian dishes. Credit cards are not accepted.

Restrictions: Smoking outside on the porch only. Will consider well-behaved pets and children.

Camping

Welcome to camping on the Oregon Coast! From north to south you will find picturesque state, federal, and private campgrounds that are set in a variety of coastal ecosystems from coastal forest and sandy beach to freshwater lakes and coastal dunes. In this section we've listed all the state park campgrounds and selected USDA Forest Service campgrounds from north to south.

North Coast

Horse enthusiasts may want to check out Nehalem Bay State Park campground located in Nehalem on the North Coast. This state park has campsites with corrals and plenty of trail options where you can take your equine friend. Many state park campgrounds also have hiker and biker camps that usually charge only $4.00 per night for backpackers traveling the Oregon Coast Trail or cyclists who are riding the Oregon Coast Bike Route.

Many state park campgrounds take reservations, and we highly recommend that you call ahead to make reservations during the peak camping season from May 1 through September 30. You'll find that many state park campgrounds have yurts, which are circular tentlike structures that are 16 feet in diameter with a wooden floor and come equipped with a lockable door, electric heater, skylight, and three beds that sleep five people. These yurts make you feel as if you're still roughing it, but they have a few amenities that make your

Insiders' Tip

You can reserve a camping site at many Oregon state parks online by visiting the Oregon State Parks and Recreation home page at www.oregonstateparks.org.

camping experience more comfortable. Yurts are very popular places to stay on the Oregon Coast so always be sure to call ahead to reserve one of these unique camping lodges. Although you are welcome to stay in a yurt, your furry friends are not permitted to stay inside with you.

Hammond

Fort Stevens State Park
Hammond
Information: (800) 551–6949, Reservations: (800) 452–5687
www.oregonstateparks.org/park_179.php

Fort Stevens State Park offers fun for everyone. As Oregon's third largest state park, Fort Stevens covers 3,763 acres of beach, sand dunes, shallow lakes, and coastal forest and is situated at the mouth of the Columbia River. Paved hiking and biking trails crisscross the park through a thick coastal forest of western hemlock, red cedar, big-leaf maple, and red alder trees. Hiking enthusiasts should also note that the Oregon Coast Trail can be accessed from the park. Fishing for brown bullhead, rainbow trout, steelhead, and yellow perch is popular at 50-acre Coffenbury Lake, situated in the park. The wreck of the *Peter Iredale* is another popular attraction. This four-masted British freighter ran aground on Clatsop Spit in a rough storm in 1906. Other activities that will tantalize you at this park are beachcombing, windsurfing, swimming, or learning about the park's history at the Fort Stevens Military Museum (see the Attractions chapter for more information about this museum). The park is open year-round. Leashed pets are allowed. Please note: Reservations Northwest charges a $6.00 fee when you make a reservation using the number given here.

Cannon Beach

Saddle Mountain State Natural Area and Campground
Cannon Beach
(800) 551-6949
www.oregonstateparks.org/park_197.php

Saddle Mountain State Park campground is located in a thickly wooded forest made primarily of red alder trees. This state park is a unique botanical area filled with bright and cheery wildflowers such as the white triangular flowers of western trillium; pink-flowered western columbine; the purple, bell-shaped flowers of the coast penstemon; vibrant orange tiger lilies; blue iris; red Indian paintbrush; white meadow chickweed; phlox; and larkspur. To see the park up close and personal, hike to the top of 3,283-foot Saddle Mountain from the campground on a 5.2-mile out-and-back trail. This steep and scenic trail takes you on a scenic tour of a unique coastal mountain landscape. Once you reach the summit you'll have spectacular views of Nehalem Bay and the Pacific Ocean to the west, the Columbia River to the north, and the snow-capped Cascade peaks of Mt. Jefferson and Mt. Hood to the east. This state park is very popular and the campground can fill up fast. The campground is open from April 1 through November 1. Leashed pets are allowed.

Manzanita

Oswald West State Park
Manzanita
(800) 551-6949
www.oregonstateparks.org/park_195.php

This campground is set in a beautiful old-growth forest, and camping sites fill up fast during the summer months. Several hiking trails lead from the campground through the old-growth forest. Trails lead to the Cape Falcon overlook, to the summit of Neahkahnie Mountain, and to a scenic path that parallels Short Sands Creek and ends at Short Sands Beach—a popular surfing and boogie boarding spot. The campground is open March 1 through November 1. Leashed pets are allowed.

Nehalem

Nehalem Bay State Park
Nehalem
Information: (800) 551-6949, Reservations: (800) 452-5687
www.oregonstateparks.org/park_201.php

Nehalem Bay State Park campground is located on a sandy spit separating the Pacific Ocean and Nehalem Bay. Six miles of beachfront lure those wanting to play on the beach. Horse enthusiasts will enjoy a first-rate 7.5-mile equestrian trail, and cyclists can hop on their two-wheel steeds to cruise on a fun 1.5-mile bike trail. Walking along the bay beachfront you can experience prime bird- and seal watching. Boating, fishing, crabbing, and clamming in the bay are also popular activities at this scenic spot on Nehalem Bay. Visit Wheeler Marina at 278 Marine

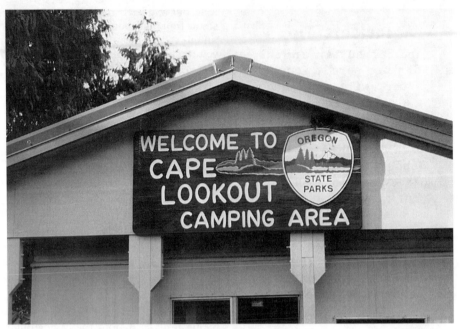

The coast has the highest concentration of state park campgrounds in Oregon. PHOTO: LIZANN DUNEGAN

Drive in Wheeler, (503) 368–5780, to rent a boat and crabbing equipment and to get advice on the fishing, crabbing, and clamming hot spots in Nehalem Bay. The park is open year-round. Leashed pets are allowed. Please note: Reservations Northwest charges a $6.00 fee when you make a reservation using the number above.

Tillamook

Cape Lookout State Park
13000 Whiskey Creek Road W., Tillamook
Information: (800) 551–6949, Reservations:
(800) 452–5687
www.oregonstateparks.org/park_186.php

This popular coastal campground is located just inland from a long, skinny sand spit that stretches for 5 miles and separates Netarts Bay from the Pacific Ocean. The sites are located within a pretty coastal forest and are spaced closely together. If you hike from the campground north to the tip of the sand spit, you'll have the opportunity to view shorebirds and harbor seals. If you want to try your luck clamming, the muddy bay

side of the sand spit is prime habitat for butter, cockle, gaper, and littleneck clams. Netarts Bay is also an excellent place to try your luck at crabbing and fishing. If you want to rent a boat and crabbing or fishing gear, stop by Bayshore RV Park and Marina, (503) 842–7774, in Netarts. You can also take a hike to the tip of Cape Lookout by driving 2.7 miles south from the campground on the Three Capes Scenic Highway to a signed parking area on the right (west) side of the road. The 5-mile out-and-back trail will take you through a thick grove of Sitka spruce trees to the tip of the cape, where you'll have a good opportunity to view migrating gray whales during their semi-annual migration that takes place during December and January and March and April. The trailhead is located in the southwest corner of the parking lot. Be sure to take the trail that goes to the left. The park is open year-round. Leashed pets are allowed. Please note: Reservations Northwest charges a $6.00 fee when you make a reservation using the number above.

Central Coast

Welcome to camping on the Central Coast! You'll find picturesque state, federal, and private campgrounds that are set in a variety of coastal ecosystems from coastal forest and sandy beach to freshwater lakes and coastal dunes. In this section we've listed all the state park campgrounds and selected USDA Forest Service campgrounds from north to south on the Central Coast.

Lincoln City

Devils Lake State Park
1452 Northeast 6th Street, Lincoln City
Information: (800) 994–2002, Reservations: (800) 452–5687
www.oregonstateparks.org/park_216.php

Devils Lake State Park campground sites are nestled among pretty shore pines just off the west shore of Devils Lake. Activities abound in this area—take your pick of swimming, fishing, canoeing, or kayaking. A boat ramp and day use area can be accessed from Northeast 1st Street off U.S. 101 in Lincoln City. You can also try exploring Lincoln City's beaches, galleries, or factory outlet stores located at 1510 East Devils Lake Road. If you want to try your luck with cards, dice, or slots, be sure to check out the Chinook Winds Casino located at 1777 Northwest 44th Street in Lincoln City. The park is open year-round. Leashed pets are allowed. Please note: Reservations Northwest charges a $6.00 fee when you make a reservation using the number above.

Newport

Beverly Beach State Park
198 Northeast 123rd Street, Newport
Information: (541) 265–9278, Reservations: (800) 452–5687
www.oregonstateparks.org/park_227.php

Campsites at this popular campground are tucked into a thick forest adjacent to pebbly Spencer Creek. Grassy picnic areas and a unique yurt village are some of the attractions at this state park campground. There is also a visitor information center, where you can learn more about the area and purchase books and souvenirs. If you want to check out the beach, a short walk from the campground proceeds under the highway and takes you to an endless expanse of sandy beach where you'll have views of Yaquina Head to the south and the headlands of Otter Rock to the north. Surfing is popular at the north end of the beach and kiteflying, sandcastle building, and beachcombing are also fun activities here. For more information about attractions around Newport area, see the Attractions chapter. The park is open year-round. Leashed pets are allowed. Please note: Reservations Northwest charges a $6.00 fee when you make a reservation using the number above.

South Beach

South Beach State Park
5580 South Coast Highway, South Beach
Information: (800) 551–6949, Reservations: (800) 452–5687
www.oregonstateparks.org/park_209.php

South Beach State Park campground is adjacent to a wide expanse of beach, and the Oregon Coast Trail traipses right through the heart of this park. If you like to hike, you can head north or south on the Oregon Coast Trail. You can also try your hand at beachcombing, kiteflying, or sandcastle building. If you make your stay at South Beach State Park your home base for a few days, you can take a deep-sea fishing charter out of Yaquina Bay in Newport (see the Fishing, Clamming, and Crabbing section of the Sports and Activities chapter for information on outfitters), visit the Oregon Coast Aquarium (see the Attractions chapter for more information), or visit the Yaquina Head Outstanding Natural Area where you can see large flocks of seabirds, explore tide pools, and visit the historic Yaquina Head Lighthouse. The park is open year-round. Leashed pets are allowed. Please note: Reservations Northwest charges a $6.00 fee when you make a reservation using the number above.

Waldport

Beachside State Park
Waldport
Information: (800) 551–6949, Reservations:
(800) 452–5687
www.oregonstateparks.org/park_122.php

This wonderful campground located right next to the beach allows beach lovers plenty of room to roam on miles of sandy beach. Winter storm watching, beach combing, kite flying, sand castle building, and whale watching are popular activities at this state park campground. There are also excellent fishing, crabbing, and clamming opportunities in Alsea Bay to the north at Waldport. The park is open March 15 through October 31. Leashed pets are allowed. Please note: Reservations Northwest charges a $6.00 fee when you make a reservation using the number above.

Florence

Cape Perpetua
Florence
(541) 563–3211
www.fs.fed.us/r6/siuslaw

This campground is set in a coastal forest along the shores of Cape Creek. More than 23 miles of trails can be found throughout the Cape Perpetua Scenic Area, which lead you through old-growth forest and to rocky tide pools filled with sea anemones, purple urchins, and bright sea stars. You'll also have the opportunity to see some historic structures built by the Civilian Conservation Corp. in the 1930s. Visit the Cape Perpetua Visitor Center to obtain a map of trails in the area. During the summer months, interpretive programs are offered on Friday and Saturday. The park is open May 10 through September 30. Leashed pets are allowed.

Tenmile Creek
Florence
(541) 563–3211
www.fs.fed.us/r6/siuslaw

This small campground is a best-kept secret that is located adjacent to Tenmile Creek. While you are in this area be sure

to head approximately 3 miles north on U.S. 101 from the junction with Forest Service Road 56 and Visit Cape Perpetua Scenic Area. Stop by the Cape Perpetua Visitor's Center to pick up a trail map and use it as a reference to hike on one of many trails that wind through coastal forest and tide pools. The facilities are open year-round. Leashed pets are permitted.

Carl G. Washburne Memorial State Park
Florence
Information: (541) 997–3641, (800) 551–6949,
Reservations: (800) 452–5687
www.oregonstateparks.org/park_123.php

The campsites in this campground are surrounded by a green expanse of coastal forest, and elk are often seen grazing in grassy areas in the campground. Hiking trails lead to a sandy beach where you have opportunities to watch for whales, build sand castles, fly kites, or look for agates. A 3-mile trail heads south from the campground to Heceta Head Lighthouse. The park is open year-round. Leashed pets are allowed. Please note: Reservations Northwest charges a $6.00 fee when you make a reservation using the number above.

Alder Dune
Florence
(541) 902–8526
www.fs.fed.us/r6/siuslaw/mapleton

This pretty campground is located between 3-acre Alder Lake and two-acre Dune Lake among pine and alder trees. Swimming, fishing, and hiking are

Insiders' Tip

Hiking and wildlife watching are present at almost all the campgrounds listed in this chapter. To be prepared for these activities, always have handy a daypack, binoculars, water bottles, and plenty of snacks.

favorite activities at this campground. You can hike on a trail around Alder Lake or take a trail that heads to Sutton Campground through a coastal sand dune ecosystem. The facilities are open Memorial Day through Labor Day. Leashed pets are allowed.

Sutton Creek
Florence
(541) 902–8526
www.fs.fed.us/r6/siuslaw/mapleton

This attractive campground offers large secluded sites surrounded by cedar, spruce, and alder trees as well as wild rhododendrons. From the campground you can explore more than 6 miles of trails in the Sutton Creek Recreation Area that give you a close-up view of a diverse coastal ecosystem made up of sand dunes, coastal forest, Sutton Lake, Sutton Creek, and sandy beach. You can take a trail to the beach—but in order to reach the beachfront you'll have to wade across Sutton Creek. This beachfront area is prime nesting habitat for the Western Snowy Plover and signs ask that you do not take your dog to the beachfront so as not to disturb the nesting activity of these birds.

You can even take a short walk through a bog located in the campground where you can view the interesting insect-eating plant, the cobra lily. Fishing and boating are also popular at Sutton Lake. Drive to Holman Vista parking area, which has a wheelchair-accessible walkway, to take in views of the rolling sand dunes, scenic beach and rambling, Sutton Creek. The facilities at Sutton Creek are open year-round. Leashed pets are permitted.

Jessie M. Honeyman State Park
84505 U.S. Highway 101, Florence
Information: (541) 997–3641, Reservations: (800) 452–5687
www.oregonstateparks.org/park_134.php

Jessie M. Honeyman State Park campground is the second-largest overnight campground in Oregon and is filled with a wealth of activities. Cleawox and Woahink Lakes are adjacent to the campground and offer great opportunities for swimming, fishing, and boating. Several interconnected trails lead through a diverse coastal ecosystem of spruce, fir, hemlock, salal, and thimbleberry. Beautiful stands of wild rhododendrons line the lakes and dunes in this popular state park and begin blooming in

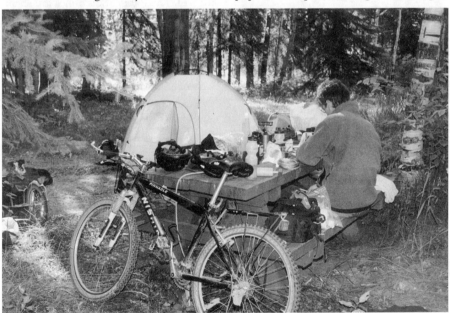

Grab your gear and get set to go camping in one of the many state, federal, county, and private parks that dot the coastline. PHOTO: LIZANN DUNEGAN

early spring. This state park also has a hiking trail where you can explore the large sand dunes that are part of the Oregon Dunes National Recreation Area. The park is open year-round. Leashed pets are allowed.

Reedsport

Carter Lake
Oregon Dunes National Recreation Area
855 U.S. Highway 101, Reedsport
Information: (541) 271–3611, Reservations:
(877) 444–6777
**www.fs.fed.us/r6/siuslaw/oregondunes/rec/
camp/carter.htm**

This campground rests in a coastal sand dune ecosystem adjacent to 28-acre Carter Lake and sites are surrounded by lush coastal vegetation. You may want to try reeling in some rainbow trout in the lake or take a refreshing swim. You can also take a wheelchair-accessible 0.75-mile trail from the campground to Taylor Dunes. Keep in mind there is no off-road vehicle use allowed in this area. The facilities at Carter Lake are open April 30 through September 28. Leashed pets are allowed.

William M. Tugman State Park
Reedsport
Information: (541) 759–3604, Reservations:
(800) 452–5687
www.oregonstateparks.org/park_98.php

William M. Tugman State Park is an undiscovered campground that is located 8 miles south of Reedsport, next to the shore of Eel Lake, a prime freshwater fishing lake that supports healthy popula-

tions of black crappie, cutthroat trout, rainbow trout, and largemouth bass. Other activities on this lake include swimming, canoeing, sailing, and boating. If you want to explore a more secluded section of the lake, you can head out on a hiking trail that takes you around the south end of the lake. The park is open year-round. Leashed pets are allowed. Please note: Reservations Northwest charges a $6.00 fee when you make a reservation using the number above.

South Coast

Coos Bay

Umpqua Lighthouse State Park
10965 Cape Arago Highway, Coos Bay
Information: (541) 271–4631, Reservations:
(800) 452–5687
www.oregonstateparks.org/park_121.php

The Umpqua State Park campground is located 6 miles south of Reedsport, not far from the mouth of the Umpqua River and has many activities that will make you want to stay and explore this beautiful area. The state park is only a mile from Salmon Harbor and excellent fishing opportunities in Winchester Bay to the north. This campground features two cozy one-room cabins that have covered porches where you can relax and enjoy the view of Lake Marie. Trails in the state park take you on a tour of towering sand dunes that are part of the Umpqua Dunes Scenic Area. You can also explore a 1-mile hiking trail that circles Lake Marie. Another unique attraction in this area is the 65-foot Umpqua River Lighthouse and museum. Tours of the lighthouse are given from May 1 to September 30. The park is open year-round. Leashed pets are allowed. Please note: Reservations Northwest charges a $6.00 fee when you make a reservation using the number above.

Sunset Bay State Park
10965 Cape Arago Highway, Coos Bay
Information: (541) 888–4902, Reservations:
(800) 452–5687
www.oregonstateparks.org/park_100.php

Rocky sandstone cliffs, rugged sea stacks, and a well-protected sandy beach await those who visit Sunset Bay State Park, located 12 miles southwest of Coos Bay. Numerous day use areas throughout this park encourage family activities and a system of well-connected trails takes you to high vistas that have spectacular views of the rugged coastline and Sunset Bay. Be sure to hike on the Oregon Coast Trail 2 miles south to Shore Acres State Park, which has a sheltered observation station and a botanical garden. Note that pets are not allowed in Shore Acres State Park. You can access this trail at the day use picnicking area inside Sunset Bay State Park. Look for the wooden Oregon Coast Trail marker located just to the right of the rest rooms that indicates the start of the trail. If you continue south on this Oregon Coast Trail from Shore Acres State Park, you'll reach Cape Arago State Park in another 2.5 miles. Other activities in this area include swimming and boating. You can also try your luck at fishing or crabbing from the small fishing village of Charleston. The park is open year-round. Leashed pets are allowed. Please note: Reservations Northwest charges a $6.00 fee when you make a reservation using the number above.

Bandon

Bullards Beach State Park
Bandon
Information: (541) 347–2209, Reservations: (800) 452–5687
www.oregonstateparks.org/park_71.php

The Bullards Beach campground rests in a grove of shore pines 2 miles north of Bandon and features a 1.5-mile paved trail to the beach that wanders through a coastal forest and changes to a dune environment before it reaches the beach. From this path you'll have views of the salmon-rich Coquille River, and if you are a wildlife lover, you should be sure to stop by the Bandon Marsh National Wildlife Refuge located just south of the park. You should also be sure to check out the Coquille River Lighthouse located on the north jetty in the park and reachable via a

Insiders' Tip

If you prefer peace and solitude and want to avoid crowds, try camping on the Central and South Coast. The North Coast is close to some of Oregon's largest population centers (Portland and Salem) and tends to attract more people than the less crowded Central and South Coast.

3-mile-long hiking path or along a paved road that ends at the lighthouse. Equestrian lovers will enjoy a 7-mile equestrian trail and miles of beach riding. If you love to fish, the Coquille River is within easy access The park is open year-round. Leashed pets are allowed. Please note: Reservations Northwest charges a $6.00 fee when you make a reservation using the number above.

Port Orford

Cape Blanco State Park
Port Orford
Information: (541) 332–6774, Reservations: (800) 452–5687
www.oregonstateparks.org/park_62.php

Large campsites protected from the coastal wind by sheltering trees and a thick understory of salal, salmonberry, and thimbleberry are what you will find at this state park campground, located 4 miles north of Port Orford. The Oregon Coast Trail can be accessed from the south end of the campground. This park has a lot of natural beauty including high chalky bluffs, black sand beach, and offshore sea stacks that are home to herds of sea lions and are also prime nesting sites for seabirds. From this campground, you

Insiders' Tip

A tasty side dish you can prepare when you are camping is red potatoes with onions and green bell pepper. For easy fixing and cleanup, wash and dice four to five red potatoes, one bell pepper, and one yellow onion into a mixing bowl. Place the mixture in foil, sprinkle with salt and pepper, and add a few pats of butter on top. Wrap the foil tightly and place on a barbecue grill for 45 to 55 minutes or in a conventional oven for 45 to 55 minutes at 400 degrees. When the potatoes are done, peel back the foil, and enjoy a tasty side dish with the rest of your evening meal. You can serve the potatoes right out of their foil wrapping to save time and cleanup.

have access to the Elk and Sixes Rivers, which offer good fishing opportunities and more than 7 miles of equestrian trails are present in the state park. In addition, you can also explore the Cape Blanco Lighthouse, which is the oldest lighthouse in Oregon, or the Hughes House Museum also located in the state park. The park is open year-round. Leashed pets are allowed. Please note: Reservations Northwest charges a $6.00 fee when you make a reservation using the number above.

Humbug Mountain State Park
Port Orford
Information: (541) 332–6774, (800) 551–6949,
Reservations: (800) 452–5687
www.oregonstateparks.org/park_56.php

This scenic state park is set in a forested setting 6 miles south of Port Orford and is adjacent to 1,756-foot Humbug Mountain. A moderate 5.5-mile loop trail will take you to the summit of Humbug Mountain. Windsurfing and scuba diving are popular activities in this area. A walkway leads from the campground under the highway to a 4-mile stretch of sandy beach where you can go beachcombing. The park is open year-round. Leashed pets are allowed. Please note: Reservations North-

west charges a $6.00 fee when you make a reservation using the number above.

Brookings

Harris Beach State Park
1655 U.S. Highway 101, Brookings
Information: (541) 469–2021, (800) 551–6949,
Reservations: (800) 452–5687
www.oregonstateparks.org/park_79.php

The campground in this state park, which is 2 miles north of Brookings, is located in a wooded area bordered with bright azaleas. Wildlife watching and beachcombing are favorite activities here. You can look for seabirds nesting on Bird Island and also watch for whales offshore during their semiannual migration. Walk along the sandy beach and admire the rocky coastline and look for sea lions and harbor seals on the offshore rocks. The park is open year-round. Leashed pets are allowed. Please note: Reservations Northwest charges a $6.00 fee when you make a reservation using the number above.

Alfred A. Loeb State Park
1655 U.S. Highway 101, Brookings
Information: (541) 469–2021, (800) 551–6949,
Reservations: (800) 452–5687
www.oregonstateparks.org/park_72.php

This park is located 7.5 miles east of Brookings, adjacent to the salmon-rich Chetco River and offers two self-guided tours through a myrtlewood forest and a small grove of magnificent redwood trees. This campground is located at the gateway to the Siskiyou National Forest and the Kalmiopsis Wilderness. Fishing opportunities abound in Chetco River and ocean fishing is available out of Brookings Harbor. The park is open year-round. Leashed pets are allowed. Please note: Reservations Northwest charges a $6.00 fee when you make a reservation using the number above.

Insiders' Tip

Always be prepared for all types of weather on the Oregon Coast, no matter what the season. Always bring a rain jacket and insulating layers of clothing, sturdy hiking shoes, mosquito repellent, sunscreen, sunglasses, and a wide-brimmed hat.

Restaurants

This chapter introduces you to many of the delicious eateries on the Oregon Coast. You'll find everything from high-end seafood restaurants to small, friendly cafes and coffeehouses that beckon you to stay for a while. Some restaurants are tucked away in historic districts and others provide you with an ocean view. We've organized the restaurants by region—North, Central, and South—and then by city from north to south. Restaurants are wheelchair accessible and accept credit cards unless noted otherwise. The price codes are listed below and will give you a hint of what your meal will cost.

Price Code

The price code below reflects the cost of a single meal excluding tips and drinks. As with other Oregon purchases, there is no sales tax.

$ . . . . $10 and less
$$ . . . . $11 to $20
$$$ . . . . $21 to $30
$$$$ . . . . more than $30

North Coast

Up on the hearty North Coast of Oregon, it is inevitable that a day jaunt on the beach or along one of the headland trails will cook up a big appetite. Here in one of the villages strung between the capes and stretches of wild sand and offshore rocks can be found a good selection of restaurants for all tastes and pocketbooks. They range from the homey and low-key Columbian Cafe in Astoria to the elegant dining at the Bay House in Lincoln City; from the legendary down-home Otis Cafe in Otis to the Grateful Bread bakery in Pacific City with its terrific pastry and fun play on words in reference to the rock band. Not only will you find some of the best-prepared seafood anywhere, you will encounter the relaxed, cheerful attitude that characterizes folks along this wind-battered, sea-pounded coastline.

Astoria

Cannery Cafe $$
1 6th Street, Astoria
(503) 325–8642
www.riverparkssuite.com/rest.html
Sitting on pilings over the bay with a great view of the Columbia River, the Cannery is a restaurant in what was once a busy processing plant for huge salmon. Now you can enjoy fresh versions of the same, other choices of seafood, and Dungeness crab cakes. Specialties include the halibut

Insiders' Tip

Curious about seafood? Want to repeat that outrageously tasty meal you just had at one of the North Coast's better eateries? How about taking a seafood cooking class at the Duncan Law Seafood Consumer Center, 2021 Marine Drive, Astoria, (503) 338–6523. Classes run $25 for a three-hour session. You will learn how to cook seafood stews, blackened fish, and seafood cooked in parchment paper.

burger, crab and shrimp cakes, and lime prawns. A full bar is available, and the restaurant is nonsmoking. The Cannery is open during the winter months Tuesday through Saturday 11:00 A.M. to 8:00 P.M. and Sunday 9:00 A.M. to 6:00 P.M. During the summer months (June through September) the restaurant is open Monday through Saturday 11:00 A.M. to 8:30 P.M. and Sunday 9:00 A.M. to 8:30 P.M.

Columbian Cafe $
1114 Marine Drive, Astoria
(503) 325–2233
www.columbianvoodoo.com/cafe.html

This little shoebox grill is one of the most famous eateries on the Coast. So, squeeze in and watch the cooks only a wild elbow away serve up some great vegetarian and seafood meals. Try the crepes! Or call upon the "Chef's Mercy," a daily concoction of the freshest seafood. The Columbian Cafe, open for breakfast, lunch, and dinner. No smoking is allowed. The hours vary, but are generally 8:00 A.M. to 2:00 P.M. Monday through Friday, 9:00 A.M. to 2:00 P.M. Saturday and Sunday. Dinner hours start at 5:00 P.M. to closing (time determined by the number of people at the restaurant) Wednesday through Saturday. Credit cards are not accepted.

Gearhart

Pacific Way Bakery and Cafe $$
601 Pacific Way, Gearhart
(503) 738–0245

This hip little scene combines lots of windows with views of downtown Gearhart, a charming hardwood floor, and a laid-back staff cheerfully dispatching cinnamon rolls, scones, and muffins from its bakery and "yuppy food," including freshly homemade sandwiches for lunch and a full selection of entrees for dinner from its cafe side. On the menu are crab cakes, cashew razor clams, macadamia roasted halibut, and vegetarian ravioli. There is an extensive list of sparkling wines, bottled beer, and nonalcoholic beer to accompany the meals. Hours are Thursday through Monday 11:00 A.M. to 3:30 P.M. for lunch and 5:00 to 9:00 P.M. for dinner.

Seaside

Premier Pasta $
1530 South U.S. Highway 101, Seaside
(503) 738–3692

This busy restaurant offers casual Italian dining with an entertaining view of the chefs working in the kitchen and windows overlooking the Necanicum River. The atmosphere is elegantly enhanced with small tables with tablecloths and candlelight and in the summer there is dining on the deck next to the river. The restaurant makes all its own pasta, featuring egg-free pasta. As well as wholesaling the pasta to many other coastal cafes and offering a cooking class, the energetic owner, Angela Sidlo, and her chefs serve up portobello mushroom ravioli, shrimp fettucine, pesto shrimp, and lots of salad and antipasto. Wine and beer are available. The restaurant is closed Sunday and Monday, its hours are Tuesday through Saturday from 4:00 to 10:00 P.M. except summer days when it is open 11:00 A.M. to 3:00 P.M.

The Stand $
220 Avenue U, Seaside
(503) 738–6592

A small, trim spot for Mexican and Tex-Mex fast food, The Stand is a serious hangout for the younger crowd with lots of hunger and little cash ambling about this youth-friendly town in their surf-splashed cutoffs. There are 10 inside tables for walk-in nibbling. No beer or wine is served, just juice. Hours are 11:00 A.M. to 8:00 P.M., closed Sundays. Credit cards are not accepted.

Dooger's $$
505 Broadway, Seaside
(503) 738–3773
1371 South Hemlock Street, Cannon Beach
(503) 436–2225
www.cannon-beach.net/doogers

With its two locations serving steaks and fresh local seafood, Dooger's is a smoke-free, cozy eatery with service so friendly it feels as if you are visiting friends or relatives for a special occasion meal. The Cannon Beach outlet has been in business for more than 16 years with this special catering focus on families and seniors. It's open for breakfast, lunch, and dinner, and if you don't mind waiting in line for a while, you'll enjoy steamer clams, scallops, and halibut. Dooger's has a full bar at the Cannon Beach site and a regionally based wine list at both restaurants.

Cannon Beach

The Bistro $$
263 North Hemlock Street, Cannon Beach
(503) 436–2661

As its name suggests, this is an intimate little bistro complete with a full bar, that serves a pleasant mix of French, Italian, and continental cuisine with seafood stew and sautéed oysters as the favorites among its return customers. It's open for dinner from 4:00 to 10:00 P.M. during the season.

Kalypso $$$
140 North Hemlock Street, Cannon Beach
(503) 436–1585

Considered the finest seafood restaurant on the North Coast, Kalypso offers an

Fine dining is available in many coastal communities. PHOTO: LIZANN DUNEGAN

upscale menu of seafood, including razor clams, petrale sole, and fresh Willapa Bay oysters; rack of lamb; and beef tenderloin. Also available are microbrews from the Pacific Northwest as well as 25 varieties of wine and champagne. The restaurant is open from 11:30 A.M. to 8:30 or 9:00 P.M. It's closed on Wednesdays in summer and on Wednesdays and Thursdays in winter.

Lazy Susan Cafe $
126 North Hemlock Street, Cannon Beach
(503) 436–2816

Breakfast is the best bet at this popular, sunny spot with its gingerbread waffles and specialty omelets. Lunches and dinners include tuna hazelnut, seafood salad, quiche, and salads served with wine or beer. Hours vary, but they're generally open from 8:00 A.M. to 8:00 P.M. during summer except on Tuesdays, and in winter, 8:00 A.M. to 2:30 P.M. Monday through Thursday and Sunday; 8:00 A.M. to 8:00 P.M. on Friday and Saturday. Credit cards are not accepted but checks are.

Pizza 'a fetta $
231 Hemlock Street, Cannon Beach
(503) 436–0333

Tucked between art galleries and gift shops in this tourist-lively town, Pizza 'a fetta serves pizza by the pie or slice, pasta, soup, and salad all made from scratch. "We specialize in taste," says the cook. Microbrewed beers or Italian wines are served by the bottle or the glass. Hours are 11:00 A.M. to 9:00 P.M. seven days a week in summer, and it closes Wednesdays and Thursdays in winter.

Manzanita

Blue Sky Cafe $$$
152 Laneda Avenue, Manzanita
(503) 368–5712

This spot offers an eclectic menu ranging from Thai peanut chicken to Mediterranean entrees to Northwest seafood, with a full bar available. Open for dinner at 5:30 P.M. on Wednesday through Sunday from April through June; from July 4 to September, all seven nights; and Friday through Sunday from October through

March. Credit cards are not accepted but checks are okay.

Bay City

ArtSpace Gallery Cafe $$
9120 5th (U.S. Highway 101 and 5th), Bay City
(503) 377–2782

As the name suggests, this charming place mixes an avant-garde art gallery with a bistro serving regional and Northwest cuisine. On the menu are seafood—especially oysters—fettuccine, and vegetarian dishes, all of which can be enjoyed with organic coffee. The cafe serves wine and beer, offers live music on Saturdays, and is entirely non-smoking. No credit cards are accepted but checks are. Hours are Thursday, Friday, and Saturday from noon to 8:00 P.M.

Oceanside

Roseanna's Oceanside Cafe $$
1490 Pacific Street, Oceanside
(503) 842–7351

In a converted old country store with a great view of the Pacific, Roseanna's is both charming and upscale. Specialties include Tillamook Bay oysters, salmon, halibut, tiger prawns, cod, red snapper, and "the best chowder around." Roseanna has a limited bar, along with wine and beer, and is open for lunch and dinner. The old building is somewhat wheelchair accessible and the owner says many in wheelchairs eat here regularly. Hours are weekends 11:00 A.M. to 9:00 P.M. and weekdays 11:00 A.M. to 8:00 P.M.

Pacific City

Grateful Bread Bakery $
34805 Brooten Road, Pacific City
(503) 965–7337

Perhaps one of the best eateries on the Oregon Coast, this always-packed spot is a haven for hungry travelers as well as a hangout for locals. With its terrific bakery supplying specialty breads, scones, brownies, and cookies, the cafe side serves up pizza, lasagna, seafood, and vegetarian options. Breakfast temptations include French toast with blackberry and apple compotes and gingerbread pancakes. There is no alcohol served. Hours are 8:00 A.M. to 6:00 P.M., closed on Wednesdays and, once in awhile, closed on Thursdays. If while touring the coast, you get a chance to stop by and enjoy this groovy eatery, consider yourself grateful.

Riverhouse Restaurant $$
34450 Brooten Road, Pacific City
(541) 965–6722

Situated on the scenic Nestucca River, this small cafe is a sanctuary from the hubbub along U.S. 101 3 miles westward. The menu is casual gourmet with sandwiches, seafood, buckets of steamer clams, and tasty apple pie. Don't miss the Riverhouse blue dressing on your salad. There is a full bar and Visa and MasterCard are accepted for the price of the meal only. Hours are 11:00 A.M. to 8:00 or 10:00 P.M. daily.

Otis Junction

Otis Cafe $
2 miles east of U.S. Highway 101 on Oregon Highway 18 at Otis Junction
(541) 994–2813

The Otis Cafe just outside of Lincoln City is a must stop for breakfast. PHOTO: LIZANN DUNEGAN

Here is a gem of an old-time country restaurant. Many folks detour in its direction just for the legendary food. The prices are cheap, the grub is terrific, and the portions are big. Try the king-size burgers with legendary fries or hash browns. One of their signature items is buttery black bread that's also sold to go. This down-home spot also offers beer and wine and is open for breakfast and lunch every day and for dinner Friday through Sunday. If you're visiting on a weekend, you'll probably have to wait for a table.

Central Coast

From Lincoln City to Florence there are lots of ports of call for the hungry visitor. The most famous is Mo's with its internationally renowned, not-to-be-missed clam chowder; the most upscale is The Whale's Tale; and the eatery that gets lots of raves is Tidal Rave. Probably Newport and Florence have the most higher-end restaurants along this portion of the Oregon Coast. Both have animated Old Towns that are usually packed with out-of-towners who are served well by local restaurateurs. The top of the try-list along this strip is definitely Dungeness crab—tasty in a crab roll or mixed in pasta, or—the ultimate coastal meal—crab with a crisp salad and a loaf of French bread.

Lincoln City

Bay House $$$
5911 Southwest U.S. Highway 101, Lincoln City
(541) 996-3222
www.bayhouserestaurant.com
Here is one of the sparkling gems of the Oregon Coast. With its classic ambience of finished wood and brass, The Bay House offers innovative entrees with an emphasis on seafood. One scrumptious example is salmon with hazelnut crust, another is pan-fried oysters in an Asian lemongrass broth. Or try the Dungeness crab legs with angel hair pasta. They have a large and impressive wine list, as well as a full bar. Open for dinner from 5:30 to 9:00 P.M., except in winter months (starting in October) when it is closed on Monday and Tuesday.

Dory Cove $
5819 Logan Road, Lincoln City
(541) 994-5180
www.dorycove.com
Nestled next to Road's End Wayside, a small state park with easy access to the beach, Dory Cove is a great place to stop when you are tired and hungry from traipsing about the coastline. A large variety of meals are offered for lunch and dinner, including clam chowder, shrimp salad, all sorts of burgers, and a very popular tenderloin steak. Wine and beer are served.

Salmon River Cafe $$
4079 Northwest Logan Road, Lincoln City
(541) 996-3663
A bistro-style restaurant with deli case and a catering service also available, the Salmon River Cafe delivers a tasty mix of ethnic foods, Pacific Northwest specialties, vegetarian and low-fat meals, fresh vegetables, pancakes, and omelets. They serve wine by the glass and bottle with a special selection of Italian, Spanish, and Northwest labels. Open for breakfast, lunch, and dinner, hours are 8:30 A.M. to 4:30 P.M. Monday and Tuesday, and 8:30 A.M. to 8:00 P.M. Wednesday through Sunday.

Gleneden Beach

The Cedar Tree at Westin Salishan Resort $
7760 North U.S. Highway 101, Gleneden Beach
(541) 764-2371
www.salishan.com
The companion to the Dining Room at Salishan, the Cedar Tree offers a more casual setting and dining fare. The menu is lively, with alder plank Pacific salmon, halibut fish and chips, smoked turkey club and crab cake sandwiches, prime rib with dip, clam chowder, and crispy calamari. A full-service bar is located between the two restaurants. Hours are breakfast: 6:30 to 11:30 A.M.; lunch: 11:30 A.M. to 2:30 P.M.; dinner: 5:00 to 9:00 P.M. Sunday through Thursday and 5:00 to 9:30 P.M. on Friday and Saturday.

The Dining Room at Westin Salishan Resort
$$$
7760 North U.S. Highway 101, Gleneden Beach
(541) 764-2371
www.salishan.com

With a spectacular view of Siletz Bay, this gourmet restaurant at the noted resort complex offers loin of lamb, duckling, venison, New York strip steak, North Coast cioppino, and grilled salmon, halibut, or scallops. Along with this upscale cuisine is a large variety of wines and cocktails. Open only for dinner, hours are 6:00 to 9:00 P.M. in winter (starting in October) and 6:00 to 10:00 P.M. in summer, which usually starts in April. It is closed Monday and Tuesday. There is no dress code, just dress comfortably.

Depoe Bay

Gracie's Sea Hag Restaurant and Lounge $$
58 U.S. Highway 101, Depoe Bay
(541) 765-2734

This spot claims that its "seafood is so fresh the ocean hasn't missed it yet." Examples of this bounty from the Pacific are baby shrimp, scallops, oysters, smoked tuna, and salmon stuffed with crab and shrimp. On Friday night there's an all-you-can-eat seafood buffet. Hours vary but they are usually open from 9:00 A.M. to 10:00 P.M.

Tidal Raves $
279 Northwest U.S. Highway 101, Depoe Bay
(541) 765-2995

A popular dining spot for folks ambling over from the Willamette Valley, Tidal Raves has one of the best views in Depoe Bay. It also has great grub including its famous Pasta Rave with crab, shrimp, and lingcod cuddling with the noodles. Another good choice is the Thai prawns. Hours are 11:00 A.M. to 9:00 P.M. daily.

Newport

Big Guy's Diner $
1801 North Coast Highway, Newport
(546) 265-5114

One of the many '50s-style restaurants that combine nostalgia and tasty fare, Big Guy's Diner offers a farm-style breakfast featuring an 8-oz. chicken breast, biscuits, and gravy; huge hamburgers; and a variety of classic dinner items all under $10. Hours are 6:00 A.M. to 9:00 P.M. daily.

Canyon Way Bookstore and Restaurant $$
1216 Southwest Canyon Way, Newport
(541) 265-8319

This lovely oasis away from the hubbub of hectic Newport has delights for the mind and body. After browsing an impressive bookstore and gift shop, settle into a tasty lunch or early dinner with selections ranging from low-priced sandwiches to fresh pasta dishes. Be sure to check out the local art adorning many of its walls. Hours are 11:00 A.M. to 3:00 P.M. and 5:30 to 9:00 P.M. Tuesday to Saturday.

Embarcadero $$
1000 Southeast Bay Boulevard, Newport
(541) 265-8521

As the eatery portion of a resort, hotel, and marina with a host of sailing options and

Insiders' Tip

A quick treat that will echo a long way back into the history of the Oregon Coast is a stop at the Siletz Tribal Smokehouse. Here you can sample smoked salmon and tuna and then take home a few cans of these delicious delicacies prepared in ancient Native American fashion. The smokehouse is at 272 U.S. Highway 101 in Depoe Bay, (541) 765-3349, www.oregonsmokedfoods.com.

a great view of Yaquina Bay, the Embarcadero offers a sumptuous Sunday brunch with champagne and fresh seafood and lunch and dinners specializing in steaks and seafood. Hours for breakfast are 7:00 to 11:00 A.M.; for lunch, 11:00 A.M. to 2:00 P.M.; and dinner, 5:00 to 10:00 P.M.

Mo's $
622 Southwest Bay Boulevard, Newport
(541) 265-2979

Easily the most famous restaurant on the Oregon Coast, Mo's is synonymous with hearty, affordable chow—particularly clam chowder and oyster stew. Other favorites are an all-you-can-eat seafood buffet and an excellent prime rib special. If this cozy spot is packed with customers, walk across the street to Mo's Annex, (541) 265-7512, for the same menu.

Rogue Ales Public House $
748 Southwest Bay Boulevard, Newport
(541) 265-3188

Tucked in Old Town Newport, this big rollicking pub is the international headquarters for sampling some great microbrews made at the Rogue Ales Brewery, also located in Newport. Tasty additions to the brew samples are hearty pizza and pasta dishes and the usual sandwich suspects, including pastrami, turkey, and ham. Hours are 11:00 A.M. to 2:30 A.M. daily.

Whale's Tale $$
452 Southwest Bay Boulevard, Newport
(541) 265-8660

Celebrated as one of the best restaurants on the West Coast, Whale's Tale has big wooden slab tables, marine memorabilia on the walls, and a delightful selection of upscale entrees. Recommended are the Cajun salmon, grilled Yaquina oysters, a German sausage and ham plate, and cioppino, a seafood mix of scallops, oysters, prawns, and mussels. Breakfast hours are 8:00 to 11:30 A.M. Monday through Saturday and 9:00 A.M. to 1:00 P.M. on Sunday. Lunch and dinner hours are 11:30 A.M. to 10:00 P.M. on Friday and Saturday and 11:30 A.M. to 9:00 P.M. Sunday through Thursday. The rest room is not wheelchair accessible.

Waldport

Grand Central Pizza $
245 U.S. Highway 101, Waldport
(541) 563-3232

Along with pizza, this popular spot offers a multicultural mix of fajitas, pasta dishes, Cajun smoked entrees, sub sandwiches, fish and chips, and seafood dishes. For dessert, try the every-berry shortcake. Hours for lunch and dinner are 11:00 A.M. to 8:00 P.M. with an extension to 9:00 P.M. in the summer.

Leroy's Blue Whale $
on U.S. Highway 101 across from Visitor Information Center, Waldport
(541) 547-3397

The Waldport franchise of this family-style restaurant offers a sumptuous menu of traditional American food with an emphasis on seafood, including prawns and calamari (squid). Hours are 7:00 A.M. to 8:00 P.M. daily in winter, and 7:00 A.M. to 9:00 P.M. in summer. Also, try the Blue Whale in Yachats.

Yachats

Adobe Resort $$
155 U.S. Highway 101, Yachats
(541) 547-3141
www.adoberesort.com

In this glass-encased dining room reaching out above Smelt Sands Beach, breakfast features Eggs Adobe, poached eggs with bay shrimp and artichoke bottoms topped with hollandaise sauce; brunch with French toast; and dinners including salmon ricotta and shrimp fettuccine. Hours are breakfast and lunch, 8:00 A.M. to 2:30 P.M. Monday through Saturday and 9:00 A.M. to 1:00 P.M. for Sunday brunch. Dinner hours are 5:00 to 9:00 P.M. Sunday through Thursday and 5:30 to 9:00 P.M. Friday and Saturday.

La Serre $$
2nd and Beach, Yachats
(541) 547-3420
www.overleaflodge.com/laserre

The name means "greenhouse," and the atmosphere is cheerful and comfy with overhead skylights and a tall, beamed ceiling. Inside, you can order gourmet as well as healthy fare including charbroiled steaks, crab cakes, cioppino, or famous Umpqua oysters.

Yachats Crab and Chowder House $
131 U.S. Highway 101, Yachats
(541) 547-4132
In every coastal village from Cape Cod to Venice, California, there are those fish and chips joints that vend quick, cheap, and tasty baskets of marine grub. The Yachats Crab and Chowder House is a solid example. Here you can grab some crab and garlic bread or rock cod and halibut fish and chips. Hours for lunch and dinner are 11:30 A.M. to 8:30 P.M. Tuesday through Thursday, 11:30 A.M. to 9:00 P.M. on Friday and Saturday and 11:30 A.M. to 8:00 P.M. on Sunday.

Yachats Leroy's Blue Whale $
580 U.S. Highway 101, Yachats
(541) 547-3397
The Yachats franchise of this family-style restaurant offers a sumptuous menu of traditional American food with an emphasis on seafood, including prawns and calamari (squid). Hours are 7:00 A.M. to 8:00 P.M. daily in winter, and 7:00 A.M. to 9:00 P.M. in summer. Also try the Blue Whale in Waldport.

Yankee Clipper $
125 Ocean Drive, Yachats
(541) 547-4004
This small sandwich parlor with a view of the Yachats Estuary offers clever soup and sandwich combos, homemade desserts, and tasty coffee. Hours are 11:00 A.M. to 3:00 P.M. daily. Credit cards are not accepted.

Florence

The Blue Hen $
1675 U.S. Highway 101, Florence
(541) 997-3907
Although there are lots of chicken dishes at this small cafe operating out of a home, it is also famous for its chowder—complete with 14 ingredients—and huge biscuits.

Wine and beer are served. Hours are seven days a week from 7:00 A.M. to 8:00 P.M.

The Bridgewater Seafood Restaurant and Oyster Bar $$
129 Bay Street, Old Town Florence
(541) 997-9405
This is the most upscale eatery in Old Town, where fresh fish is often cooked with a Cajun flavor. Some claim that it is the winner in the clam chowder contest with Mo's. But only your palate can win that contest! Another hit here is the All-You-Can-Eat seafood dinner buffet for $10 or slightly more. Hours are 11:30 A.M. to 9:00 P.M. during the week and 9:00 A.M. to 9:00 P.M. on weekends.

Clawson's Windward Inn $$
3757 U.S. Highway 101, Florence
(541) 997-8243
This highly acclaimed gourmet restaurant has a sophisticated ambiance in which you can sample an innovative menu including fresh mussels broiled with hazelnuts and chicken and veal sausage, lobster, and steak. Hours for breakfast, lunch, and dinner are 7:00 A.M. to 10:00 P.M. in the summer and 7:00 A.M. to 9:00 P.M. in winter. There is a full bar.

Mo's $
1436 Bay Street, Old Town Florence
(541) 997-2185
There are six Mo's Restaurants along the Oregon Coast at Cannon Beach, Lincoln City, two at Otter Crest, Newport, and here at Florence. Located along the Siuslaw River dock, this particular outlet of the notable chowder palace chain is a big rambling place. With its reasonable prices, a large variety of seafood dishes, bustling service, and an atmosphere of fun at the beach, Mo's is probably the most attractive restaurant in Old Town. Hours are 11:00 A.M. to 8:00 P.M. Sunday through Thursday and 11:00 A.M. to 9:00 P.M. Friday and Saturday.

Traveler's Cove $$
1362 Bay Street, Florence
(541) 997-8194
Crab is a big part of the menu here at this combination gift shop and restaurant. There are crab enchiladas, crab quiche, and

Caesar salad loaded with Oregon's legendary Dungeness crab. If this creeping cuisine makes you crabby, try other sandwiches and salads that are also tasty. Take your lunch out to the dining deck with a river view.

Lakeside

Lakeshore Lodge $$
290 South 8th Street, Lakeside
(541) 759-3161, (800) 759-3951
Dining on the lakefront of the many-fingered Ten-Mile Lake in a big-windowed room enhances the choice of a family-style chicken dinner, prime rib, fresh local seafood, steaks, homemade pizza, and fresh pastas. Hours are 8:00 A.M. to 9:00 P.M. daily, with earlier openings on the weekends for fisherfolk.

South Coast

Down on Oregon's South Coast are dozens of great restaurants, particularly in Bandon, a revitalized destination resort town that suffered a devastating fire in the 1930s. Back in the mid-to-late 1970s, Bandon government officials and local boosters worked hard to get funding to rebuild much of Old Town. Now, in this historic and charming strip along with the scenic Beach Loop Drive that winds along the bluff overlooking some of the loveliest beach and offshore rocks in the Pacific Northwest, lots of new eateries help to amplify Bandon's new reputation as a hot spot to visit. But don't ignore the fine eateries in Coos Bay and Charleston to the north and Gold Beach and Brookings to the south. There are lots of great choices for repast as you pass by these salty towns.

North Bend

The Mill Casino $$
East side U.S. Highway 101, North Bend
(800) 953-4800
www.themillcasino.com
On the bay side of the Coquille tribe's humming casino, beyond the video poker and gaming tables, is a sizable restaurant open 24 hours a day. The best bet here is a $7.00 prime rib dinner. The Mill also serves seafood as well as traditional sandwiches.

Alder SmokeHouse $
1055 Virginia Avenue, North Bend
(541) 756-9599
This specialty spot offers lip-smacking smoked and barbecue meals for dining in or taking out. Their most popular item is a tri-tip sandwich with sides of pasta salad, potato salad, or cole saw. A popular sidedish is their smokehouse chili beans. Hours are Tuesday through Thursday 11:00 A.M. to 3:00 P.M. and Friday and Saturday 11:00 A.M. to 7:00 P.M.

Coos Bay

Blue Heron Bistro $$
110 West Commercial, Coos Bay
(541) 267-3933
Probably the most European-flavored and -furnished eatery in Coos County, the Blue Heron Bistro offers healthy and affordable eatables from waffles and genuinely good coffee to nitrate-free German sausage to prime rib. Hours are 11:00 A.M. to 9:00 P.M. Monday through Friday and 11:00 A.M. to 10:00 P.M. on Saturday and Sunday.

Gourmet Coastal Coffees $$
273 Curtis Avenue, Coos Bay
(541) 267-5004

Located a few blocks off the main drag in Coos Bay, this very popular coffee shop and sandwich parlor has a wide variety of coffee drinks, pastries, and their big hit, the Zestie Veggie Sandwich. This is known as a place where you can stop by and read all the Sunday paper, meet with friends for a lively discussion, or amble back to a charming little patio for a quiet sip of java among the greenery. Live music is a casual affair with drum circle on Thursday night. Hours are 6:00 A.M. to 6:00 P.M. Credit cards are not accepted.

Kum-Yon's $
835 South Broadway, Coos Bay
(541) 269-2662

Although there are a number of Asian restaurants in Coos Bay and North Bend, most are nondescript and not worth a traveler's effort. Except for Kum-Yon's, a pleasant little spot featuring South Korean cuisine. They also serve sushi, sashimi, chow mein, and yakitori in sizable portions. They offer beer and wine. Hours are 11:00 A.M. to 9:00 P.M. weekdays and 11:00 A.M. to 9:30 P.M. on Friday and Saturday.

Sumin's $
298 South Broadway, Coos Bay
(541) 267-0119

The first sign that this is a hot spot for fans of sushi and other Asian cuisine is a packed house of smiling customers. But be patient and wait for seats. Your reward is some of the finest sushi on the Oregon Coast. The service is swift and cordial and the food is fresh and innovative. Open seven days a week.

Charleston

Portside $$
63383 Kingfisher Road, Charleston
(541) 888-5544

Lots of folks from "The Bay Area" come over the bridge at the Charleston Boat Basin to dine at the Portside. Here in this darkly lit room, you can get a window seat and watch the fishing boats come and go as you sample dishes of fresh seafood including shrimp, crab, and smoked salmon accompanied by cucumber dressing. On Friday the chef prepares a generous Chinese seafood buffet. Hours are weekdays 11:00 A.M. to 9:00 P.M. and weekends 11:00 A.M. to 11:00 P.M.

Bandon

Bandon Bill's Steak & Seafood $$
3225 Beach Loop Drive, Bandon
(541) 347-7302

Located at the Inn at Face Rock out on the scenic Beach Loop Drive overlooking a gorgeous strip of beach and offshore rocks, Bandon Bill's offers a terrific view and opulent cuisine. Examples are mesquite chicken quesadilla, shrimp and crab stuffed scallops, and Kalhua honey-smoked game hen. The chef is also very proud of his special clam chowder! Hours are 7:00 to 11:00 A.M. for breakfast, 11:00 A.M. to 2:00 P.M. for lunch, and dinners run from 5:00 to 9:00 P.M. during the winter and 5:00 to 10:00 P.M. during the summer season.

Bandon Dunes $$
57744 Round Lake Drive, Bandon
(888) 345-6008

Whether you are trying out this new golf course along the bluff north of Bandon, designed in the spirit of Scotland's ancient links tradition, enjoying its spa; staying at one of the suites at the lodge or at their Lily Pond Cottages, or just stopping by for a meal, their restaurant has lots to offer the hungry duffer or visitor. Breakfast features the Bandon Dunes Scramble—smoked lox salmon scrambled with eggs, capers, red onions, and the famous Bandon cheddar cheese. Lunch ranges from crispy oysters to Grandma Thayer's meatloaf sandwich, and dinners offer aged prime New York steak, steamed Oregon little-neck clams and fried calamari. Hours are 6:00 A.M. to 10:00 P.M. daily.

Harp's Restaurant and the Hideaway Lounge $$
480 1st Street SW, Bandon
(541) 347-9057

The latest culinary incarnation in this small building that once housed an art gallery and three restaurants, Harp's is its biggest hit. With fresh pasta made every day, a unique seasoning to go with its grilled oysters, and a hot New York strip steak basted with Tabasco sauce, this comfy little spot is one of the best options for fine dining in Bandon. Open Tuesday

Insiders' Tip
Coos Bay folks in the know head for the Scenery in the morning for a brisk cup of java and their choice of a freshly baked scone. They also have soup and sandwiches later in the day for lunch. The Scenery is at 190 Central Avenue, Coos Bay, (541) 267-5600.

through Saturday from 5:00 to 9:00 P.M. daily. There is a full service bar.

Lord Bennett's $$
1695 Beach Loop Road, Bandon
(541) 347-3663

Named after the dour Irish lord who established the town of Bandon, this fine eatery poised on the bluff along Beach Loop Road with a stunning view of the Pacific Ocean, offers a wide range of entrees. Lunch items include shrimp omelet, broiled red snapper, and a crab sandwich with avocado and melted jack cheese; dinner specialties are stuffed sole, blackened red snapper, lobster, and a combination seafood plate. They are open for Sunday brunch and lunch from 11:00 A.M. to 3:00 P.M. and for dinner daily from 5:00 to 9:00 P.M.

Sea Star Bistro $$
375 2nd Street, Bandon
(541) 347-9632

At the entrance to Bandon's Old Town, the Sea Star Bistro, attached to a bed-and-breakfast, is a creative dining spot for guests of the Sea Star Bed and Breakfast, with everything made from scratch in creative ways. Breakfasts include salmon hash, vegetarian home fries, and Greek omelets; lunch choices include seafood burritos, grilled prawns with pesto, and black bean chili; and dinners offer poached salmon, smoked game hen, herb fettuccine with prawns, and a tempting cannelloni. It is worth an effort to try out this charming lodging and bistro. It is not wheelchair accessible.

Wheelhouse Restaurant & Crow's Nest Lounge $
125 Chicago Avenue, Old Town Mall, Bandon
(541) 347-9331

With its nautical theme and close view of the local working fishing fleet moored across the street, the Wheelhouse is a lively and tasty spot to dine while visiting this friendly, cheerful tourist stop. Try fresh native seafood, local lamb, or the homemade clam chowder. Another hit is the fish fried in a beer batter. Hours are daily from 11:30 A.M. to 9:00 or 10:00 P.M. depending on the crowd.

Beach Junction Market & Deli $
Bandon
(541) 347-6978.

At the corner of U.S. 101 and the southern end of Beach Loop Road, this market and deli is handy for picnic fixings, a quick snack, or stocking up for camping. They have homemade biscuits & gravy, specialty sandwiches, cold beverages, and gourmet coffees.

Wedderburn

Rod 'n' Reel $
94321 River Road, Wedderburn
(541) 247-6823

A neat little cafe close to the jet boat docks where you begin your adventure zooming up the Rogue River, Rod 'n' Reel serves breakfast, lunch and dinner—all tasty and all low cost. Try the grilled shrimp or crab sandwiches. Hours are 6:00 A.M. to 2:00 P.M.

Brookings

Chives $$
1025 Chetco Avenue, Brookings
(541) 247-4121

Here's a surprisingly upscale restaurant in a town that's a charming little coastal burg with no pretensions. Their specialties include a rock shrimp risotto appetizer, steamer clams in white wine and garlic butter broth, oysters in pesto, and baked king salmon. Chives is closed Monday and Tuesday.

Hog Wild Cafe $
16158 U.S. Highway 101 S., Brookings
(541) 469-8869

They have fun with the porcine theme at this eatery. Portions are large and there are items with names like Hog Slop (chocolate-caramel mochas). They also serve zesty breakfast fajitas, Belgian waffles with fresh berries, and an innovative selection of omelets. Hours are 7:00 A.M. to 2:00 P.M. every day but Monday.

Rubio's Mexican Restaurant $
1136 Chetco Avenue, Brookings
(541) 469-4919

Rubio's is a good bet if you are craving Mexican or Tex-Mex cuisine. The salsa is a big hit, and the house specialty is seafood doused with jalapeño sauce, butter, garlic, and wine. Also, try their chiles rellenos. Hours for lunch are 11:00 A.M. to 5:00 P.M. and dinner is served concurrently from 11:00 A.M. to 8:00 P.M. on weekdays and 11:00 A.M. to 9:00 P.M. on the weekends.

Wild River Pizza $
16279 U.S. Highway 101, Brookings
(541) 469-7454

This big and bustling pizza parlor is a great spot to feed the family that's starved after a hearty time at the beach. Along with the usual choices for pizza is a selection of microbrews. Hours are 11:00 A.M. to 10:00 P.M. daily.

Nightlife

After a fun day at the beach or touring a historic shopping district, you may be ready to check out the lively nightlife on the Oregon Coast. This chapter provides you with a variety of entertainment choices including clubs with dancing and live music, playhouses featuring local theatrical productions, and casinos with cards and slots. The entertainment possibilities are listed north to south by region and then by city.

North Coast

Oregon's tame but pleasing beach world is a far distance from the bright lights of Atlantic City or Las Vegas, but there are a few choices of nightlife that will entertain visitors as well as introduce them to the local cultural flavor. In Astoria, the oldest village in Oregon, you can catch the antics of the Astor Street Opry Company or join the gang at Cafe Uniontown, the hot spot for live music here. Farther south, there are some great shows at the Coaster Theater in Cannon Beach for folks who have stopped by this artsy town to view the painting and crafts.

Astoria

Astor Street Opry Company
Elks Hall, 453 11th Street, Astoria
(503) 325–6104

A local theater troupe presents *Shanghaied in Astoria* Thursday through Saturday nights, mid-July through mid-August. The play, with chase scenes, bar fights, and lots of Scandinavian jokes, is based on Astoria's dubious distinction as a notorious shanghai port during the late 1800s. Buy tickets in the lobby of the John Jacob Astor Apartments, a renovated 1920s hotel at 14th and Commercial Street or at the Elks Hall box office. Tickets run between $5.00 and $12.00.

Cafe Uniontown
218 West Marine Drive, Astoria
(503) 325–8708

This hot spot under the Astoria Bridge is the town's jazz scene with both jazz and blues performed by Northwest notables such as jazz singer Nancy King. Also fun are the piano sing-alongs in the bar. The cafe is host to live music Tuesday through

Insiders' Tip

To zero in on your tastes in evening entertainment, here are two sparkly Web sites that will give you plenty of choices: The Oregon Coast Council for the Arts lists concerts, plays, and other events on its www.coastarts.org. On the far side of guidance, the Alternacoast Guide is a wild and wacky take on local arts and entertainment down the Coast. Examples include news of the most inexpensive bar on the West Coast and the reason why Lincoln City is now a lot more fun after dark. This site can be reached at www.navicom.com/~andrehage/alternacoast.html.

Be sure to attend a play while you are visiting the scenic Coast. PHOTO: LIZANN DUNEGAN

Saturday night. There is usually a cover charge of $3.00 to $5.00.

The Wet Dog Cafe
144 11th Street, Astoria
(503) 325-6975

This haven for both old hipsters and Gen-X types has local and regional groups playing blues to alternative rock on Friday and Saturday. There are free billiards on Saturday and Sunday until 5:00 P.M. On tap are Sow Your Wild Oatmeal Stout and Rye PA, an amber ale produced by the Pacific Rim Brewing Company. For snacks there are lots of pasta dishes, pizzas, and great halibut fish and chips.

Seaside

Girtle's Restaurant & Lounge
311 Broadway, Seaside
(503) 738-8417

On weekends, Girtle's presents bands from nearby and from Portland having fun with current pop favorites as well as golden oldies. After a day of beachcombing, it's fun to shake off the sand while dancing at Girtle's.

Cannon Beach

Bill's Tavern
188 North Hemlock Street, Cannon Beach
(503) 436-2202

This legendary lounge was recently renovated and has emerged as the center of Cannon Beach nightlife. A hand-carved sign with a wooden crow perched on top is a relic from the original tavern founded 65 years ago. Now it is home to local blues and rock groups who take the stage once or twice a month.

Coaster Theater
108 North Hemlock Street, Cannon Beach
(503) 436-1242

This lively theater company runs its plays on Friday and Saturday with tickets ranging from $10 to $15. Recent productions included Neil Simon's comedy *Barefoot in the Park* and *Love Letters,* a play about letters exchanged over a lifetime between two people.

Manzanita

Gales Bar & Grill
165 Laneda Avenue, Manzanita
(503) 368-4253

On Friday and Saturday night, this cozy little nook offers live rock music by local and Portland bands with dinners of steaks, pasta, and seafood—particularly their popular Captain's Platter of mixed seafood. The live music continues after dinner from 9:00 P.M. to 1:00 A.M.

Pacific City

Tidewaters
34455 Brooten Road, Pacific City
(503) 965-6960

Musicians of all flavors are brought in from Portland and other urban zones to perform at the Tidewaters with no cover charge. Along with a 50-seat restaurant, there is a lounge with a festive maritime motif and a wide view of the bay at Pacific City. There is also a wild karaoke party on Friday night.

Otis

Cascade Head Chamber Music Festival
P.O. Box 145, Otis 97368
Tickets: (541) 994-5333.
Held at St. Peter the Fisherman Lutheran Church (1226 Southwest 13th Street, Lincoln City, 541-994-2007) Thursday through Saturday for two weeks in June each year. Noted violinist Sergiu Luca directs a host of talented musicians who flock to the Oregon Coast to perform classical music.

Central Coast

From Lincoln City down to Florence, the Oregon Coast hums both day and night with scenic wonder and lively entertainment. In just about every town there is a performing arts center, if only a modest renovation of a grange hall. It's a great way to meet the locals and you may be surprised by the quality of entertainment particularly in the realm of community theater.

Lincoln City

Chinook Winds Casino
1777 Northwest 44th Street, Lincoln City
Casino information: (888) 244-6665
Entertainment and bus reservations:
(888) 624-6228
www.chinookwindscasino.com
One of the most successful Native American gaming ventures in Oregon, Chinook Winds Casino offers a variety of games including blackjack, poker, bingo, slots, keno, and a large stage and entertainment theater. Newer entertainments include craps, roulette, Pai Gow poker, Let-it-Ride, Caribbean Stud, Aruba Stud, Progressive Blackjack, and Big 6 Wheel. It all adds up to gambling fun of all flavors. Other amenities include a restaurant and lounge: The Rogue River Room, with live

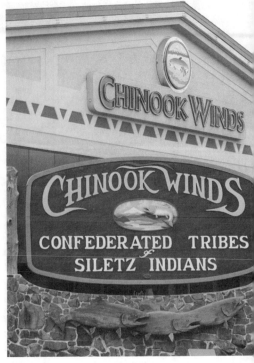

Enjoy live entertainment several nights each week at Chinook Winds Casino in Lincoln City. PHOTO: LIZANN DUNEGAN

entertainment several nights each week and a sumptuous dance floor. Hours are 10:00 A.M. to 1:00 A.M. Sunday and Monday 8:00 A.M. to 2:00 A.M. Tuesday through Saturday. There is child care available, a video arcade for kids, and a gift shop.

Newport

The Newport Performing Arts Center
777 West Olive, Newport
(541) 265-9231
www.coastarts.org/pac
In 1986, they burned down the historic Bluebird Cottages at Nye Beach to make room for the Newport Performing Arts Center. With its 400-seat Alice Silverman Theater and auxiliary Studio Theatre, the center is the largest performing arts venue on the Oregon Coast. While traveling through Newport, it is always a good idea to check its schedule for music, theater, or lectures. One of the popular events is a

monthly Nye Beach Writers Series that runs spring through fall with two designated writers reading each month, followed by an "open mike."

Bay Haven Tavern
608 Southwest Bay Boulevard, Newport
(541) 265–7271

Established in 1908, this ancient fisherman's saloon has served all sorts of folks, including Jack London and John Steinbeck. Perhaps its greatest claim to fame was as a location in the screen version of Ken Kesey's *Sometimes a Great Notion.* Nowadays and nights, its identity is as "Home of the Blues." If you stop by on Sunday afternoon after 3:00 P.M., you'll find a musical assembly mixed with a down-home potluck called the Bay Haven BBQ Blues Jam. There isn't a cover but a couple of bucks in the tip jar will keep everything alive and well.

Port Dock One
325 Southwest Bay Boulevard, Newport
(541) 265–2911

A large restaurant and lounge reminiscent of the three-story, stick-porched hostels of the Caribbean, the Port Dock One is on Newport's bayfront next to the Undersea Gardens. Stop by in the evening for live and usually danceable music.

Yachats

Yachats Commons
101 2nd Street, Yachats
(541) 547–3935

Sponsored by the Friends of Yachats Commons, this cozy little venue for jazz, acoustic, and classical music offers visitors a treat for a modest charge of $5.00 to $10.00.

Florence

The Fisherman's Wharf Restaurant & Lounge
1341 Bay Street, Florence
(541) 997–2613

The most legendary item in this rustic old saloon is a long bar with seashells gleaming from beneath a thick slab of Verathaned plastic. Also in this classic coastal tavern is a lounge that presents a variety of rock bands that play the old tunes from the '70s and '80s. There are also pool tables for those who want to shoot a few games.

The Lotus
1150 Bay Street, Florence
(541) 997–7168

Nestled under the bridge crossing the Siuslaw River, The Lotus is a calmer night scene than the Fisherman's Wharf but just as fun for its live music of local bands covering '50s rock 'n' roll and blues.

Florence Events Center
715 Quince Street, Florence
(541) 997–1994, (888) 968–4086
www.eventcenter.org

Here at the Events Center you can find a wide variety of evening entertainment including brass orchestra concerts, storybook theater by the Last Resort Players, rhododendron shows, and art exhibits. While in town, call for current events on tap.

South Coast

North Bend

North Bend Lanes Bowling Center
1225 Virginia Avenue, North Bend
(541) 756–0571

This modern bowling center is a complete operation with pool tables and a giant-screen TV and is a luncheon spot with salads, sandwiches, and homemade soup.

Little Theater on the Bay
2100 Sherman Avenue (U.S. 101 & Washington), North Bend
(541) 756–4336

Maybe it's the legendary grey skies or the communal energy of a coastal village, but it seems that live theater is a booming force in North Bend, Coos Bay, Bandon, and Coquille. A good example is Little Theatre on the Bay. This ambitious outfit has been mounting full-scale musicals as well as serious drama for decades. Examples of their shows include *One Flew Over the*

Cuckoo's Nest, Grease, and *The Grapes of Wrath.* Tickets range from $7.00 to $10.00.

The Mill Casino
3201 Tremond Avenue, North Bend
(541) 756–8800, (800) 953–4800
www.themillcasino.com

Here in the sprawl of a renovated plywood mill along U.S. 101 is a lively yet perfectly safe gambling parlor operated by the Coquille Tribe. You can stop by every night and play slots, bingo, blackjack, and poker. There is also live entertainment six nights a week with rock, country and western, and oldies to dance to while the house bags up your winnings. There is free RV parking.

Roger's Zoo
2047 Sherman Avenue, North Bend
(541) 756–2550

This smoke-free pub has great pizza and often has live music with a $3.00 cover. The sounds are usually rock or jazz. This is a haunt of locals who want a quiet good time.

Coos Bay

Bank Brewing Company
201 Central Avenue, Coos Bay
(541) 267–0963

Located in a classic old bank building, this local brewery is a popular hangout for tame but tasty brew (Coast Golden Ale and Sweet Wheat), innovative pub grub including fajitas and pastas, and entertainment. Live music on Saturday starts at 7:00 P.M. with no cover. One of the favorite events is an Irish sing-along with local musicians. Also on tap are local jazz quartets, acoustic guitar blues, and one performer billed as the "Don Rickles of Rock."

Blue Moon Restaurant and Lounge
871 South Broadway, Coos Bay
(541) 269–9004

This old saloon is a bit rough around the edges but is the real McCoy as a country tavern in downtown Coos Bay. Live country music fills the saloon on Friday and Saturday nights with no cover charge. It also offers free pool on Mondays 5:00 P.M. to close.

Old City Hall Grand Ballroom
375 Central Avenue, Coos Bay
(541) 267–5897

The old seat of power only a block away from the new city hall has been remodeled into a dance hall. Dancing lessons run $5.00 for students and $7.00 for adults. Bands play rock 'n' roll and Big Band sounds. There is a $5.00 cover charge for events.

Gooney's Sports Bar & Grill
3290 Ocean Boulevard, Coos Bay
(541) 266–8815

This full-service bar has good grub, 10 satellite-access TVs, pool tables, darts, a jukebox, video golf, and Oregon lottery games. There is live music every other weekend at 9:00 P.M., no cover charge. The sounds include highly danceable Cajun swamp rock and a local band that calls itself the Beat Dragons.

Gussie's
1088 Newmark Avenue, Coos Bay
(541) 888–2022

An old institution located en route to the Coast from downtown Coos Bay, Gussie's has family-style dining as well as live music and DJ's spinning CDs on Friday and Saturday.

On Broadway Theater
226 South Broadway, Coos Bay
(541) 269–2501
www.geocities.com/obthespian

As well as presenting adult drama, this lively group also mounts shows with teenage thespians involved in Alternative Youth Activities. There is also a Children's Theatre for younger children. A recent example of the shows produced with one act plays be Tennessee Williams including *Portrait of a Madonna, Lord Byron's Love Letter,* and *Hello from Bertha.* Tickets usually run $10.

Wanda's
740 Koos Bay Boulevard, Coos Bay
(541) 267–6293

Wanda's is another reliable venue for the best of local bands playing blues and rock on Friday and Saturday night usually with no cover.

Insiders' Tip

A handy way to find out about theater and concert events along the South Coast is a call to The Ticket Connection, (541) 266–9180, at 265 South Bayshore Drive in Coos Bay. This outlet in the downtown stretch of U.S. 101 will alert you to and sell tickets to local performances.

Coquille

Sawdust Theatre
38 East 1st Street, Coquille
(541) 396–4563
www.sawdusttheatre.com

This hilarious and highly entertaining theater group is worth a side jaunt east from U.S. 101 to Coquille. Their specialty is a theatrical form called an "olio," in which the audience is encouraged to hiss at the villains and cheer the heroes and heroines. Examples of the plays they perform are *The Colossal Cranberry Caper* and *Boondoogled in the Bog.* Call for current schedule and ticket prices.

Bandon

Bandon Playhouse
City Park, Bandon
(541) 347–4529

After struggling along as a small amateur theater group presenting plays at the local grade school and other temporary venues, the Bandon Playhouse has a brand-new home built for $1 million in Bandon City Park. For a schedule of upcoming plays, call or write to Bandon Playhouse, P.O. Box 1047, Bandon 97411. Tickets range from $7.00 to $10.00. Recent performances have included *Fiddler on the Roof, Oklahoma, The King and I,* and *My Fair Lady.*

Fraser's Restaurant and Quarterdeck Lounge
1032 Oregon Avenue SW, Bandon
(541) 347–9024

Just about the only nightlife venue on the upper side of Bandon-by-the-Sea, Fraser's offers a full service bar, lottery games, social gaming, electronic darts, circular fireplace, and a big-screen TV for sports action. There is usually a pool tournament in February.

Lloyd's
119 2nd Street, Bandon
(541) 347–4211

Fondly known as "Lloyd's of Bandon," this venerable pub has been the scene of lots of live music brought in from Portland and other larger scenes. The bands play every other Friday and Saturday from

9:00 P.M. to 2:00 A.M. The restaurant side menu is available in the lounge side. Best bet is classic cheeseburger and fries.

Pistol River

Pistol River Friendship Hall
P.O. Box 6086, Pistol River 97444
(541) 247–2848
www.pistolriver.com
In the old country tradition of grange halls and barn dances, the Pistol River Friendship Hall stages lots of great entertainment. Located along a small river flowing to the ocean halfway between Gold Beach and Brookings, the hall has recently featured nationally renowned jazz pianist Scott Cossu. Call or visit the Web site for current show schedules and ticket prices.

Pistol River is located 10 miles south of Gold Beach off U.S. 101.

Brookings

Redwood Theater
621 Chetco Avenue, Brookings
(541) 469–4632
www.redwoodtheater.com
Probably the most southern nightlife venue on the Oregon Coast, the Redwood Theater, an old movie house actually constructed with redwood, shows films and presents live music concerts. The Friends of Music schedule five concerts of classical chamber music on Sunday afternoons in spring and fall. Another musical event recently held was Celtic music by The Golden Bough.

Shopping

The Oregon Coast offers a variety of shopping experiences. You'll find everything from outlet malls to small upscale shops in quaint historic districts. Many shops are locally owned and feature one-of-a-kind arts and crafts, toys, clothing, jewelry, candy, and everything in between. The shops in this chapter are listed from north to south.

North Coast

The shopping ambiance varies considerably on the North Coast of Oregon. You'll find outlet centers and main streets, crowded tourist strips and destination stops, and everything in between. Each of the towns on the Oregon Coast has a distinctive retail character. Cannon Beach, for instance, has many fine, upscale shops and galleries; Seaside's colorful shopping district serves customer demand for candy, beach toys, and souvenirs; Astoria's old-fashioned main street–style downtown area demands hours of browsing and exploring. In fact, many of the towns on the Coast have lively main streets to investigate, areas that retain their qualities of independence and eclecticism. While Cannon Beach is a tourist mecca, it also doesn't allow franchises, so family-owned businesses are common and the town is attractively idiosyncratic. The main street area of Tillamook (actually called Main Avenue) is worth exploring for the opposite reason: because apparently tourists hardly ever do. It has a distinctively local flavor, with Sears, hardware stores, building supplies, second-hand stores, groovy record shops, and farmers' co-ops all mixed up together. These districts are full of surprises, adding adventure to the other pleasures of buying local.

Astoria

Maybe it's because downtown Astoria looks like the movie set of a small midcentury town, or maybe it's because this shopping district is for everyone, locals and tourists alike, but whatever the secret ingredient to the retail charm of this area, it works. From Marine Drive south to Franklin and from 16th west to 8th, you'll find all sorts of places to spend your time and money. Scrapbookers and stamp maniacs will be hard-pressed to leave **Paper Moon Rubber Stamps,** 229 14th Street, while chocolate fiends will linger in **Columbia Chocolates,** 1396 Duane Street, where they sell candy made right there in town. **Let It Rain,** 1124 Commercial Street, sells everything to keep you dry in coastal storms. **Finn Ware,** 1116 Commercial Street, is the source for all things Scandinavian, from sauna supplies to crystal. **Custom Threads,** 1282 Commercial Street, will keep you in splendid yarns and needles and hooks during all your knitting and crochet projects. Notable bookstores in the area include **Lucy's Books, Godfather's Books** and **Espresso,** 1108 Commercial Street; and right nearby, the **Backroom Bookstore** at 1052 Commercial Street. The *Daily Astorian,* the local newspaper, also maintains a bookstore that specializes in local history; you can find them at 949 Exchange Street.

Columbia River Maritime Museum
1792 Marine Drive, Astoria
(503) 325-2323

Museum gift shops are often excellent resources for unusual birthday, anniversary, and wedding gifts, and the shop at this well-planned museum is no exception. Comprehensive books and monographs on Indian art, Oregon history, maritime history, fishing, shipwrecks, lighthouses, and other water-related items are for sale, and so are elegant sand glasses and ships' lanterns. Their teaching resources are outstanding;

in addition to all the books, there are maps, charts, graphs, and videos. If none of those sound like the right gift, try the jewelry.

Lucy's Books
348 12th Street, Astoria
(503) 325–4210

Lucy's is a bookstore with a strong local focus, and Astoria is a town with a lot of writers. Lucy's has not only an excellent selection of books about the Pacific Northwest but carries the local writers too; you can find things here that you cannot find anywhere else, like anthologies of poems collected from the Fisher Poets Gathering, which takes place in February. Lucy's also has a good section on women's writing and a decent travel section. It's closed Sundays.

Seaside

Seaside Antique Mall
39 South Holladay, Seaside
(503) 717–9312
www.myantiquemall.com

There are about a dozen stores in Seaside that sell antiques; the Seaside Antique Mall is the largest, and browsing here is a splendid way to spend a rainy Oregon day. In addition to the usual china, glass, and linens, you can also score some great finds in the advertising, Indian artifact, and art pottery departments. You can find a lot more than that, too: 88 antiques and collectibles dealers have pooled their resources at this mall. Open Sunday to Friday 10:00 A.M. to 5:00 P.M.; Saturday 10:00 A.M. to 8:00 P.M.

Seaside Carousel Mall
300 Broadway, Seaside
(503) 738–6728

Broadway is Seaside's waterfront shopping district, and there you will find many candy, souvenir, and wacky T-shirt shops. In the middle of it all is the appropriately named Seaside Carousel Mall, which houses a beautiful carousel in addition to the shops. After the little ones go for a ride on a big ginger cat or a unicorn, take them to **Under the Big Top Toys** for more indulgence. Then perhaps something for you is in order from **Signature Imports,**

which sells furniture and decorating items in addition to beautiful leather bags, hand knit sweaters, and batik sarongs. **Mary Anna's $12 Store** carries nothing that costs more than $12 and much of it is surprisingly chic; **Mostly Hats** carries, well, mostly hats, but it's awfully convenient when you've forgotten yours.

Seaside Factory Outlet Center
111 North Roosevelt, Seaside
(503) 717–1603
www.seasideoutlets.com

One of the favorite activities of visitors to the North Coast is spending the day at the shopping mall, and in this case big savings are in store. You'll see some familiar outlet names at this 25-store complex—**Kitchen Collection, OshKosh B'Gosh, Nine West,** and **Dress Barn** all have spaces here. Our favorites include the **Black & Decker** store for small appliances, **Nike** and **Adidas** for sportswear and shoes, and **Coldwater Creek** for clothes, jewelry, and more. **The Wine Haus** carries a respectably large selection of wines, excellent cigars, and more than 300 kinds of beer from here and abroad. Wine tastings are held daily; they also serve soup and sandwiches.

Cleanline Surf Shop
719 First Avenue, Seaside
(503) 738–7888
171 Sunset Boulevard, Cannon Beach
(503) 436–9726
www.cleanlinesurf.com

Both branches of this store sell surfboards, skateboards, and snowboards. But that's not all: You can also repair your board or rent one for the day—they feature complete surf rental packages. Or if you'd feel safer in a kayak, they can help you get set up with that too. In addition to gear, Cleanline also sells wet suits and simple shoes; you'll keep warm with the Ugg sheepskin boots and the Patagonia jackets. Or you'll cool down with Billabong shorts.

Cannon Beach

Animal Crackers Toys and Gifts
123 South Hemlock Street, Cannon Beach
(503) 436–0536

A cute shop in the two-story Ecola Square, Animal Crackers features educational toys for children and those who play with them. Children like the shop because of the great mix of traditional and modern toys it carries; parents like it because it's attached to the Lite Bites deli and espresso shop, so when they weary of all the playing and toy-testing, respite is only a few steps away.

Bruce's Candy Kitchen
256 North Hemlock Street, Cannon Beach
(503) 436–2641
www.brucescandy.com

This plank-floored, false-fronted building sells handmade chocolate and saltwater taffy and it's a Cannon Beach institution. It's a full-service candy store; you can get swirly rainbow lollipops and gummi bears. You can watch them make the candy right there, and watching it being made imparts an even more delicious flavor. They don't pull every flavor in their saltwater taffy line; that means that the butterscotch, root beer, butter, and cinnamon varieties are stickier and harder (and usually the first ones eaten, as long as no dental work is in jeopardy). Bruce's also makes a line of sugar-free candy; it's quite good.

Cannon Beach Book Company
132 Hemlock #2, Cannon Beach
(503) 436–1301, (877) 312–5045
www.cannonbeachbooks.com

A fine bookstore, the Cannon Beach Book Company is a great supporter of writers and literary events in the area, so stop by to see what's happening and what local writers have published lately. While you're there, check out the contemporary fiction and literary nonfiction—and anything else, for this is a shop that believes in browsing. You'll also find a good mystery section and books for children.

Center Diamond
1065 South Hemlock Street, Cannon Beach
(503) 436–0833
www.centerdiamond.com

This shop is helping to feed the mania for quilting, and after a visit, it's easy to see why. It's a must-stop for North Coast quilters. The Center Diamond really is a center—not only do they sell beautiful fabrics, patterns, and notions for quilting, but they also feature classes and workshops. You might try a "Slumber party," which is an extended retreatlike workshop on doll making, quilting, or related topics.

Ecola Square
123 South Hemlock Street, Cannon Beach

Ecola Square has some of the most interesting shops in Cannon Beach. Its attractively faded, white-trimmed exterior just begs to be visited. Some highlights of this village mall are **Ecola Square Books,** which specializes in books for children as well as books about the region and **Refuge,** which features rustic decorations and supplies for your house. Three other shops worth noting are **Shorelines Northwest**—it sells local and exotic shells and ocean-themed gifts; the **Wild Bird Shop,** which features everything you need to learn about birds; and **Nature Arts and Sounds,** which will supply you with fountains and nature-related gifts. Ecola Square is very Cannon Beach, and a great place to spend a rainy day when you can't have the real thing.

El Mundo for Men
231 North Hemlock Street, Cannon Beach
(503) 436–1002
319 Broadway, Seaside
(503) 738–6551

El Mundo for men was doing Casual Friday long before anyone else; in 1975, the owner, George Vetter, was convincing college students that they should skip the necktie and mellow out. Now he carries a lot of attractive natural-fiber clothing for men; he also has quite a selection of joke T-shirts. When the beach look won't do, El Mundo's can also spiff you up in a dinner jacket by Ralph Lauren or Christian Dior; they have all sizes, including those for children.

Geppetto's Toy Shoppe
299 North Hemlock Street, Cannon Beach
(503) 436–2467

This shop is a longtime favorite of vacationers to Cannon Beach, and those families know that Geppetto's is a must-stop before a long car trip home. It specializes in entertaining and educational toys, and the folks who work there are imaginative about travel and rainy-day activities. Also noteworthy is the good selection of arts-and-crafts kits appropriate for different ages and all the sand toys a child could ever want.

Jupiter's Rare and Used Books
244 North Spruce Street, Cannon Beach
(503) 436-0549

Used bookstores are awfully fun, and Jupiter's is no exception. You can find that copy of Plato you were looking for or pick up last month's Stephen King novel, all for really great prices. And like many of the bookstores on the Coast, they feature local writers, especially hard-to-find editions of them. You'll also find some first editions.

M. Sellin
215 North Hemlock Street, Cannon Beach
(503) 436-1572

This clothing shop for women features natural-fiber garb that is as stylish as it is comfortable. In addition to the wonderful dresses, skirts, trousers, and shirts, M. Sellin carries a good selection of fashionable shoes and jewelry. Recently, they have started featuring yummy-smelling skin care products too. M. Sellin is an institu-

tion here in Cannon Beach, and so is its sister store on Hawthorne in Portland.

Spicy Bambu
231 North Hemlock Street, Cannon Beach
(503) 436-0774

This fabulous store, which has a corresponding branch in Portland, sells clothing, accessories, and things for your house made by artisans primarily from Mexico, Indonesia, and Nepal. The items are directly imported from the people who make them, returning profits right to the communities that produced them. Beautiful cotton dresses, hemp bags, and hand-knit sweaters will entice you to refresh your wardrobe, while rugs, blankets, and art objects will inspire you to redecorate. And you don't even have to feel guilty since it's all going to a good cause.

Manzanita

Manzanita News and Espresso
500 Laneda Avenue, Manzanita
(503) 368-7450
www.neahkahnie.net/newsespresso.html

Manzanita News is a dangerous and distracting heaven for magazine fanatics, who probably should stop reading them and get outdoors. But no one could break the habit with the 435 titles here to tempt them. Not only does the shop carry *Martha Stewart Living* and *Atlantic Monthly*, but it also carries the *Sun* and *Film Quarterly*. And there are lots of maps and newspapers and very inviting spaces to sit and read. Add to this the Portland Roasting Company coffee and the cookies, muffins, and scones by Temptations, a local baking company, and you might forget to go back out to the beach (we'd tell you how good the gingerbread scones were, only then there might not be any left for us).

Mother Nature's Natural Foods
298 Laneda Avenue, Manzanita
(503) 368-5316
www.neahkahnie.net

In 1997, when Judson Moore and Susie Freeman took over the natural foods store that used to be where Mother Nature's is now, they decided to give it a whole new look and feel. So they added a cafe that serves delicious, seasonal organic food made right there, a fresh produce case, and organic wine, and suddenly people who had balked at the very idea of "natural foods" were shopping there regularly. Mother Nature's is a full-service natural foods store that sells vitamins, health supplements, beauty aids, cards, and gifts in addition to the groceries. The produce is excellent; they try to buy as much as they can from local producers. The cafe is great—one of few alternatives for a healthful lunch in Manzanita. But the ambience is the real secret here: The owners are unbelievably friendly and welcoming.

Tillamook

Latimer Center Gift Shop
2105 Wilson River Loop Road, Tillamook
(503) 842–8622

The Gift Shop at the Latimer Center helps to pay for the extraordinary conservation and study of the textile arts that the Latimer Center has undertaken. You can purchase patterns for Latimer-designed quilts, baskets, wall hangings, bags, and handmade papers. If you're a textile artist

yourself, you can purchase Northwest plant fibers; if you'd like to become a textile artist, you can take classes. And this doesn't even count the works by local textile artists that you can purchase and take home with you.

Pacific City

Migrations
33105 Cape Kiwanda Drive, Suite 1, Pacific City
(503) 965–4661

So much more than a shop, this space is actually a coffee shop that features organic coffees and teas and delicious bakery things in addition to being a book and nature store. The bookstore has a wide assortment of books and magazines for vacationing travelers and serious readers, while the nature store carries everything you'll need when you put the book down and venture out on your own. Field guides, binoculars, knives, some rain gear, and day packs are among the featured items; for backyard adventurers there are bird baths and feeders. Sip some coffee while you look over your purchases and enjoy the lovely ocean view from this interesting store.

Textile artists and quilt makers will love exploring the Latimer Quilt and Textile Center in Tillamook.
PHOTO: LIZANN DUNEGAN

Like the North Coast, the Central Coast has enough variety in its shopping to keep it lively. Those who love shopping malls will like the Lincoln City Factory Stores and the Marketplace at Salishan. Those who adore exploring old-fashioned main street shopping will enjoy the Nye Beach area in Newport with its funky shops in Victorian buildings and the Old Town district of Florence. And all along U.S. 101 you'll find little shops that will have you making U-turns.

Lincoln City

The Factory Stores at Lincoln City
1500 Southeast East Devils Lake Road,
Lincoln City
(541) 996–5000
www.shoplincolncity.com

You can spend a whole day exploring the 65 stores at the factory outlet mall in Lincoln City. PHOTO: LIZANN DUNEGAN

Built to resemble a village, the Factory Stores at Lincoln City, which are at the intersection of Devils Lake Road and U.S. 101, have lawns and benches and courtyards. It's pleasant and rare to encounter grass at 65-store outlet mall; that alone makes this one worth a visit. You'll find the staples of outlet mall shopping here: **Carter's** for children's clothing, **Kitchen Collection, G. H. Bass,** and **Mikasa** are some familiar names, but there are many more. You'll find a lot of great clothing deals at **Eddie Bauer, Dress Barn, Pendleton Woolen Mills, Gap Kids,** and the **Gap Outlet.** The **Rockport** store carries well-priced dress shoes in addition to casual wear. Other compelling reasons to shop here: outlets for **Columbia Sportswear** and **Norm Thompson. Willamette Valley Chateau Benoit** sells good wine at their shop in the mall, and they run a deli there too. Stop in for some wine and cheese to take back to your hotel.

Book End Books
4095 A Logan Road, Lincoln City
(541) 994–9393
The perfect place to spend a rainy afternoon in Lincoln City, Book End offers free coffee to its customers, encourages browsing, and carries a wide selection of magazines and new books. It's also a good source for a miscellany of cards and CDs. Book End is a pleasant space; you may get so absorbed stocking up on beach reading that you'll forget to go to the beach to read it once the sun comes out.

Judith Anne Antiques
412 Southeast U.S. Highway 101, Lincoln City
(541) 994–9912
Judith Anne Antiques is the place to go if you find your mouth watering at the idea of good dishes—without any food on them. She carries a great selection of china, art pottery, and jewelry. Some delicious-looking Victorian necklaces are available and from time to time she'll get her hands on a cameo. Here you'll also find American art pottery from Fiesta, Weller, Franciscan, Bauer, Roseville, and even Rookwood, as well as Belleek porcelain, older Royal Doulton, and other imports. And she has a

number of interesting oyster plates. A good stop for collectors.

Gleneden Beach

The Marketplace at Salishan
7760 U.S. Highway 101 N., Gleneden Beach
(541) 764–2371, (888) SALISHAN (725–4742),
(541) 764–3282
www.salishan.com/marketplace

Shopping the Marketplace at Salishan brings many advantages—not only are there fabulous stores, but if you're staying at the Westin Salishan, you don't even need to leave the premises to see them. Start off at the **Coast Roast Coffee Company** for a cup of joe and a pastry, then (after you've finished) begin your wandering. **Le Domaine** carries beautiful linens, accessories, and furniture for the beach house, while **Hot Pots** will outfit the kitchen. After you've dressed your house, dress yourself at **Warm Coverings** specializing in hand-knit sweaters, hats, and jackets. The **Wooden Duck** carries toys, puzzles, and games for the little ones, and **Scribbles** offers a fine selection of writing paper so you can tell your friends at home what they're missing. Complete your shopping trip by trying some handmade chocolates at **Sweet Delights.**

Newport

There are two appealing areas for shopping in Newport, the waterfront and Nye Beach. The waterfront has a selection of shops mostly geared toward tourists (everybody else down there is too hard at work to go shopping) but still worth visiting. If you're there, you can check out **Cat House** (which advertises "an unexpected variety of gifts from around the world for cats and their slaves"), 410 Southwest Bay Boulevard; **Charisma Gifts** for good-smelling soaps and lotions and cute home decor items, 424 Southwest Bay Boulevard; the **Dockside,** 333 Southwest Bay Boulevard, for myrtlewood and sea-related artifacts; and **Northwest Kitchens,** 420 Southwest Bay Boulevard, which stocks Oregon wines and gourmet food in addition to an ample supply of kitchen gadgets.

Insiders' Tip
Oregon has no sales tax, making shopping even more fun than usual.

Turn off U.S. 101 and drive toward the ocean anywhere from 6th to 2nd Streets in Newport, and you will run right into Nye Beach, the historic district that was the summering spot for well-to-do residents of the Willamette Valley and the home of a sanatorium run by Herbert Hoover's step-father. People still summer here, and you might say they come here for their mental health. Now in these blocks you will find the impressive **Newport Performing Arts Center** (777 West Olive) and the **Yaquina Art Center** (839 Northwest Beach), lovely hotels and inns, and some great shopping. The stores here are really delectable. The gift shop at the **Sylvia Beach Hotel,** 267 Northwest Cliff, is worth checking out: It carries books, gifts, and cards. **Toujours Boutique,** 704 Northwest Beach, has beach-stylish clothing in natural fibers. **Tsunami Ceramics,** 310 Northwest Coast, has bisqueware ready for you to paint, as well as a potter's wheel and clay to play with—the perfect activity for a blustery coastal day. And then there is **Tea and Tomes,** 716 Northwest Beach, which will appease your appetite for British imports and serve you tea as well. On the outskirts, at 156 Southwest Coast Street, you'll find **Green Gables,** which is both a bed-and-breakfast inn and a bookstore featuring books for children, books on the Northwest, and many books for women. They also have a commanding collection of second-hand mystery novels.

Canyon Way Bookstore
1216 Southwest Canyon Way, Newport
(541) 265–8319

This independent bookstore has been feeding opinions, brains, and souls since the early 1970s and keeping the flame of thoughtful bookselling alive for coastal residents. In addition to the more than 30,000 titles in stock, Canyon Way Bookstore also carries interesting cards and calendars and an eclectic collection of CDs. They don't just feed your soul here, though; there is also a little restaurant for the rest of you. Don't miss this Newport institution.

Cheap Frills
817 Southwest Hurbert, Newport
(541) 265–9588

You'll find really great vintage clothing at this shop, and these days really great vintage clothing is hard to come by. Some standouts are the collections of delicate, frothy lingerie and becoming Victorian hats. Also look for Victorian and Art Nouveau jewelry; it is worth the trip to search through these collections. Men may find suits, leather jackets, and funky ties.

Cottage Gardenware at Nye Beach
732 Northwest Beach Drive, Newport
(541) 574–7706

Paradise for Martha Stewart fans: That sums up the atmosphere and product lines of this delightful shop. Look for fine tools, hats, and gloves; look for a variety of seeds; look for wonderful garden-themed gifts. But you don't have to actually have a garden to enjoy this shop; it also features a gorgeous selection of furniture and decorating items, beautifully displayed. Choose wisely and you can feel like you're in a garden without doing any of the work.

Craft Warehouse & Antique Mall
116 South Coast Highway (U.S. 101), Newport
(541) 265–2642

Thirty thousand square feet of antiques, collectibles, and craft supplies ensure that you'll find something if money is burning a hole in your pocket. You'll find the usual assortment of shells, dolls, glass, porcelain, linens, and so on; what's more, you'll find all the supplies you need to make your own family heirlooms and future collectibles. Worth visiting just for the sheer vastness of it all.

Sea Towne
1670 North Coast Highway (U.S. 101), Newport

Another Newport collection of shops is at the north of town in the Sea Towne Courtyards. Some notable shops here are

Queen of Hearts for fabulous lingerie from Donna Karan to Wacoal; **Sea Towne Books,** which has an outstanding selection of magazines; and **Cheri's at Sea Towne.** Cheri's features a number of local artists and craftspersons who make everything from jewelry to dolls to kelp wall pouches.

Yachats

Grandma & Me
430 U.S. Highway 101, Yachats
(541) 547–3224

This charming shop with a large front porch begs you to move right in with Grandma, or at least stop and browse through her antiques, collectibles, and gifts. Grandma (Barbara Adkinson) is a genius at display, so it's fun to wander about and see what combination of china, doilies, and dolls she has worked her magic on lately. As you wander, you'll also find bears, kitchen stuff, memorabilia, silver, Victoriana, and flowers. Lending their gentle scents are candles and sachets scattered throughout the shop. You won't want to go home.

Luna Sea Products
245 Aqua Vista Loop, Yachats
(541) 547–4794

The Luna is a tough old fishing boat built in 1925 and restored to picturesque working condition. The folks who own it process their own fish rather than selling it to a processor; that way the product is as fresh as possible. They marinate and smoke their catch right away, and the result is incredibly delicious smoked salmon, smoked tuna, and all kinds of cheeses and spreads. You can't get much fresher than this.

Planet Yachats
Corner of 4th and U.S. Highway 101, Yachats
(541) 547–4410

Yachats really is sometimes like another planet, and for those times, check out Planet Yachats. This lapidary sells amazing crystals, minerals, and fossils for when you're feeling in tune with terrestrial forces. It also features beautiful jewelry made of polished stones. Planet

Yachats is an inspired choice for unusual gifts for life's big ceremonies.

Old Town Florence

The Old Town district of Florence is a wonderful place to hang out. Attractions and public facilities, art galleries and antiques shops, food and drink, hotels, clothing stores, gift stores, bookshops, and specialty stores all combine to form an atmosphere that is charming and festive. It's much more than a shopping district; like all good market squares, it provides a center for village social life (even though it's not actually a square). It's a fun place to hang out, read the paper at a sidewalk or riverside cafe, and get caught up on the local news. Old Town is fun for visitors too. Wander leisurely through and watch the glassblowers make raindrops at the **Raindrop Factory,** 1287 Bay Street or watch a new movie at the vintage **Harbor Theater,** 1377 Bay Street. See if you can score any deals at **Thrifty Threads Consignment Shop,** 168 Maple Street, or blow your paycheck on jewelry at **Divine Decadence,** 1297 Bay Street (see below). Need some amusements for the kids? Try **Treasures by the Bay,** 1312 Bay Street, an excellent toy store that carries Playmobil, Disney toys, and Gotz dolls, as well as perfect toys for the beach. Or pick up a kite at **Catch the Wind,** 1250 Bay Street. The adults in the family may prefer to souvenir shop at **End of the Trail Trading Post,** 175 Nopaul Street, for clothing and decor inspired by the American West. Finish up your day with a sternwheeler cruise on the Siuslaw at **Mo's,** 1436 Bay Street, have an ice cream at **BJ's,** 1441 Bay Street, and go home.

Divine Decadence
1297 Bay Street, Florence
(541) 997-7200

A scrumptious shop in Old Town Florence, Divine Decadence will incite drooling in the most dignified jewelry lover. Divine Decadence carries both costume jewelry and the real stuff, both modern and vintage confections. This is definitely a browsing store: also look here for vintage clothes, for gifts, and for other kinds of unclassifiable "eclectica." This shop is an excellent source for gifts for those you love, especially you.

Grape Leaf
1368 Bay Street, Florence
(541) 997-1646

This shop showcases regional wines but it also features an excellent selection of international wines. And it sells the accessories to go along with the wine: openers, good glassware, wine guides, and everything else you need to sample and compare. Grape Leaf sells high-end food and gifts as well—and you can try before you buy at the charming riverside winetasting room and deli.

Lovejoy's Imports
Best Western Pier Point Inn, 85625 U.S. Highway 101, Florence
(541) 902-0502

Maybe it's all the rain, maybe it's the seaside, but something about the Oregon Coast reminds people of England. For those times when you'd rather be in Bristol, check out Lovejoy's Imports, which is the retail section of the pub and tearoom within the Best Western Pierpoint Inn, just south of the Siuslaw River bridge. There you'll find delicious English teas, gifts, and imported foods, as well as other edible delights from other parts of the world. And if you can't wait to get home to try them, you can visit the tearoom instead.

Northwest Passage
1308 Bay Street, Florence
(541) 902-1466

This shop right on the water specializes in men's, women's, and unisex seasonal clothing in natural fibers. Browsing in the store is a pleasure not just because of the clothes, however. The decorator accents and beautiful handcrafted furniture you see around the store are also for sale. You'll find the perfect chairs for the beach house or the front porch at home, locally made from native cedar, in addition to that Hawaiian shirt you've been needing.

South Coast

The shopping areas on the South Coast are stretched out with miles of road separating them, though you'll sometimes find an interesting store in between centers of population. The major shopping areas are in Coos Bay/North Bend, Bandon, and Brookings. Coos Bay has a pedestrian-friendly, old-fashioned downtown area with charming street lamps; this district was recently renovated and is in the process of reinventing itself. Near the Coos Art Museum, just up from the waterfront, this district sports a tidy, bustling Rite-Aid, cafes and pubs, and some shops worth seeing (see below). Bandon's Old Town district, just off U.S. 101, is especially charming and popular; in addition to the many shops, with souvenirs and luxury items as well as books, gifts, and clothes, are funky diners and bars and a nice boardwalk along the harbor where you can get fresh seafood. Brookings has two main shopping areas, one along U.S. 101 and one at the Port of Brookings (technically known as "Harbor"). To get there, take Harbor Drive west off U.S. 101. Some excellent shops lie along the main strip of U.S. 101 but they can be hard to spot, for it's an area that suffers from minimall sprawl. Still, there's a little core of buildings in the middle of town that provide a coherent shopping experience.

Coos Bay

The Headlands Country Mercantile
63336 Boat Basin Road, Coos Bay
(541) 888–0505

This attractive store has great curb appeal. The pleasantly cluttered store sells china, bath products, cards, collectibles, and gifts, and if you have a passion for collectible porcelain, this is the store for you. The Headlands has extensive collections of Mary Engelbreit items and Margaret Furlong figurines, and more. Popular bath lines like Crabtree and Evelyn are well represented, too, and make the store smell really good.

Harvest Book Shoppe and The Coffee Corner
756 North 9th Street, Coos Bay
(541) 267–5824

A friendly and wide-ranging bookstore in downtown Coos Bay and run by knowledgeable people, the Harvest Book Shoppe has everything from Robert Ludlum to Plato, Stephen King to Shakespeare. Especially notable are the works on Northwest and local history, culture, and natural history. The Harvest is a steady supporter of downtown Coos Bay and does all it can to increase knowledge about this richly historical area and the whole community. Stop there before or after a visit to the Coos Art Museum up the street.

Threads That Bind
120 Central, Coos Bay
(541) 267–0749

This vigorous store provides all that the quilter needs to be in heaven. Lovely fabrics, helpful books, thread, and notions are all here so you can stock up for the winter. They carry a special collection of lighthouse quilt patterns based on lighthouses on the coasts of Oregon, Washington, and California. Threads That Bind is well connected, too, so they can set you up with sewing circles and lessons. They provide a machine quilting service, too, making life simple for you.

Bandon

Bandon Mercantile Company
U.S. Highway 101 and Elmira, Bandon
(541) 347–4341
www.bandonmercantile.com

The Bandon Mercantile is an excellent stop for brides-to-be, cooks, gardeners, or anyone else seeking gifts for others and themselves. High-end kitchen supplies from Krups and Chantal, aromatherapy bath products from Pre de Provence, cushy Egyptian cotton towels, April Cornell linens, fountains for the garden, and simple linen dresses are a fraction of the goodies in this attractive and friendly shop. They also stock stoneware, rugs, baskets, and potpourri. The little sample of coffee they give you is another reason to stop by.

Big Wheel General Store
130 Baltimore Street, Bandon
(541) 347–3719
www.bandonbythesea.com/bigwheel.htm

Few stores are like this one, which supplies the weary tourist with delicious fudge and the local with pet food. The Big Wheel General Store is in an old building with a wide-planked floor that creaks delightfully as you walk around to look at the free driftwood museum or decide whether you should buy a wooden lighthouse, marbles, or shells. In addition to many tourist items, the Big Wheel also sells some old stuff—farm implements, glass, and other oddities—and some practical things like dog flea spray. There is a very decent selection of guidebooks and field guides.

Cranberry Sweets
Bandon Waterfront, Bandon
(541) 347–9475, (800) 527–5748

The sweets here are made with cranberries and other local products. (There are plush toys and gifts, too, to round out the picture.) Every kind of cranberry candy you could imagine is here, along with other fruit candies and chocolates, and they're all handmade and delicious. The most renowned, and deservedly so, are the chewy jelly candies called Cranberry Nut. Try the cheddar cheese fudge.

The Cobbler's Bench
110 2nd Street, Bandon
(541) 347–9012
www.bandonbythesea.com/cobblar.htm

Wolf Daniel Braun has been a leathersmith since 1977, and he branched out and opened the Cobbler's Bench in 1985. He will resole your Justins or custom design a wallet. But he'll also provide you with ready-made leather products from a variety of respected suppliers, a number of them from Oregon. The Cobbler's Bench has a notably good a selection of belts, briefcases, and bags. They carry Birkenstocks and other name brands and an attractive selection of men's and women's clothing and Native American jewelry. This is an excellent store for personal gifts for women and men.

Forget Me Knots Quilting & Needlework
125 Baltimore Street, Bandon
(541) 347–9021

Our spies tell us that quilting is very big in the South Coast area, perhaps, the theory goes, because winters can be long and lonely and quilting brings people together. When they do get together, chances are it's at this homey shop to pick up supplies. Patterns, notions, fabric paint, and even precut squares are all available here.

Harbor Lights Books
175 2nd Street, Bandon
(541) 347–2371
www.bandonbythesea.com/harbor_b.htm

A delightfully musty little bookshop that specializes in used books and book searches, Harbor Lights carries a broad selection of usefully organized materials. You can find things here that are hard to find in cities, where the bookstores are gleaned more thoroughly. Harbor Lights seems to prompt interesting conversations between strangers; it must be the wild selection of books in a small space.

Browsing the shops, galleries, and restaurants in Bandon's Old Town is a fun afternoon adventure.

PHOTO: LIZANN DUNEGAN

Winter River Books
170 2nd Street, Bandon
(541) 347–4111

This bookstore is bright and light, just the thing for a gray day. Leisurely browsing is required. Winter River carries bestsellers and a number of sale books and remainders, and the selection is quite broad, from gardening to mysteries to classics. There's a good children's section and, like many bookstores on the Coast, a competent section of books about the Oregon Coast. Winter River also carries a nice selection of cards, crystals, music, and pottery, and they occasionally have author events.

Oregon Coast Jams
48053 U.S. Highway 101, Bandon
(888) 795–1719
www.oregonjam.com

This newly built store replaces the roadside stand that the family has used to sell their excellent Misty Meadows jam since 1971 (and it's about time). You should go into the store just to smell the new-split logs. But you won't be able to leave without stocking up on some of the best jam around. They make every kind—hot pepper, pumpkin, pomegranate, even jelly made out of beer. They specialize in local fruit jams, though—cranberry, wild huckleberry, wild blackberry, and Marionberry are perennial favorites. They also make exceptional honeys (try the Lemon Blossom). They never use corn syrup or coloring. They're open every day except Christmas and they close early on Thanksgiving.

Port Orford

Timeworn Treasures
345 West 6th Street (U.S. 101),
Port Orford
(541) 332–2046

This little gem is in an old house on U.S. 101 just down the hill from the Castaway. The treasures are not too timeworn—they look good—but you'll find some Victorian furniture pieces; pretty, embroidered old linens; china dishes; memorabilia; and things like the glasses that gas stations gave away when you filled your tank. And

the owner, Deborah Beck, is very friendly and will make you an espresso while you look around. (You have to pay for the espresso though.)

Gold Beach

The Bookworm
29401 South Ellensburg Avenue (U.S. 101),
Gold Beach
(541) 247–9033

The Bookworm is one of those bookstores that is part merchant, part community service. It is a friendly gathering place that serves many needs in addition to the need for literature, and its storefront appearance belies its true nature. They sell both new and used books and you can make trades; they have a very good children's section; they sell periodicals, gifts, pottery, and lots of kaleidoscopes. They serve "white coffee" for those who desire (white coffee is coffee that has not been roasted and it is extra-loaded with caffeine), and once you're wired on coffee, you can wire yourself to the Internet for an hourly fee. There's also a tiny reading room, but it's more fun to read at the espresso counter.

Brookings

At Home... by the sea
519 Chetco Avenue, Suite A, Brookings
(541) 412–3220

Brookings residents are grateful to Hazel Wilcher Allen for bringing her designer sensibilities to the urbane shop she founded in 1999. Stumbling upon this lovely space in San Francisco or Seattle would not surprise anyone, but to find something this "downtown" on the South Coast is somewhat of a shock. At Home... by the sea carries an integrated mixture of antiques, decorator items, gifts, house furnishings, and aromatherapy, all beautifully and effectively displayed. you'll find beautiful wreaths of dried flowers and hand-embroidered linens. Bottles of clean-lined aromatherapy products are clustered on antique tables with distressed paint. A small space in the back provides a kind of feng shui laboratory and a peaceful place to hang out for a moment. It's all in the mix of things (and if you like it, Allen provides design services too). Yet Allen's prices are very reasonable, especially compared to what you'd pay for the same thing in Seattle; even those on a limited budget can find a little treasure here.

Banana Belt Trading Company
654 Chetco Avenue (U.S. 101), Brookings
(541) 469–6087, (877) 276–3141

The Banana Belt Trading Company is the place to go for the person who has everything, because you'll find something here that he definitely doesn't have. Oregon products—especially, but not exclusively, gourmet food items—are featured in this interesting and eclectic shop on Brookings's main strip. It carries an unusual assortment of souvenirs and gifts. There are some good aromatherapy products, fun T-shirts, leather goods, and the only risqué card collection in town.

Beachfront Gifts
16011 Boat Basin Road, Brookings
(541) 469–8025

The mania for fudge on the South Coast is matched only by the mania for saltwater taffy on the North Coast. But after eating the fudge at Beachfront Gifts, you can see how a mania would develop. Beachfront Gifts sells T-shirts and other souvenirs, but the focus is on Oregon crafts and other products. This is an excellent gift shop; it has everything from plastic pails and shovels for your kids to fine baubles for you, and everything is attractively displayed.

Book Dock
16364 Lower Harbor Road, Brookings
(541) 469–6070, (800) 230–3591

The Book Dock is in the Port of Brookings Harbor and it takes advantage of its pleasant location by offering fireside chats, book discussions, and author events in addition to its new and used books. The fireside chats are favorite events: Local experts are asked to present talks on topics of interest (like lighthouses or whales), tea is served, and the place is jammed with interested listeners. The Book Dock sells music and gifts in addition to their books; books on Oregon history and natural history are especially well represented but there are also lots of mysteries and other vacation reading.

Flora Pacifica
15447 Ocean View Drive, Brookings
(800) 877–9741
www.florapacifica.com

Flora Pacifica is the place for flowers: fresh, dried, preserved, or wreathed. They supply cut flowers and bouquets, as well as plants for landscaping or potting, from their own 11-acre farm. They also grow and sell herbs; books, crystals, and floral arts and crafts are for sale as well. The wreaths, swags, garlands, potpourri, and other dried flowers are extraordinary, as are the flower arrangements—these are the reasons that brides and businesses alike flock to Flora Pacifica. The shop also maintains an experimental viewing garden and offers classes on flower arranging, herb growing, wreath making, and more.

Good For You!
15352 U.S. Highway 101 S., Brookings
(541) 412–9027

A cooperative natural foods grocery store, Good For You! not only sells quinoa muesli and tofu dogs, but it also offers a range of services that include massage, ear candling, and wellness retreats. You don't have to be a member to shop here, but members save more money. The store carries everything for the natural foods consumer. Bulk items are plentiful. Vitamins and natural beauty products are often offered at a deep discount, and organic food is astonishingly well priced too. This is the natural foods mecca of the South Coast. Closed Sundays.

Sandy's Kitchen and Gift Shop
97900 Shopping Center Avenue, Brookings
(541) 469–3355

Right next door to Sandy's Restaurant in the Brookings-Harbor Shopping Center is her Kitchen and Gift Shop. Don't let that fool you: This is a serious store for serious cooks, full of china, cookware, linens, and other enticing kitchen paraphernalia. If you've just moved to Brookings, you'll find everything you got rid of that you thought you wouldn't need anymore, like ricers and egg separators. Sandy carries Calphalon and Tramontina cookware, and any cookie cutter you ever thought of is probably here. The kitchen towels and potholders are attractive and reasonably priced. Sandy's is a pleasant gift venue and a necessity if you're setting up house.

Stuff for Guys
16340 Lower Harbor Road, Suite 201, Brookings
(541) 412–3823

Finally, somewhere to find something for your dad who never answers questions about what he wants for his birthday. Everything here is for guys, and the people who love them, including cigars and lighters, gnarly knives, handmade belts and wallets, WEK Clothing, and a supply of masculine food items, like barbecue sauce and chili, and rolls of yellow tape that say "Danger: Men Cooking." The landscape paintings and still lifes hanging on the wall are also for sale. There are some gag gifts, too—our favorite was the faux spilled latte.

Windjammer Windborne & Nautical Gifts
660 Chetco Avenue (U.S. Highway 101), Brookings
(541) 469–1227, (800) 295–4663

This is the store for "windy things," says owner Mary Friesen. And that's what you'll find here—a wonderful selection of things that move, like kites, windsocks, mobiles, and whirligigs, will delay you for quite a while before you wander over to the shell or the T-shirt section. Windjammer has been supplying souvenir hunters and nautical-theme fanatics since 1994; it has a good, representative selection of myrtlewood products, lighthouses, cards, and candles. But the dual- or single-line kites in every color are the real draw.

Words and Pictures
407 Oak Street, Brookings
(541) 469–7067

Words and Pictures is both an art gallery and a bookstore. The bookstore part, which also sells alluring gifts and CDs, features a good range of new books, "from best-sellers to special treasures," in the words of owner Pat Stewart. Some highlights of her collection are pleasantly crowded shelves of cooking and gardening books, as well as an excellent children's book section. You can also find audio books—occasionally good bargains are to be found among them. After stocking up on best-sellers and blank books, wander into the next room and look at the art.

Attractions

If you're a history buff, like to find unique and out-of-the way places, and enjoy a variety of and things to see and do, then this chapter is for you! In this chapter we've listed a wide range of attractions including museums and historic monuments, lighthouses, casinos, cheese factories, microbreweries, wineries, interpretive areas, and a few other odds and ends. We've organized these attractions by region of the Coast—North, Central, and South—and then by city from north to south.

While we've done our best to make sure times and admission prices are up to date we recommend that you call ahead to verify times and prices for the attractions listed. Also, many of the attractions in this chapter have seasonal hours and have longer, more extended hours usually from May 1 through September 30.

If you still want to find out more things to see and do on the amazing Coast, be sure to check out fun ideas in our other chapters on Kidstuff, Annual Events and Festivals, The Great Outdoors, and Day Trips.

North Coast

Astoria

Astoria Column
1 Coxcomb Drive, Astoria
(503) 325–2963
Built in 1926, the 125-foot Astoria Column rises prominently from its high vantage point from the top of Coxcomb Hill and offers outstanding views of the mouth of the Columbia River where it meets the Pacific Ocean, Mount Saint Helens, Youngs Bay, downtown Astoria, and the Astoria Bridge, which links Oregon and Washington. To reach the top of the column, you'll climb up a narrow 166-step spiral staircase to a viewing platform. The outside of the column features painted murals of the settlement and exploration of this area. The Astoria Column is open from 9:00 A.M. to dusk seven days a week.

Columbia River Maritime Museum
1792 Marine Drive, Astoria
(503) 325–2323
www.crmm.org
The Columbia River Maritime Museum is a 37,000-square-foot facility that celebrates the seafaring history of the Astoria area. The museum has seven galleries that include displays about the history of the salmon-packing industry, specifics on different types of boat design, and artifacts from the *Peter Iredale* shipwreck that occurred near the mouth of the Columbia in 1906. The museum is located at the edge of the scenic Columbia River and also has a dock where you can tour the lightship *Columbia*—a historic floating lighthouse. This museum also has some modern maritime artifacts from the *New Carissa*, a wood-chip freighter that ran aground off of Coos Bay in February of 1999. The museum is open 9:30 A.M. to 5:30 P.M. daily. The admission fee is $8.00 for adults; $7.00 for seniors 65 and up; $4.00 for children ages 6 to 17; and children under 6 are free.

Flavel House
441 8th Street, Astoria
(503) 325–2203
If you want to take a step back in time to view the wealthy life-style of shipping tycoon George Flavel, be sure to visit the Flavel House. This Queen Ann Victorian-style mansion was finished in 1885 and from its three-story octagon tower you'll have outstanding views of downtown Astoria and the Columbia River. When you tour the inside of this magnificent house, you'll find winding staircases, Persian rugs, 14-foot ceilings, and exquisite

fireplaces. You'll also find clothing displays, artwork, and other household items from this opulent era. The Flavel House is open daily from 10:00 A.M. to 5:00 P.M. from May through September and from 10:00 A.M. to 4:00 P.M. October through April. The admission price is $5.00 for adults, $4.00 for seniors and AAA members, $2.00 for children ages 6 to 17, and free for children 6 and under. This admission fee also includes entrance to the Heritage Center Museum and the Uppertown Fire Fighters Museum.

Fort Clatsop National Memorial
92343 Fort Clatsop Road, Astoria
(503) 861–2471
www.nps.gov/focl

The Fort Clatsop National Memorial is administered by the National Park Service and is a memorial to the camp set up by Lewis and Clark, who spent the winter of 1805–1806 in this area. The members of the expedition befriended the Clatsop Indians and decided to name their encampment after this resident Native American tribe. The national memorial is a reconstruction of the expedition's camp based on sketches made by Lewis and Clark. One of the main attractions at this memorial is the reenactment of the day-to-day activities of Lewis and Clark's party. Park rangers wearing 19th-century garb demonstrate how members of the expedition tanned hides; made candles, moccasins and clothing, jerky, canoes, and lead bullets; loaded muskets; used flint and steel to make fires; and much more. The memorial also has a visitor center adjacent to the fort with interesting displays that recount the events of the expedition, artifacts from the Clatsop Indians, and video and slide presentations. Well-maintained trails and picnic areas are also present at the memorial, making this a fun place to spend the day. Fort Clatsop is open every day year-round except Christmas Day. The visitor center is open 8:00 A.M. to 5:00 P.M. from mid-September through mid-June and from 8:00 A.M. to 6:00 P.M. from mid-June through mid-September. Admission prices are $3.00 for those 17 and older or $5.00 per car.

Heritage Center Museum
1618 Exchange Street, Astoria
(503) 325–2203

The Heritage Museum is made up of two stories of exhibits that explore the history and the cultural diversity of the Astoria area. Several galleries in the museum contain weapons, tools, photos, and other mementos depicting Astoria's colorful past. An entire room explores the rich history of the Clatsop tribe. The museum is open 10:00 A.M. to 5:00 P.M. daily May through September and 11:00 A.M. to 5:00 P.M. the rest of the year. The admission price is $5.00 for adults, $4.00 for seniors and AAA members, $2.00 for children ages 6 to 17, and free for children 6 and under. This admission fee includes entrance to the Flavel House and the Uppertown Fire Fighters Museum (see the write-ups in this chapter).

Historical Tours of Astoria
612 Florence Avenue, Astoria
(503) 325–3005

Rae Goforth is the owner and operator of Historical Tours of Astoria. She offers two- to three-hour van tours of the Astoria area—as well as tailor-made tours, depending on your time and interest. Her basic van tour includes a trip through an area of historic Astoria homes and a visit to Fort Clatsop (see the description of Fort Clatsop in this chapter). In addition, the tour includes admission to the Flavel House, a highly ornamented Victorian-style mansion located at 441 8th Street. This house was originally owned and built by Captain George Flavel, a prominent shipping tycoon and citizen of Astoria in the 1870s and 1880s (see the write-up in this chapter). She gives tours by appointment only. Call for information and rates.

Uppertown Firefighters Museum
2986 Marine Drive, Astoria
(503) 325–2203

This museum houses a fine collection of vintage fire fighting equipment including horse-drawn and motorized vehicles that were in service from 1877 to 1921 as well as an interesting collection of fire extinguishers and photos from some of Astoria's most devastating fires. The museum is open 10:00 A.M. to 5:00 P.M. daily May through September and 11:00 A.M. to 5:00 P.M. from the rest of the year. Admission is $5.00 for adults, $4.00 for seniors and AAA members, $2.00 for children ages 6 to 17, and free for children 6 and under. This admission fee also includes entrance to the Flavel House and the Heritage Center Museum.

Seaside

The Promenade
Prom Street, Seaside
(503) 738-6391

Seaside is famous for its concrete boardwalk, known as "The Promenade," which parallels the Pacific Ocean along an endless sandy beach. When you walk on the promenade, you'll see miles of flat, sandy beach, bikers, skaters, and other visitors enjoying the view. This spot is a classic tourist trap, but this adds to its charm. Benches and rest rooms are present along this 1.5-mile boardwalk. You can get to the Promenade by turning west onto Avenue A from U.S. Highway 101 in downtown Seaside and following it west until you reach Prom Street. Expect crowds during the height of the summer months and be patient, because finding a parking spot can prove to be challenging.

Seaside Historical Museum
570 Necanicum Drive, Seaside
(503) 738-7065
www.seasurf.net/~smhs

The Seaside Historical Museum has many informative displays that document the history of the Seaside area beginning with Native American artifacts and moving on to displays from the 19th century. An antique print shop display demonstrates how newspapers were printed at the turn of the 19th century, and a display of century-old fire fighting equipment demonstrates how firefighters equipped themselves. Next to the museum is a beach cottage display called "The Butterfield Cottage." This cottage is a wonderful restoration of one of the original beach cottages in Seaside at the beginning of the 19th century and gives you a feel for what it was like to live in a beach town in a simpler time. The museum is open 10:00 A.M. to 4:00 P.M. Monday through Saturday and noon to 3:00 P.M. on Sunday mid-March through October 31. From November 1 through mid-March, the museum is open noon to 3:00 P.M. daily. The admission charge is $2.00 for adults, $1.50 for seniors age 62 and older, $1.00 for children ages 13 to 18, and children under the age of 12 are admitted free.

Cannon Beach

Haystack Rock
Cannon Beach
(503) 436-2623

Located 0.5 mile south of downtown Cannon Beach, 235-foot Haystack Rock can be accessed by parking in downtown Cannon Beach and walking west on Harris Street to the beach and then walking 0.5 mile south. Haystack Rock is part of the Oregon Islands Wildlife Refuge and is an important nesting site for pigeon guillemots, tufted puffins, pelagic cormorants, and western gulls. At the base of this monolith are rocky tide pools that are fun to explore. You may see bright green sea anemones, orange starfish, purple crabs, chitons, and limpets.

Tillamook

Blue Heron Cheese Company
2001 Blue Heron Drive, Tillamook
(503) 842-8281
www.blueheronoregon.com

You can taste fine wines and cheese at the Blue Heron Cheese Company. Specialty cheeses such as Brie and Camembert are popular, and this company also sells specialty fruit products, mustard, honey, and jams. The Blue Heron Cheese Company is open from 9:00 A.M. to 5:00 P.M. October through February and from 8:00 A.M. to 8:00 P.M. March through September.

Latimer Quilt and Textile Center
2105 Wilson River Loop Road, Tillamook
(503) 842-8622
www.oregoncoast.com/latimertextile

A fine collection of pioneer quilts can be seen at the Latimer Quilt and Textile Center.

The center is housed in the historic Maple Leaf School and features a research library. Demonstrations on quilting, rug making, basketry, spinning, and weaving are also given at the center. The center is open 10:00 A.M. to 4:00 P.M. Tuesday through Saturday and noon to 4:00 P.M. Sunday (March 1 through October 31). Admission is $2.50 for adults, $2.00 for seniors, and $1.00 for children ages 13 to 17. Children age 12 and under are admitted free.

Tillamook Cheese Factory
4175 U.S. Highway 101 N., Tillamook
(503) 815–1300
www.tillamookcheese.com

Tillamook Cheese factory makes some of the finest cheddar cheese in the world. Tillamook County has a mild climate and plenty of moisture to support large herds of Holstein, Guernsey, and Jersey cows that produce fresh, sweet milk. When you visit the Tillamook Cheese Factory, you can get a first-hand glimpse at how the cheese is actually made. A glass viewing area lets you watch the master cheese makers at work. In addition, you can learn about the history of cheese making in Tillamook County. This facility also makes high-quality butter, ice cream, and cheese spreads. If you want to taste-test some ice cream, visit the ice cream counter, or if you want to purchase their products and take some souvenirs home, check out the gift shop. The Tillamook Cheese Factory is located 2 miles north of Tillamook on U.S. 101 on the east side of the highway. It is open 8:00 A.M. to 6:00 P.M. October through May and 8:00 A.M. to 8:00 P.M. June through September. Admission is free.

Tillamook Air Museum
6030 Hangar Road, Tillamook
(503) 842–1130
www.tillamookair.com

The Tillamook Air Museum features more than two dozen vintage aircraft that are housed in a World War II blimp hangar. Some examples of planes you'll see at this interesting museum are the B-25 Mitchell Bomber, A-26 Invader, Mk-8 Spitfire, FM-2 Wildcat, Mig-17, P-47, and T-6 Texan. The museum also features a 1940s-style cafe, gift shop, theater, and exhibits that display World War II artifacts. To get to the museum, drive 2 miles south of Tillamook on U.S. 101 to a blinking yellow light. Turn left onto Long Prairie Road and follow the signs to the museum. The museum is open from 10:00 A.M. to 5:00 P.M. year-round. The museum is closed Thanksgiving and Christmas Day. Admission is $9.50 for adults, $8.50 for seniors, $5.50 for children ages 13 to 17, $2.00 for children ages 7 to 12, and kids under 7 are free.

Tillamook Pioneer Museum
2106 2nd Street, Tillamook
(503) 842–4553
www.tcpm.org

The Tillamook Pioneer Museum is located in the old courthouse and features an interesting mix of exhibits that are worth checking out. The museum has displays that give the history of the Tillamook tribe; a rock and mineral collection; a pioneer home and workshop; replicas of early automobiles; a natural science display of shorebirds and waterfowl; beeswax candles from a 17th-century shipwreck; and carved stones that are thought to be related to a buried treasure at the base of Neahkahnie Mountain. Travel and history books about the Tillamook area are available in the museum's bookstore. The museum is open 8:00 A.M. to 5:00 P.M. Monday through Saturday and 11:00 A.M. to 5:00 P.M. on Sunday. Admission is $3.00 for adults, $2.00 for seniors 62 and older, 50 cents for children ages 12 to 17, and kids under 12 are free.

Pacific City

Cape Kiwanda
Pacific City

Cape Kiwanda is a golden sandstone headland sculpted by the frothy ocean waves of the Pacific and is located at Pacific City. Pacific City is 25 miles south of Tillamook and 20 miles north of Lincoln City off U.S. 101 on the Three Capes Scenic Loop. Pacific City is most well known for its fleet of Dory boats. Dory boats are flat-bottomed fishing

Cape Kiwanda consists of soft sandstones that reveal its interesting geologic past. PHOTO: LIZANN DUNEGAN

boats that are launched off the flat, sandy beach at the base of Cape Kiwanda. Locals still launch these boats into the calm morning surf to fish for halibut, lingcod, and other commercial fish species that are plentiful around offshore Haystack Rock. If you want to experience fishing from a dory boat, call Haystack Fishing, owned by Joe & Wendy Hay, (888) 965-7555. This state-licensed outfitter offers chartered trips where you can catch halibut, sturgeon, salmon, and lingcod. If you just want to look and not catch, this outfitter also offers chartered whale-watching trips. Many visitors come to Cape Kiwanda beach to watch the dory boats ride the ocean waves back into shore and come to a sliding stop on the sand. Mixed in with the Dory fleet, you will also see surfers and ocean kayakers playing in the waves. Walk along Kiwanda Beach at the base of Cape Kiwanda and investigate the rocky tide pools that are home to anemones, sea stars, mussels, and hermit crabs. You may also find sand dollars, mussel shells, and other beach treasures by walking along the flat, sandy beach south from Cape Kiwanda. If you like hiking up steep sand

dunes, you can hike to the top of Cape Kiwanda from Cape Kiwanda beach. The soft, sandy, strenuous trek to the top of Cape Kiwanda is well worth the effort. You will have spectacular views of Haystack Rock, Nestucca Bay to the south, and Cape Lookout to the north. Kids can spend hours climbing, jumping, and running down the face of this expansive sand dune. A public parking area and rest rooms are available at Cape Kiwanda beach. If you want to try a local microbrew, check out the Pelican Pub & Brewery located adjacent to the public parking area.

Pelican Pub & Brewery
33180 Cape Kiwanda Drive, Pacific City
(503) 965-7007
www.pelicanbrewery.com

To taste an Oregon-made microbrew and have a fantastic ocean view, you should visit the Pelican Pub & Brewery. This brewery features award-winning beers and fresh fish and seafood. Examples of featured beers include Blackbird lager and Mount Hebo mild. The brewery also offers a good breakfast menu. The brewery is open from 8:00 A.M. to 9:00 P.M. daily.

Oregon Lighthouses

Oregon's lighthouses are a direct link to our maritime past, and there are nine lighthouses along the coastline that were built close to estuaries or major headlands between 1870 and 1896 as dictated by the former U.S. Lighthouse Board. The U.S. Corps of Engineers built the lighthouses and maintenance of the lighthouses was given to the Coast Guard. In the 1960s, the Coast Guard installed automated beacons in the lighthouses and ownership of many of the lighthouses was handed over to state and federal agencies. This prompted a movement to protect and preserve these beautiful historic structures. All the lighthouses on the Oregon Coast are on the National Register of Historic Places and many are open for tours.

Tillamook Rock Lighthouse
Cannon Beach

Nicknamed "Terrible Tilly," the Tillamook Rock Lighthouse stands 62 feet high and rests on a large chunk of basalt rock that is more than a mile offshore from Tillamook Head. This lighthouse was built in 1881 and acted as a lifesaving beacon for ships headed for the Columbia River. The lighthouse is privately owned and does not allow public access. You can view this lighthouse from Indian Beach at Ecola State Park located 3 miles north of Cannon Beach. There is a $3.00 day use fee at this state park and you need to purchase a day use permit at the entrance station.

Cape Meares Lighthouse
Tillamook, (800) 551–6949

The 38-foot-tall Cape Meares Lighthouse was built in 1890 and is the shortest lighthouse tower on the Oregon Coast. The lighthouse is open daily May through September and on the weekends in October, March and April. A gift shop is located in the lighthouse and is open from 11:00 A.M. to 4:00 P.M. daily from May through September. This lighthouse is on a scenic headland in Cape Meares State Park, 10 miles west of Tillamook on the Three Capes Scenic Highway.

Yaquina Head Lighthouse
Newport, (541) 574–3100

The Yaquina Head Lighthouse stands 93 feet tall and was commissioned in 1873. This lighthouse is the tallest on the Oregon Coast and was built to aid the navigation of ships entering Yaquina Bay. This lighthouse is located in the Yaquina Head Outstanding Natural Area 4 miles northwest of Newport off U.S. 101. Drive north 3 miles on U.S. 101 and turn left onto Lighthouse Drive. Drive 1 mile on Lighthouse Drive to the Yaquina Head Lighthouse parking area. Note there is a $5.00 entrance fee to

At 38 feet tall, Cape Meares lighthouse is the shortest lighthouse on the Oregon Coast. PHOTO: LIZANN DUNEGAN

enter this area, which has trails to tide pools, a rocky beach, and spectacular viewpoints. It is recommended that you begin your tour by stopping by the Interpretive Center that is located 0.7 mile from U.S. 101 on Lighthouse Drive. The Interpretive Center has exhibits, video presentations, and hands-on displays about the geology and cultural and natural history of Yaquina Head. The Interpretive Center is open in the summer months from 10:00 A.M. to 6:00 P.M. and in the winter months from 10:00 A.M. to 4:00 P.M.

Yaquina Bay Lighthouse and Museum
Newport, (541) 574–3100
Commissioned for service from 1871 to 1874, the 40-foot-tall Yaquina Bay Lighthouse is one of the rare lighthouses on the Pacific Coast that was built with a Cape Cod style light keeper's house as part of its tower. Located in scenic Yaquina Bay State Park, this lighthouse—filled with period furniture and with great views from every window—is one of the most visited on the Oregon Coast. In addition, the bottom portion of light-house houses a gift shop that has books on coastal lighthouses, wildlife, and much more. Visiting hours are from 10:00 A.M. to 4:00 P.M. daily from Memorial Day through Labor Day and from noon to 4:00 P.M. the rest of the year (weather permitting). The lighthouse is located in Yaquina Bay State Park at the north end of the Yaquina Bay Bridge off U.S. 101 in Newport.

Heceta Head Lighthouse
Florence, (541) 547–3696
The 56-foot Heceta Head Lighthouse was commissioned in 1894 and rests on a rocky headland 205 feet above the ocean. Adjacent to the lighthouse is the Heceta House, the original light keeper's house which was built in 1893 and now is operated as a bed-and-breakfast. The lighthouse can be accessed from the Heceta Head Lighthouse State Viewpoint parking area located 12 miles north of Florence on U.S. 101 on the west side of the highway. There is a $3.00 day use fee at this site. You can purchase a permit from the automated pay station in the parking area.

Umpqua River Lighthouse
Reedsport, (541) 271–4631
The 65-foot Umpqua River Lighthouse is located at the entrance to Winchester Bay and is adjacent to Umpqua Lighthouse State Park. This lighthouse was illuminated in 1894 and replaced an earlier lighthouse that was built on the north spit of the Umpqua River in 1857. You can get to the lighthouse by driving 6 miles south of Reedsport on U.S. 101 to the Umpqua Lighthouse State Park entrance.

Cape Arago Lighthouse
Coos Bay, (541) 756–0100
The 44-foot Cape Arago Lighthouse was commissioned in 1934 and is located 12 miles southwest of Coos Bay adjacent to Gregory Point. This lighthouse is the most recent lighthouse in service on the Coast and it replaced lighthouses that were built in 1866 and 1908. This lighthouse is not open to the public but it can be seen from trails at Sunset Bay State Park. To get to Sunset Bay State Park from U.S. 101 in Coos Bay, fol-low the signs to Charleston Harbor and Ocean Beaches and drive on the Cape Arago Highway 12 miles southwest to the park.

Coquille River Lighthouse
Bandon, (541) 347–2209
The Coquille River Lighthouse is located on the north bank of the Coquille River in Bullards Beach State Park. The lighthouse was illuminated in 1896 to help steer mariners across the hazardous bar. Interestingly, this lighthouse is powered by solar energy. The lighthouse is open year-round during daylight hours and you can tour the tower watch room by request. To get to the lighthouse, drive 2 miles north of Bandon on U.S. 101 to the entrance to Bullards Beach State Park.

Cape Blanco Lighthouse
Port Orford, (541) 756–0100
The 59-foot tower of the Cape Blanco Lighthouse is located on Cape Blanco, the westernmost point in Oregon. The lighthouse is in Cape Blanco State Park. To reach Cape Blanco State Park drive 46 miles south of Coos Bay or 4 miles north of Port Orford on U.S. 101 to the junction with Cape Blanco Road. Turn west and drive 5 miles on Cape Blanco Road to the state park entrance. For more information about Cape Blanco State Park see The Great Outdoors chapter.

Contact these organizations for more information about coastal lighthouses:

Oregon Chapter, U.S. Lighthouse Society
P.O. Box 600, Lakeside 97449; (541) 759–3920

Yaquina Lights, Inc.
P.O. Box 410, Newport 97365; (541) 574–3100

Friends of Cape Meares
P.O. Box 282, Oceanside 97134; (503) 842–5270

Central Coast

Lincoln City

Alder House II
611 South Immonen Road, Lincoln City
(541) 996–2483
www.alderhouse.com
Alder House II is a glassblowing studio that welcomes visitors to view the ancient art of turning molten glass into vases, bowls, paperweights, and so on. The studio is open from 10:00 A.M. to 5:00 P.M. March 15 through the end of November. The studio is located 4 miles south of Lincoln City off U.S. 101 on Immonen Road. If you are coming from the south, drive 0.5 mile past the entrance to Salishan Lodge on U.S. 101 and turn right on Immonen Road. If you are coming from the north through Lincoln City on U.S.

101, you'll cross the Siletz River Bridge and you'll see Immonen Road approximately 0.5 mile from the end of the bridge. Turn left and the studio entrance is approximately 0.75 mile from U.S. 101.

Chinook Winds Casino
1777 Northwest 44th Street, Lincoln City
(888) CHINOOK (244–6665)
www.chinookwindscasino.com
Chinook Winds Casino is owned and operated by the Confederated Tribes of the Siletz Indians of Oregon and is packed full of fun activities. The inside decor of the casino is filled with wood beams that reflect its rustic outdoor theme, a pond with a cascading waterfall, and great views of the Pacific Ocean. The casino is 20,000 square feet in size and contains convention facilities, guest rooms, and gaming areas for blackjack, Caribbean stud poker, craps, roulette,

keno, bingo, and slot machines. Complimentary Starbucks coffee and soft drinks are also available to visitors. The casino also has a gift shop, day-care center, and video arcade, as well as three restaurants. If you are staying at a local Lincoln City motel or RV Park, Chinook Winds offers a complimentary shuttle service to and from the facility you are staying at. You can request shuttle service between 9:00 A.M. and 1:00 A.M. by calling (541) 992-4137. This casino also attracts well-known entertainers such as Kenny Loggins, the Beach Boys, and Julio Iglesias.

North Lincoln County Museum
4907 Southwest Highway 101, Lincoln City
(541) 996-6614
www.lincolncity.com/nlch/default.html
The North Lincoln County Museum has exhibits and artifacts that depict the lives of the first homesteaders that came to the Lincoln City area. Exhibits of an early day classroom, bedroom, and kitchen with period pieces and handmade furniture can be seen. Native American artifacts and logging implements are also present in this museum. The museum is open from noon to 4:00 P.M. Tuesday through Saturday and admission is free.

Grand Ronde

Spirit Mountain Casino
P.O. Box 39, Grand Ronde 97347
(800) 760-7977
www.spirit-mountain.com
Spirit Mountain Casino is owned by the Confederated Tribes of the Grand Ronde Community of Oregon. This facility on Oregon Highway 18 is more than 90,000 square feet and houses a casino (smoking and nonsmoking) with 1,100 slot machines, craps tables, roulette tables, blackjack tables, Let It Ride poker tables, Pai Gow poker tables, and a Big 6 Wheel. In addition to the fun gaming activities, the casino has the 100-room Spirit Mountain Lodge, a SuperPlay Kids Club which provides supervision for children from the ages 18 months to 12 years, four restaurants, and first-class entertainment. Spirit Casino is open 24 hours a day, seven days a week, all year round.

Otter Rock

Flying Dutchman Winery
915 1st Street, Otter Rock
(541) 765-2060
www.dutchmanwinery.com
This winery produces fine Pinot Noir, Chardonnay, and Pinot Gris wines. The winery is located in a spectacular setting overlooking the ocean and has picnic facilities. The winery is open from 11:00 A.M. to 6:00 P.M. (May through October) and 11:00 A.M. to 5:00 P.M. November through April. They offer free samples of all their fine wines.

Newport

Hatfield Marine Science Center
2030 Southeast Marine Science Drive, Newport
(541) 867-0271
hmsc.orst.edu/visitor
The Hatfield Marine Science Center offers a variety of displays that give you a closer look at the plants and animals that live on the Oregon Coast. You'll find tide pools filled with colorful starfish, sea anemones, sea urchins, and mollusks, and one of the main attractions is a display

Insiders' Tip
If you are traveling with your pet, remember not to leave him locked in the car in hot weather—it only takes a few minutes before he can die of heat exhaustion. Also, always carry a leash with you and plastic bags. Many attractions on the Oregon Coast require that your dog be leashed and that you pick up and dispose of your pet's waste.

with a large octopus that often captivates kids. A whale skeleton gives you an idea of how large these mammals really are and informative marine science films also further educate you about Northwest marine life. You can also hike on the 1-mile paved Estuary Trail that begins on the left side of the chain-link fence on the south side of the parking lot. The center is open Thursday through Monday from 10:00 A.M. to 5:00 P.M. May through September and Thursday through Monday from 10:00 A.M. to 4:00 P.M. the rest of the year. Admission is by donation.

Lincoln County Historical Society Museums
545 Southwest 9th Street, Newport
(541) 265–7509

Be sure to stop and explore two museums run by the Lincoln County Historical Society. The Log Cabin museum contains maritime displays, a logging display, and exhibits that contain Siletz Indian artifacts such as beaded robes, headdresses, baskets, and tools. Adjacent to the museum is the Burrows House, which was originally a boarding house and now displays a collection of household items and furniture from the early part of the 20th century.

You should also browse through the bookstore, which features many local history titles. The museum is open from 10:00 A.M. to 5:00 P.M. Tuesday through Sunday (June to September). They are open 11:00 A.M. to 4:00 P.M. Tuesday through Sunday the rest of the year. Admission is free although donations are encouraged.

Oregon Coast Aquarium
2820 Southeast Ferry Slip Road, Newport
(541) 867–3474
www.aquarium.org

The Oregon Coast Aquarium is a special place that everyone should visit. This aquarium contains several indoor and outdoor displays about Northwest plant and animal marine life. One of the most popular displays in the jellyfish tank—dozens of beautiful jellyfish swim freely in a circular tank in the middle of a large room filled with huge aquarium displays. Another favorite is the touch tank where you can touch tidal pool creatures such as sea anemones, starfish, and other mollusks. The outside displays are just as interesting. You can view California sea otters, harbor seals, and sea lions and walk through an outdoor aviary where you can watch tufted

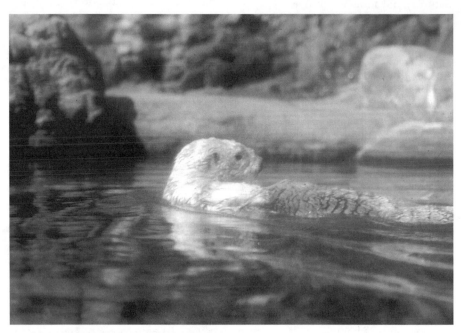

A California sea otter swims and plays at the Oregon Coast Aquarium in Newport. PHOTO: LIZANN DUNEGAN

puffins, pigeon guillemots, common murres, and other seabirds swimming and feeding in a natural environment. The *Passages of the Deep* exhibit lets you view three underwater habitats. As you walk through a clear acrylic tunnel, you'll have a close-up view of a southern Oregon reef; Halibut Flats, which introduces you to bottom-dwelling fish; and the Open Sea, which features large sharks, salmon, and bat rays. Trails outside the aquarium lead through gardens of native plants with interpretive signs. The aquarium also has a bookstore and cafe. The aquarium is open from 10:00 A.M. to 5:00 P.M. daily from mid-September through the end of May and 9:00 A.M. to 6:00 P.M. June through mid-September. Admission is $8.75 for ages 14 to 64, seniors 65 and older are $7.75, children ages 4 to 13 are $4.50, and children age 3 and under are free.

Waldport

Alsea Bay Bridge Historical Interpretive Center
Waldport
(541) 563–2002

Stop at this interpretive center to learn about the history of travel routes on the Oregon Coast beginning with Indian trails and leading to road routes. Photos of different coastal bridges are on display and there is also a model of the Alsea Bay Bridge. Located at the southern end of the Alsea Bay Bridge off U.S. 101, the center is open from 9:00 A.M. to 4:00 P.M. daily from Memorial Day through Labor Day and from 9:00 A.M. to 4:00 P.M. Wednesday through Sunday during the rest of the year. Admission is free.

Yachats

Cape Perpetua Interpretive Center
Yachats
(541) 547–3289
www.newportnet.com/cape perpetua

The Cape Perpetua Interpretive Center is located 3 miles south of Yachats off U.S. 101 on the east side of the highway. This center provides you with a wealth of information about coastal ecology, coastal tides and weather, whale migration, and exhibits about the Alsea tribe. You can also pick up a trail brochure that describes all the trails in the Cape Perpetua area. The center has a bookstore that has a good collection of titles on local history. The center is open from 9:00 A.M. to 6:00 P.M. daily from May to September and from 10:00 A.M. to 4:00 P.M. on Saturday and Sunday from October through April.

Sea Lion Caves
91560 U.S. Highway 101, Yachats
(541) 547–3111
www.sealioncaves.com

When you visit Sea Lion Caves, you'll descend 208-feet in an elevator to an observation point about 50 feet above a large sea grotto where sea lions gather in large groups and reverberate their raucous barks in a large natural amphitheater. The lions are present in this rocky cave in the fall and winter months and during the rest of the year they occupy the offshore rocks. Note that you access the elevator through the gift shop. This Oregon Coast attraction is sometimes called an overrated tourist trap, but is worth a stop if you are curious. Admission prices are $7.00 for those age 16 and up, $4.50 for children between ages 6 and 15, and children age 5 and under are free. Visiting hours are 9:00 A.M. to 6:00 P.M. July and August and 9:00 A.M. to 3:30 P.M. the rest of the year. Sea Lion Caves is located 10 miles north of Florence on U.S. 101.

Florence

Siuslaw Pioneer Museum
85294 U.S. Highway 101 S., Florence
(541) 997–7884
www.florencechamber.com/recatt_pioneerm.htm/

Located in a historic church, the Siuslaw Pioneer Museum contains a good collection of artifacts from the Siuslaw tribe. In addition, there are exhibits depicting the early life of those who settled in this area including a kitchen exhibit from the beginning of the 20th century. The museum is open noon to 4:00 P.M. Tuesday through Sunday. Admission is free but donations are encouraged.

Chambers of Commerce/Visitor Centers

Be sure to stop by one of the following chamber of commerce offices or visitor centers for the area you are visiting. The helpful staff at these centers can provide you with information on things to see and do and with brochures and coupons for attractions and meals.

Astoria/Warrenton Highway 101 Visitor Center
143 South U.S. Highway 101, Warrenton, (541) 861–1031, www.oldoregon.com

Bandon Chamber of Commerce
300 Southeast Second Street, Bandon, (541) 347–9616, www.bandon.com

Bay Area Chamber of Commerce
50 East Central, Coos Bay, (800) 824–8486, www.oregonsbayareachamber.com

Brookings-Harbor Chamber of Commerce
16330 Lower Harbor Road, Brookings, (800) 535–9469, www.brookingsor.com

Cannon Beach Chamber of Commerce
207 North Spruce, Cannon Beach, (503) 436–2623, www.cannonbeach.org

Charleston Information Center
P.O. Box 5735, Charleston 97420, Boat Basin and Cape Arago Highway, (800) 824–8486

Coquille Chamber of Commerce
119 North Birch, Coquille, (541) 396–3414, www.coquillechamber.com

Depoe Bay Chamber of Commerce
70 Northeast U.S. Highway 101, Depoe Bay, (541) 765–2889,
www.depoebaychamber.org

Florence Area Chamber of Commerce
270 U.S. Highway 101, Florence, (800) 524–4864, www.florencechamber.com

Garibaldi Chamber of Commerce
235 Garibaldi Avenue, Garibaldi, (503) 322–0301, www.garibaldioregon.com

Gold Beach Chamber of Commerce/Visitors Center
29279 Ellensburg Avenue, #3, Gold Beach, (800) 525–2334,
www.goldbeachchamber.com

Lakeside Chamber of Commerce
P.O. Box 333, Lakeside 97449, (541) 759–3981,
www.presys.com/ps-home/cty/lakeside/lakeside.html

Lincoln City Visitors & Convention Bureau
801 Southwest U.S. Highway 101, Lincoln City, (800) 452–2151, www.oregoncoast.org

Myrtle Point Chamber of Commerce
424 5th Street, Myrtle Point, (541) 572–2626

Nehalem Bay Area Chamber of Commerce/Visitors Center
8th and Tohl Streets, Nehalem, (503) 368–5100, www.nehalembaychamber.com

Nestucca Valley Chamber of Commerce
P.O. Box 75, Cloverdale 97112, (503) 392–3445

Newport Chamber of Commerce
555 Southwest Coast Highway, Newport, (800) 262–7844, www.newportchamber.org

North Bend Information Center
1380 Sherman Avenue, North Bend, (541) 756–4613

Oregon Coast Visitors Association
609 Southwest Hurbert Street, Suite B, Newport, (888) 628–2101,
www.visittheoregoncoast.com

Pacific City Chamber of Commerce
P.O. Box 331, Pacific City 97135, (503) 965–6161, www.pacificcity.net

Port Orford Chamber of Commerce
520 Jefferson & U.S. Highway 101, Port Orford, (541) 332–8055,
www.portorfordoregon.com

Reedsport/Winchester Bay Chamber of Commerce
Junction of U.S. Highway 101 and Oregon Highway 38, Reedsport, (800) 247–2155,
www.reedsportcc.org

Rockaway Beach Chamber of Commerce
103 South 1st Street, Rockaway Beach, (503) 355–8108, www.rockawaybeach.net

Seaside Visitors Bureau
7 North Roosevelt, Seaside, (888) 306–2326, www.seasideor.com

Tillamook Chamber of Commerce
3705 U.S. Highway 101 N., Tillamook, (503) 842–7525, www.tillamookchamber.org

Toledo Chamber of Commerce
311 Northeast 1st Street, Toledo, (541) 336–3183

Waldport Chamber of Commerce & Visitors Center
620 Northwest Spring Street, Waldport, (541) 563–2133, www.cqsco.net/~waldport

Yachats Area Chamber of Commerce & Visitors Center
241 U.S. Highway 101, Yachats, (541) 547–3530, www.yachats.org

Reedsport

Dean Creek Elk Viewing Area
Reedsport
(541) 888–5515

Learn more about the magnificent Roosevelt elk by stopping at this interpretive area to read the interesting facts about these beautiful animals—best of all you get to see a herd of 100 elk that feed in the adjacent meadow. Other wildlife residents you may see in this area include black-tailed deer, osprey, blue herons, and Canada geese. The best viewing times are early morning and evening. The interpretive area is located 3 miles east of Reedsport on Oregon Highway 38.

Oregon Dunes Visitor Center
855 Highway Avenue, Reedsport
(541) 271–3611

The Oregon Dunes Visitor Center is a must-stop to find out about all the activities available in the Oregon Dunes National Recreational Area. The center has a film that gives you an interesting look into dune formation and numerous brochures that describe plant and animal life, hiking opportunities, and information on off-road vehicle use and recommended places to camp. Many interpretive programs are offered during the summer months. The center is open from 8:00 A.M. to 4:30 P.M. Monday through Friday and from 10:00

A.M. to 4:00 P.M. Saturday and Sunday from May 28th through Labor Day. During the rest of the year, the center is open 8:00 A.M. to 4:30 P.M. Monday through Friday.

Umpqua Discover Center Museum
409 Riverfront Way, Reedsport
(541) 271–4816

Visit this museum to learn about the culture of the Umpqua Indians and early explorers and the natural history of the Umpqua River Valley. The center is open from 9:00 A.M. to 5:00 P.M. daily from June 1 through September 30 and from 10:00 A.M. to 4:00 P.M. the rest of the year. Admission is $5.00 for adults, $4.50 for seniors, $3.00 for children between the ages of 6 and 15, and kids age 5 and under are free.

South Slough Estuary Interpretive Center
61907 Seven Devils Road, Reedsport
(541) 888–5558

This interpretive center offers a first-hand glance at an estuary ecosystem. The center is located adjacent to a large estuary that is filled with a variety of shorebirds and other wildlife. Several interpretive trails lead you through the rich maze of life that is present here. Then center is open Monday through Saturday from 8:30 A.M. to 4:30 P.M. from Memorial Day weekend through Labor Day weekend and from 8:30 A.M. to 4:30 P.M. Monday through Friday the rest of the year.

South Coast

North Bend

Coos County Historical Museum
1220 Sherman Avenue, North Bend
(541) 756–6320
www.cooshistory.org

This museum contains a diverse collection of artifacts and exhibits that tell the history of the Coos tribe as well as well as those who originally settled here. You'll find intricately beaded aprons, ceremonial robes, baskets, and shells, as well as finely chiseled arrowheads. You also find pioneer implements and artifacts from the area's prominent shipping past. The museum is open 10:00 A.M. to 4:00 P.M. Tuesday through Saturday. Admission is $2.00 for adults and $1.00 for children ages 7 to 11.

Coos Bay

Oregon Connection House of Myrtlewood
1125 South 1st Street, Coos Bay
(541) 267–7804
www.oregonconnection.com

If you want to see how myrtlewood souvenirs and other products are produced, stop by the House of Myrtlewood, take a free factory tour, and view a 12-minute video that shows the production of bowls, clocks, and other myrtlewood souvenirs. A gift shop sells the items made in the factory as well as other Oregon-made products. Business hours are 9:00 A.M. to 5:00 P.M. Monday through Saturday and 11:00 A.M. to 4:00 P.M. on Sunday.

Bandon

The Wool Company
990 U.S. Highway 101, Bandon
(541) 347–2912
www.woolcompany.com

You'll be impressed by the inventory of wool products in this unique spinning, knitting, and weaving shop. You'll find natural fiber yarns, books, equipment, dyes, fibers, buttons, and patterns. The shop also offers classes and individual lessons. The Wool Company is open from 9:00 A.M. to 5:00 P.M. Monday through Saturday.

Port Orford

Hughes House
91814 Cape Blanco Road, Port Orford
(541) 332–6774

Built in 1898 by Patrick Hughes, the 11-room, two-story Victorian-style house was built out of old-growth Port Orford cedar at a cost of $3,800. This Victorian mansion is open for tours from 10:00 A.M. to 3:30 P.M. Thursday through Monday during the summer and is filled with delightful antique furniture and old photos depicting the life of the former 1,000-acre dairy ranch that the house sits on.

Gold Beach

Curry County Museum
920 South Ellensburg Avenue, Gold Beach
(541) 247–6113

At this museum you can find out about the gold fever that struck this area during the late 1880s. You'll also learn about what the interior of a gold miner's cabin looked like and other interesting gold rush trivia. In addition, you'll learn about the history of the Native Americans and other settlers who came to this area. The museum is open 10:00 A.M. to 4:00 P.M. Tuesday through Saturday. Donations are encouraged.

Brookings

Brandy Peak Distillery
18526 Tetley Road, Brookings
(541) 469–0194

If you want to learn about brandy making, be sure to visit the Brandy Peak Distillery. This facility makes delicious blackberry liqueur, brandies, and grappa, and their products are available in most Oregon liquor stores. You can visit the distillery from March 1 through the first week in January from 1:00 to 5:00 P.M. Tuesday through Saturday. Call for an appointment during the rest of the year.

Chetco Valley Historical Society
15461 Museum Road, Brookings
(541) 469–6651

To see an ancient cypress tree with a trunk diameter of 27 feet, be sure to stop by the Chetco Valley Historical Society Museum. The 100-foot-tall tree is adjacent to the museum and is thought to be the oldest cypress tree in the world. This museum is located inside the old stagecoach station and trading post and has displays of 20th century Japanese swords and a dugout canoe in addition to late 19th-century furniture, tools, and arrowheads. The museum is open noon to 5:00 P.M. Friday through Sunday from November through March and from noon to 5:00 P.M. Wednesday through Sunday during the rest of the year. Admission is free but donations are encouraged.

The Arts

The natural beauty of the Oregon Coast inspires writers, artists, and musicians to express themselves in a variety of ways. Use this chapter as your stepping stone into the Oregon Coast art and culture scene, where you'll find dozens of activities that will satisfy your artistic cravings.

In this section you'll find a listing of Art Museums that feature traditional and contemporary artwork, and writing events and retreats where you'll find out about workshops you can attend. Also you'll find eclectic events such as the Fisher Poets Gathering, which features the lyrics of salty seafarers and gives you a chance to recite your own verse, and an overview of selected stages where you can attend theater and music performances plus the rich offering of music festivals and events that are present throughout the year. You'll also find a comprehensive listing of art galleries that showcase the talents of Northwest artists in a variety of mediums. The galleries listed are a mix of working studios, traditional art galleries, and galleries that are often combined with a bookstore, gift shop, or other retail enterprise. Many of these galleries hold art shows during the summer months but may have shorter hours during the winter months. Keep your eyes and ears open, for every place you visit on the scenic Oregon Coast you'll find that the arts are alive and are celebrated year-round.

Art Museums

Newport Visual Arts Center
777 Northwest Beach Drive, Newport
(541) 265–6540
www.coastarts.org/vac

The Newport Visual Arts Center showcases the art of many Northwest artists in the 1,000-square-foot Runyan Gallery and the 300-square-foot Upstairs Gallery. Examples of artwork you'll see at this impressive cultural center include Paintings of the Oregon Territory by Jim Shull, photography from local photographers, and selected pieces from local glass artists. The William Runyan Gallery hosts 12 shows per year featuring new artists from the Northwest. Admission to the center is free. The Runyan Gallery is open from 11:00 A.M. to 6:00 P.M. Tuesday through Sunday, and the Upstairs Gallery is open from noon to 4:00 P.M. Tuesday through Saturday.

Coos Art Museum
235 Anderson, Coos Bay
(541) 267–3901
www.coosart.org

The Coos Art Museum is housed in an art deco–style building and has a permanent collection of nearly 400 pieces of artwork. The interior of the museum is decorated in a modernistic style and has three galleries. The Maggie Karl Gallery is downstairs and the Oregon Gallery and Mabel Hansen Gallery are upstairs. These galleries display paintings, prints, and photographs by Northwest artists and all of the art pieces are available for purchase. The gallery also has the Prefontaine Memorial Gallery, which displays photos, trophies, and awards of Olympic runner Steve Prefontaine of Coos Bay. The museum has an additional permanent collection of paintings, prints, and sculptures with the highlight of this collection being 110 original graphics from well-known artists such as Robert Rauschenberg, Alexander Calder, Red Groms, Larry Rivers, James Rosenquist, and Warrington Colescott. Many pieces of the permanent collection can be viewed on-line at the museum's Web site. The museum is open 10:00 A.M. to 4:00 P.M. Tuesday through Friday and from 1:00 to 4:00 P.M. on Saturday.

Art Galleries

North Coast

Art Center Gallery
Clatsop Community College, 1653 Jerome, Astoria
(503) 338–2473
www.clatsopcollege.com

The Art Center Gallery at Clatsop Community College features a collection of sculpture, photography, painting, drawing, printmaking, and mixed media artwork by local and regional artists.

Pacific Rim Gallery
108 10th Street, Astoria
(503) 325–5450

Stop by the Pacific Rim Gallery to find a unique blend of fine arts and crafts combined with a small espresso bar and deli. The gallery holds art shows every eight weeks featuring different mediums, such as bronze sculpture.

RiverSea Gallery
1160 Commercial Street, Astoria
(503) 325–1270

This local gallery features contemporary works by Northwest and national artists in a variety of mediums including prints, paintings, pastels, photos, glass, clay, wood, fiber, sculpture, and an extensive selection of jewelry.

Burke Gallery
1111 Irvine Place, Seaside
(503) 738–3937

This gallery is a working studio that features the work of Burke family members as well as other artists. The highlights of this gallery are Alisa Burke's acrylics, clay, collage, oils, and watercolors, and Jon and Linda Burke's unique clay, metal, and wood pieces.

The Purple Pelican
210 Broadway Street, Seaside
(503) 738–5799
www.rarediscovery.com

This gallery showcases the work of local and international artists featuring jewelry, pottery, glass, and wood pieces. The gallery is open daily from 10:00 A.M. to 6:00 P.M.

ExposureArt Gallery
609 Broadway Street, Seaside
(503) 738–8030
www.shopseaside.com/ea

The ExposureArt Gallery features original works by local and regional artists. In this gallery you'll find a wonderful collection of art glass, intricate basketry, candles and scents, beautiful bronze and clay sculptures, jewelry, and dazzling pottery.

Fine Art Gallery
111 Broadway Street, Seaside
(503) 738–0328

The Fine Art Gallery features the work of northwest national and international artists in a variety of mediums including ceramics, etchings, fabric, furniture, glass jewelry, mixed media, paintings, pastels, prints, and sculptures. Local Seaside art featured at this gallery include Michial Freigang's oils, Philip Mancil's watercolors, Kel Toomb's mixed media pieces, Shannon Symond's whimsical watercolors, and Lynne Artiste's etchings and acrylics. The gallery features "Paint Ins" during the summer months, where local artists paint in the gallery for seven hours on Saturdays. In addition, they hold art shows for individual artists in the spring and fall months.

Necanicum Gallery & Picture Framing
1928 South Holladay Drive, Seaside
(503) 738–3168

The Necanicum gallery features wonderful watercolor prints by Rie Munoz and Nancy Loukkula.

Artists Gallerie
271 North Hemlock Street, #3, Cannon Beach
(503) 436–0336
www.cannon-beach.net

This is a working artists' gallery, which features original pieces in oils, acrylics, woodblock prints, and watercolors.

Ballantyne & Douglass Fine Art
123 South Hemlock Street, Cannon Beach
(503) 436–0507

This fine art gallery showcases a special collection of artwork in oils and watercolors and limited edition bronzes by regional and national artists.

Bronze Coast Gallery
224 North Hemlock Street, Suite #2, Cannon Beach
(503) 436–1055
www.cannon-beach.net
Representing Northwest artists, this gallery features limited edition bronzes, paintings, giclees, photographs, and life-size heroic monuments.

Cannon Beach Arts Association Gallery
1064 South Hemlock Street, Cannon Beach
(503) 436–0744
www.cannonbeach.org/main/cbaa.html
The Cannon Beach Gallery was founded in 1986 and represents local professional and non-professional artists. The Cannon Beach Arts Association sponsors the gallery and features solo artist exhibits and also hosts juried shows throughout the year. The gallery promotes excellence in visual art through education and exhibition. It sponsors an internship program for Seaside High School students and also sponsors students from Clatsop Community College. Featured artists at this gallery have included Gerri Ondrizek, who uses organic forms to create installations using drawings, prints, and real objects; Steve McLeod, who creates pieces ranging from utilitarian lamps to figurative sculpture; Barbara Grant, who creates beautiful paintings of land, sea, and sky; Gary Callaway, who uses watercolors to create intricate patterns of a botanical nature; and Betsy Priddy, who is well know for the saturated color and bold lines of her unique paintings.

Collide
172 North Hemlock Street, Cannon Beach
(503) 436–0402
When you visit this gallery, you'll find intricate pen drawings, a variety of unique prints, fun cards, incense, candles, and other eclectic items.

Dragonfire Interactive Studio and Gallery
23 South Hemlock Street, Cannon Beach
(503) 436–1533
www.dragonfirestudio.com
This gallery features acrylic art by Robyn Waters, wood turnings of Bob Moyer, the glass creations of Greg Lauch, the color and semiprecious stone-woven jewelry of Eeva Lantel, and beautiful stained glass mosaic artwork by Amy Gunn. The gallery promotes local artists and also offers classes for beginners and professionals.

Ernst & Ernst Collectors Gallery
224 North Hemlock Street, Cannon Beach
(503) 436–1819 or (800) 289–1819
www.cannonbeach.net
This Cannon Beach gallery features fine art prints, canvases, porcelains, ornaments, and gifts by Northwest and international artists.

Greaver Gallery
739 South Hemlock Street, Cannon Beach
(503) 436–1185
Original lithographs and paintings by the owners of the gallery, Hanne and Harry Greaver, are featured.

Haystack Gallery
183 North Hemlock Street, Cannon Beach
(503) 436–2547
The Haystack Gallery features a collection of original lithographs and watercolors.

House of the Potter
183 North Hemlock Street, Cannon Beach
(503) 436–2504
www.houseofthepotter.com
The House of the Potter in the Cannon Beach Mall features hand-thrown stoneware by Jay Steward and also sells a wide variety of nondenominational Christian books, gift cards, and inspirational gifts.

The Jeffrey Hull Gallery
P.O. Box 272, Cannon Beach 97110
(503) 436–2600, (888) 436–2606
www.hullgallery.com
This spacious second-floor gallery at Sandpiper Square showcases original

watercolors, limited edition lithographs, mini-cards, and boxed cards by featured artist Jeffrey Hull. Jeffrey Hull is a member of the American Society of Marine Artists and is one of Oregon's premier seascape watercolorists. The gallery participates in the Story Weather Art Festival events held the first weekend in November by hosting an open house to unveil their newest prints.

Icefire Glassworks
116 East Gower Street, Cannon Beach
(503) 436–2359

Icefire Glassworks is a working studio where you'll be able to see James Kingwell and Suzanne Kindland making free-blown glass vases, bowls, weights, and sculptures through a glass observation window.

Nature Art & Sounds
123 South Hemlock Street, Cannon Beach
(503) 436–9806 or (800) 281–9806
www.wildbirdshop.com

If you are a nature lover, you should be sure to visit Nature Art & Sounds in Ecola Square. This shop features birding supplies, decorative fountains, nature-oriented art, crafts and gifts, music, and wildlife arts and crafts by local Oregon artists.

Northwest By Northwest Gallery
239 North Hemlock Street, Cannon Beach
(503) 436–0741

This Cannon Beach gallery houses variety of arts and crafts that focus on glass media.

Oregon Gallery
223 North Hemlock Street, Cannon Beach
(503) 436–0817

This gallery houses a good collection of scenic Northwest photography, wall decor, and a large selection of gifts made in Oregon. If you want to bring home a special gift that was made in Oregon be sure to stop by this gallery.

The Purple Pelican
140 South Hemlock Street, Cannon Beach
(503) 436–1390
www.rarediscovery.com

The Purple Pelican features metal garden art by Tom Torrens that includes bells, bird feeders, and gongs. The Purple Pelican also has a fine collection baskets, ceramics, glass, pottery, sculpture, and woodcarvings by international artists.

The Radmacher Gallery
172 North Hemlock Street, Cannon Beach
(503) 436–2774

This gallery features the multimedia work of Maryanne Radmacher and also showcases a strong collection of fine art collage and prints, paintings, and handblown glass by local artists. It is located upstairs at Sandpiper Square.

Rare Discovery
148 North Hemlock Street, Cannon Beach
(503) 436–0119
www.rarediscovery.com

Rare Discovery features glass art by Richard Satava, Stephen Schlanser, Peter Vanderlaan, William McGrath, Sabino Crystal, Caithness Glass, Miller Glass, Glass Eye Studio, and Round-the-House. The garden art works of Tom Torrens are also featured. His pieces are made using recycled and industrial materials and are formed and welded steel with a protective industrial sealant. Materials such as cedar, weathered steel, handspun copper, and powder-coated aluminum are also used to form sundials, bells, gongs, fountains, bird feeders, and birdbaths. Rare Discovery also carries a fine collection of Swarovski crystal, animal sculptures by Mill Creek Studios, artwork by Thomas Kinkade, and box figurines from Harmony Kingdom. Business hours are daily 10:00 A.M. to 6:00 P.M.

Steidel's Art/S. Clay's Designs
116 South Hemlock Street, Cannon Beach
(503) 436–1757

The gallery features watercolors and pastels by William M. Steidel and specialized matting and framing by Sam Steidel.

Valley Bronze of Oregon, Inc.
186 North Hemlock Street, Cannon Beach
(503) 436–2118
www.valleybronze.com

When you visit this gallery at Sandpiper Square, you'll find beautiful bronze sculptures, original paintings, limited edition serigraphs, and photographs by well-known regional and national artists.

White Bird Gallery
251 North Hemlock Street, Cannon Beach
(503) 436–2681
www.whitebirdgallery.com

Evelyn Georges established the White Bird Gallery in 1970 and has represented the finest local, regional, national, and international artists for the past 30 years. When you visit this gallery, you'll be able to view oil, watercolor, and acrylic paintings, and clay, glass, and wood sculptures. Some of the artists represented by this gallery include Royal Nebeker, Norman La Liberte, and Grace Bishko. Artwork by these artists and others is featured during art shows given throughout the year. The gallery is open daily from 11:00 A.M. to 6:00 P.M. during the summer months and is open from 11:00 A.M. to 6:00 P.M. Thursday through Monday during the winter months. All major credit cards are accepted.

Windridge Gallery
224 North Hemlock Street, Cannon Beach
(503) 436–2406

This gallery features a variety of art mediums including art furniture, black and white photography, original watercolors, oils, mixed media, limited edition prints, and sculpture.

Osborne Studio & Gallery
635 Manzanita Avenue, Manzanita
(503) 368–7518
www.osbornestudio.com

This gallery exhibits the paintings of Donald Osborne. Visit his Web site to view the current painting available.

River Gallery
35820 U.S. Highway 101, Nehalem
(503) 368–5295

The River Gallery exhibits original oils, watercolors, stoneware, and sculpture by talented Northwest artists.

Shepherd Gallery
12905 U.S. Highway 101, Nehalem
(503) 368–6247

The Shepherd Gallery showcases beautiful goldsmith work, paintings, and fine crafts.

Three Village Gallery
35995 U.S. Highway 101, Nehalem
(503) 368–5885
www.threevillagegallery.com

Dr. Kenneth McGough, D.V.M., established The Three Village Gallery in 1989 as a way to spend some of his free time during his retirement. This gallery specializes in Native American art pieces, wildlife prints, Alaskan art, painted gourds, Tiffany lamps, Swedish crystal, Pendleton robes and blankets, Mexican rugs and wall hangings, and Taos drums, baskets, and jewelry.

Carvers & Designers
19485 U.S. Highway 101, Rockaway Beach
(503) 355–8508

Unique woodcarvings, photography, furniture, and paintings are exhibited at the Carvers & Designers gallery.

Pacific Moon Gallery
111 South Miller Street, Rockaway Beach
(503) 355–2212

Photography, oils, watercolors, pottery, and stained glass are some of the art mediums you'll find at the Pacific Moon Gallery.

ArtSpace Gallery & Cafe
9120 5th Street (U.S. 101 and 5th Street), Bay City
(541) 377–2782

This gallery showcases contemporary Northwest art including colorful multimedia paintings, marble sculptures, and interesting wood carvings. In addition, this gallery has a cafe that serves fresh seafood and other daily specials.

Beppu Gallery
34930 Brooten Road, Pacific City
(503) 392–3983
www.beppugallery.com

The Beppu Gallery exhibits clay, oil, etchings, woodcuts, watercolor, pastels, photographs, and glass. Featured artists include Stan Beppu, Gail Beppu, Donna Fountain, Kathy Haydon, Jonathan Dukehart, and Jeff White.

Soaring Crane Gallery
33105 Cape Kiwanda Drive, Pacific City
(503) 965–7848
www.pacificcityart.com/soaring-crane/
gallery.html

Featured artwork at the this gallery includes art quilts, wood, paper, antler carvings, recycled glass dishware, a fine jewelry collection, and panoramic photography.

Pacific City Gallery
35350 Brooten Road, Pacific City
(503) 965–7181
www.pc-gallery.com

This gallery features the artwork of over 100 Northwest artists. You can find glass, pottery, wall art, jewelry, and beautiful handmade gifts at this large gallery.

Westwind Gallery
35030 Brooten Road, Pacific City
(541) 965–4559

Westwind features local and regional artists in the following mediums: oils, acrylics, watercolors, pastels, steel sculptures, pottery, handblown glass, and prints. Subjects include seascapes, lighthouses, coastal seabirds and wildlife.

Hawk Creek Gallery
48460 U.S. Highway 101, Neskowin
(541) 392–3879
www.michaelschlicting.com/hawkcreek
gallery.html

This gallery exhibits the acrylic and watercolor paintings of Michael Schlicting.

Central Coast

Alder House II
611 South Immonen Road, Lincoln City
(541) 996–2483
www.alderhouse.com

The Alder House II is a glassblowing studio that welcomes visitors to view the ancient art of turning molten glass into vases, bowls, paperweights, and so on.

American Shadows
825 Northwest U.S. Highway 101, Lincoln City
(541) 996–6887 or (800) 215–3781

This gallery was established in Arizona in

Many galleries feature handblown glass pieces.
PHOTO: LIZANN DUNEGAN

1990 and then moved to the Oregon Coast in 1993 where its Southwest art collection was expanded to include the artwork of the Northwest Coastal Native Americans. This gallery proudly exhibits woodcarvings by the following Native American artists: Ken Hatch (Siletz tribe), Micah Vogel (Makah tribe), and Odin Lonning (Tlingit tribe). The gallery also features the watercolors of April White and Linda Nelson. Other artists featured include Barry Herem, J. D. Challenger, and Howard Terpning. Some of the mediums you'll find at the gallery include original paintings, hand-pulled and offset lithographs, bronze and alabaster sculptures, kachina carvings, American Indian artifacts, Northwest Coastal carvings, masks, Brentwood boxes and Western and wildlife art. This gallery also has one of the largest selections of traditional and contemporary jewelry on the Oregon Coast.

Earthworks
620 Northeast U.S. Highway 101, Lincoln City
(541) 557–4148

The Earthworks gallery features blown and fused glass and functional and decorative ceramics. In addition, you'll find handmade baskets, fine wood pieces, and paintings.

Frame Cellar & Gallery
2150 Northwest Mast Place, Lincoln City
(541) 994-8556

The Frame Cellar & Gallery houses a collection of oil paintings, sculptures, and watercolors.

Freed Gallery
6119 Southwest U.S. Highway 101, Lincoln City
(541) 994-5600
www.freedgallery.com

The Freed Gallery exhibits furniture, pottery, jewelry, glass, sculpture, clay, wood, and photography. The gallery features the contemporary paintings by Beth Ames Swartz, unique clay pieces by Brian Mackin, and glass art by Andrea Mullans Weir.

Ryan Gallery
4270 North U.S. Highway 101, Lincoln City
(541) 994-5391

The Ryan Gallery displays a good collection of oils, acrylics, watercolors, pastel and mixed media paintings, ceramics, glass, sculpture, and jewelry.

Gallery at Salishan
P.O. Box 148, Gleneden Beach 97388
(541) 764-2318

Located not far from the beautiful Salishan Links golf course at the Marketplace at Salishan, the Gallery at Salishan exhibits contemporary fine arts and crafts from national and international artists.

Mossy Creek Pottery
483 Immonen Road, Gleneden Beach
(541) 996-2415

Mossy Creek Pottery features unique handmade earthenware, stoneware, and porcelain pottery.

Cheri's at Sea Towne
1658 North Coast Highway, Newport
(541) 265-8476

Cheri's at Sea Towne has a good selection of Oregon crafts and other handcrafted wood, pottery, fiber, jewelry, and basketry pieces. In addition, you'll also find photography, art dolls, toys, and puppets.

Cosmos Gallery
740 West Olive Street, Newport
(541) 265-4040

The Cosmos Gallery specializes in fused glass, jewelry, and pottery.

Forinash Gallery
3438 Southeast Chestnut Street, Newport
(541) 867-3430

This gallery specializes in photography by Chuck Forinash and prints of scenic coastal images featuring lighthouses and bridges.

Insiders' Tip
You can find out about performances and upcoming exhibits by reading the local newspaper in the community you are visiting. See the Media chapter for more information about local newspapers. Another good source for finding out about art and musical events is the local chamber of commerce or visitor center. You can find a complete listing of chamber of commerce offices and visitor centers for the entire Oregon Coast in the Attractions chapter.

Nye Beach Gallery
715 Northwest 3rd Street, Newport
(541) 265-3292

This gallery features the beautiful bronze, copper, and concrete sculpture artist Lon Brusselback.

Oceanic Arts
444 Southwest Bay Boulevard, Newport
(541) 265-5963

Stan Pickens established the Oceanic Arts gallery in 1974 to showcase art pieces with Northwest flair. This gallery features fine art prints and contemporary crafts in wood, glass, pottery, metal, and other mediums.

Original Bard
28 Northwest Coast Street, Newport
(541) 265-5842

If you like beadwork, you should visit the Original Bard, which showcases original beadwork pieces from Native American, African, and European artists.

Rickert Gallery
640 Southwest Bay Boulevard, Newport
(541) 265-5430
www.rickertart.com

The Rickert Gallery features the seascapes of Sharon Rickert, landscapes by Lyn Lasneski, watercolors by Jan Kunz, and metal sculptures by John Cabalas. In addition, the gallery exhibits original bronzes, lithographs, pastels, and prints.

Wood Gallery, Inc.
818 Southwest Bay Boulevard, Newport
(541) 265-6843, (800) 359-1419

Located on Newport's historic bayfront, the Wood Gallery features oil originals and other art pieces from more than 400 artists. At the gallery, you'll find bronze and glass pieces, metal sculpture, jewelry, handmade wood furniture, and scrimshaw.

Yaquina Art Center
P.O. Box 274, Newport 97365
(541) 265-5387

The Yaquina Art Center at the Nye Beach Turnaround features original acrylics, oils, pastels, watercolors, photos, and cards.

Michael Gibbons Gallery: The Vicarage
140 Northeast Alder Street, Toledo
(541) 336-2797

This gallery is housed in a historic home built in 1926. The gallery features the paintings in oil and reproductions of the Pacific Northwest and Southwest desert by Michael Gibbons.

Brian McEneny Woodcarving Gallery
10727 U.S. Highway 101, Seal Rock
(541) 563-2452
www.woodcarvinggallery.com

You don't want to miss the unique wildlife carvings made out of black walnut, cedar, hibiscus, maple, myrtle wood, and redwood at this unique gallery.

Triad Gallery
5667 Northwest Pacific Coast Highway, Seal Rock
(541) 563-5442
www.triadgallery.com

The Triad Gallery displays regional, national, and international artists in fine art media such as painting, printmaking, sculpture, fiber art, jewelry, crafts, wearable art, handmade furniture, and carpets. The first thing you'll notice about this gallery is the sculptured building with a blue neon horse in front. Architect Glen Howard Small, one of the founders of the Sci-Arc Institute for Architecture and Design in Los Angeles, designed the building, and its wave-shaped exterior reflects the motion and form of the natural forces on the Coast. The gallery features monthly shows with an opening reception given the first week of the month, and posts its schedule on its Web site. This gallery has featured Martin Anderson's neon sculpture, Carl Nieder's acrylics, David Vala's carpet designs, and Sarah Wauzynski's unique jewelry.

Westlight Gallery
5174 Southwest Pacific Highway 101, Waldport
(541) 563-2125

This gallery specializes in traditional oils featuring landscapes and seascapes, and florals.

Earthworks Gallery
2222 U.S. Highway 101 N., Yachats
(541) 547-4300

Steve Dennis established the Earthworks Gallery in 1990. Steve has exhibited his functional and artistic ceramics nationally and many of his pieces are represented in public, corporate, and private collections. This gallery represents more than 150 artists working in clay, glass, wood, and metal, and it has one of the largest showings of glass pieces in Oregon. The gallery also features landscape paintings, watercolors, oils, and pastels.

Touchstone Gallery
2118 U.S. Highway 101 N., Yachats
(541) 547-4121
www.touchstonegallery.com

Robin Mathews fulfilled a lifelong dream when she opened the Touchstone Gallery in 1998. Her gallery specializes in ceramics, glass, wearable art, sculpture, and paintings.

Blue Heron Gallery
1385 Bay Street, Florence
(541) 997-7993

Established in 1990, the Blue Heron Gallery showcases a mix of different mediums from local and internationally acclaimed artists. You'll see woodcarvings, bronze sculpture, jewelry, glassworks, and metalwork pieces that are shown with award-winning presentation. In 1999, *Niche* magazine rated this gallery as one of the top 100 galleries in the United States, and if you stop by you'll see why.

Frames of Florence–Gallery 101
1361 1st Street, Old Town Florence
(541) 997-2043

While you are browsing through the shops in Old Town Florence, be sure to stop by the Frames of Florence–Gallery 101. This gallery exhibits Charles Draper's color photos, Dan Looney's watercolors and mixed media, Stephanie Lochow's pottery, Tom Turk's scrimshaw, Don Jenson's gyotaku (fish rubbings), Lane Sharkey's limited edition prints of dried flowers, and a permanent display of Barclay Cook's black and white photographs of local scenes.

Florence Events Center Gallery
715 Quince Street, Florence
(541) 997-1994, (888) 968-4086
www.eventcenter.org/gallery/gallery.html

The Florence Events Center Gallery features the artwork of local and regional artists throughout the year. Visit their Web site to view the current gallery schedule.

Mindpower Gallery
417 Fir Avenue, Reedsport
(541) 271-2485, (800) 644-2485
www.mindpowergallery.com

The Mindpower gallery features original artwork in 2-D and 3-D. The gallery also has a gift shop that carries music, books, and original handmade crafts and offers custom framing services.

Myrtlewood Gallery
1125 U.S. Highway 101, Reedsport
(541) 271-4222
www.myrtlewoodgallery.com

The Myrtlewood Gallery features gifts and art pieces made from wood as well as original paintings. This gallery features woodcarvings by Terry Woodall, Kim King, Ervin Besler, Burt Holden, Rong Foster, Richard Rombold, and Lee Fisher. Also featured are jewelry boxes made by Chuck Stewart, Dick Smith, as well as paintings by Erma Todd, Alix Mosieur, and Gina Femrite. You'll also find handmade furniture created by Al Redding, Jack Barnes, and Richard Howell.

South Coast

Crystal Dolphin Gallery
1901 Sherman Avenue, North Bend
(541) 756-1989

You'll find many unique art items at the Crystal Dolphin Gallery. This gallery features contemporary jewelry, glass, paintings, and sculpture.

Frogblossom Studio & Gallery
1554 Sherman Avenue, North Bend
(541) 756-2844

Emily Ashworth established the Frogblossom Studio & Gallery and gift shop in 1998 to market her own artwork, which includes abstract, architectural, floral, and whimsical original framed and unframed acrylic paintings, cards, bookmarks, and frog collectibles. Emily is usually creating a new painting in her studio, and she asks that you call before you visit or knock on the door of her studio to view her artwork.

Bay Moss Studio
180 Central, Coos Bay
(541) 269–0965
www.geocities.com/soho/gallery/7582

You'll find ceramics, glass, furniture, jewelry, paintings, woodturnings, and much more by local and regional artists at Bay Moss Studio.

Clock Tower Gallery
198 2nd Street SE, Bandon
(541) 347–4721

Located in downtown Bandon, the Clock Tower Gallery exhibits artwork in a variety of mediums including prints, posters, watercolors, oils, drawings, stained glass, ceramics, and myrtlewood.

Bandon Glass Art Studio and Gallery
240 U.S. Highway 101, Bandon
(541) 347–4723

Be sure to stop by this working glassblowing studio. Through an observation window you can watch master glassblowers create colorful glass vessels and paperweights. In this hot glass shop, you'll find the amazing work of Dutch Schulze, who creates vases that are characterized by the flow of complex multicolored strands and orbs against a background of vibrant color. Another featured artist is Aro Schulze, who is well known for his coral glass paperweights.

Second Street Gallery
210 2nd Street, Old Town, Bandon
(541) 347–4133
www.bandon.com/gallery

This gallery proudly exhibits the artwork of more than 100 artists, including paintings in oil, acrylic, and watercolors; sculptures in stone, bronze, steel, wood and clay; fine furniture; blown glass, fused glass; wearable art; contemporary jewelry; decorative ceramics; functional pottery; basketry; and weavings.

Spirit of Oregon
112 2nd Street, Bandon
(541) 347–4311

The Spirit of Oregon is an artists' cooperative that displays handmade pottery, sea kelp and sea grass baskets, paintings, jewelry, wearable art, sculptures, fiber, and African arts.

Cook Gallery
705 Oregon Street, Port Orford
(541) 332–0045

This gallery focuses on the wood art and also exhibits contemporary and traditional paintings, sculpture, and fine crafts.

Grantland Mayfield Gallery
246 Sixth Street (U.S. 101), Port Orford
(541) 332–6610

Artwork is celebrated in all shapes and forms along the Oregon Coast. PHOTO: LIZANN DUNEGAN

This gallery contains an eclectic mix of art pieces, including blown glass, silk ensembles, jewelry, paintings, and sculpture.

Art & Sign
29282 Ellensburg Avenue, Gold Beach
(541) 247–6528

Art & Sign is a working studio that showcases acrylics and watercolors by Magda Druzdzel.

Gallery 101 at the Bookworm Bookstore
29401 Ellensburg Avenue, Gold Beach
(541) 247–9033

This gallery features oils, watercolors, multimedia, photography, ceramics, jewelry, photography, and woodworking by local and regional artists.

J. Ader Gallery
29272 Ellensburg Avenue, Gold Beach
(541) 247–0148

Jean Ader's original oils of local scenes, wildlife, and birds are featured.

The Gray Whales Gallery
29830 Ellensburg Avenue, Gold Beach
(541) 247–7514

The Gray Whales is a gallery and gift shop that is owned and operated by Ed and Maggi Frazier. The gallery features a variety of mediums from local artists including pottery; watercolor, oil, and acrylic mixed media paintings; bronze, stone, wood, and clay sculptures; stained glass; weavings; basketry; Native American drums and rattles; and gyotaku or fish rubbings.

Judy's Corner Frame Shop
15608 U.S. Highway 101, Unit One, Brookings
(541) 469–5839

This shop exhibits collage work, jewelry, pastels, watercolors, and stained glass.

Mory's Mini Gallery
810 Chetco Avenue, Brookings
(541) 469–4856, (800) 782–8578

Mory's Mini Gallery features a variety of art pieces by local coastal artists. The gallery exhibits acrylic, oil, and watercolor paintings, ink drawings, mixed media, sculpture, pottery, and prints.

Pelican Bay Arts Association
509 Pine Street, Brookings
(541) 469–1807

The Pelican Bay Arts Association displays visual arts, porcelain, textile, and sculpture artwork by member artists. The Pelican Bay Arts association is a nonprofit organization and is supported by an endowment fund, membership dues, gifts, and donations.

Words and Pictures
407 Oak Street, Brookings
(541) 469–7067

This combined gallery and bookstore features the work of more than 50 local and regional artists in a wide variety of mediums. Paintings, sculptures, carvings, glass, photography, basketry, pottery, fiber art, and prints are some of the types of artwork you'll find on display in this warm and friendly gallery. In addition to browsing the gallery, you may also want to browse through her vast collection of book titles, greeting cards, and music titles.

Writing Events/Retreats

Fisher Poets Gathering
Astoria
(503) 325–7972

The three-day Fisher Poets Gathering is a get together of salty seafarers who recite their lyrics at places like the Wet Dog Cafe in downtown Astoria. This workingperson's poetry revival entices anglers from up and down the West Coast from California to Alaska to recite stories about their experiences at sea. Jon Broderick, a one-time commercial fisherman turned high school teacher in Astoria, started this event in an effort to preserve the seafarer's verse, which is much like cowboy poetry. The gathering features 15 hours of readings and various workshops on history, photography, and poetry about life at sea. One of the favorite events at this gathering is the limerick contest, where contestants write passages under the clock. Call ahead for specific times and locations.

Haystack Program in the Arts & Sciences
P.O. Box 1491, Portland 97201
(503) 725–4832, (800) 547–8887 ext. 4832
www.haystack.pdx.edu

The Haystack Program is an ensemble of weekend and weeklong workshops held during the summer months in Cannon Beach that focuses on art, music, and writing. The Portland State University School of Extended Studies sponsors this landmark program and undergraduate and graduate credit can be earned for most courses. A variety of writing workshops are offered such as "Poet's Choice: Crafting Lines and Stanzas," "Finding the Language of Loss," and "Fiction Writing for the Restless." Examples of art-photography workshops given include "Pastels: The Portable Medium," "Plateau Basketry Twining Techniques," and "Playing with Paint." Music offerings include classes such as "Songunting: The Lure of the Lyric" and "Explorations in Rhythm." Call to request a workshop schedule or visit the program's Web site.

Neahkahnie Institute
P.O. Box 447, Manzanita 97130
(503) 368–7878

The Neahkahnie Institute offers a variety of writing workshops for new and published authors. Examples of workshop topics include: "Manuscript Workshop," "Writing and the Natural World," "Mystery Writing," and "Tell Me a Story: Dramatic Structure and the Secret of the Scene." Call for a schedule of current classes.

Onion Peak Reading Series
Pine Grove Community Club, 225 Laneda Street, Manzanita
(503) 368–7463

The Pine Grove Community Club hosts the Onion Peak Reading Series, which features monthly readings by writers and poets. Featured poets have included Lois Baker and James Bertolino. Featured writers have included John Murray and M. K. Wren. The readings are held on Saturday nights at 7:30 P.M. Admittance is free but donations are encouraged.

Oregon Writer's Colony
P.O. Box 15200, Portland 97293-5200
(503) 827–8072
www.oregonwriterscolony.org

The Oregon Writer's Colony was formed to support writers, establish a permanent writers' retreat on the Oregon Coast called the Colony House, and sponsor a variety of writing workshops throughout the year. The Colony House is a log house located in Rockaway Beach with great views of the Pacific Ocean and Lake Lytle. The house has four bedrooms, two full bathrooms, a well-equipped kitchen, and many windows with views. From October through May members of the Oregon Writer's Colony can reserve a room with a shared bathroom and kitchen for $100 (Sunday evening through Friday afternoon). To reserve a room you need to call Marlene Howard at (503) 771–0428.

Sitka Center for Art and Ecology
P.O. Box 65, Otis 97368
(541) 994–5485
www.sitkacenter.org

Tucked into the slopes of Cascade Head on the central Oregon Coast, Sitka Center for Art and Ecology is a unique educational facility and working artists' studio that celebrates the relationship between nature and art. This special facility is located in a beautiful natural setting adjacent to the a Nature Conservancy preserve, in the midst of an 8,000-acre national scenic area and

Insiders' Tip

To view an events calendar that covers the arts and cultural scene for the entire Coast, visit the Oregon Coast Council for the Arts Calendar of Events Web site at www.coast arts.org/schedule/OCCA schedule.html.

overlooking the Salmon River estuary, which inspires artists with its natural beauty. The Sitka Center is operated by the Neskowin Coast Foundation and offers a variety of workshops and special residency programs for artists, writers, and naturalists. The facilities at the center consist of studios where classes and workshops are held. The facility itself is surrounded by the Harold Hirsch Garden, which provides a natural setting for conducting outdoor workshops. Classes and workshops are offered throughout the year in books and journaling, drawing, ecology, fibers, photography, printmaking, sculpture, and other art media, and writing. The center also hosts various shows, readings, and music events. Visit the centers Web site for a current course catalog and a current list of events.

Newport Performing Arts Center
777 West Olive Street, Newport
(541) 265–9231
www.coastarts.org/pac
The Nye Beach Writers series features readings from award-winning poets and writers throughout the year. Visit the Web site for a list of current events in this series.

Music

Newport Performing Arts Center
777 West Olive Street, Newport
(541) 265–9231
www.coastarts.org/pac
The 23,000-square-foot Newport Performing Arts Center is the pride of Newport and was opened in 1988 to promote performing, literary, and visual arts, and as part of its offering features a variety of musical as well as theater, film, and literary events throughout the year. To see the current calendar of musical events, you can visit the center's Web site.

Florence Events Center
715 Quince Street, Florence
(541) 997–2051
www.eventcenter.org
The 8,000-square-foot Florence Events Center is a modern, state-of-the-art facility that combines meeting and exhibit

space with a 500-seat theater. The center is a community venue for theater, ballet, art shows, concerts, and a variety of other community events. Call for a schedule of current concerts or visit the Web site.

Theater

North Coast

Astor Street Opry Company
Elk Hall, 453 11th Street, Astoria
(503) 325–6104
The Astor Street Opry Company features Shanghaied in Astoria, a melodrama about Astoria's colorful past featuring 28 local entertainers. The play is a family affair and encourages participation from the audience—you can boo the villain and cheer for the play's hero. This show is given on Thursday, Friday, and Saturday nights from mid-July through August. Ticket prices range from $5.00 to $12.00.

Coaster Theatre
108 North Hemlock Street, Cannon Beach
(541) 436–1242
The Coaster Theatre often features chamber music, drama, and musical comedies throughout the year. An average ticket price at this theater runs $15.

Cedar Bay Restaurant
2605 12th Street, Tillamook
(503) 815–8272
The Cedar Bay Restaurant often hosts fun dinner shows such as *The Odd Couple*. Shows usually begin at 7:30 P.M. and an average ticket price is $20 per person. Call ahead for a current show schedule.

Tillamook Bay Community College
2510 1st Street, Tillamook
(503) 815–8272
Tillamook Bay Community College often hosts plays throughout the year. *Pirates of Penzance* is an example of a classic that is hosted by the college and is sure to please all who attend. Shows usually start at 7:00 P.M. on Friday and Saturday nights and a matinee show is held at 2:00 P.M. on Sunday. Ticket prices are $8.00 for adults,

$5.00 for students and seniors, and $20.00 for a group of four people. Call ahead for a current show schedule.

Central Coast

Theater West
3536 Southwest U.S. Highway 101, Lincoln City
(541) 994–5663

Theater West entertains the local community by featuring different plays throughout the year such as *Habeas Corpus*, a comedy about mistaken identity and middle age. Shows are usually held Thursday, Friday, and Saturday nights at 8:00 P.M. Call for a current show schedule and ticket prices.

Newport Performing Arts Center
777 West Olive Street, Newport
(541) 265–ARTS (265–2787)
www.coastarts.org/pac

The Newport Performing Arts Center features a variety of plays throughout the year. Examples of works featured at the center include *The Diary of Anne Frank* and *Mad Woman of Chaillot*. An average ticket price runs about $10. To see the current schedule of plays, visit the center's Web site.

Florence Events Center
715 Quince Street, Florence
(541) 997–2051
www.eventcenter.org

The Florence Events Center hosts several plays throughout the year, including such classics as *The Wizard of Oz*, with an all-star cast from The Last Resort Players Storybook Theatre. Visit the events center Web site to find out about current show offerings or call for more information.

South Coast

Little Theater on the Bay
2100 Sherman Street, North Bend
(541) 756–4336

This community theater features plays throughout the year such as *The Grapes of Wrath* by John Steinbeck. Call ahead for a current schedule and for ticket prices.

On Broadway Theater
226 South Broadway, Coos Bay
(541) 269–2501

This community theater hosts a variety of plays throughout the year that people of all ages will enjoy. A sample of an evening show or matinee includes *Tennessee Williams a la Mode*, which is made up of five one-act plays: *Hello From Bertha*, a tragic story of a lady of the night; *The Lady of Larkspur Lotion*, a tragic comedy of a landlady who tries to collect rents from some manipulative renters; *Something Unspoken*, set in the 1930s, a woman seeks the presidency of a social club; *Portrait of a Madonna*, an aging southern woman must be committed to an institution due to her deep grief over a lost love; and *Lord Byron's Love Letter*, a romance set in New Orleans during Mardi Gras. Average ticket prices are $8.00 for adults and $7.00 for students and seniors. Call ahead for a current schedule and for ticket prices.

The Dusty Saw Theatre
38 East 1st Street, Coquille
(541) 396–4563
www.sawdusttheatre.com

Coquille residents and visitors alike enjoy plays at the community theater such as *Mail-Order Brides Beware* (or) *Lured to a Villain's Lair*—a whimsical extravaganza of dapper gentlemen and winsome ladies. An average ticket price is $10. Call ahead for a current show schedule.

Bandon Playhouse
Route 1, Box 1555, Bandon 97411
(541) 347–4529

The Bandon is a community theater that features a variety of plays throughout the year at different locations in Bandon. Shows have included *Molière by the Sea—A Royal Command Performance for the Sun King*, a set of two one-act comedies by the French playwright; *Dinner with Heather*, a one-woman play that explores the ages and stages of life, featuring Heather Bouher, a native of Bandon who studied theater and arts at Portland State University; *The Singing Company*, featuring songs from folk to opera; and *Night Watch*, a mystery thriller. You can purchase tickets at the Coast-to-

Coast (541) 347–3230 or the Bandon Mercantile in Bandon (541) 347–4341. You can call or write to be added to the mailing list to receive a calendar of events.

Music Festivals and Events

Oregon Dixieland Jubilee
Seaside Convention Center, 415 1st Avenue, Seaside
(800) 394–3303
www.jazzseaside.com

The Oregon Dixieland Jubilee is a huge event where nine bands play Dixieland-style music at the Seaside Convention Center and other locations in Seaside. This event has included bands such as The Titan Hot Seven, New Pacific Jazz Band, Clint Baker's New Orleans Jazz Band, and Chicago Six with Yve Evans. This annual event takes place during the last part of February and you can purchase a three-day badge that admits you to all the music events for $55. Call ahead for specific locations and times.

Cascade Head Music Festival
Peter the Fisherman Lutheran Church, Campus Building, 1226 Southwest 13th Street, Lincoln City
(877) 994–5333
www.cascadeheadmusic.org

This festival features beautiful orchestral pieces from orchestras from all over the world. Different orchestras are featured and play on weekday and weekend evenings during the month of June. Delicious Oregon wines, cheeses, and handmade desserts are offered at each concert. Call ahead for specific locations and times.

Ernest Bloch Music Festival
Newport Performing Arts Center, 777 West Olive Street, Newport
(541) 265–2787
www.baymusic.org

This annual music festival commemorates composer Ernest Bloch who lived and composed on the Oregon Coast from 1940 to 1959. During the festival you'll hear music composed by Block, Richard Strauss, Saint-Saëns, Poulenc, Chen Yi,

and many others. The festival is held from the end of June through mid-July. Call or visit the Web site for specific dates, times, and ticket prices.

Oregon Coast Music Festival
P.O. Box 663, Coos Bay 97420
(877) 894–9350
www.coosnet.com/music

This music festival is one of the big events of the summer season on the Oregon Coast. This two-week event is held in mid-July and features chamber, choral, and symphony music as well as performances that feature the sounds of big band, bluegrass, blues, and jazz. Call for specific locations and times.

Art Festivals and Events

Glastonbury Renaissance Faire
South Beach State Park, Newport
(541) 265–9231
www.oregonstateparks.org/park_209.php

Held the second weekend in May at South Beach State Park, the Glastonbury (pronounced GLOSS-on-brie) Renaissance Faire includes over 30 booths that feature unique pieces made by regional artists. This art fair is sponsored by the Oregon Coast Arts Association and has a medieval theme where the myths, history, and legends of this time in history are celebrated. The Glastonbury Renaissance Faire is open from 10:00 A.M. to 6:00 P.M. Saturday and Sunday. Call for current admission prices.

Yachats Original Arts and Crafts Fair
Yachats Commons, 4th Street and U.S. Highway 101, Yachats
(800) 929–0477
www.yachats.org

Held the third weekend in March, the Yachats Original Arts and Crafts Fair features over 70 exhibitors displaying items such as paintings, drawings and photos, glasswork, pottery, ceramics, woodworking, furniture, and lamps. Local artists featured at this event include Jenny Connor and Rusty and Janine Summy of Yachats; Bryan Duncan and John Bradley of Waldport; Pamela Parker of Seal Rock; Cheri

Aldrich, Lu Ramundt, and Gloria and David Pozniak of Newport; and Michael and Linda Soeby of Otis. Event hours are from 9:00 A.M. to 5:00 P.M. on Saturday and from 10:00 A.M. to 4:00 P.M. on Sunday. Admission is free.

Art Faire
Florence Events Center, 715 Quince Street, Florence
(541) 997–2051
www.eventcenter.org

The last weekend in August the Florence Events Center sponsors an art show and sale from local and regional artists working with all media and high-quality crafts. You can support local artists by attending this fun event.

Cranberry Festival
Cranberry Festival Association, P.O. Box 348, Bandon 97411
(541) 347–9616
www.bandon.com

Be sure to attend the annual Cranberry Festival held the third weekend in September. At this historic Bandon festival, you can view a variety of arts, crafts, and photography and enjoy on-stage music and entertainment as well as a street fair and Grand Parade.

Azalea Festival Art Show
Azalea Park, Brookings
(800) 535–9469
www.brookingsor.com

Held during the last weekend in May, this festival celebrates the brightly flowered Azaleas that are at their peak bloom during May in Azalea Park. Held since 1939, this festival features a floral parade and queen coronation, arts and crafts, and food booths. The art show features pieces in watercolor, oil and acrylic, pastel, mixed media/collage, drawing, and graphics.

In Support of the Arts

Oregon Arts Commission
775 Summer Street NE, Suite 200, Salem
(503) 986–0123
www.oregonartscommission.org

Established in 1967, the Oregon Arts Commission supports the arts to ensure their excellence in the state of Oregon. Nine commissioners in this organization determine policies, establish long-range plans, and review applications to grants programs to determine funding levels. The commission provides ongoing funding for the operations for almost 100 nonprofit arts organizations. This organization's Web site has links to dozens of arts organizations and also lists internship and grant opportunities for Oregon writers and artists.

Oregon Coast Council for the Arts (OCCA)
P.O. Box 1315, Newport 97365
(888) 701–7123
www.coastarts.org

The Oregon Coast Council for the Arts is a nonprofit organization that is part of a national network of local arts agencies that serves the entire coastal region. The organization assists arts and humanities organizations and individual artists by providing grants, cultural planning and programs, and management expertise for arts facilities. Their Web site includes a comprehensive events listing of cultural and art happenings for the entire Coast and also includes links to other arts organizations.

Oregon Coast Extended Arts Network (OCEAN)
P.O. Box 1315, Newport 97365
(888) 701–7123
www.coastarts.org/ocean/home.html

The Oregon Coast Extended Arts Network is one of 10 regional art councils that serve under the Oregon Arts Commission. This organization is an eight-county arts advocacy organization that promotes the arts for Oregon's coastal communities. This organization provides grants and funding; marketing; cultural facilities planning; community and downtown renewal; art education, classes, residencies, and training; and promotes performances and exhibits.

Kidstuff

For kids, the more than 300-mile stretch of the Oregon Coast is one long playground with all sorts of fun stuff to do, from gazing up at huge concrete dinosaurs to peering down closely at the strange critters in a small puddle of a tide pool. There are lots of sand dunes to romp on, docks to try your skill at crabbing and fishing, and neat spots for hiking, biking, horseback riding, wading, and walking where pioneers, explorers, sailors, and Native Americans once trod. We've organized the activities by region and city from north to south. So bring along jeans or cutoffs for your own adventure, buckets and scoops for sandcastle building, toss in a couple of kites for flying on a breezy day, fishing gear for when the perch or flounders are biting, and of course, rain gear for every day of the year. It's pretty hard for a kid to have a bad day on the Oregon Coast.

North Coast

Astoria

Astoria's Riverfront
Starts at 1700 block of Marine Drive, Astoria
(503) 325–6311

Astoria's riverfront promenade has 2.8 miles of shoreline where you can walk along plank docks and watch freighters heading for the Columbia Bar or out to sea to Japan and China. There are also chances to watch fishing boats bringing in their catch. A nifty Sixth Street Pier viewing tower is a fun spot to observe the ships and boats as well as climb high enough to look down at the crowds.

Columbia River Maritime Museum
1792 Marine Drive, Astoria
(503) 325–2323
www.crmm.org

At this terrific museum, there's lots of interactive stuff, including a replica of a steamboat pilothouse in which kids can man the helm, operate a 5-foot-high wheel, and send commands to the engine room through a voice tube. The navigation bridge from the USS *Knapp,* a World War II destroyer, is also a great place to scramble about. Near this intriguing museum with its professionally presented exhibits is the lightship *Columbia,* which once served as a floating lighthouse near

the river of the same name. Kids can also climb about the *Columbia.* Hours are 9:30 A.M. to 5:00 P.M. seven days a week; closed Thanksgiving and Christmas. Admission is $8.00 for adults, $7.00 for seniors, $4.00 for children ages 6 to 17, and children age 5 and under are free.

Uppertown Firefighters Museum
30th and Marine Drive, Astoria
(503) 325–2203

This 1890s fire station houses a horse-drawn fire engine built in 1878 and a 1912 fire truck that was America's first motorized fire engine. Also at the museum are other examples of fire fighting equipment. The museum is open 10:00 A.M. to 5:00 P.M. daily May through September and 11:00 A.M. to 5:00 P.M. the rest of the year. Admission is $5.00 for adults, $4.00 for seniors, $2.00 for children ages 6 to 17, and free for children under 6. This admission includes entrance to the Flavel House and the Heritage Center Museum (see the Attractions chapter).

Fort Clatsop
92343 Fort Clatsop Road, Astoria
(503) 861–2471
www.nps.gov/focl

Fort Clatsop is a precise replica of the fort where Meriwether Lewis, William Clark, and their Corps of Discovery wintered during the winter of 1805–06. Summers are great times to visit the fort to watch the rangers in costume enact "living history," make candles and moccasins, and demonstrate how to shoot a muzzle-loader. Of particular interest to kids is the Junior Ranger Program in which children can participate in pioneer activities to earn a certificate. At the Interpretive Center there's a 32-minute film and a 17-minute slide show. Located off U.S. Highway 101, 6 miles south of Astoria, the fort is open daily except for Christmas. Admission is $3.00 per visitor or a maximum charge of $5.00 per family. Admission is free on winter weekends.

Fort Stevens State Park
Astoria
(503) 861–1671
www.oregonstateparks.org/park_179.php

Named for a Union General killed in the Civil War, this fortification dates from

that era. Located 10 miles west of Astoria off U.S. Highway 101, it was used to keep a lookout for Confederate warships. There was also concern that British ships-of-war would appear as a response to Britain's possible alliance with the Southern Confederacy. During World War II, Japanese submarines shelled the area, making it the only spot in the continental United States that received fire. Shortly after World War II, the battery was dismantled but there is still enough for kids to clamber about on. There are 6 miles of bike trails, guided tours, and summer reenactments of the Civil War. Except for tour fees, the fort admission is free.

Seaside

The Saltworks
Lewis and Clark Way, Seaside

This monument, reproduced from descriptions in the journals of the Lewis and Clark expedition and located 8 blocks south of Broadway, between Beach Drive and the Promenade, commemorates the work of boiling seawater into salt. It took seven weeks to make four bushels of salt. Kids will learn about the some of the difficulties the Lewis and Clark expedition faced out west.

Seaside Aquarium
200 North Promenade, Seaside
(503) 738–6211
www.seasideaquarium.com

An old-time building that served as a swimming pool (natatorium) 60 years ago, this aquarium is home to seals that the kids can feed. There are also sea stars, wolf eels, a sand shark, and many other types of marine life. Open daily from 9:00 A.M. to 5:00 P.M. in summer; 9:00 A.M. to 5:00 P.M. Wednesday through Sunday from November through February.

Town Center Carousel
300 Broadway, Seaside
(503) 738–6728

Seaside's antique carousel was exchanged for a newer model in 1990. Located near the beach at the center of Seaside Town Center, the carousel is a real kid pleaser. This wild ride has a dozen horses, a flying pig, and a huge rabbit.

Tillamook

Blue Heron Cheese Company
2001 Blue Heron Drive, Tillamook
(503) 842–8281
www.blueheronoregon.com

A somewhat smaller establishment than the Tillamook Cheese Factory, this is just as fun—with lots of free samples of cheese, syrups, and jams. A delicatessen and gift shop are on-site, as well. Open from 9:00 A.M. to 5:00 P.M. October through February and 8:00 A.M. to 8:00 P.M. March through September.

Tillamook Cheese Factory
4175 U.S. Highway 101 N., Tillamook
(503) 815–1300
www.tillamookcheese.com

Opened in 1949, the Tillamook Cheese Factory is renowned for its delicious cheese rendered from dairy farms in the county, where the land is too salty to grow crops. There are self-guided tours with lots of great old photos, free cheese, and an ice cream bar. A restaurant and gift shop are available for tasty meals and nifty mementos. Open daily, 8:00 A.M. to 8:00 P.M. from June through September and 8:00 A.M. to 6:00 P.M. the rest of the year.

Central Coast

Newport

Yaquina Head Lighthouse, Interpretive Center, and Tidal Basin
750 Lighthouse Road, Newport
(541) 574–3100, www.or.blm.gov/salem

Yaquina Head is home to more than 25,000 shorebirds that nest on nearby offshore islands during spring and summer and a wide variety of marine life including a fairly new population of whelkins, sea stars, anenomes, sculpins, shore crabs, and other rockgrippers setting up shop in tidal basins scooped out of the quarry by the Bureau of Land Management.

Quarry Cove, at the base of Yaquina Head, a promontory of lava flow and basaltic cliffs, juts out a mile into the Pacific 3 miles north of Newport on Oregon's Central Coast and was once an abandoned rock quarry. Now, along with the lighthouse on the bluff above, it has been designated as an Outstanding Natural Area by the BLM. Specially built to be wheelchair accessible, the cove is a natural spot (well, not quite natural) to observe the growth of tide pools.

The black and white faces of Holstein cows are a common sight in Tillamook County, home to the world-famous Tillamook Cheese Factory. PHOTO: LIZANN DUNEGAN

Up the hill, the Interpretive Center has kid-friendly, hands-on exhibits and lively videos that present the geological, biological, and social chronicles of the area. Tourists and townspeople from nearby Newport get a chance to learn about the first Americans who lived here 4,000 years ago and consider the lonely, vigilant lives of the lighthouse keepers who kept ships at sea safe from the rocky lips of the Oregon shore.

If visitors have any time or energy left after visiting the tide pools, lighthouse, and museum, there are trails crisscrossing the 100-acre site worth investigating. Salal Hill Trail is a short but steep 12-minute hike leading to terrific views and wildflowers in the spring. A walk up Communications Hill Trail takes a hiker into a woodsy flank of shore pine, Sitka spruce, and a lively neighborhood of chipmunks, chickadees, and wrens. The Coast Guard maintains navigation communications equipment on top of the hill. A third trail leads down from the lighthouse bluff to Cobble Beach. It's an easy, five-minute descent to a shore composed of tons of cobbles the size of baseballs. A while back, 14 million years or so, boiling hot lava rushed to the sea and exploded into shards that have slowly been ground smooth by the tides.

Yaquina Bay lighthouse was built in 1871 and the Yaquina Head lighthouse was constructed in 1873. After three years, the lighthouse down at the harbor was extinguished, leaving the other lighthouse, at 162-feet above sea level, a higher, brighter beacon reaching 19 miles out to sea. A glimpse of its 9-foot high, 6-foot wide, two-ton fresnel lens is a visual cue that this light is indeed powerful. The lens was first illuminated by burning 2½ gallons of lard oil each night. This was replaced by a kerosene/mineral oil combination that lighted up the lamp until 1911, when a kerosene mist similar to a Coleman stove was used. In 1933, an electrical element was installed. Eventually, the lighthouse was automated and is now staffed by BLM tour guides. The lighthouse is Newport's oldest building. In 1869, Congress set aside money for harbor improvements that included two lighthouses. One would be at the harbor entrance and the other was to be built on Yaquina Head, then known as Little Cape Foulweather.

Thousands of school kids have been bussed to Yaquina Head to spend mesmerizing moments staring down into these quietly undulant lagoons and later to wander about a cool museum with lots of buttons to push and stuff to play with and out to the tip of the cliff to this lighthouse that has a gigantic light bulb in a window at the top.

Also, there's a neat deck where you can watch for whales. Look for spouts and what they call breaching when those big guys roll around on the surface of the water. The ranger says that not only are there migrating whales going by but also a resident pod of gray whales that likes it here better than

Insiders' Tip

If the weather turns really rough while you are out and about along the Oregon Coast, and you're looking for ways to entertain disappointed kids, give the local library a call for a schedule of its children's events. Most libraries sponsor storytelling, crafts, sing-alongs, and puppet shows. They are always free of charge. Even if there is no event planned for when you are in town, the library is always a fun sanctuary from the downpours.

Alaska or Baja California. You can also scope out those fat and happy harbor seals lying around on Seal Island down below and, starting in March and going through summer, check out the birds on Colony Island and other offshore rocks just below the lighthouse on the northwest side of the bluff. There's a "starwheel" on the deck to help identify Brandt comorants, tufted puffins, oystercatchers, pelicans, and other feathered characters.

Yaquina Head Outstanding Natural Area is not only a terrific spot for kids but also eminently worthy of a visit for adults, particularly those intrigued by natural history. Yaquina Head, open from dawn to dusk, is 4 miles northwest of Newport, off U.S. Highway 101 on Lighthouse Drive. The Interpretive Center is open daily; hours change during different seasons.

Oregon Coast Aquarium
2820 Southeast Ferry Road, Newport
(541) 867-3474
www.aquarium.org

In the 40,000 square feet devoted to marine life, this famous aquarium off U.S. Highway 101 has a giant octopus, sea otters, and sea lions cavorting about in front of your wide eyes. There are also lots of fluffing puffins and other seabirds in a huge outdoor aviary. As well as learning lots about the life of an ocean and its residents, you can watch the feeding of the animals and observe various special programs. A special alert: If you read in other guidebooks that Keiko, the legendary orca, is housed here, they are behind the times. Keiko was airlifted to Iceland where he is getting adjusted to the notion of eventually swimming free. Tickets are $8.75 for adults, $7.75 for seniors, $4.50 for children ages 4 to 13. The aquarium is open from 10:00 A.M. to 5:00 P.M. daily from mid-September through the end of May and 9:00 A.M. to 6:00 P.M. June through mid-September.

Hatfield Marine Science Center
2030 South Marine Science Drive, Newport
(541) 867-0226

A splendid companion to the Oregon Coast Aquarium, this science center opened in 1996. Primarily designed as a place to research and study marine life, it is also a great place for kids to get the real feel for

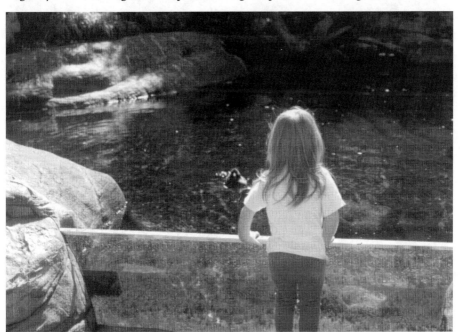

The Oregon Coast Aquarium has many exhibits that allow small children to learn about coastal wildlife.
PHOTO: LIZANN DUNEGAN

the ocean via hands-on activities, such as petting the octopus, playing with sea anemones, and handling starfish. Also in this intriguing spot are exhibits, demonstrations, and field trips. The center is open daily 10:00 A.M. to 6:00 P.M. in the summer and Thursday through Tuesday 10:00 A.M. to 6:00 P.M. during the rest of the year. There is no admission charge but a $3.00 donation is a good idea.

Ripley's Believe It Or Not!
250 Southwest Bay Boulevard, Newport
(541) 265–2206

Ripley's Believe It Or Not! is packed with strange items that will appeal to the kid in all of us. For example, children get a chance to pretend they are astronauts speeding through space. Be careful that younger ones aren't too spooked. Open daily, except for Christmas. Summer hours are 9:00 A.M. to 8:00 P.M.; the rest of the year, it's 10:00 A.M. to 5:00 P.M.

The Wax Works—A Living Museum
250 Southwest Bay Boulevard, Newport
(541) 265–2206

Insiders' Tip

Another terrific jaunt is pounding down a hard, sandy beach on a well-seasoned pony. Try the Bandon Beach Riding Stables, (541) 347-3423, 2640 Beach Loop Drive, ¼ mile south of the Inn at Face Rock. They are open all year come rain or shine. While you're there, take a peek at Face Rock and see if your kids can see that famous brow, nose, and lips jutting out of the Pacific waters.

Another roadside attraction that will certainly entertain kids is The Wax Works, where legendary and famous characters, some animated, seem to come alive. Open daily, except for Christmas, the summer hours are 9:00 A.M. to 8:00 P.M., the rest of the year, 10:00 A.M. to 5:00 P.M.

Florence

Sea Lion Caves
Florence
(541) 547–3111

This special location, 11 miles north of Florence, on U.S. Highway 101, is a natural wonder worth visiting. An elevator will take you 208 feet down to the world's largest sea cave—it's the size of a football field. Safe behind glass (and keeping the seals safe), you can still hear the uproar from the seals as you watch them loll and swim and cavort in large heaps. Up on top there is a gift shop and an observation deck to try and sight a whale spouting. Open 9:00 a.m. to dusk, admission is $6.50 for adults, $4.50 for children ages 6 to 15.

Darlingtonia Wayside
Florence

As you walk along wooden platforms through a patch of skunk cabbage in a steamy bog, you will encounter a collection of pitcher plants called Darlingtonia. These exotic cobra lilies are freakish carnivorous plants that lure insects by enchanting them with their sweet smell. The bugs crawl into the mouth of the Darlingtonia, can't crawl back up, and eventually fall to the base of the stem where they are digested. Most all adults and surely all kids will be fascinated with these little critters that are plants that eat animals! Located 5 miles north of Florence, on U.S. Highway 101 on the east side of the road, the wayside is for day use only. There are nearby picnic benches and tables if the visit makes you hungry.

Dolly Ware's Doll Museum
On U.S. Highway 101 at 36th Street, Florence
(541) 997–3391

If you have kids who like dolls, you may want to stop and visit this museum, which houses 2,500 dolls of all ages and descriptions. This collection of dolls from Germany, France, and Italy also includes a pre-Columbian doll. Collector's items such as Kewpie dolls and Shirley Temple dolls are also on display. The museum is open daily except Mondays from 10:00 A.M. to 5:00 P.M.

Sandland Adventures
85366 U.S. Highway 101, Florence
(541) 997–8087
www.sandland.com

This wild and wooly adventure gives kids a chance to scoot about the dunes in a dune buggy. You can hire a guide or rent a buggy for yourself to pilot. If no one wants to go dune buggying, there are also go-cards, miniature golf and bumper boats. Open daily 9:00 A.M. to 7:30 P.M. from June 1 to Labor Day. Open 9:00 A.M. to 5:00 P.M. during the rest of the year. Closed January 1 and December 25.

Jessie M. Honeyman State Park
Florence
(800) 551–6949, (541) 997–3641
www.oregonstateparks.org/park_134.php

This charming old state park is one of the most child-friendly spots on the Oregon Coast. Kids can swim, hike, beachcomb, and build sandcastles or you can rent a boat or canoe for a family cruise. If you have a boat or canoe with you, you will find a boat launch available, or you can rent a canoe, rowboat, or paddle boat at the concession stand in the park. Located 3 miles south of Florence on U.S. Highway 101, the park is open year-round. For a campsite reservation, call (800) 452–5687.

Sand Dunes Frontier and Theme Park
Florence
(541) 997–8087

Dune buggy rides operated by trained drivers will escort your family on an exciting outing to the world-famous dunes 4 miles south of Florence on U.S. Highway 101. Licensed drivers can also rent buggies for their own excursions. Open daily from March 1 to November 1.

South Coast

Coos Bay

Blossom Gulch Nature Trail
Coos Bay

The trail can be found by turning left off U.S. 101 onto Central just as you enter downtown Coos Bay. Follow Central to 10th Street, turn left and continue to the Blossom Gulch Elementary School at 10th and Anderson. Walk along the north side of the school past the playground to signs welcoming you to the trail.

Blossom Gulch sounds like the title of a western novel written for young adults. In real life, it's a boggy grove on the outskirts of Coos Bay laced with trails and dotted with signs explaining the nature of watershed enhancement.

Located behind Blossom Gulch Elementary School in a mixed thicket of fir, cedar, and alder, the Blossom Gulch Nature Trail starts with a boardwalk built over a swamp of cattails, skunk cabbage, and bunchgrass. A few steps along the trail, a covered deck offers information about Watershed Connections, a local wetland enhancement project. A collaboration between Oregon Department of Fish and Wildlife, South Slough Estuarine Reserve, and other local agencies, the project mobilized school children who spent many hours cleansing the gulch of invasive plants like English ivy.

Beyond the deck, the boardwalk passes by a slow brook rippled only by a Lilliputian cavalcade of a mother duck and five youngsters scurrying to catch up. Then the trail heads uphill switching back along a ridge trail of sun-dappled duff—a fecund mélange of twigs, needles, and decaying wood pulp strewn on hard-packed soil. Alongside the trail are thick carpets of tangy wood-sorrel, spiky clusters of bracken fern, and broad-leafed stalks bereft of their orange-sweet salmonberries. Above all this, slim Douglas firs billow and creak in the whisper of a southwesterly wind.

The walk ends at its entry point or continues on a spur along the south side of the school's playground. A modest, educational trek through a microcosm that serves as a gallery of broader environmental restoration, Blossom Gulch Nature Trail is also a natural for younger children who may not grasp watershed rehabilitation at work but will enjoy an up-close look at life in a swamp.

Charleston

South Slough National Estuarine Reserve
61907 Seven Devils Road, Charleston
(541) 888–5558
www.southsloughestuary.com

A glossy bit of trickery takes place on a micro-scale at South Slough, a 4,700-acre estuary on the southern Oregon Coast off Cape Arago Highway just west of Charleston. On one of those remarkable coastal days when the sun chooses to power through the clouds, thousands of little sundew plants sparkle with what appear to be baubles of dew. Unfortunately for thirsty insects, the tasty drops are actually sticky digestive juice that renders bugs into snacks for carnivores with roots. Folks who have been to Darlingtonia Wayside will get a sense of déjà vu.

These critter-gobbling plants and lots more intriguing flora and fauna are on view at a place still close to its original wild and natural state that scientists have dubbed "The Richest Place on Earth." One of the few estuaries in the world to have escaped development into a large port city, this arm of the Coos Bay estuarine system offers a rare chance to see a fresh watershed blending into a saltwater bay.

Here in this tranquil locale, visitors can trace the trickle of a small freshwater stream down a hillside of cedar and fir; through tunnels of alder to a valley floor carpeted with pickleweed, a succulent that holds freshwater in its fleshy leaves to dilute inundations of salt; through waving eelgrass meadows to a saltmarsh combed with saltgrass, a slender weed that excretes salt through its leaves. Beyond this adaptive vegetation lie the tideflats—ancient sediment replenished by the moving waters of ocean and stream where a vast community of shellfish, shrimp, and worms burp and wiggle out their quiet lives.

First stop is the interpretive center at the top of the hill. Inside are several exhibits about estuarine ecology and displays of plants and animals that live in or near South Slough. Staff members will happily answer questions about upcoming programs, direct you toward appropriate nature walks, and introduce you to live feathered or furry animals that are often hanging around the center. Slide shows and films are scheduled almost daily and a bookstore offers books, T-shirts and other related gifts.

Next, it's time to choose a trail down the hill. There are three basic paths, each with a particular slant: A 1.5- to 3-mile-long Estuary Study Trail—this easy-down, puffer-up trek is the most notable of South Slough's hikes. It follows Hidden Creek as it tumbles 100 feet down from the uplands to the slough. The trail starts

> ## Insiders' Tip
>
> How about a trip of a lifetime for young folks? Try a kayak paddle excursion along Nehalem Bay, a 6-mile estuary about 20 miles south of Cannon Beach. Not only do you get to take a great boating excursion with your kids, you also get to observe lots of birds and seals who live in this lovely spot. Call the Nehalem Bay Kayak Company at (503) 368-6055. They are at 395 U.S. Highway 101, Wheeler. Kayak rental is $30 for a full day on the water.

in the parking lot of the Interpretive Center (follow the sign marked trailhead). The trail then meanders through a series of habitats, crisscrossing the creek a number of times until it becomes a boardwalk across a wetland. One of the most dramatic stretches along the boardwalk is a stroll through a squat jungle of skunk cabbage with huge rubbery leaves that conjure up the dinosaur days. Shortly after this delightful journey through the Pleistocene, you'll come to an observation platform that offers a vista of fresh- and saltwater marshes. Beyond the platform, the trail emerges from the forest to spread out into a braid of paths. One leads to agricultural dikes built by farmers to keep salt water out of their fields. Another leads to Sloughside Pilings—once an elevated railroad for log trains chugging down from high ridges to dump logs into the slough for a boom-tow down to the mills at Empire, North Bend, and Coos Bay.

Ten Minute Loop is an easier 0.25-mile hike particularly suitable for young children. Starting at the interpretive center, this loop offers a glimpse of recovering forest habitat. Along the trail, local flora are labeled for easy identification and a short way down this path you'll come to a viewpoint overlooking the slough and surrounding watershed.

Wasson Creek Trail is a moderate 0.75-mile trail that covers a variety of habitats in a short distance. The trail begins at a freshwater wetland, crosses the valley, and returns through an upland forest. Hawks, songbirds, beaver, elk, and deer are all common citizens of the Wasson Creek drainage. To get there, head south from the interpretative center on Seven Devils Road to another preserve sign. Take this left turn onto Hinch Road and travel for about a mile, then turn right at a small binocular sign. This is the trailhead for Wasson Creek Trail.

Hoofing is not the only way to tour South Slough. Many visitors canoe South Slough to get to habitats inaccessible by trail. Canoe launch areas are available in the preserve and at Charleston, but it's a good idea to call or stop by the Interpretive Center first for information about tides and winds. One great way to slide through the slough is with a trained interpretive guide paddling his own canoe. To participate in this 6-mile trip, bring along your own canoe, paddles, lifejackets, and sack lunch.

Although the preserve is open all year, the interpretive canoe trip and most organized events are held during the summer. Don't be shocked by the news that it gets seriously damp at the slough. But also, if you want to take your chances, it can also be blessed by a perfectly mild and sunny day deep in the middle of winter.

A trek that kids really like is "Mudflat Mysteries," a goopy hands-on examination of clams and other critters that live below the muddy surface. Another program for young students (age 6 to 12) is "Slough Safari," a hike that gives children a chance to learn about the science of this magical spot.

Lastly, "Big Cedar Guided Walks" offers an access trail for individuals with physical disabilities. These free walks lead groups on a 0.5-mile, easy journey to the observation platform near the edge of the marsh.

The slough is also an educational experience for biologists and ecologists, who use the area as a living laboratory. As one of the most active biological areas on the planet, it is a rare locale where scientists can observe and research the nature of the beasts and their habitat. The interpretive center is open 8:30 A.M. to 4:30 P.M. Monday through Saturday from Memorial Day weekend to Labor Day and from 8:30 A.M. to 4:30 P.M. Monday through Friday the rest of the year. For more information, write to South Slough National Estuarine Reserve, P.O. Box 5417, Charleston, OR 97420.

Bandon

West Coast Game Park Safari
Bandon
(541) 347-3106
www.gameparksafari.com

Here in what is claimed to be the largest wild animal petting zoo in America, kids get a chance to pet little critters and observe the bigger wildlife. Included in the roaming tribe you can observe as you drive through are tigers, bears, cougars, lions, buffalo, elk, zebras, and camels. Free-roamers include goats, llamas, deer, and peacocks. Located 7 miles south of Bandon on U.S. Highway 101, it is open daily in the summer from 9:00 a.m. to 7:00 p.m. Open spring and fall from 9:00 a.m. to 5:00 p.m. Open in January and February on weekends and holidays only. Admission is $11.00 for those 13 years and older, $8.00 for kids age 7 to 12, $5.00 for kids age 2 to 6; seniors are $10.00.

Port Orford

Prehistoric Gardens
36848 U.S. Highway 101 S., Port Orford
(541) 332–4463
This melodramatic roadside attraction with its looming dinosaurs is a bit startling to those driving by. In operation since the mid-1950s, the garden presents these ancient reptiles in a rain forest setting.

Built to the correct shape and size, the dinos are also accompanied with interpretive signage. It's a self-guided tour through the garden so it's easy to take your time to absorb the knowledge as well as the fun. Open all year, daily from 8:00 A.M. until dusk.

Brookings

Alfred A. Loeb State Park
Brookings
(541) 469–2021
www.oregonstateparks.com
Located 6 miles north of the California-Oregon border is a stretch of mild climate on both sides of Brookings that the locals proudly call the Banana Belt. Alfred A. Loeb State Park has a good sampling of the famed myrtle tree (it's actually the largest grove in Oregon). There are some good swimming holes in the Chetco River and lots of picnic nooks.

Annual Events and Festivals

You'll be amazed at the variety of annual events and festivals that are held on the Oregon Coast. Many feature arts and crafts by local artisans, delicious seafood such as crab and salmon, and live entertainment. Other events are centered on favorite beach pastimes such as sandcastle building or kiteflying. Or they focus on the natural beauty of the plants and animals present on the coastline. For example, twice a year you can participate in whale-watching week and look for spouting gray whales on their semiannual migration, or if you love flowers you should check out the Azalea Festival in Brookings or the Rhododendron Festival in Florence, both during the month of May. If you want to combine great seafood with fine Oregon wines, then you should be sure to attend the Newport Seafood and Wine Festival held in February in Newport. We've tried to include events that are big crowd pleasers as well as small-town gatherings, and we've also included events such as the Great Oregon Beach Cleanup where you can volunteer to help keep the Oregon Coast beautiful.

In this chapter we've listed annual events and festivals alphabetically in the months that they occur. We've noted the time of the month the event is taking place and we always recommend that you call ahead to verify specific places and times. Note that concerts and writing events are not included in this chapter, but, instead, are listed in the Arts chapter.

January

Crustacean Classics Crab Festival
Factory Outlet Stores, 1500 East Devils Lake Road, Lincoln City
(800) 452-2151
www.oregoncoast.org

At this fun racing event you can buy or rent your own crab to compete in a unique race just for crustaceans. Winners of each heat earn a prize and the grand prizewinner receives a handblown glass float. Food vendors offer a variety of seafood and nonseafood dishes and a dozen Oregon wineries showcase delicious wines to taste. Clowns, music, and face painting are some of the additional highlights of this annual festival. This event is held the third week in January and admission is $5.00 per person or $10.00 per family.

Winter Whale Watch Week
Along the Oregon Coast
(541) 563-2002
www.whalespoken.org

During Winter Whale Watch Week you can stop by more than 29 locations on the Oregon Coast from December 26 through January 2 and watch for gray whales migrating south. Trained volunteers can help you spot these magnificent creatures and can provide you with information about gray whale migration. Volunteers are present from 10:00 A.M. to 1:00 P.M. at designated sites that are identified by a WHALE WATCHING SPOKEN HERE sign. You can find out where the designated whale-watching locations are by visiting www.whalespoken. org. The Oregon Parks and Recreation District, the Oregon Coast Aquarium, and other private and governmental agencies sponsor this semiannual event.

February

Antique Week/Lincoln Days
Lincoln City
(800) 452-2151
www.oregoncoast.org

Held in the middle of February, Antique Week and Lincoln Days is a 10-day-long multi-venue event in Lincoln City. Some of the events include a two-day quilt and craft fair is held at Taft High School; a four-day sidewalk sale at the Lincoln City Factory Outlet stores where you can purchase a variety of items from outdoor gear to kitchenware; an Estate Sale held at the Connie Hansen Garden located at 1933 Northwest 33rd Street; and several free history lectures given at different locations in Lincoln City.

Charleston Merchants' Annual Crab Feed
Charleston Elementary School, 5200 Seven Devils Road, Charleston
(541) 888-4875
www.charlestonmarina.com

Join the fun at the annual Charleston Merchants' Crab Feed held in mid-February. The local Charleston Merchants sponsor a dinner of a whole or half crab, fresh green beans, fluffy French bread, and a beverage. The dinner is held from 11:00 A.M. to 4:00 P.M. and proceeds from this event benefit the Charleston Visitors Association.

Insiders' Tip

You'll have better luck spotting gray whales on calm days with the sun at your back. Look for the signature "blows" the whales give when they are surfacing for air. Be sure to dress warmly and bring a pair of binoculars.

Newport Seafood & Wine Festival
Newport Marina Exhibit Hall, Newport
(541) 265-8801
www.newportchamber.org/swf

This festival was established in 1976 and is one of the premier festivals on the Oregon Coast. Held the last weekend in February, this event features more than 100 exhibitors including the food booths that cook up sinfully delicious seafood specials. You'll also be able to taste-test a variety of wines from representatives from most of Oregon's wineries as well as well-known wineries from California and Washington. Arts and crafts booths filled with photography, original paintings, handcrafted jewelry, woodcarvings, wall hangings, and handcrafted pottery are part of the fun. The festival hours are Friday from 2:00 to 8:00 P.M., Saturday 10:00 A.M. to 5:00 P.M., and Sunday from 10:00 A.M. to 4:00 P.M. You must be over 21 years of age to attend and the admission price is $6.00 Friday and Sunday and $9.00 on Saturday.

Seaside Chocolate Festival and Bridal Show
Seaside Convention Center, 415 1st Avenue, Seaside
(800) 444-6740
www.seasideconvention.com

You can sample all kinds of sumptuous chocolate and view gorgeous bridal gowns at this annual event held the second weekend in February at the Seaside Convention Center.

March

Oregon Dune Mushers Mail Run
P.O. Box 841, North Bend 97459
(541) 269-1269
www.oregondunemushers.com

Held the second weekend in March, this annual three-day event is a 70-mile endurance mush from North Bend to Florence through the Oregon Dunes National Recreation Area. Dryland dog teams (dogs pulling a cart on wheels) and their owners brave sand dunes, trails, hard-packed roads, and sandy beaches.

Spring Whale Watch Week
Along the Oregon Coast
(541) 563-2002
www.whalespoken.org

During Spring Whale Watch Week you can stop at more than 29 locations on the Oregon Coast during the third week in March and watch for gray whales migrating north. Trained volunteers can help you spot these magnificent creatures and can provide you with information about gray whale migration. Volunteers are present from 10:00 A.M. to 1:00 P.M. at designated sites that are identified by a WHALE WATCHING SPOKEN HERE sign. You can find out the 29 designated whale-watching locations that are part of this program by visiting www.whalespoken.org. The Oregon Parks and Recreation District, the Oregon Coast Aquarium, and other private and governmental agencies sponsor this semiannual event.

Yachats Arts & Crafts Fair
Yachats Commons, 4th Street and U.S.
Highway 101, Yachats
(541) 547-3530
www.yachats.org

Held the third week in March, the annual Yachats Arts & Crafts Fair is filled with fun sights and sounds for everyone. Cruise through booths filled with handcrafted wares made from clay, leather, and fabric. If you get hungry, be sure to stop by the food booths filled with fresh seafood delicacies, yummy desserts, and other concoctions that will make you want to go back for seconds. The arts and crafts fair is open from 9:00 A.M. to 5:00 P.M. on Saturday and from 10:00 A.M. to 4:00 P.M. on Sunday.

April

Astoria-Warrenton Crab & Seafood Festival
Hammond Mooring Basin, Hammond
(503) 325-6311
www.oldoregon.com/crabfestandevents.htm

Thousands of people attend the annual Astoria-Warrenton Crab & Seafood Festival held the last weekend in April. More than 150 craft, food, and wine vendors are present, with the main event being the traditional crab dinner. This festival features a variety of entertainment, a colorful carnival, a kids corner, and many more activities that will appeal to all members of the family. The admission fee is $5.00 on Friday and Sunday and $7.00 on Saturday. The festival is open Friday evening from 4:00 to 9:00 P.M., Saturday from 10:00 A.M. to 8:00 P.M. and Sunday from 11:00 A.M. to 4:00 P.M.

Great Oregon Beach Cleanup
Entire Coast
(503) 844-9571
www.solv.org

You can help keep the Oregon coastline beautiful by joining more than 5,000 volunteers to take part in the Oregon Beach Cleanup that takes place the first Saturday in April and the second Saturday in October to collect 20 to 30 tons of debris along the scenic coastline. Dozens of designated cleanup sites are available all along the Coast and you are asked to pick up trash between 10:00 A.M. and 1:00 P.M. Plastic bags are provided. Bring rubber gloves to protect your hands from sharp objects. Call ahead for specific locations.

May

Azalea Festival
Azalea Park, Brookings
(800) 535-9469
www.brookingsor.com

Held during the third weekend in May, this festival celebrates the brightly flowered Azaleas that are at their peak bloom during May in Azalea Park. Held since 1939, this festival features a floral parade and queen coronation, arts and crafts, and food booths.

Rhododendron Festival
Florence
(800) 524-4864
www.florencechamber.com

The beautiful blooms of the rhododendron are celebrated at this annual event held during the third weekend in May. A variety of events such as an arts and crafts fair, floral parade and queen's coronation, flower show, and Rhodie Run are some of the fun events at this festival.

June

Beachcomber Days
Waldport
(541) 563–2133
www.waldport-chamber.com

Beachcomber Days is an annual celebration held during the third weekend in June for the community of Waldport and sponsored by the Waldport Chamber of Commerce. The whole town comes alive with arts and crafts vendors selling unique items, food booths featuring seafood delicacies, and live entertainment. Kids will love the parade and carnival that is also held in conjunction with this annual event.

Cannon Beach Sandcastle Contest
Cannon Beach
(503) 436–2973
www.cannonbeach.org

This annual event is held in Cannon Beach on the second Saturday in June and draws sandcastle builders and spectators from all over Oregon. The event is held from 6:30 to 10:00 A.M. and is limited to 150 participants organized into divisions by age, individual or team, and type of building implements used. Each individual or team is assigned a building plot and can use only natural materials such as rocks, seaweed, shells, and sticks to build their sandcastle.

Cascade Head Music Festival
Peter the Fisherman Lutheran Church,
Campus Building, 1226 Southwest 13th
Street, Lincoln City
(877) 994–5333
www.cascadeheadmusic.org

This annual event is held in mid-June and features musicians from all over the world that play compositions by classic Viennese masters such as Beethoven and Schubert. Delicious Oregon wines, cheeses, and handmade desserts are offered at each concert. Call for specific dates and times.

Chainsaw Sculpture Championships
Rainbow Plaza, Reedsport
(541) 271–3495
www.reedsportcc.org

This annual event is held the second weekend in June and features professional chainsaw carvers who create one-of-a-kind wood sculptures in timed events. Wood sculptures are offered for sale after the contest. Call for specific dates and times.

Tillamook County Rodeo
P.O. Box 65, Tillamook 97141
(503) 842–7525
www.tillamookrodeo.com

This fun family event is held the last weekend in June and features the Dairy Parade, rodeo, dance, and Buckaroo Breakfast. Reserve seats for the rodeo are $9.00 for adults and $6.00 for children in the grandstand. Bleacher seats are $7.00 for adults and $4.00 for children. Call for specific dates and times.

July

Fourth of July Celebration
Rockaway Beach
(503) 355–8108
www.rockawaybeach.net

Join in the festivities at Rockaway Beach, which include a parade, auction, races, games, and treasure hunt. End the day by watching a grand display of colorful fireworks on the beach at dusk.

Insiders' Tip

To find out about more events and festivals held on the Oregon Coast, call the Oregon Tourism Commission at (800) 547-7842 and request *The Events Calendar—Oregon* or you can write to them at 775 Summer Street NE, Salem, OR 97301-1282 or visit their Web site at www.traveloregon.com.

Ocean Festival
Beach Boulevard, Winchester Bay
(541) 271–3495
www.reedsportcc.org

The Ocean Festival has a rich set of activities that will satisfy anyone. Arts and Crafts booths, a children's carnival, a classic car show, a quilt show, a dance, and a seafood dinner are some of the highlights of this annual event that is held the fourth weekend in July.

Pancake Breakfast & Parade
Downtown Manzanita
(503) 368–5100

Come join the rest of the Manzanita community for a homemade pancake breakfast and a small-town Fourth of July parade. The communities of Wheeler, Nehalem, and Manzanita participate in this fun annual event. Local seniors have their own float and kids dressed up in brightly colored costumes march proudly for their parents in this small-town parade. The pancake breakfast is held from 8:30 to 11:00 A.M. and the parade starts at 1:30 P.M. Be sure to stick around for the fireworks off the beach at Manzanita at dusk.

Toledo Summer Festival
Memorial Field, Toledo
(541) 336–9550

This fun community event is held the last weekend in July and features a logging show, carnival, parade, dances, delicious food, and Toledo's famous fireworks display. Call for specific dates and times.

August

Blackberry Arts Festival
50 East Central, Coos Bay
(541) 269–0935
www.pcncommunity.com/pch/blackberry

Juicy, sweet blackberries are the heart and soul of this arts and crafts festival that is held the last weekend in August in downtown Coos Bay. At this fun festival you can taste-test blackberry pie, blackberry cookies, blackberry scones and blackberry jams and jellies—just for starters. You can also check out almost 100 booths that are filled with local arts and crafts. Many of these talented craftspeople will demonstrate how they make their wares and if you ever wanted a handmade German leather cap, you'll find it here.

Sandcastle Contest
Southwest 51st Avenue, Lincoln City
(541) 996–3800
www.oregoncoast.org

Building sandcastles is a favorite beach activity and at this event you'll find some of the best and most creative sandcastle builders around competing for different prizes. This event takes place during the first part of August and has been an annual event for more than 20 years.

September

Bandon Cranberry Festival
Bandon
(541) 347–9616

This annual festival is held the first weekend in September in Bandon's Old Town and features arts and crafts, food vendors, live music, a parade and queen's coronation, and the Cranberry Bowl Football game.

Chowder Blues and Brews Festival
Florence Events Center, 715 Quince Street, Florence
(800) 355–8018
www.florencechamber.org

This three-day festival is held at the end of September and features a chowder cook-off, microbrew tasting and competition, food booths, and live music. Event hours are 5:00 to 11:00 P.M. on Friday, 11:00 A.M. to 11:00 P.M. on Saturday, and 11:00 A.M. to 5:00 P.M. on Sunday. Call for current ticket prices.

Fall Kite Festival
Lincoln City
(800) 452–2151
www.oregoncoast.org

You'll be amazed at all the colorful kites that come in all shapes and sizes and are flown at this annual kite festival that is held the third weekend in September.

Kiteflyers from all over the world participate in a variety of contests including team kiteflying, lighted kite night fly, and many more. Call ahead for specific times and location.

Indian Style Salmon Bake
City Park, Depoe Bay
(541) 765–2889
www.stateoforegon.com/depoe_bay

If you love salmon and want to participate in a more than 40-year-old annual event, than you should plan on spending the third Saturday in September at this salmon fest. Hundreds of pounds of salmon are baked on the beach in a festive atmosphere filled with music, clowns, and other fun happenings.

October

Dog Show at the Beach
Surfsand Resort, 148 West Gower, Cannon Beach
(800) 547–6100, (503) 436–2274
www.surfsand.com

This community event is held in mid-October and is sponsored by the Surfsand Resort. You and your dog can participate in 14 events, such as cutest dog, oldest dog, biggest dog, and smallest dog. Others include Frisbee catch, best bark, an obstacle course race, best tail wag, the 25-yard doggy dash, obedience trials, best trick, a "so ugly you're cute!" award, best costume, and a pet/owner look-alike contest. In addition to the events and awards ceremony is the auction/raffle and Parade of Champions at the day's end. Proceeds go to the Clatsop County Animal Shelter.

Oregon Coast Aquarium's "Creatures of the Night" Halloween Party
2820 Southeast Ferry Slip Road, Newport
(541) 867–3474
www.aquarium.org

From 7:00 to 9:00 P.M. you can bring your kids to join the fun on Halloween night at the annual spook fest at the Oregon Coast

Aquarium. A haunted shipwreck, haunted caves and caverns, chilling ghost stories, ghouls, and goblins fill the aquarium with Halloween fun. Sip on some witch's brew or create Halloween crafts. This event is filled with family fun for all ages. Call ahead for the admission price.

Oregon Shorebird Festival
Charleston
(541) 267–7208

Learn about Oregon's shorebirds at this annual festival sponsored by the Cape Arago Audubon Chapter. You can participate in boat birding trips, land field trips, and informative lectures. Call for specific dates and times.

November

Holiday Gift Fair
Seaside Convention Center, 415 1st Avenue, Seaside
(800) 444–6740
www.seasidechamber.com

During this gift fair, held the last weekend in November, you can shop for handmade crafts and holiday decorations at more than 130 booths. Additional highlights of this event include holiday caroling, a visit from Santa, and a tree lighting ceremony at Quatat Park in Seaside.

Stormy Weather Arts Festival
Cannon Beach
(503) 436–2623
www.cannonbeach.org

This festival celebrates drama, poetry, music, and artwork of Oregon artists at different locations in Cannon Beach. You can listen to hot country fiddles, classical piano music, or attend a variety of short plays. Another crowd pleaser is the Quick Draw Event where 14 artists have one hour to paint and frame their artwork in front of an audience. The art is then sold by auction. This festival is held the second weekend in November. Call ahead for event times, ticket prices, and locations.

December

Newport Lighted Boat Parade
Newport Harbor, Newport
(800) 262–3183
www.christmasboatparade.com

During the third week in December, the Christmas Boat Parade lights up Newport Harbor with an array of colorful holiday lights. Some boats are decorated with animated Christmas scenes and carolers. The boats travel 14 miles around Newport Harbor allowing viewers to enjoy the lights from restaurants, public beaches, and private homes. The parade takes place five consecutive nights and starts at 6:30 P.M. each night.

Oregon Coast Aquarium's "Sea of Lights"
2820 Southeast Ferry Slip Road, Newport
(541) 867–3474
www.aquarium.org

Twinkling lights, traditional caroling, and a gingerbread village are part of the holiday magic that takes place the first weekend in December from 6:30 to 9:30 P.M. at the Oregon Coast Aquarium. Kids can make holiday crafts and visit Santa and his elves and adults can enjoy hot chocolate and other holiday goodies while looking at the fascinating exhibits at the aquarium.

Insiders' Tip

There are many celebrations and events happening in all coastal cities during the Fourth of July weekend and the Christmas holidays. To find out more about holiday events and celebrations, call the local chamber of commerce for the city you are visiting. See the Attractions chapter for a listing of chamber of commerce office locations and phone numbers.

The Great Outdoors

The recreational opportunities along the Oregon Coast are as limitless as your imagination. In this chapter you'll find information on the coastal landscape, geology, climate, plants, and animals. In addition, you'll find detailed listings of state parks, recreation sites, and natural areas. The beach is the big attraction at many state parks. You can fly a kite along the shore, play Frisbee or beach volleyball, build sandcastles, play in the surf, or watch for wildlife. Almost all state parks have hiking trails that wander through scenic coastal forest, along wide, sandy beaches, or on scenic bluffs that overlook the ocean. You'll have the chance to watch for whales, explore tide pools, and learn about coastal plants and animals by reading interpretive signs. In addition to beach access, many state parks and recreation areas have picnic areas nestled in a coastal forest or perched above the beach offering scenic ocean views.

Natural World

The natural world of the Oregon Coast is a kaleidoscope of sights, sounds, and smells. With a diverse landscape made up of mountains, beaches, rivers, dunes, bays, and estuaries, the Oregon Coast is filled with colorful plants and viewable wildlife waiting to be experienced. If you were to paint a canvas of the Oregon Coast, you would begin by painting the north-south running Coast Range of mountains that are covered by a patchwork of deep green cedar and fir forest. This young mountain range separates the Oregon coastline from the green Willamette Valley to the east. Roaming this lush, green range of mountains you would find majestic Roosevelt elk, swift black-tailed deer, and lumbering black bear. Flowing from the mountains you would paint the wide-running coastal rivers like the Nehalem, Wilson, Siuslaw, Rogue, and Chetco that are stocked by fish hatcheries with salmon, trout, and steelhead. Mixed in with these major waterways you would draw outlines of large, rounded coastal bays, lakes and estuaries that support a myriad of bird species such as blue herons, Canada geese, kingfishers, loons, and mallard ducks.

As you near the edge of the Pacific Ocean, you would paint high cliff walls, spectacular headlands, and rocky islands that are home to colonies of seabirds like common murres, pigeon guillemots, gulls, cormorants, and tufted puffins. Mixed between the high rocky cliffs you would paint long, flat strokes for sandy beaches and swift strokes for the high, sweeping sand dunes that change with wind and tide. Chasing the tides on the sandy beaches you would sketch black oystercatchers, sanderlings, snowy plovers, and western sandpipers. Flying just above the break you draw a group of stately brown pelicans scouting for their next meal. Along the shoreline, you would also capture the intricate shadows of craggy tide pools that are home to creatures like sea-green anemones, bright orange starfish, prickly purple sea urchins, gregarious crabs, black oval mussels, and rough-shelled barnacles. And last, you would apply brushstrokes for the Pacific Ocean that pulses with the rise and fall of the tide with its undulating swells and pounding waves. This blue-green ocean is home to migrating gray whales, harbor seals, and barking Stellar's sea lions.

The sights and sounds of the Oregon Coast natural world are waiting to be discovered by you. With more than 300 miles of scenic coastline, there are dozens of opportunities to pull off U.S. Highway 101, the main coast arterial highway, into a scenic viewpoint or state park where you may have the opportunity to observe sea lions resting on offshore rocks, nesting seabirds catching fish and feeding young, a bald eagle soaring high above on the lofty air currents, the spout of a gray whale, or interesting tide pools that serve as a window to the undersea world.

In this chapter we will introduce you to the geologic events that shaped the coastal landscape, give you a taste of what the climate has in store for you, and tell you about some of the diverse plants and animals you may see while you are on your journey through this rugged and magnificent place. We'll also guide you through our wonderful state parks, which all have something unique to offer.

Geology

Molded and shaped by a series of geologic events, the Oregon Coast mountains are relatively young in relation to their Cascade mountain cousins located in the central part of the state. The Coast mountain range began as seafloor sediments and basalt seamounts. When the North American con-

tinent collided with these seamounts more than 45 million years ago, a shallow sea floor was created that filled with sediment over the next 20 million years. About 25 million years ago, the Coast Range was pushed upward from the sea and over the next 7 million years the Oregon Coast landscape evolved into what you see today.

Other volcanic episodes also shaped the basalt headlands along the coast. Over 15 million years ago, as many as 12 huge basalt lava flows, originating in eastern Oregon and Washington, traveled west to the Pacific Ocean through the ancient Columbia River channel and formed Tillamook Head, Cape Falcon, Cape Meares, Cape Lookout, Cape Kiwanda, Yaquina Head, Depoe Bay, Otter Rocks, and Seal Rocks.

Climate

There is no disputing the fact that it is wet in Oregon. As a matter of fact, the coastline has the highest rainfall in the entire state. For example, Astoria and Newport receive an annual rainfall of over 80 inches, and Brookings, nicknamed "the banana belt of

Sea stars inhabit coastal tide pools and feed on shellfish by using their tube feet to pull apart the shell of their prey. PHOTO: LIZANN DUNEGAN

the Oregon Coast" for its often warm and sunny weather, comes in with an average rainfall of about 10 inches less. You can expect average temperatures on the Coast in the low to mid-60s in the summer months with occasional warm sunny days that reach into the mid-70s. In the winter months, you can expect average tempera-tures to be in the 40s and 50s. Remember, the weather on the Coast can resemble the moods of a two-year-old—it can be sunny and bright; cloudy and foggy; rainy and windy or a combination of any of the above. With this thought in mind, it is always best to be prepared for all types of weather. In the winter months, bring along a sturdy rain jacket and insulating layers such as polar fleece or a wool sweater as well as sturdy, waterproof shoes and insulating socks. In the summer months, be sure to wear sunscreen and sunglasses and a wide brimmed hat, and keep a rain jacket and other insulating layers on hand in case the weather decides to turn on you.

The climate on the Coast is influenced by a variety of natural forces, including sun, wind, and tides. Heavy winter rain-storms create green coastal forests, and salt-laden winds constantly reshape sand dunes, beaches, and coastal vegetation. The moody weather is all a part of the area's attraction. Walking through a forest filled with sea-green fog and mist captures the mystery of the woods. Walking along the rocky coast on a stormy day, you can watch huge, white, frothy breakers crash into offshore rocks creating a thundering roar. Or, you may happen to be walking on a long, flat, sandy beach on a bright, sum-mer day with the salty wind whipping

your hair, surfers catching fast waves, and kids flying brightly colored kites. These images are all possibilities along the scenic Oregon Coast.

The Coastal Landscape

Forests

The Oregon Coast landscape is dynamic and always changing. The coastal moun-tains are laden with a patchwork forest made up of western hemlock, Sitka spruce, red cedar, and Douglas fir. In southern coastal forests there are small islands of orange-barked madrone trees, Port Orford cedar, coastal redwood trees, and myrtle trees. The myrtle tree is a mem-ber of the laurel family and is related to avocado, camphor, cinnamon, and sas-safras. Scented candles and perfumes are made from the oil present in the myrtle's fragrant and spicy leaves. The leaves also serve as an excellent seasoning for soups and sauces. Furniture and souvenirs are made from the beautiful wood of this tree, and dotted along the Oregon Coast you'll find souvenir shops selling myriad prod-ucts made from it. Large areas of coastal forest are a patchwork of different ages and types of trees due to logging. It is not uncommon to see large tracts of clearcuts that have been replanted with young seedlings. In areas that have been heavily cut, you'll find thick groves of big-leaf maple and red alder trees. You can recog-nize red alders by their grayish white bark and thick covering of green moss and lichens. The coastal Indian tribes made utensils and carvings from the wood of this tree and also steeped the bark in hot water to cure rheumatic fever.

To see a rare grove of myrtle and red-wood trees, visit **Alfred A. Loeb State Park** located 7.5 miles east of Brookings off of North Bank Chetco River Road. Walk on the River View Nature Trail to view the myr-tle trees and the Redwood Nature Trail to view the 600- to 800-year-old grove of red-wood trees. An informative brochure that corresponds to numbered trail markers along each trail is available at the trailhead.

Insiders' Tip

To learn more about weather on the Oregon Coast, visit the Oregon Climate Service home page on the World Wide Web at wwww.ocs.oce. orst.edu/.

There are only a few pockets of old-growth trees on the Oregon Coast. One of the best places to walk through a grove of old-growth trees is **Oswald West State Park** located 9 miles west of Cannon Beach off U.S. 101.

The coastal forests have a rich variety of understory plants. In the spring months you'll have the opportunity to view many wildflowers such as the delicate, white triangular flowers of western trillium; the pink-flowered western columbine; the purple, bell-shaped flowers of the coast penstemon; and the cloverlike leaves and delicate white flowers of wood sorrel. Woven into this forest recipe are the distinctly shaped leaves of sword fern, deer fern, and maidenhair fern that thrive in the cool, wet environment. Wildflowers that grow in sunny, open areas include vibrant orange tiger lilies, blue iris, red Indian paintbrush, white meadow chickweed, phlox, and larkspur. **Saddle Mountain State Park** is a rich botanical area featuring many different species of wildflowers. It is east of Cannon Beach off U.S. Highway 26.

Many coastal headlands are covered with a variety of grasses and unique wildflowers such as red fescue, wild rye, goldenrod, coastal paintbrush, wild iris, blue violet, lupine, and yarrow. **Cascade Head** is designated as a National Scenic Preserve and is haven to a rare meadowland ecosystem that protects the threatened Oregon silverspot butterfly. Cascade Head is one of six remaining areas where this butterfly is found. Its current range is along the coasts of northern California, Oregon, and Washington. The best time to see the butterfly is from August through September when it is in the adult stage. Adults lay eggs on the tall grasses in August and September and the caterpillar emerges in early spring. The caterpillar forms a cocoon in early summer and reaches the adult butterfly stage in midsummer. The butterfly is about 1 inch wide and has orange and brown markings on the top of the wings and silver spots under the wings. Cascade Head is located 4 miles north of Lincoln City on U.S. 101.

Black-tailed deer inhabit the coastal forests and feed on bark, buds, leaves, and grasses. These graceful mammals are named for the distinctive dark brown tail with black trim, which has a white underside. Smaller than their mule deer cousins, black-tailed deer can be most frequently seen grazing in open clearings in the evening and early morning hours.

Black bears can also be found roaming the mountains and valleys of the Coast Range. Varying in color from rich, dark brown to light cinnamon, these bears range from 35 to 40 inches tall when on all fours and have a length of 4½ to 6 feet. Depending on area and level of nutrition, black bears weigh from 125 to 600 pounds, with males being about a third larger than females. Black bears have taste buds for virtually anything that is edible. About 75 percent of their diet is made up of roots, berries, flowers, grasses, sedges, herbs, and tubers. They also feed on decaying animal carcasses, fish, small marine animals, insects, and small mammals.

One of the most magnificent mammals you may see is the Roosevelt elk. Mature bull elk can weigh up to 1,000 pounds and are usually reddish-brown in color. Roosevelt elk are primarily grazers and tend to congregate in open meadows where grasses are plentiful. A dominant bull elk is usually in charge of a herd of about 20 cows. Every spring, the bulls grow a set of antlers that are used to ward off rival males during the fall breeding season. Once the breeding season is over, the antlers are shed. To see a herd of Roosevelt elk, visit Cascade Head or the **Jewell Meadows Wildlife Area** located 1.5 miles west of Jewell off Oregon Highway 202. The best viewing months are September through March. Another place to view Roosevelt elk and black-tailed deer is the **Dean Creek Elk Viewing Area** located on the south side of Oregon Highway 38 three miles east of Reedsport.

Estuaries

As you move down from the mountains, coastal rivers meander through lush coastal valleys and eventually flow into the transitional zone of estuaries. The Oregon coastline is rich with estuaries that are formed when tides cause seawater to flood the mouths of coastal rivers, mixing freshwater and seawater. The level of the water in estuaries rises and falls with the tide. Estuaries are very productive places due to the fairly calm rise and fall of the water that creates a safe haven for estuarine plants and animals to live. Estuaries have a flat, muddy bottom that is created from the accumulation of decaying plants, animal matter, and fine sediment that is brought down from the coastal mountains in the rivers. Shellfish such as butter clams, razor clams, and oysters thrive in this rich, muddy environment and, in turn, shorebirds find an ample supply of crustaceans, fish, snails, and worms. Estuaries are an excellent place to view different varieties of birds such as blue herons, belted kingfishers, loons, grebes, and a variety of geese and ducks. Plants that thrive in the nutrient-rich soil include arrow grass, giant vetch, salt rush, cattails, bull rushes, and bull thistle.

If you'd like to view birds and other wildlife in this rich coastal zone, visit **Bayocean Peninsula** at Tillamook Bay, **Netarts Bay** or **Siletz Bay Park** in Lincoln City, **Yaquina Bay** in Newport, the **South Slough National Estuarine Reserve** south of Charleston, and the **Bandon Marsh National Wildlife Refuge** located across the river from Bullards Beach State Park, located 2 miles north of Bandon on U.S. 101.

Sand Dunes

Oregon's sand dunes form desertlike landscapes that intermingle with coastal forest and freshwater lakes creating different types of coastal ecosystems. The Oregon Dunes stretch from Heceta Head south to Cape Arago and are protected as part of the Oregon Dunes National Recreation Area, established in 1972. This recreation area protects more than 50 square miles of dunes between Florence and Coos Bay. These ever-changing dunes sit on top of a marine sandstone layer called the Coos Bay Dune Sheet. Wind, tides, and wave action have pushed sand as far inland as 2.5 miles over thousands of years to create some of the world's largest dunes. The wind sculpts and shapes the dunes by blowing at a constant rate of about 14 miles per hour from the northwest. Winter storm winds that

blow in from the southwest can exceed 100 miles per hour and also have a great influence on dune formation. Ocean currents flowing north in the winter months and south in the summer months also act as a partner in sculpting the dunes by keeping sand deposited by coastal rivers at the shoreline. Large waves then push the sand onto shore and strong winds blow the sand inland.

Rocky Shore

The rocky shore has been shaped by its never-ending struggle with the sea. Winter storms and high tides form pounding waves that crash into rocky islands, arches, sea stacks, and cliffs. During this process, the ocean carves out its own masterpiece for all of us to enjoy. Atop the headlands and bluffs you'll find the twisted and bent trunks of shore pines often referred to as *krumholz* that are sculpted by the relentless winds that whip in from the sea. Among these sturdy trees, hardy salal and ceanothus bushes make their stand in the wet, windy environment. Open meadows of grasses and bright wildflowers also grace the slopes along the rocky coast and brave succulents gain a foothold on the steep cliff faces and rocky outcroppings.

Where the ocean meets the rocky shore, sea caves, tide pools, and cobblestone beaches are home to a variety of seashore animals and birds. The most common bird we all associate with the seashore is the vivacious gull. Five different species of gulls live along the coastline, the glaucous-winged gull being the largest and most common. You can identify this gull species by its white head and chest, gray wings, and yellow bill with a distinctive red spot. Sharing the rocky cliffs with the gulls are the penguinlike common murres, which can be identified by their dark brown feathers and white undersides, and pigeon guillemots, which are distinguished by their black bodies, white wing patches, and bright red beaks and feet. Tufted puffins also nest on rocky cliffs and offshore islands. The males have bright orange beaks, white eye patches, yellow feather tufts, and dark plumage. They feed on small minnowlike fish that

Offshore sea stacks are favorite nesting sites for thousands of seabirds that nest along the Oregon Coast each year. PHOTO: LIZANN DUNEGAN

they catch by diving underwater and swimming with their wings. Other birds that nest on the rocky ledges and offshore islands are pelagic and brandt's cormorants. These long-necked birds have dark, iridescent plumage and can often be seen resting on rocks with their wings outstretched. This curious behavior is due to the fact that their feathers become saturated with water after they have been diving for fish. In order to regain flight, these birds have to dry out their waterlogged feathers in the sun. Bald eagles also soar on the air currents above the rocky shoreline searching for ill or injured fish. The bald eagle has beautiful dark brown plumage and distinctive white head, neck, and tail feathers. The rocky coast also supports large groups of Stellar's sea lions, which rest and breed on offshore islands. They feed on fish and squid, and males can weigh up to 2,200 pounds and reach lengths of up to 11 feet. You can hear the barklike sounds of large herds of Stellar's sea lions up to a mile away.

Another common sight along the coastline is the spout of migrating gray whales during their semiannual migra-

tion. Gray whales can be seen migrating south to their breeding lagoons in Baja California during December and January and migrating north during March and April to feed in the rich Arctic seas. Mature gray whales are about 35 to 45 feet long, weigh 22 to 35 tons, and can live up to 60 years. These gentle giants feed on shrimp-like amphipods by scraping up mud from the ocean bottom and then filtering unwanted material through their baleen (a horny substance in their jaws) leaving the tasty amphipods behind, which they then swallow.

If you are exploring the rocky shoreline in the tidal zone, you'll have a unique opportunity to view a wealth of plant and animal life. The black stain you see on some rock faces in the tidal zone is hardy black lichen that consists of algae and fungi that have developed a symbiotic partnership. Rough-shelled acorn barnacles also cluster closely on exposed rocks. When the tide is out, these small creatures seem lifeless, but when the tide comes back in and the shells become submerged, these tiny creatures thrust out a netlike appendage that catches microscopic

Dune Walk

To walk among some amazing dunes in the Oregon Dunes National Recreation Area, check out these trails:

Taylor Dunes Trail

This 3.2-mile moderate out-and-back trail takes you through a beautiful coastal forest and dune environment. Start by hiking north from the parking area and crossing the Carter Campground entrance road. Follow the forest path as it parallels quiet Taylor Lake on the right. At 0.3 mile you'll arrive at a trail junction. Go left and continue 0.2 mile to a viewing platform surrounded by big Sitka spruce trees. After enjoying views of the dunes and far-off beach, head back to the trail junction and turn left. Follow the blue-banded posts for 0.5 mile to a beautiful beach (your turnaround point). Retrace the route back to the trailhead. To get there from Reedsport, travel 12 miles north (or 9 miles south of Florence) on U.S. 101 to the Taylor Lake Trailhead.

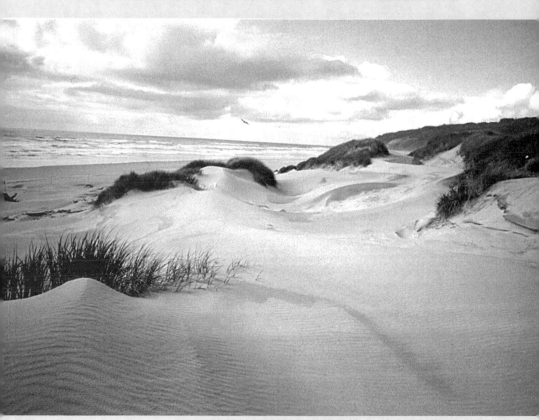

Sculpted sand dunes and a sandy beach are some of the highlights of Sutton Creek Recreation Area. PHOTO: LIZANN DUNEGAN

Dunes Overlook

This easy 2-mile hike takes you to a scenic viewpoint overlooking expansive dunes in the Oregon Dunes National Recreation Area. From the parking area walk out to a viewing platform and then take a paved sidewalk and long wooden ramp to the start of the sandy hiking trail. Use the guideposts to find your way across the dunes to a secluded beach (your turnaround point). To get there from Reedsport, travel 11 miles north (or 10 miles south of Florence) on U.S. 101 to the Dunes Overlook Trailhead.

Umpqua Dunes

This 1-mile interpretive loop takes you through a madrone and manzanita forest, wetlands, and magnificent coastal dunes. If you feel like a longer hiking adventure, continue through the dunes 2.5 miles to the beach. Look for posts with blue bands to guide your way. To get to this hike, travel 10.5 miles south of Reedsport on U.S. 101 (or 12 miles north of North Bend) to the signed Umpqua Dunes Trailhead.

Tahkenitch Creek Loop

This pleasant 1.5-mile loop route takes you through a coastal dune environment along picturesque Tahkenitch Creek in the Oregon Dunes National Recreation Area. To get there from the junction of OR 38 and U.S. 101 in Reedsport, travel 9.2 miles north (or 12 miles south of Florence) on U.S. 101 to the Tahkenitch Creek Trailhead.

Sutton Creek Recreation Area

The 2,700-acre Sutton Creek Recreation Area has over 6 miles of trails to explore, giving you a close-up view of a diverse coastal ecosystem made of sand dunes, coastal forest, freshwater lakes, coastal stream, and sandy beach. The Sutton Creek Campground has a short walk through a bog where you can view the insect-eating plant, cobra lily. To get to the Sutton Creek Campground Trailhead, drive 4.2 miles north of Florence on U.S. 101 to Sutton Beach Road and turn left (west) at the SUTTON RECREATION sign.

For more information on these trails contact the Oregon Dunes National Recreation Area, 855 Highway Avenue, Reedsport, OR 97467; call (541) 271–3611; or visit www.fs.fed.us/r6/siuslaw/odnra.htm.

plankton. Acorn barnacles share their rocky home with limpets and snails that are also especially adapted to live with the changing tide. In the tidal zone you'll also find greenish yellow rock weed and bright green sea lettuce, whose wrinkled fronds resemble a head of Romaine lettuce. In tide pools, black oval-shelled mussels cluster tightly together on the craggy rocks, sharing their underwater habitat with vibrant orange starfish, prickly purple sea urchins, and emerald-green sea anemones. Other plants that live here include the light yellowish brown sea cauliflower, green sea cabbage, and olive-brown crisp leather seaweed. Bustling about in these craggy pools are hermit crabs, purple shore crabs, and Oregon rock crabs.

The Oregon Islands National Wildlife Refuge protects all these species and many more. More than 56 islands are part of this system and stretch along the entire Oregon Coast. You can view birds and mammals from many designated viewpoints along our coastline. Some of the best viewing areas are **Ecola State Park,** located 3 miles north of Cannon Beach; **Cape Meares State Park,** located 9 miles west of Tillamook on the Three Capes Scenic Highway; **Oceanside State Park,** located 2 miles south of Cape Meares on the Three Capes Scenic Highway; **Cape Lookout State Park,** located 11 miles southwest of Tillamook on the Three Capes Scenic Highway; **Yaquina Head Outstanding Natural Area,** located 3 miles north of Newport on U.S. 101; and **Devil's Elbow State Park** and **Oregon Islands National Wildlife Refuge,** located 12 miles north of Florence on U.S. 101. To learn more about coastal species and to see them up close, we highly recommended that you visit the **Oregon Coast Aquarium,** which has interactive displays, hands-on exhibits, and natural outdoor displays that house a variety of species

Insiders' Tip

When you are visiting Oregon's scenic beaches, keep the following in mind:

• Avoid hiking to isolated rocks, tide pools, beaches, or headlands during the incoming tide. You can download tide table information by visiting www.oregonstateparks.org/images/pdf/tidetable.pdf. You can also view tide tables on-line at www.hmc.orst.edu/weather/tides/tides.html

• Be aware that water-saturated logs weigh several tons and could crush you should they roll on you.

• Don't wade out too far in the surf. Strong currents and waves can swiftly carry you offshore. In addition, ocean temperatures are very cold and can quickly sap your strength.

• Watch for sneaker waves that can knock you off exposed rocks, headlands, and jetties.

• Don't climb on steep cliffs or rocks. Always assume that all cliff edges are unstable and stay away from them.

that live on the coast. The Oregon Coast Aquarium is located just south of Newport's Yaquina Bay Bridge, off U.S. 101. To find out more about the aquarium, see the Attractions chapter.

Coastal Parks

North Coast

Fort Stevens State Park (Camping and Day Use)
www.oregonstateparks.org/park_179.php

Located about 1 mile south of Hammond, Fort Stevens State Park encompasses 3,763 acres and offers a coastal habitat with a wonderful mix of shallow lakes, wetlands, coastal forest, and sandy beach. Paved biking trails and hiking trails are present throughout the park. You can hike 2 miles around scenic Coffenbury Lake, and a 1-mile trail takes you from the campground to the wreck of the *Peter Iredale*, a four-masted British freighter that ran aground on Clatsop Spit in a rough storm in 1906. Watch for whales at a viewing tower located in parking lot C at the north end of the park.

You may also want to explore the abandoned gun batteries of the Fort Stevens Military Reservation, which guarded the mouth of the Columbia River from the Civil War until World War II. You can view military artifacts and interpretive displays at the Fort Stevens Military Museum, (503) 861–2000, which is located off of Ridge Road adjacent to the park and is open from 10:00 A.M. to 6:00 P.M. from June through September and 10:00 A.M. to 4:00 P.M. the rest of the year. The Oregon Coast Hiking Trail passes through the park and if you are backpacking on this trail, hiker/biker campsites are available at Fort Stevens. Other popular activities in the park are swimming, windsurfing, picnicking, and beachcombing. The day use fee is $3.00.

Del Rey Beach State Recreation Site (Day Use)
www.oregonstateparks.org/park_177.php

Del Rey Beach is located 2 miles north of Gearhart off U.S. 101. You'll find a flat, sandy beach only a short walk from your car at the Del Rey Beach State Recreation Site. This beach is a great place to watch the surf, take a long walk, fly kites, play Frisbee, build sandcastles, or play in the surf on a hot summer day. There is access to the Oregon Coast Trail. There is no day use fee.

Saddle Mountain State Natural Area (Camping and Day Use)
www.oregonstateparks.org/park_197.php

Saddle Mountain State Natural Area is located 17 miles northeast of Cannon Beach off U.S. 26. The area encompasses 2,911 acres and is rich in botanical diversity. Saddle Mountain rises 3,283 feet above the park, and a 5.2-mile out-and-back strenuous hiking trail leads you to the summit of this lofty peak. If you plan on hiking to the summit, note that the upper section of the trail can be somewhat treacherous. Wooden walkways and handrails have been put in place to help you reach your goal, but some parts of the trail are precipitous. However, once you arrive at the top you'll have far-reaching views to the west of Nehalem Bay, Onion Peak, Tillamook Head, and the coastline from Seaside to Clatsop Spit. To the east, you'll be able to see the Cascade Mountains as well as the surrounding Coast Range. This natural area is home to more than 300 species of plants. Ten primitive campsites are present in this park and they tend to fill up fast. Rest rooms, picnic facilities, and water are available. There is no day use fee.

Ecola State Park (Day Use)
www.oregonstateparks.org/park_188.php

Ecola State Park is located off U.S. 101 2.5 miles north of Cannon Beach on Tillamook Head. The park covers 1,304 acres and affords many breathtaking views from several different viewpoints. From the main parking area, a short, paved trail leads you to viewpoints looking south toward Cannon Beach and Haystack Rock. There are several picnic tables located in a grassy area adjacent to the parking area where you can soak in the view while enjoying your lunch. Also from the main parking area, you can hook up with the Oregon Coast Trail and hike 1.5 miles north through a pretty coastal forest to Indian tures, such as sea anemones, starfish, mussels, and hermit crabs. The flat, sandy beach is a great place to take a bike ride. If you need to rent a bike go to **Mike's Bike Shop** at 248 North Spruce Street in Cannon Beach, (503) 436–1266.

Other activities include picnicking, fishing, and kiteflying. There is access to the Oregon Coast Trail. There is no use fee.

Arcadia Beach State Recreation Site (Day Use)
www.oregonstateparks.org/park_187.php

Arcadia Beach is located 3 miles south of Cannon Beach off U.S. 101. The long, flat, sandy stretch of beach offers picnicking, fishing, beachcombing, and kiteflying, as well as access to the Oregon Coast Trail. Arcadia beach is a great place to spend the afternoon after exploring the shops, galleries, and restaurants in nearby Cannon Beach. There is no day use fee.

Hug Point State Recreation Site (Day Use)
www.oregonstateparks.org/park_191.php

Hug Point is located 5 miles south of Cannon Beach off U.S. 101. The beach at Hug Point State Recreation Site is a historic wagon route and settlers headed south on the beach at low tide to reach the town of Arch Cape. Settlers had to "hug" closely to the headland to get around the point at low tide. Hug Point is a pretty beachside cove that houses two sea caves that are fun to explore. Fall Creek runs through this area. A great hike is to head north on the Oregon Coast Trail 5.2 miles north to Third Street in Cannon Beach. If you plan on completing this hike, make sure it is at low tide so you can trek around several of the headlands. Other activities include picnicking, fishing, kiteflying, and sandcastle building. There is no day use fee.

Beach. Along the way, you'll pass three spectacular viewpoints. From Indian Beach, you'll have great views of the 62-foot-high Tillamook Rock Lighthouse that rests on a large chunk of basalt rock that is more than a mile offshore from Tillamook Head. This lighthouse was built in 1881 and acted as a lifesaving beacon for ships headed for the Columbia River.

Instead of parking in the main parking area, you can continue driving to the Indian Beach parking area. This scenic, rocky beach is popular with surfers and boogie boarders. If you need to rent surfing or boogie boarding gear, stop by **Cleanline Surf Shop,** 171 Sunset Boulevard, Cannon Beach, (503) 436-9726; www.cleanlinesurf.com.

There is fishing at the park as well as a hike-in camp at Indian Creek. The day use fee is $3.00.

Tolovana Beach State Recreation Site (Day Use)
www.oregonstateparks.org/park_199.php

Tolovana Beach is located 1 mile south of Cannon Beach off U.S. 101. It is a flat, sandy beach that offers access to Haystack Rock. This interesting rock formation is the basalt remnant of volcanic eruptions that occurred 17 million years ago. It is also part of the Oregon Islands Wildlife Refuge and is an important nesting site for puffins, pelagic cormorants, pigeon guillemots, and western gulls. At the base of Haystack Rock, you'll find tide pools filled with a variety of colorful crea-

Oswald West State Park (Camping and Day Use)
www.oregonstateparks.org/park_195.php

Oswald West State Park, located 10 miles south of Cannon Beach on U.S. 101, covers 2,474 acres and offers breathtaking scenery. Arch Cape, Neahkahnie Mountain, Cape Falcon, and Smuggler's Cove are all contained within this park. You can camp here but need to haul your gear

Short Sand Creek in Oswald West State Park.

PHOTO: LIZANN DUNEGAN

to the campground in wheelbarrows. A 1-mile out-and-back hiking trail leads you to Short Sands Beach—a popular beach for surfers and boogie boarders. The Oregon Coast Trail passes through the park and if you go north you can hike a 5-mile out-and-back trail to Cape Falcon. If you hike south on the Oregon Coast Trail, you can take a strenuous trek to the top of Neahkahnie Mountain, which is about 3.6 miles from the parking lot. The views from the summit are some of the best on the coast. There is no day use fee.

Nehalem Bay State Park (Camping and Day Use)
www.oregonstateparks.org/park_201.php

Nehalem Bay State Park covers 890 acres and is located adjacent to Nehalem Bay and the Pacific Ocean, about 3 miles south of Monzanita. The campground in this park has sites for camping with horses. On one side of the campground is scenic Nehalem Bay and on the other side are sand dunes that lead to a sandy beach that extends for 4 miles to the end of the Nehalem Bay Spit. If you want to crab in the bay, you can launch your boat at the boat ramp located in the park. You may also want to launch your kayak or canoe in the bay. You can ride your bike on the 1.7-mile bike path that winds through open dunes adjacent to the bay. While riding on this bike path, you may see deer, elk, and a variety of other wildlife. Horseback riders can enjoy the 7.5-mile equestrian trail that takes you to the end of Nehalem Bay Spit. Hikers who walk along the bay beachfront can experience prime bird- and seal-watching. The Oregon Coast Trail passes through the park and there is a hiker/biker camp here. Try horseback riding by renting a horse from **Northwest Equine Outfitters,** (503) 801–RIDE (801-7433), which operates a horse concession Memorial Day through Labor Day. Find them at the day use area in the park. There is a $3.00 day use fee at the park.

Manhattan Beach State Recreation Site (Day Use)
www.oregonstateparks.org/park_193.php

Manhattan Beach is located 2 miles north of Rockaway Beach off U.S. 101. This day use park offers several picnic tables nestled among beautiful shore pines. A short access trail leads to a pretty beach where you can go beachcombing, fly a kite, build a sandcastle, or play Frisbee. There is also fishing and access to the Oregon Coast Trail. There is no day use fee.

Cape Meares State Scenic Viewpoint (Day Use)
www.oregonstateparks.org/park_181.php

Cape Meares is located 10 miles west of Tillamook on the Three Capes Scenic Loop. One of the park's main attractions is the Cape Meares Lighthouse that was built in 1890. You can tour the lighthouse daily May through September and on the weekends in October, March, and April. A gift shop is located in the lighthouse and is open from 11:00 A.M. to 4:00 P.M. daily from May through September. A wide, paved path leads from the parking area to the lighthouse and along the way you'll have the opportunity to stop at several different viewpoints where you'll be able to see nesting seabirds that include common murres, tufted puffins, pigeon guillemots, cormorants, and gulls. In addition, 3 miles of hiking trails take you through an old-growth spruce forest where you can view a tree shaped like an octopus. There is no fee for day use.

Oceanside Beach State Recreation Site (Day Use)
www.oregonstateparks.org/park_182.php

Oceanside Beach is located 11 miles west of Tillamook off U.S. 101 in the small community of Oceanside. When you visit this area, you can walk on the beach and hunt for agates, fly a kite, try surfing or kayaking in the fun waves off the beach, or check out the wildlife. A half-mile offshore is Three Arch Rocks, home to 13 species of seabirds that nest on these sea stacks. The rocks are designated wilderness and all animals that live here are protected. While you're visiting the Oceanside area, be sure to stop at **Roseanna's Oceanside Cafe,** 1490 Pacific Street, Oceanside, (503) 842-7351. This local restaurant has a mouth-watering seafood menu and a great view of Three Arch Rocks and the pounding surf.

Other popular activities include hang gliding and fishing. There is no day use fee.

Cape Lookout State Park (Camping and Day Use)
www.oregonstateparks.org/park_186.php

Located 12 miles southwest of Tillamook, Cape Lookout State Park covers 2,014 acres that include Netarts Spit and the jutting headland of Cape Lookout that is covered with a fern-filled coastal forest. Hiker and biker campsites are available. The campground is located adjacent to the ocean and has a few sites with an ocean view. A variety of hiking trails in the park will satisfy all levels of hikers. A very scenic trail is the 5.4-mile out-and-back Cape Trail that takes you to the tip of Cape Lookout, which is a good spot to look for whales. This trailhead is located 2.7 miles south of the state park campground entrance on the Three Capes Scenic Loop. If you're looking for a shorter hike, two nature trails are also present in the park. The 0.25-mile self-guided nature trail begins adjacent to the campground registration booth. The Jackson Loop Nature Trail begins off the park entrance road east of the RV dump station.

Other activities include picnicking, fishing, and kayaking. There is access to the Oregon Coast Trail. The day use fee is $3.00.

Cape Kiwanda State Natural Area (Day Use)
www.oregonstateparks.org/park_180.php

Cape Kiwanda State Natural Area, about 15 miles north of Lincoln City, encompasses 185 acres and is composed of a pretty beach adjacent to Cape Kiwanda, which is made of a spectacular sand dune. This area is best known for its fleet of dory boats that are launched from the beach. Once they're in the surf, it takes a bit of skilled maneuvering to start their engines; then they're off, racing over the waves. Bottom fishing in this area is excellent next to offshore Haystack Rock. If you want to fish from a dory, you can rent a charter boat; call **The Haystack Fishing Club** at (888) 965-7555. Kids love to climb up the sand dune and have races down the hill as well as explore the tide pools at the base of Cape Kiwanda. Surfers and kayakers also enjoy playing in the surf off Cape Kiwanda beach. You'll also find hiking, kiteflying, sandcastle building, and paragliding. If you want to rent surfing or boogie boarding gear, stop by **South County Surf,** 33310 Cape Kiwanda Drive, Pacific City, (503) 965-7505. Public rest rooms and a parking area are adjacent to the beach.

Robert ("Bob") Straub State Park (Day Use)
www.oregonstateparks.org/park_183.php

At this flat, sandy beach in Pacific City you can explore Nestucca Spit. Go to the end of the spit by turning left (south) and hiking about 2.3 miles. Good fishing opportunities exist at the tip of the spit. Clamming is also good along the shores of Nestucca Bay. There is no day use fee.

Neskowin Beach State Recreation Site (Day Use)
www.oregonstateparks.org/park_223.php

Neskowin Beach is located in the community of Neskowin on U.S. 101, 33 miles south of Tillamook and 10 miles north of Lincoln City. Kids can enjoy wading in Neskowin Creek as it skirts the base of Proposal Rock. If you feel like taking a hike, you can head north up the beach that ends at the Nestucca River. While you are here be sure to check out the town of Neskowin. There is no day use fee.

Central Coast

Roads End State Recreation Area (Day Use)
www.oregonstateparks.org/park_225.php

Located about 3 miles south of Lincoln City, Roads End offers a popular spot for windsurfing, surfing, and boogie boarding. To rent surfing or boogie board gear, visit **Safari Town Surf Shop**, 3026 Northeast U.S. 101, Lincoln City, (541) 996-6335. A short trail takes you to the beach that is nestled in a sheltered cove. From here you'll have views of Cascade Head and at low tide you can explore the tide pools. If you go north along the beach for about 1.5 miles, you can hike around the tip of the headland to a secluded cove that can only be accessed during low tide. If you hike to the cove, be sure you return before the tide comes back in! There is no day use fee.

D River State Recreation Site (Day Use)
www.oregonstateparks.org/park_214.php

D River is located in Lincoln City just off U.S. 101, adjacent to the D River (the shortest river in the world) that flows 200 yards from Devils Lake to the ocean. A fall kite festival is held here the last weekend in September. If you need a kite, visit **Catch the Wind Kite Shop**, 266 Southeast U.S. 101, (541) 994-9500. Other popular activities include fishing and hiking. There is no day use fee.

Devils Lake State Park (Camping and Day Use)
www.oregonstateparks.org/park_216.php

If you love watersports, you'll enjoy your stay at Devils Lake, which covers 678 acres and has an average depth of 10 feet. Docks are adjacent to the campground, and boat launches in the park's day use areas are located west of the campground and across the lake in the park's East Devils Lake location. Picnicking, windsurfing, water skiing, knee boarding, jet boating, sailing, hiking and fishing are also fun activities here. The lake is home to rainbow trout, bluegill, yellow perch, catfish, black crappie, and Chinese grass carp.

Located in Lincoln City, this park is surrounded by wetlands and marshes that attract migratory geese and ducks. Bald eagles are known to nest here. There is no day use fee.

Gleneden Beach State Recreation Site (Day Use)
www.oregonstateparks.org/park_221.php

Gleneden Beach is located 7 miles south of Lincoln City off U.S. 101. This recreation area has a nice picnic area set against a backdrop of shore pines. A paved path leads to a sandy beach where surfers and boogie boarders like to catch a few waves. You may get lucky and spot sea lions playing in the surf or try your hand at fishing. If you want to rent surfing or boogie boarding gear, stop by the **Safari Town Surf Shop,** 3026 Northeast U.S. 101, Lincoln City, (541) 996-6335. There is no day use fee.

Fogarty Creek State Recreation Area (Day Use)
www.oregonstateparks.org/park_220.php

Fogarty Creek State Recreation Area is located 2 miles north of Depoe Bay off U.S. 101. Bubbling Fogarty Creek meets the sea at this scenic state park. Picnic tables are scattered across a grassy lawn that is bordered by a forest canopy of western hemlock, Sitka spruce, and shore pine. Trails cross charming footbridges over the creek and lead to the sandy beach. On the beach you'll have plenty of opportunities to watch waves crashing into offshore rocks, watch seabirds, or enjoy other beach activities, such as fishing. There is a $3.00 day use fee.

Boiler Bay State Scenic Viewpoint (Day Use)
www.oregonstateparks.org/park_213.php

Boiler Bay is located 1 mile north of Depoe Bay off U.S. 101. The viewpoint rests atop scenic rocky bluffs and has picnic tables. From here you'll more than likely see gray whales spouting in the far distance (be sure to bring your binoculars!). Another popular activity here is watching waves crash into the rocky cliffs during the winter months. There is no day use fee.

Otter Crest State Scenic Viewpoint (Day Use)
www.oregonstateparks.org/park_224.php

Otter Crest is located 10 miles north of Newport off U.S. 101. From this scenic viewpoint perched 500 feet above the ocean, you'll have spectacular views of Cape Foulweather and Devils Punchbowl, and you may also spot some gray whales. There is no day use fee.

Devils Punch Bowl State Natural Area (Day Use)
www.oregonstateparks.org/park_217.php

Located about 8 miles north of Newport, Devils Punchbowl is aptly named after its punch bowl–shaped rock formation that is thought to be the remnants of a sea cave. Waves come crashing into the rocky bowl creating a frothy white brew. This small park has picnic tables and a hiking trail that leads down to a rocky tide pool area. You have the option of heading down a set of stairs and walking south on scenic Beverly Beach. Surfers also brave the surf off the rocky shoreline. You'll have a good chance at spotting whales at this park. There is no day use fee.

Beverly Beach State Park (Camping and Day Use)
www.oregonstateparks.org/park_227.php

Beverly Beach State Park, about 7 miles north of Newport, has a large campground and day use area with picnic tables in a grassy area surrounded by coastal forest. A trail leads under the highway to a broad sandy beach. Surfers should check out the north section of the beach that promises a good break. The Oregon Coast Trail passes right through the park and if you are backpacking, you'll be happy to know that in addition to biker and horse campsites, this park has hiker campsites and showers. If you feel like a short hike, take a leisurely 0.75-mile self-guided nature trail that parallels Spencer Creek. The trail can be accessed between campsites C3 and C5. If you have kids, you may want to take them to the playground that is adjacent to campsite E9. Other popular activities include fishing, whale watching, and wildlife viewing. There is no day use fee.

Agate Beach State Recreation Site (Day Use)
www.oregonstateparks.org/park_212.php

Agate Beach is located 1 mile north of Newport off U.S. 101. This day use area

Devils Punchbowl. PHOTO: LIZANN DUNEGAN

offers picnicking and beach access and is a good clam digging and surfing beach. If you want to go surfing or boogie boarding, get local advice and gear from **Ocean Pulse Surfboards,** 429 Southwest Coast Highway, Newport, (541) 265–7745. There is no day use fee.

Yaquina Bay State Recreation Site (Day Use)
www.oregonstateparks.org/park_208.php

Yaquina Bay State Park in Newport covers 32 acres and its star attraction is the 40-foot-tall Yaquina Bay Lighthouse that was commissioned for service from 1871 to 1874. The lighthouse also has a gift shop that has books on coastal lighthouses, wildlife, and much more. Visiting hours are from 10:00 A.M. to 5:00 P.M. daily from Memorial Day through Labor Day and from noon to 4:00 P.M. the rest of the year (weather permitting). The lighthouse stands on a scenic bluff that has views of the Yaquina River and the Pacific Ocean. The park also has several picnic tables that are set among shore pine and spruce trees. There is no day use fee.

Paved trails lead to sand dunes along the north jetty. If you go north, you can walk along the beach all the way to Yaquina Head. Keep your eye out for a variety of shorebirds including sandpipers and dunlins. From the park you can also head east to Newport's bayfront where you can watch the fishing fleet or try fishing off the docks. You are also in the close vicinity of the **Oregon Coast Aquarium** and the **Hatfield Marine Science Center** that are worth visiting (see the Attractions chapter for more information).

Another area to visit is the **Yaquina Head Outstanding Natural Area** that is managed by the Bureau of Land Management (BLM), (541) 574–3100, www.or.blm.gov/salem. At this scenic stop you'll learn about the natural history of this part of the Central Coast and you'll be able to view the 93-foot **Yaquina Head Lighthouse** that was commissioned in 1873. A visitor center and hiking trails take you on a journey to tide pools, rocky beach, and grassy headlands.

The Yaquina Head Outstanding Natural Area is located 4 miles northwest of Newport off of U.S. 101. Drive north on U.S. 101 for 3 miles and turn left onto Lighthouse Drive. You'll reach the interpretive

Insiders' Tip

Watch for brown highway signs with a binocular symbol that indicate wildlife viewing areas.

center in 0.7 mile. Note there is a $5.00 entrance fee to visit this area.

South Beach State Park (Camping and Day Use)
www.oregonstateparks.org/park_209.php

South Beach State Park, which offers a long stretch of sandy beach, encompasses 434 acres and is located at the southern end of Yaquina Bay, about 2 miles south of Newport on U.S. 101. The park has a large campground with a playground. If you like to hike, be sure to check out the 1-mile Cooper Ridge Trail that can be accessed at the hiker/biker camp or at campsite C37. Cyclists may want to try the South Jetty Trail, which has a paved 10-foot-wide pedestrian/bicycle path connecting the park's day use area to South Jetty Road. Other trails lead to the beach where you can participate in all kinds of fun beach activities including beachcombing, kiteflying, and sandcastle building. Windsurfers and surfers may like the waves off this beach. If you need to rent gear, visit **Ocean Pulse Surfboards,** located at 429 Southwest Coast Highway, Newport , (541) 265-7745.

Fishing is popular off the south jetty. You may catch lingcod, sea bass, perch, and salmon. There is no day use fee at the park.

Lost Creek State Recreation Site (Day Use)
www.oregonstateparks.org/park_205.php

Lost Creek State Recreation site is located 7 miles south of Newport off U.S. 101. You'll be able to have a picnic with an ocean view as well as views of Yaquina Head and Seal Rock. From the parking area a trail leads to a long expanse of sandy beach. The Oregon Coast Trail passes

through this state park and can be hiked as a day hike or as a longer backpack trip. Other activities include kiteflying and surf fishing. There is no day use fee.

Ona Beach State Park (Day Use)
www.oregonstateparks.org/park_206.php

Covering 237 acres, 8 miles south of Newport, Ona Beach State Park offers a wide sandy beach for swimming and other recreational opportunities on Beaver Creek, which empties into the ocean at Ona Beach. Ona is a Native American word that translates to "razor clam." At one point in time these tasty clams were abundant at this beach. A boat ramp is located on the east side of the highway and allows you access for launching a canoe or kayak on the creek. Picnic sites are located along the creek in a large grassy area. While you are paddling you may spot otters, blue herons, mallard ducks, and other wildlife. There is no day use fee at the park.

Seal Rock State Recreation Site (Day Use)
www.oregonstateparks.org/park_207.php

The scenic recreation site is located atop a bluff about 10 miles south of Newport, with fantastic views of offshore rocks where you can view sea lions and seabirds. Before you begin exploring this spot, you can have lunch in the picnic area that is surrounded by shore pines and thick stands of salal. After lunch hike down a short path to explore the beach and rocky tide pools. There is no day use fee.

Driftwood Beach State Recreation Site (Day Use)
www.oregonstateparks.org/park_203.php

Located 3 miles north of Waldport, Driftwood Beach has scenic picnic spots set among pretty shore pine trees. You have direct access to a flat sandy beach that is perfect for a variety of beach activities, such as fishing. There is no day use fee.

Governor Patterson Memorial State Recreation Site (Day Use)
www.oregonstateparks.org/park_117.php

This recreation site is located along a scenic stretch of sandy beach 1 mile south of

Waldport. From the parking area you can walk north to Yaquina John Point located at the edge of Alsea Bay where you'll have a good chance of seeing seals lounging on the sandy shore. You'll also have a good chance of spotting brown pelicans flying overhead. Some windsurfers try their luck at the mouth of the bay if the wind conditions are right. You may also want to try surf fishing in this area. At the picnic area you can take a break and enjoy ocean views. If you are hiking the Oregon Coast Trail, you'll continue walking south on the beach through this recreation area toward Yachats. While you're here, be sure to visit the **Alsea Bay Bridge Historical Interpretive Center,** (541) 563-2002, located at the southern end of the Alsea Bay Bridge off U.S. 101 in Waldport. At this interpretive center, you'll learn about the history of travel routes on the Oregon Coast beginning with Indian trails and leading to road routes. There is no day use fee.

Beachside State Park (Camping and Day Use)
www.oregonstateparks.org/park_122.php

The park is located 4 miles south of Waldport on U.S. 101 right next to a wide expanse of sandy beach and is one of the few campgrounds on the Oregon Coast that has campsites with an ocean view. A bubbling creek is the dividing line between the campground and the day use area. Beach activities are the highlight here. You can fly a kite, build a sandcastle, play Frisbee or volleyball, or go beachcombing. A wealth of other activities is close by. You can try clamming or crabbing in Alsea Bay 4 miles north of the park or try fishing in the Alsea River for steelhead and salmon. You should also be sure to stop by the **Cape Perpetua Visitor Center,** (541) 547-3289, located 7 miles south off U.S. 101. At the interpretive center you'll learn about coastal ecology, coastal tides and weather, whale migration, and the Alsea tribe. You can also pick up a trail brochure and map that describes all the trails in the Cape Perpetua area. The center is open from 9:00 A.M. to 6:00 P.M. daily from May to September and from 10:00 A.M. to 4:00 P.M. on Saturday and Sunday from October through April. There is a $3.00 day use fee at Cape Perpetua. There is no day use fee for the park.

Smelt Sands State Recreation Area (Day Use)
www.oregonstateparks.org/park_128.php

This recreation area in north Yachats is well known for its annual smelt run (small silvery fish related to salmon) and is also a good whale-watching spot. At this recreation area you can also hike on the historic 804 Trail. The 0.75-mile trail starts from the parking area, takes you past two spouting horns (areas where the ocean is pushed through cracks in the lava rock and sends sprays of water into the air), and then through a wind-blown coastal ecosystem. After 0.75 mile you'll reach the beach, but if you continue hiking you'll get to Vingie Creek in another 0.8 mile, Tillicum Beach picnic area in another 2.7 miles, or, if you really feel like walking, the Governor Patterson Memorial State Recreation Site in 6.3 miles. The Oregon Coast Trail is accessible from Smelt Sands. There is no day use fee.

Yachats State Recreation Area (Day Use)
www.oregonstateparks.org/park_133.php

This recreation area is located in the heart of Yachats, it has a nice picnic area and views of the Yachats River as it meets the ocean. You can explore tide pools, watch for whales, or try your luck at fishing from this scenic spot. There is no day use fee.

> ## Insiders' Tip
> Visit the Oregon State Parks and Recreation Web site at www.oregon stateparks.org for a wealth of information about coastal state parks including maps, descriptions, camping information, reservation information, and much more.

Yachats Ocean Road State Natural Site (Day Use)
www.oregonstateparks.org/park_132.php

This scenic natural area in Yachats has many viewpoints of Yachats Bay and the Pacific Ocean. Trails give you access to the beach and tide pools. You'll also have a good chance at spotting whales. There is no day use fee.

Neptune State Scenic Viewpoint (Day Use)
www.oregonstateparks.org/park_126.php

Neptune State Scenic Viewpoint covers 302 acres and is located adjacent to the Cummins Creek Wilderness 3 miles south of Yachats. Cummins Creek meets the ocean here and hiking trails offer beach access from both sides of this stream. If you hike south on the beach, you can explore the rocky shore and tide pools. You'll also have good opportunities to see whales and other sea mammals here. Other activities include picnicking, fishing, and windsurfing. If you want to hike a strenuous 8.5-mile loop to the Cape Perpetua Visitor Center from Neptune, you can hook up with the Cummins Creek Trailhead that is located east of U.S. 101 and follow the Cummins Creek Trail to the Cooks Ridge Trail to the visitor center. From the visitor center, you can access the Oregon Coast Trail to return to your starting point. There is no day use fee.

Stonefield Beach State Recreation Site
www.oregonstateparks.org/park_130.php

You can enjoy beach activities and watching for wildlife on this uncrowded beach just south of Yachats. There is no day use fee.

Muriel O. Ponsler Memorial State Scenic Viewpoint (Day Use)
www.oregonstateparks.org/park_125.php

This scenic viewpoint, located 16 miles north of Florence on U.S. 101, has access to 5 miles of wide sandy beach that is a great stop for all kinds of beach activities including windsurfing and fishing. This is also a good spot to watch for whales. There is no day use fee.

Carl G. Washburne Memorial State Park (Camping and Day Use)
www.oregonstateparks.org/park_123.php

One of the highlights of this park, located 12.5 miles north of Florence, is a 6-mile out-and-back hike to Heceta Head Lighthouse from the campground. You'll begin this hike on the Valley Trail that is located before the pay station to the campground. The trail follows China Creek and then leads you to an open, grassy meadow where you may get to see some Roosevelt elk. The trail then takes you through a boggy area, and then you'll reach U.S. 101. Cross the highway and continue your adventure by turning onto Hobbit Trail. You'll hike for a short way on this trail and then come to a trail junction. Turn left onto the Heceta Head Trail that will take you to the Heceta Head Lighthouse. Once you reach the lighthouse, you can watch for seabirds nesting in the high cliffs surrounding the lighthouse. If you aren't up for such a long hiking adventure, you can hike 0.5 mile to the beach and enjoy beach activities, such as fishing. The Beach trail can be accessed between campsites B40 and B42. There is no day use fee.

Heceta Head Lighthouse State Scenic Viewpoint (Day Use)
www.oregonstateparks.org/park_124.php

The Heceta Head Lighthouse State Scenic Viewpoint is located 12 miles north of Florence and 14 miles south of Yachats off U.S. 101. The 56-foot lighthouse was commissioned in 1894 and it rests on a rocky headland 205 feet above the ocean. Adjacent to the lighthouse is the Heceta House, the original light keeper's house that was built in 1893 and now is operated as a bed-and-breakfast. To reach the lighthouse you can take a gravel path from the parking lot and walk 0.5 mile through a thick coastal cedar and fir forest dotted with sword fern, wild iris, and salal. You'll also enjoy the view of the rocky shore and the Cape Creek Bridge from the picnic tables along the path. From the lighthouse you'll have great views of puffins, cormorants, and other seabirds nesting on the offshore cliffs. You can also hike to the beach and enjoy exploring tide pools and other beach activities. You can hike to Carl G. Washburne State Park from the lighthouse on the Heceta Head Trail. Tours of the lighthouse are given daily from 11:00 A.M. to 5:00 P.M. Memorial Day through Labor Day. There is a $3.00 day use fee at the viewpoint.

Darlingtonia State Natural Site (Day Use)
www.oregonstateparks.org/park_115.php

When you stop at this 18-acre state natural site, located 5 miles north of Florence, you'll be able to take a short walk on a boardwalk through a bog to view the interesting insect-eating plant *Darlingtonia californica.* This hungry plant traps flies and other insects into its tubelike opening and then digests the insects to get much-needed nutrients. After you take your tour, you can eat your lunch at the picnic area in a shady forest setting. There is no day use fee.

Jessie M. Honeyman Memorial State Park (Camping and Day Use)
www.oregonstateparks.org/

Jessie M. Honeyman has something to offer everyone. Located 3 miles south of Florence on U.S. 101, this popular state park is next to scenic sand dunes and also provides camping and access to 82-acre Cleawox Lake and 350-acre Woahink Lake. These lakes offer all kinds of water activities, including swimming, boating, water-skiing, and fishing. Boat ramps and picnic sites are available on both lakes. Windsurfers may want to try these lakes. Canoeing and kayaking are other fun activities.

Or you can hike on one of the park's many hiking trails. A 0.5-mile trail takes you from the Cleawox Lake picnic areas to the shore of Lily Lake that is bordered by colorful rhododendrons. A second nature trail connects the Cleawox day use area with the group camp on Woahink Lake. To reach the beach you'll have to hike over 2 miles of dunes from the Cleawox area. There is a $3.00 day use fee at the park.

Bolon Island Tideways State Scenic Corridor (Day Use)
www.oregonstateparks.org/park_114.php

This scenic spot 5 miles north of Reedsport has a hiking trail that takes you on a

Insiders' Tip

To be sure you're prepared for all kinds of coastal adventures, keep a day pack in your car with the following essentials: water, snacks, camera and extra film, sunscreen, sunglasses, hat, comfortable walking shoes or boots, extra pair of sandals for wading through creeks or playing in the surf, rain jacket, fleece jacket or some kind of insulating layer, beach toys (Frisbee, volleyball, kite), and towel.

tour of the island. On this trail you'll have a good chance at spotting a variety of birds. You'll also have a scenic view of the Umpqua River. There is no day use fee.

Umpqua Lighthouse State Park (Camping and Day Use)
www.oregonstateparks.org/park_121.php

This state park, about 5 miles north of Reedsport, has a campground and day use area that is centered on scenic Lake Marie and hilly sand dunes. Lake Marie offers fishing and nonmotorized boating, making canoeing and kayaking a popular activity. Canoeists and kayakers enjoy exploring the mouth of the nearby Umpqua River where different species of birds can be observed. Swimmers like the small sandy beach that provides good access to the lake. If you want to look for whales, check out the whale-viewing platform located just north of the lake—this viewpoint has interpretive signs that fill you in on the migration and feeding patterns of gray whales. If you feel like a short hike you can walk on one of three paths from the campground that take you to the 1.4-mile lakeshore loop. A short trail leads off the lakeshore loop to a viewpoint of the sand dunes. If you are feeling ambitious, you can hike over the dunes to the beach.

The other highlight of this area is the 65-foot Umpqua River Lighthouse. The lighthouse is within walking distance of the state park and you can tour the lighthouse May 1 through September 30. Call Douglas County Parks, (541) 271-4631, for the current tour schedule. There is no day use fee.

South Coast

William M. Tugman State Park (Camping and Day Use)
www.oregonstateparks.org/park_98.php

This state park and campground is located 8 miles south of Reedsport on U.S. 101, next to 350-acre Eel Lake, which supports healthy populations of black crappie, cutthroat trout, rainbow trout, largemouth bass, and brown bullhead. The lake has a boat ramp as well as a fishing dock set up for anglers with disabilities. Windsurfing, canoeing, and kayaking are also popular here. If you like to picnic, you'll like this state park's large, grassy lawns with facilities set against a backdrop of shore pines and other coastal forest vegetation. If you're a hiker, you'll enjoy exploring a trail that leads around the south end of the lake where you might see ospreys, eagles, and black-tailed deer. Other activities include swimming and bicycling. There is no day use fee.

Sunset Bay State Park (Camping and Day Use)
www.oregonstateparks.org/park_100.php

Sunset State Park is nestled in a scenic cove between sandstone cliffs 12 miles southwest of Coos Bay. The campground here is located on the east side of the highway, and Big Creek meanders through it, which may explain its popularity. Day use facilities along the bays have picnic tables set on a grassy expanse of lawn. Beach lovers have access to a sandy beach and there are also facilities to launch boats.

From the day use picnic area, you can hook up with the Oregon Coast Trail and hike south to Shore Acres State Park and Cape Arago State Park. You'll reach Shore Acres State Park in a little over 2 miles. Along the way, you'll have spectacular views of the 44-foot Cape Arago Lighthouse, which was commissioned in 1934. After approximately 4.5 miles you'll reach Cape Arago State Park. There is no day use fee at the park.

Shore Acres State Park (Day Use)
www.oregonstateparks.org/park_97.php

Shore Acres State Park, located on a high bluff above the Pacific Ocean about 13 miles southwest of Coos Bay, was once the private estate of lumberman and ship builder Louis B. Simpson. He built a summer home here that boasted three stories, a ballroom, and a heated indoor swimming pool. He also cultivated five acres of formal gardens.

You can tour the grounds that contain two spectacular rose gardens, a Japanese garden with a lily pond, and other formal flower gardens. During December, the gardens are festooned with colored lights and holiday decorations. Different flowers are planted at different times of year for a garden that blooms almost year-round. Peak blooming time for bulbs and daffodils is late February through March; the tulips open late March through April; rhododendrons and azaleas flower from April through mid-May; annuals and perennials are the attraction from May through September and roses from June through September; and dahlias bloom August through mid-October. The gift store and information center are situated at the entrance to the gardens. The Friends of Shore Acres State Park sponsor a variety of horticultural and cultural events here throughout the year.

In addition to the gardens, you'll find an observation building perched atop a rugged bluff. From this point you'll have spectacular views of the waves crashing into the sandstone cliffs and you'll also have the opportunity to spot whales from December through June. You'll have access to the Oregon Coast Trail and Simpson Beach, where you can participate in all kinds of beach activities. The day use fee is $3.00.

Cape Arago State Park
www.oregonstateparks.org/park_94.php

Cape Arago State Park is located 14 miles southwest of Coos Bay on a rocky headland that rises 200 feet above the Pacific. Picnic tables are located on scenic viewpoints along the bluff offering good opportunities for whale watching and for spotting nesting seabirds in the spring months. Simpson Reef is located off this cape and is the home of seals and sea lions. You can access the beach at North, Middle, and South coves. Note that North Cove is closed March 1 to June 30 while sea lions are birthing and raising their pups. South Cove has numerous tide pools that are fun to explore. A 4.5-mile section of the Oregon Coast Trail links this park to Shore Acres State Park and Sunset Bay State Park (located to the north). There is no day use fee.

Seven Devils State Recreation Site (Day Use)
www.oregonstateparks.org/park_69.php

Located 7 miles north of Bandon, the Seven Devils recreation area has a picnic area adjacent to Merchants Beach where you can participate in all kinds of activities, such as fishing, beachcombing, kite-flying, and sandcastle building. There is no day use fee.

Bullards Beach State Park (Camping and Day Use)
www.oregonstateparks.org/park_71.php

Bullards Beach State Park, located 2 miles north of Bandon, has a campground with hiker/biker campsites as well as horse campsites and also a 7-mile equestrian trail. The park is sandwiched between the Coquille River and the Pacific. A 1.5-mile trail gives hikers and bikers access from the campground to the beach where you can participate in all kinds of beach activities. Another 3-mile trail takes you to the North Jetty that is home to the historic Coquille River Lighthouse, built in 1896. Memorial Day through Labor Day you'll find interpreters who will tell you about the lighthouse's history. You can fish in the Coquille River for steelhead, coho, and chinook salmon. Kayakers will also enjoy exploring the estuary at the mouth of the Coquille River, which has been designated as the Bandon Marsh National Wildlife Refuge. If you need to rent kayaks and gear, visit **Adventure Kayak,** 315 First Street, Bandon, (541) 347–3480, http://adventurekayak.com. The park has a boat launch and access to the Oregon Coast Trail. There is no day use fee.

Face Rock State Scenic Viewpoint (Day Use)
www.oregonstateparks.org/park_66.php

This park is located 1 mile southwest of Bandon off U.S. 101. Here you'll have wonderful views of Face Rock and a series of pointed sea stacks. You'll also be able to take a trail to the beach where you can explore tide pools and participate in other beach activities, such as fishing. If you are looking for a longer hike, you can trek 3 miles north on the beach to downtown Bandon. There is no day use fee.

Bandon State Natural Area (Day Use)
www.oregonstateparks.org/park_64.php

This park has several access points off of U.S. 101 from 1 to 5 miles south of Bandon. The first access point is a viewpoint overlooking Face Rock. The face on this rock is supposed to represent Ewauna the daughter of Chief Siskiyou. You'll also be able to see a series of sea stacks that are part of the National Wildlife Refuge System. From here a trail leads down to the beach and to a picnic area with tables.

If you continue south on U.S. 101, the next access point is the Devil's Kitchen area. Hiking trails lead to the beach and a picnic area next to a pretty creek. Continuing south on U.S. 101, you'll come to two more access points, that feature beach access but do not have picnic or rest room facilities. There is no day use fee at these areas.

Boice Cope County Park (Camping and Day Use)

Located 2 miles south of Langlois on U.S. 101, Boice Cope County Park features a campground at Floras Lake with 22 paved spaces with water but no hookups. There are also 12 tent sites. Rest rooms and showers are available. You cannot reserve these sites; they are first come first served. Rates are $16 per night. On summer weekends this park fills up fast, and you'll have the best luck finding a camping site during the middle of the week. Floras Lake is popular with windsurfers due to its warm temperature, sandy bottom, and strong 15 to 25 mph northwest winds. You can rent windsurfing gear and take lessons March through mid-October from **Floras Lake Windsurfing,** which is owned by the same people who run **Floras Lake House by the Sea Bed and Breakfast,** 92870 Boice Cope Road, Langlois, (541) 348-2573, www.floras lake.com. You can take a beginning lesson that includes equipment, wet suit, booties, and instruction for $60 per person. A private lesson will cost you $65. If you just want to rent gear, rates for a board, boom, sail, and mast run $20 per hour, $40 for a half day, and $50 per day. You can also rent a wet suit and booties for $15.00 per day or $5.00 per hour. Sea kayak rentals are also available. There is no day use fee at the park.

Floras Lake State Park (Day Use)
www.oregonstateparks.org

Located about 7 miles north of Port Orford, Floras Lake State Park is wild and undeveloped. The 1,371-acre park encompasses 2.5 miles of ocean, including Blacklock Point, and also includes the west side of Floras Lake. Wild rhododendrons and salal thrive here along with wild blueberries and huckleberries. If you want to explore this area, you can start hiking on a dirt road that is located to the left of the gated entrance to the airport You'll hike through hardy coastal forest. After 0.8 mile cross a creek and turn left at the trail junction. Follow the Oregon Coast Trail marker signs at the next three junctions and you'll arrive at Blacklock Point in a little over a mile. To reach the beach, which is filled with driftwood logs and huge boulders, stay to the left and navigate your way down—note this can be a bit tricky There are other trail options that take you to Floras Lake—but be forewarned that the trails are not maintained and the intersections are confusing. There is no day use fee at the park.

Cape Blanco State Park (Camping and Day Use)
www.oregonstateparks.org/park_62.php

Cape Blanco State Park is host to large campsites protected from the coastal wind by sheltering trees and a thick understory of salal, salmonberry, and thimbleberry. The Oregon Coast Trail can be accessed from the south end of the campground. Additional hiking trails lead to several viewpoints and the beach. Horse owners will love exploring a series of horse trail loops that take you through coastal forest and to the beach. A 150-acre area is also designated as an open riding area. Photographers and wildlife lovers will enjoy the natural beauty of this park with its high chalky bluffs, black sand beach, and offshore sea stacks, which are home to herds of sea lions and prime nesting sites for seabirds. From this campground, you have access to the Elk and Sixes Rivers, which offer good fishing. A boat ramp is present on the Sixes River if you want to launch your boat. If you're a history buff, don't miss exploring the 59-foot Cape Blanco Lighthouse, which is the oldest lighthouse in Oregon. Another historical structure at this state park is the Hughes House Museum built in 1898 by Patrick Hughes.

Insiders' Tip

Visit Fish Mill Lodges & RV Park, 4844 Fish Mill Way, Westlake, (541) 997-2511, to rent a boat and stock up on fishing supplies or to rent a cottage that is close by this prime fishing scene of Siltcoos Lake. To get there from Florence, drive 5.5 miles south of Florence on U.S. Highway 101, turn east between milepost 196 and 197, and follow the signs a quarter of a mile to the resort.

Western Snowy Plovers

The Pacific Coast breeding colonies of western snowy plovers can be found from southern Washington to Baja California. Snowy plovers are sparrow-sized birds with a dusty, sand-colored back and a white underside with a black chest band. They like to nest in open, sandy areas next to the water, where they usually lay two to three greenish brown eggs in a sandy depression above the beach. The nesting season is from mid-March through mid-September. In 2001, 110 nesting adults were counted along the Southern Oregon Coast. Out of 110 nests, only 34 were successful, producing 94 hatchlings. Sturdy areas include Necanicum Spit, Bayocean Spit, Sutton Beach, Siltcoos, Dunes Overlook, Takenitch, Tenmile, Coos Bay north Spit, Bandon State Natural Area, New River, and Floras Lake.

The snowy plover's rapid decline is due to several factors. The encroachment of European beach grass has caused a large amount of habitat loss. The grass stabilizes dunes and reduces the amount of unvegetated area above the tide line, making the sandy beach narrower and steeper and ultimately rendering the nesting area less suitable for the birds. Predators are one of the main reasons for the decline in snowy plover populations. Major predators include gulls, crows, ravens, skunks, dogs, cats, coyotes, foxes, opossums, raccoons, hawks, and owls. The most controllable factor is human impact on nesting habitat. Off-road vehicle use, loose dogs, walking and running on the beach, and beach raking have all taken their toll.

Unfortunately, the nesting season for the snowy plover coincides with the highest traffic of beachgoers. Measures have been introduced to help protect this tiny bird. Nesting sites are now fenced off, thereby minimizing human impact, and nest enclosures have been introduced to protect the birds from predators. After you reach the beach, keep a lookout for these quick birds as they run up and down the beach feeding on crabs, marine worms, beetles, sand hoppers, shore flies, and other insects.

This 11-room, two-story Victorian-style mansion was built out of old-growth Port Orford cedar at a cost of $3,800. It's open for tours during the summer and is filled with delightful antique furniture and old photos depicting the life of the former 1,000-acre dairy ranch that the house sits on. There is no day use fee at the park.

Port Orford Heads State Park (Day Use)
www.oregonstateparks.org/park_61.php

Port Orford Heads State Park in Port Orford features a wind-sheltered picnic area adjacent to the historic Port Orford Heads United States Coast Guard Lifeboat Station that was decommissioned in 1939. A 0.3-mile path takes you to a scenic viewpoint. There is no day use fee.

Humbug Mountain State Park (Camping and Day Use)
www.oregonstateparks.org/park_56.php

The centerpiece of Humbug Mountain State Park, located 6 miles south of Port Orford, is 1,761-foot Humbug Mountain, which is the highest point on the coast. A 5.5-mile strenuous loop hike takes you to the summit of this mountain from the campground. To reach the trailhead from the campground, cross a bridge over Brush Creek and then proceed through the tunnel under U.S. 101. The trail passes through maple and myrtle trees and then leads you through sections of old-growth Douglas fir. You'll come to a junction in about a mile that is the start of the loop portion of the trail. If you go to the right, you'll come to a viewpoint. Looking north you'll see Redfish Rocks, Port Orford, and Cape Blanco. Keep following the trail as it loops back around to rejoin the main trail. At this junction, you can hike up a short, steep trail that leads to a viewpoint looking south toward Gold Beach. Another hiking trail worth exploring is part of the Oregon Coast Trail. Start on this section of the Oregon Coast Trail by walking east in the campground and watching for the 2.5-mile signed Recreation Trail. The trail follows the old highway to where it ends at U.S. 101 just south of Rocky Point. You can reach the beach by walking on a trail that begins near campsite C7. On the beach you may see windsurfers braving the offshore break. There is no day use fee at the park.

Geisel Monument State Heritage Site (Day Use)
www.oregonstateparks.org/park_55.php

This historic site, located 7 miles north of Gold Beach, has interpretive signs that give details about the Rogue Indian war skirmish that took place here. If you are traveling along the South Coast, this is a perfect spot to take a break, have a picnic, and learn about this area's colorful history. There is no day use fee.

Otter Point State Recreation Site (Day Use)
www.oregonstateparks.org/park_58.php

At this recreation site, 4 miles north of Gold Beach, you'll have the opportunity to hike on different trails that have spectacular views of sandstone rock formations. You'll also have access to the beach where you can enjoy all kinds of beach activities. There is no day use fee.

Cape Sebastian State Scenic Corridor (Day Use)
www.oregonstateparks.org/park_73.php

Located 7 miles south of gold Beach, this recreation area has two parking areas with scenic viewpoints that are located on bluffs 200 feet above the ocean. From the south parking area you can see Humbug Mountain 43 miles to the north and Crescent City 50 miles to the south. A hiking trail leads you 1.5 miles out to the tip of Cape Sebastian through a thick Sitka spruce for-

est. From the tip of the cape you'll have a good chance at spotting migrating gray whales from December through June. Beach access and fishing are also available. There is no day use fee.

Pistol River State Scenic Viewpoint (Day Use)
www.oregonstateparks.org/park_76.php

Pistol River is located 11 miles south of Gold Beach on U.S. 101. At the north parking area you'll have access to Myers Beach, which is strewn with huge boulders, making it a very scenic spot. From the south parking area, you'll see the Pistol River carving its way to the Pacific through a series of sand dunes. Bring your binoculars to spot birds in the estuary. Windsurfing is very popular in this park and the conditions are so good that national championships have been held here. Horseback riders will love riding on the beach. There is no day use fee.

Samuel H. Boardman State Scenic Corridor (Day Use)
www.oregonstateparks.org/park_77.php

This scenic corridor covers 1,471 acres and stretches from Burnt Hill Creek 11 miles south. The coastline here is rugged and wild and filled with offshore rocks and sea stacks, secluded sandy beaches, and wild coastal headlands. The first access point is Lone Ranch, located 4 miles north of Brookings. Lone Ranch has scenic picnic sites and rest rooms adjacent to the beach. A hike that should not be missed is a 7-mile section of the Oregon Coast Trail that begins at the Cape Ferrelo parking area just north of Lone Ranch off U.S. 101. The trail begins in the northwest corner of the parking area and takes you 1.5 miles through a coastal forest to the House

Insiders' Tip
The following state parks have horse camping sites: Nehalem Bay, Bullards Beach, and Cape Blanco.

Rock Viewpoint, which can also be accessed from U.S. 101. From this point you'll have a good chance of spotting migrating whales and a variety of seabirds. Continue walking north on the trail through a spruce-filled forest. The trail eventually begins a steep descent through an open, grassy area to the sandy beach. You'll walk 1.5 miles on the beach to Whalehead Cove, which is the next developed access point off U.S. 101. From here you'll be able to see Whalehead Island, which is just offshore. This area has picnic sites and rest rooms. As you continue walking, look for the Oregon Coast Trail marker that is located off a side road leading toward U.S. 101. On this section of the trail you'll hike up a headland to a scenic viewpoint. After a mile you'll reach Indian Sands, another access viewpoint off U.S. 101. Shore pines dominate the scene in this area. You can also see a Native American midden (a pile of shells and bones leftover from meals) at this spot. If you continue north on the trail, you'll wind around headlands that offer more outstanding vistas. After Indian Sands there are many more viewpoints off U.S. 101 as you continue north. Plan on spending the day exploring this park—you won't be disappointed. There is no day use fee.

Alfred A. Loeb State Park (Camping and Day Use)

www.oregonstateparks.org/park_72.php

This park is located adjacent to the salmon-rich Chetco River, 7.5 miles east of Brookings, and is the starting point for two self-guided nature walks. The 0.7-mile River View Trail takes you along the banks of the scenic Chetco River through an old grove of myrtle trees, and the 1.2-mile Redwood Nature Trail loops you through a grove of immense 300- to 800-year old coastal redwood trees. The River View Trail can be accessed from the picnic area adjacent to the campground. Be sure to pick up an interpretive brochure that corresponds to numbered trail markers along this nature trail. You'll hike on this trail for 0.7

mile and cross a paved road where you'll begin the 1.2-mile Redwood Nature Trail. If you are visiting this area for a few days, you can camp at this state park (see the South Coast section in the Camping chapter for more information). There is also excellent swimming holes on the Chetco River and great fishing opportunities abound in Chetco River and ocean fishing is available out of Brookings Harbor (see the Fishing, Clamming, and Crabbing section in the Sports and Activities chapter for recommended outfitters in the Brookings area). There is no day use fee at the park.

Harris Beach State Park (Camping and Day Use)

www.oregonstateparks.org/park_79.php

The campground in this state park is located in a wooded area bordered with bright azaleas 2 miles north of Brookings. Wildlife watching and beachcombing are favorite activities at this state park. You can look for seabirds nesting on Bird Island and also watch for whales offshore during their semiannual migration. Walk along the sandy beach and admire the rocky coastline and look for sea lions and harbor seals on the offshore rocks. If you have a bicycle, you'll want to try the park's scenic bike path. There is no day use fee.

Sports and Activities

This chapter covers a variety of activities that you can enjoy on the Oregon Coast. You can cycle on the Oregon Coast Route; hike on shady forest trails to view scenic waterfalls; kayak quiet creeks, bays, and lakes; and go horseback riding on the beach. It also lists surfing and windsurfing hot spots; fishing, clamming, and crabbing opportunities; and outfitters that offer whale-watching and fishing trips, jet boat tours, and dune buggy rides.

ATV and Dune Buggy Rentals and Tours

Sandland Adventures
85366 U.S. Highway 101, Florence
(541) 759-3313

Located 1 mile south of Florence on U.S. Highway 101, Sandland Adventures offers all kinds of family fun including go-carts, bumper boats, miniature golf, ATV rentals, and dune tours. Up to five people can take a sand rail tour for $12 per person for a 30-minute tour. It costs $17 per person for a 60-minute tour of the beach and dunes (half-hour tours have a $36 minimum and one-hour tours have a $55 minimum). A sandrail tour is like taking a ride in a tour bus but instead it is a dune buggy outfitted with seats for several people—a tour leader takes a large group on a scenic tour of the dunes and beach. All you have to do is sit back, relax, and enjoy the scenery. For large groups (up to 27 people) who want to tour the dunes at a slower pace, the rate is $10 per person. ATV rentals range in price from $35 to $40 per hour. Sandland Adventures is open from 9:00 A.M. to 5:00 P.M. during the winter months and 9:00 A.M. to dusk in the summer months.

Spinreel Dunebuggy Rentals, Inc.
67045 Spinreel Road, North Bend
(541) 759-3313
www.spinreel.com

Located next to the Oregon Dunes National Recreational Area, Spinreel Dunebuggy Rentals offers ATV rentals

for $30 for one hour, $95 for a half day, and $155 for a full day. Dune buggy tours across the scenic dunes and to the beach range in price from $15 to $55 per hour. Hours are 9:00 A.M. to 6:00 P.M. during the winter and 9:00 A.M. to dusk during the summer months.

Bicycling

The Oregon Coast Bike Route
355 Capitol Street NE, Room 210, Salem
(503) 986-3556
www.odot.state.or.us/techserv/bikewalk/ocbr.htm

Traveling from north to south, the Oregon Coast Bike Route covers 368 miles (378 miles if you opt to ride on the Three Capes Scenic Loop) following U.S. 101 beginning in Astoria and ending in Brookings. Most cyclists can complete the route in six to eight days by cycling 50 to 65 miles per day. The Oregon Department of Transportation recommends that you travel the route from north to south from May through October due to prevailing winds that blow from the northwest. This ride offers stunning ocean views, scenic beaches, and great camping facilities. However, it also has heavy car and truck traffic during the summer season, steep ascents and descents, and many narrow, dangerous sections. You can obtain a free map of the Oregon Coast Bike Route by writing or calling the address above or visiting their Web site. If you would like to take day trips along this route, here are some suggestions:

• Astoria Bridge to Nehalem Bay State Park (44 miles)
• Nehalem Bay State Park to Cape Lookout State Park (48 miles)
• Cape Lookout State Park to Beverly Beach State Park (57.5 miles)
• Beverly Beach State Park to Jessie M. Honeyman Memorial State Park (60.3 miles)
• Jessie M. Honeyman Memorial State Park to Sunset Bay State Park (54.9 miles)
• Sunset Bay State Park to Humbug Mountain State Park (57 miles)
• Humbug Mountain State Park to the California border (56 miles)

Bike Shops

Prom Bike Shop
622 12th Avenue, Seaside
(503) 738–8251
You can rent a variety of bikes from the Prom Bike Shop, including surreys that two to four people can ride. A variety of other fun beach mobiles are also available. The bike shop is open from 10:00 A.M. to 6:00 P.M. daily.

Mike's Bike Shop
248 North Spruce Street, Cannon Beach
(503) 436–1266
Mike's Bike Shop offers bike rentals for those wanting to ride on the beach and trails around Cannon Beach. You can rent a three-wheel recumbent bike popular for beach cruising, a one-speed beach cruiser, or a mountain bike. The shop is open from 10:00 A.M. to 5:30 P.M. Thursday through Monday.

The Bike Shop
223 Northwest Nye Street, Newport
(541) 265–7824
This bike shop sells and rents mountain bikes and also carries cycling accessories and equipment. Call for hours and rental information.

Bicycles 101
1537 8th Street, Florence
(541) 997–5717
This friendly shop will help you find some of the best biking routes on the South

Insiders' Tip
The following state parks have paved bike paths: Fort Stevens State Park, Nehalem Bay State Park, and South Beach State Park.

Coast. They rent and sell road and mountain bikes.

Mountain Bike Trails

Neahkahnie Mountain (Moderate)
Getting There: Drive 9 miles south of Cannon Beach on U.S. 101 to Oswald West State Park campground located on the right side of the road.
Length: 8.6 miles (out and back)
Ride south out of the parking lot on U.S. 101. Ride 2.7 miles on the highway and then turn left onto Road 38555 and begin a steep climb up a double-track dirt road. Ride 1.6 miles on this road to where the road intersects with a hiking trail. This is where the bike ride ends and you can opt to hike 0.4 mile to the summit of 1,631-foot Neahkahnie Mountain.

Cummins Creek Loop (Difficult)
Getting There: Drive 28 miles south of Newport on U.S. 101. Turn left and drive to the Cape Perpetua Visitor's Center parking area.
Length: 10.4-mile loop
From the parking area ride back out to U.S. 101 and turn right (north). Ride 0.5 mile on U.S. 101 to the intersection with Forest Service Road 55. Take a right onto Forest Service Road 55 and ascend steeply for 4 miles to a gravel parking area on the right side of the road at the Cooks Ridge Trailhead. Turn onto this trail and ride for 0.2 mile to a trail junction. Turn left at this junction onto the Cummins Creek Trail. Ride about 0.5 mile and turn left at the next trail junction. At the next junction stay to the right and continue to follow the Cummins Creek Trail. After approximately

Bicycling the State Parks

These state park campgrounds have hiker/biker campsites, which charge $4.00 a night for you and your two-wheel steed. We've listed the state parks from north to south and also directions on how to get there:

Fort Stevens—From U.S. 101/Highway 30 in Astoria drive south on U.S. 101 for approximately 2.5 miles and turn right (west) onto East Harbor Drive. Proceed about 4.5 miles on East Harbor to Hammond. From Hammond drive south about a mile on Lake Drive to the state park.

Nehalem Bay—From Manzanita go 3 miles south on U.S. 101 to Carey Street. Turn west onto Carey Street and head 1.5 miles to the park.

Cape Lookout—From Tillamook go 12 miles southwest on Netarts Highway (Three Capes Scenic Loop) to the entrance to the state park.

Devils Lake—You can access Devils Lake State Park by turning east from U.S. 101 in Lincoln City onto Northeast 6th Street and proceeding 0.1 mile to the campground.

Beverly Beach—From Newport go 7 miles north on U.S. 101 to the park entrance.

South Beach—From Newport go 2 miles south on U.S. 101 to the park entrance.

Beachside—Go 4 miles south of Waldport on U.S. 101 to the park entrance.

Carl G. Washburne—From Florence go 12.5 miles north on U.S. 101 to the park entrance.

Jessie M. Honeyman—From Florence go 3 miles south on U.S. 101 to the park entrance.

William M. Tugman—From Reedsport go 8 miles south on U.S. 101 to the park entrance.

Bullards Beach—From Coos Bay drive approximately 22 miles south on U.S. 101 to the park entrance located on the west (right) side of the road. If you are in Bandon, the park is 2 miles north on the left (west) side of U.S. 101.

Sunset Bay—From U.S. 101 in Coos Bay, follow the signs to Charleston Harbor and Ocean Beaches and drive on the Cape Arago Highway 12 miles southwest to Sunset Bay State Park.

Cape Blanco—To reach Cape Blanco State Park, go 46 miles south of Coos Bay or 4 miles north of Port Orford on U.S. 101 to the junction with Cape Blanco Road. Turn west and go 5 miles on Cape Blanco Road to Cape Blanco State Park.

Humbug Mountain—From Port Orford go 6 miles south on U.S. 101 to the park entrance on the left (east) side of the highway.

Harris Beach—From Brookings go 2 miles north on U.S. 101 to the park entrance located on the left (west) side of the highway.

8.5 miles the trail intersects with a paved road. Follow the paved road back to U.S. 101 where you'll turn right (north) and head back to your car at the visitor center.

Siltcoos Lake Trail (Moderate)
Getting There: Drive 7 miles south of Florence on U.S. 101 and turn left at the Siltcoos Lake Trail sign. If you are coming from Reedsport, drive 13 miles north on U.S. 101 to the Siltcoos Lake Trail sign.
Length: 4.5-mile loop

This short, fun loop trail takes you by the shore of Siltcoos Lake and has short, intense hills. The trail starts at the Siltcoos Lake Trailhead sign adjacent to the parking lot.

Canoeing and Kayaking

Many coastal bays and rivers offer great kayaking and canoeing opportunities. We recommend calling one of the outfitters listed below to rent gear and get advice on where to spend the day on the water.

Nehalem Bay Kayak Company
395 U.S. Highway 101, Wheeler
(503) 368–6055
www.nbkayak.com
Nehalem Bay Kayak Company rents kayaks for $40 a day. They also offer lessons and lead tours. Call for rates and times.

Blue Heron Landing
4006 West Devils Lake Road, Lincoln City
(541) 994–4708
You can rent a canoe from Blue Heron Landing and paddle around scenic Devils Lake. Canoe rentals are available March through September.

Central Coast Water Sports
1901 U.S. Highway 101, Florence
(541) 997–1812, (800) 789–3483
Central Coast Water Sports rents all kinds of water gear to maximize your fun. Scuba equipment, canoes, kayaks, ocean kayaks (sit on top style), wet suits, surfboards, and boogie boards. Call for hours and rental information.

Adventure Kayak
315 1st Street, Bandon
(541) 347–3480
http://adventurekayak.com
Adventure Kayak, located adjacent to the scenic Coquille River and the Bandon Marsh National Wildlife Refuge, offers sea kayak rentals, classes, and tours. You can rent a double sea kayak for $30 for two hours or a single sea kayak for $24 for two hours. Full-day rates are $45 for a single sea kayak and $60 for a double. Adventure Kayak also sells new kayaks, kayaking accessories and equipment, kayaking books and videos, T-shirts, hats, and much more. Business hours during the winter months are Monday through Saturday 10:00 A.M. to 5:00 P.M. and Sunday 10:00 A.M. to 4:00 P.M. with extended hours in the summer months.

Fishing

Fresh coastal lakes interspersed amongst sand dunes and burgeoning coastal forest produce prize-winning largemouth bass, bluegill, black crappie, and yellow perch. Coffenbury Lake, located at Fort Stevens State Park, is stocked with rainbow trout and steelhead. Other species that are fun to catch are the brown bullhead and panfish that thrive in Cullaby Lake, located 4 miles north of Gearhart. Siltcoos, Takenitch, Sutton, and Woahink Lakes are only a small sample of the freshwater lakes that offer dozens of angling opportunities. See the Freshwater Lakes section in this chapter for information about these lakes and many more.

More than a dozen coastal rivers rush to the Pacific Ocean from the Coast Range and each has its own secret fishing holes and runs of wild and hatchery-raised salmon and steelhead. Even though wild salmon and steelhead runs in coastal rivers and streams have been on a rapid decline for many years, you can still find some good salmon, steelhead, and trout fishing holes. See the Bays, Rivers, and Streams section for detailed information about individual rivers and streams.

Sturgeon is a good catch in coastal bays and rivers. This ancient fish species is caught from an anchored boat with bait cast to the bottom of the river. Strong sturgeon fisheries can be found in the Lower Columbia River and Winchester Bay. Spring and summer are the best seasons to catch these fish, although the season is open year-round.

If you like to surf fish, you can catch perch, rockfish, and greenling off many of coastal beaches and jetties. See the Bays, Rivers, and Streams section of this chapter for information about jetty fishing hot spots.

Bottom fishing on the Oregon Coast produces healthy catches of halibut, cabezon, lingcod, red snapper, and sea bass. Late summer is also the time albacore tuna are running offshore and you can catch these feisty fish by renting a charter boat (see the Ocean Charters and River Outfitters section). Also keep in mind that most fishing charters also offer whale-watching tours. See the Ocean Charters and River Outfitters section for details on individual outfitters and guide services in each area. Popular bottom fishing and deep-sea fishing hot spots along the coastline include the Lower Columbia River, Nehalem Bay, Garibaldi, Netarts Bay, Nestucca Bay, Depoe Bay, Newport Harbor, Waldport, Florence, Winchester Bay, Charleston, Bandon, and Brookings Harbor.

North Coast

Freshwater Lakes

Cape Meares Lake

Cape Meares Lake covers 90 acres and is known for its fun catches of rainbow trout, bass, bluegill, and an occasional steelhead. The lake has an average depth of about 10 feet and can be filled with an excess of aquatic plants, especially around its perimeter, in the warmer months of the year. The lake is located approximately 10 miles northwest of Tillamook off of Bayocean Road.

Coffenbury Lake

Covering 50 acres, Coffenbury Lake in Fort Stevens State Park is a popular freshwater lake that has good stocks of brown bullhead, rainbow trout, steelhead, and yellow perch. There is good road access near the north end of the lake, and a trail circles the perimeter of the lake. Fun family camping is available in the state park. Coffenbury Lake is located 2 miles west of Warrenton in Fort Stevens State Park. For more information about Fort Stevens State Park, see the Coastal Parks section of The Great Outdoors chapter.

Columbia River

The Columbia River ends its mighty 1,200-mile journey west of Astoria where it meets the ocean. The Columbia is home to large runs of migratory coho, chinook, and steelhead salmon and sea-run cutthroat trout. Some of the best salmon fishing in the river occurs at Buoy 10 from early August through Labor Day. You can fish off the bank for salmon at Clatsop Spit. The Columbia River also has a strong white and green sturgeon fishery with white sturgeon dominating. Sturgeon fishing is open all year but spring and summer are the best seasons to try your luck. Desdemona Sands to Grays Bay Point are sturgeon hot spots. If you like to surf fish, you can try your luck at the north or south jetties for lingcod, greenling, rockfish, or perch.

Cullaby Lake

Cullaby Lake covers 200 acres and has an average depth of 6 to 12 feet. This lake is well known for its excellent panfish stock as well as bluegill, brown bullhead, black crappie, largemouth bass, and perch. You'll have the best luck at landing these

Insiders' Tip

Bring along a pair of binoculars or a spotting scope to get a close-up view of wildlife. Remember that some of the best times to view wildlife are dawn and dusk.

fish from early spring through the late fall. The lake is located 4 miles north of Gearhart on the east side of U.S. 101 via Cullaby Lake Road or about 12 miles south of Astoria off U.S. 101.

Hebo Lake

If you like to catch cutthroat trout, you may want to take a trip to Hebo Lake, which is stocked with cutthroat trout every spring. There is a campground at the lake and there are wheelchair-accessible fishing spots. The lake is located approximately 20 miles southeast of Tillamook off of Oregon Highway 22. From the intersection of Hebo and U.S. 101, drive east on OR 22 for 0.1 mile, and turn left on to Mt. Hebo Road (Forest Service Road 14). You'll reach the lake in approximately 4.5 miles.

Sand Lake

Sand Lake is a tidal basin that has formed at the mouth of Sand Creek. During July and August you can try your chances at catching some sea-run cutthroat trout, or go for steelhead during February and March. In rare cases you may be able to catch flounder using mud shrimp or night crawlers—the hot spots are near the outlet. There are also good opportunities to do some surf fishing for perch on either side of the outlet. You can reach Sand Lake by driving approximately 11 miles south on U.S. 101 from Tillamook to the junction with Sand Lake Road. Turn west on Sand Lake Road and follow this road for 4 miles to the junction with Cape Lookout Road. Turn south onto Sand Lake Road and you'll reach the lake in about 2 more miles.

Smith Lake (Clatsop County)

Largemouth bass, yellow perch, bluegill, white crappie, and black crappie are present in decent numbers in 41-acre Smith Lake. You'll have the best luck fishing from a boat early in the spring. The lake is located 2 miles south of Warrenton off of Ridge Road. Warrenton is located approximately 8 miles southwest of Astoria via the Warrenton-Astoria Highway. This highway can be accessed by following U.S. 101 south from Astoria.

Smith Lake (Tillamook County)

You may want to try your luck at landing some rainbow trout at 35-acre Smith Lake. The water in this lake averages 8 to 12 feet in depth and provides good bait and lure angling. Brown bullheads thrive in this lake, and largemouth bass can be found in small numbers. The lake is located less than a mile north of Barview on the west side of U.S. 101. Barview is located 12 miles north of Tillamook on U.S. 101.

Spring Lake

Spring Lake is a small 13-acre lake that supports fair numbers of largemouth bass, rainbow trout, and cutthroat trout. The lake is located about a mile north of Barview on the east side of U.S. 101. Barview is located 12 miles north of Tillamook on U.S. 101.

Sunset Lake

Good trout, largemouth bass, black crappie, brown bullhead, and yellow perch can be found at Sunset Lake. Also known as Neacoxie Lake, this pencil-thin lake is only 500 feet wide and 2 miles long and covers approximately 107 acres. You can reach the lake by driving 4 miles north of Gearhart on U.S. 101. Turn west on to Sunset Beach Road and drive 0.25 mile to the lake.

Bays, Rivers, and Streams

Depoe Bay

Good chinook fishing can be found near the buoys marking the entrance to Depoe Bay. This scenic bay is located right in the heart of the community of Depoe Bay, 12 miles south of Lincoln City and 10 miles north of Newport on U.S. 101. Trolling with herring or spinners often works well. Bottom fishing is also good off the reefs to the north of Depoe Bay. Use jigs or herring to catch rockfish, lingcod, red snapper, perch, and other common bottom fish. The entrance to the ocean is one of the most dangerous on the Oregon Coast and it is recommended that you hire a charter boat to take you ocean fishing. See the Ocean Charter Services and River Outfitters

Cabezon is a common bottom fish caught along the coastline. PHOTO: LIZANN DUNEGAN

section in this chapter for recommendations for finding a guide for Depoe Bay.

Ecola Creek

This little stream has good catches of steelhead and cutthroat trout, with January and February being the best times to catch steelhead. The stream empties into the ocean at Cannon Beach.

Fogarty Creek

This small stream produces some good catches of hatchery steelhead and small numbers of cutthroat trout. The creek meets the ocean at Fogarty State Park located approximately located 2 miles north of Depoe Bay and 8 miles south of Lincoln City.

Kilchis River

Fall chinook fishing in November is popular on the Kilchis River. Winter steelhead are also strong in this 20-mile-long river, with the peak runs occurring November through March. This river can be accessed via Alderbrook Road north of Tillamook off U.S. 101.

Necanicum River

Try fishing the Necanicum for winter steelhead from November through January. The Necanicum River parallels U.S. 26 and some of its best access points are on the river's upper stretches. To reach some of these access points, drive east from Cannon Beach on U.S. 26 toward Portland.

Nehalem Bay

If you like to bottom-fish and surf fish, Nehalem Bay is a good fishing destination. Try casting for greenling, perch, or rockfish off the south jetty or the beaches located north and south of the bar. Nehalem Bay that is located approximately 15 miles south of Cannon Beach off U.S. 101.

Nehalem River

The Nehalem River stretches for more than 100 miles from its origin near the town of Timber off U.S. 26 to where it meets the ocean at Nehalem Bay and the community of Nehalem. This fun fishing river has good runs of steelhead, cutthroat trout, and salmon. The best time to try for steelhead is

December through March, with the lower section being the most productive. The Nehalem River is located approximately 15 miles south of Cannon Beach off U.S. 101.

Nestucca Bay

Fall chinook have a strong presence in Nestucca Bay during August and September. Sea-run cutthroat also make their way into the bay near the end of the summer. Surf fishing for perch and greenling is recommended at the beach located in Robert Straub State Park. Nestucca Bay is located south of Pacific City off Brooten Road.

The Big Nestucca River

Sea-run cutthroat trout are present on the Nestucca River and August is the peak month to catch these fish. Spring and fall chinook runs are also strong, with June and July being the peak months for the spring chinook and September and October for the fall chinook. Most anglers find the best salmon fishing on the river below Hebo. Steelhead also have a strong presence in the river year-round. The river can be accessed at Beaver off U.S. 101. The community of Beaver is located approximately 15 miles south of Tillamook and about 30 miles north of Lincoln City.

Salmon River

The Salmon River has a strong fall chinook run and fair runs of winter steelhead, coho, and sea-run cutthroat. Your best bet for bank angling is at the U.S. 101 bridge located a few miles north of Lincoln City.

Wilson River

The Wilson River empties into Tillamook Bay and produces large runs of steelhead that are at their prime from December through March. Spring chinook runs peak in June and July and the peak of the fall run is November. Sea-run cutthroat are also present in this award-winning stream. The Wilson River can be accessed via Oregon Highway 6, which heads east from Tillamook.

Central Coast

Freshwater Lakes

Alder Lake

You can find good rainbow trout fishing in three-acre Alder Lake. Alder Lake is a part of a unique system of freshwater lakes around the Florence area. If you want to stay and fish for a while, there is a campground at the north end of the lake. To reach the lake, drive 4.1 miles north of Florence on U.S. 101 to the Alder Dune Campground turnoff. Turn west and you'll reach the lake in about 0.5 mile.

Cleawox Lake

Cleawox Lake is a best bet to catch rainbow trout and you might also reel in some largemouth bass, black crappie, brown bullhead, bluegill, or yellow perch. This 82-acre lake tends to get crowded during the height of the summer because it is located in the popular Jessie M. Honeyman State Park. The park is located 3 miles south of Florence off U.S. 101. See the Coastal Parks section of The Great Outdoors chapter for more information about this state park.

Devils Lake

Devils Lake provides some good opportunities to reel in rainbow trout, brown bullhead, black crappie, panfish, and yellow perch. A campground and a boat ramp are on the west side of the lake. The campground can be found by turning east on to Northeast 6th Street from U.S. 101 in Lincoln City and driving 0.1 mile to the campground entrance. The day use area and boat ramp can be accessed by turning east on to Northeast 1st Street from U.S. 101 in Lincoln City and driving to the end of the road.

Elbow Lake

Rainbow trout and yellow perch are good catches at 13-acre Elbow Lake. The lake is located on the west side of U.S. 101 about 4 miles north of Reedsport.

Erhart Lake

Erhart is a small gem of a lake that provides excellent rainbow trout fishing. The lake is located approximately 8 miles south of Florence on the east side of U.S. 101.

Mercer Lake

Largemouth bass prove a challenging catch on the 340-acre Mercer Lake. Other fish that may bite your line include bluegill, panfish, rainbow trout, and yellow perch. You can rent a boat from the resort that is located on the lake. Mercer Lake is located about 5 miles north of Florence on the east side of U.S. 101 via Mercer Lake Road.

Munsel Lake

Munsel Lake is a good trolling lake where you may get bites from rainbow or brook trout. Other likely catches are bluegill, brown bullhead, yellow perch, and largemouth bass. To get there, drive approximately 2.5 miles north of Florence on U.S. 101. Turn east onto Munsel Lake Road N. and you'll reach the lake in about a mile.

Siltcoos Lake

Siltcoos Lake is bursting at the seams with brown bullhead, bass, bluegill, black crappie, yellow perch, trout, steelhead, and salmon. This 3,500-acre lake is the largest lake on the Oregon Coast and offers some of the best wild cutthroat trout fishing around this area. Native steelhead can be caught as they migrate to their spawning grounds on the Siltcoos River. All steelhead fishing is catch-and-release only, with the best times to catch the feisty fish is during the months of December and January. To get there, drive 6 miles south of Florence on U.S. 101. The lake is located on the east side of the highway.

Sutton Lake

Sutton Lake has a good stock of rainbow trout, largemouth bass, bluegill, panfish, and yellow perch. At 100 acres in size, there is plenty of room for everyone to try their luck. The lake is located approximately 6 miles north of Florence via U.S. 101.

Takenitch Lake

Covering more than 1,600 acres, Takenitch Lake is a good family fishing spot. You'll need to fish from a boat because the shore is not very accessible due to thick brush. The boat ramp is located about 9 miles north of Reedsport at the north end of the lake. Best catches on this lake are yellow perch, crappie, and bluegill. Small numbers of largemouth bass can also be found in this lake, as well as wild cutthroat trout and rainbow trout. The lake is located approximately 13 miles south of Florence on the east side of U.S. 101.

Woahink Lake

Woahink Lake provides fair fishing opportunities for largemouth bass, brown bullhead, black crappie, bluegill, rainbow trout, wild cutthroat trout, and yellow perch. The lake is most well known for its yellow perch fishing and 15-inch fish are usually caught in water depths over 30 feet. This lake is located in Jessie M. Honeyman State Park, 3 miles south of Florence off U.S. 101. Camping facilities are available in this popular state park. See the Coastal Parks section of The Great Outdoors chapter for more information.

Bays, Rivers, and Streams

Alsea Bay

Alsea Bay offers a strong fall chinook run during September and October. Hot spots for these lively catches are at the mouth of the Alsea River and the lower main channel of the bay. Coho may also be caught but this fishery is subject to closure and you should always check the most current regulations to see if it is open. Trolling with feather spinners and herring works well for adult salmon. Perch are also abundant in the bay and can be caught using kelp worms and sand crabs. Alsea Bay can be accessed via U.S. 101 at Waldport. Waldport is located 17 miles south of Newport and 8 miles north of Yachats on U.S. 101.

Alsea River

Good steelhead fishing can be found on the Alsea River beginning in November

Fishing Guides and Bait Shops

Fishing Guides

Master Guides, Astoria; (503) 458–5450
Charleton Deep Sea Charters, Warrenton; (503) 861–2429
Salmon Master Guide Service, Seaside; (503) 717–9901
J.R. Amicks Guide Service, Tillamook; (503) 842–3775
Haystack Fishing Club, Pacific City; (888) 965–7555
Tradewinds Charters, Depoe Bay; (800) 445–8730
Newport Sport Fishing, Newport; (541) 867–7200
Newport Tradewinds, Newport; (800) 676–7819
Betty Kay Charters, Charleston; (800) 752–6303
Strike Zone Marine & Charters, Winchester Bay; (800) 230–5350
Mark Van Hook Guide Service, Gold Beach; (541) 247–6702
Rick Howard Guide Service, Bandon; (541) 347–3280
Critters Sporthaven Charters, Brookings; (541) 412–9990
Tide Wind Sportfishing, Brookings; (800) 799–0337

Tackle and Bait Shops

Tackle Time Bait Shop, Warrenton; (503) 861–3693
Wheeler Marina, Wheeler; (503) 368–5780
The Guide Shop, Tillamook; (503) 842–3474
Lyster Bait & Tackle, Garibaldi; (503) 322–3242
Garibaldi Marina, Garibaldi; (503) 322–3312
Bayshore RV Park & Marina, Netarts; (503) 842–7774
Rose Lodge Park Store & Feed Store, Lincoln City; (541) 994–2415
Victory Fishing Gear, Newport; (541) 867–4531
Newport Marina Store and Charters, Newport; (541) 867–4470
Hillco Bait, Waldport; (541) 563–6730
The Dock of the Bay Marina, Waldport; (541) 563–2003
The Sportsman, Florence; (541) 997–3336
The Reedsport Outdoor Store, Reedsport; (541) 271–2311
Winchester Bay Market, Winchester Bay; (541) 271–2632
Lakeside Marina, Lakeside; (541) 759–3312
Basin Tackle Shop, Coos Bay; (541) 888–3881
Bandon Bait, Bandon; (541) 347–3905
The Dock Tackle, Port Orford; (541) 332–8985
Rogue Outdoor Store, Gold Beach; (541) 247–7142
Sporthaven Marina, Brookings; (541) 469–3301

and running through the end of March. The rule is that they can only be caught using barbless hooks. The peak time to catch fall chinook is late September. The Alsea River can be accessed via U.S. 101 at Waldport. Waldport is located 17 miles south of Newport and 8 miles north of Yachats on U.S. 101.

Siletz Bay

During early spring and summer, anglers use sand shrimp, kelp worms, and clam pieces to catch bottom fish in Siletz Bay. Fall chinook fishing begins in late September and October with a large majority of fish caught in the upper bay. Spinners with feathered hooks work well. Siletz Bay is located 5 miles south of Lincoln City via U.S. 101.

Siletz River

Good runs of fall chinook and summer and winter steelhead can be found on the Siletz River. The river meets Siletz Bay at Kernville, which is 5 miles south of Lincoln City via U.S. 101.

Siuslaw River

The Siuslaw River offers strong fall chinook and winter steelhead fishing. The fall chinook hit their highest numbers September through December and the winter steelhead runs begin in late November and last through February. Other good catches on this river are hatchery-raised cutthroat trout in the early spring. The Siuslaw runs into Siuslaw Bay at Florence.

Yaquina Bay

Good bottom fishing is present in Yaquina Bay. Cabezon, striped perch, rockfish, and greenling are landed from the north and south jetties. South Beach Marina offers good opportunities to jig for herring with the best catches landed during February and March. Fall chinook also enter the bay from September through November. Fair numbers of sturgeon are also available in the bay during the winter and spring. Yaquina Bay is located in the community of Newport.

South Coast

Freshwater Lakes

Clear Lake

This small 15-acre lake is a local's favorite for cutthroat trout and yellow perch. The lake is located approximately 5 miles south of Reedsport on the east side of U.S. 101.

Eel Lake

Eel Lake covers 350 acres and supports healthy populations of black crappie, cutthroat trout, rainbow trout, and largemouth bass. It also has a smaller population of brown bullhead. The southwest section of this lake is part of William M. Tugman State Park, which has camping facilities. This lake is located approximately 7 miles south of Reedsport on the east side U.S. 101.

Floras Lake

Floras Lake is a popular 250-acre lake that is well stocked with rainbow trout. You may also reel in some largemouth bass, chinook, or steelhead. You can reach this lake by driving 17 miles south of Bandon, turning west on Floras Lake Loop Road, and then continuing west on Floras Lake Road to the lake.

Garrison Lake

Largemouth bass, rainbow trout, wild cutthroat trout, and good stocks of yellow perch can be found at 134-acre Garrison Lake. This lake follows the lead of many other coastal lakes that tend to be weedy, so it is recommended that you fish from a boat. There are boat ramps and the north and south ends of the lake. The lake is just west of Port Orford off U.S. 101.

Saunders Lake

Saunders Lake covers 55 acres and boasts prime fishing for bluegill, crappie, yellow perch, rainbow trout, largemouth bass, and panfish. Your best bet for catching rainbows is in early spring when the lake has been freshly stocked. A boat ramp and park are located at the south end of the lake. To get to the lake, drive approximately 15 miles south of Reedsport on U.S. 101. The lake is located on the west side of U.S. 101.

Tenmile Lakes (North and South)

You can catch your limit of largemouth bass, brown bullhead, rainbow trout, cutthroat trout, and bluegill at Tenmile Lakes, which cover over 1,700 acres. You may also land some hybrid bass (a cross between white and striped bass) that are great fighters and can weigh up to 15 pounds. If you don't have a boat, you can fish off the dock at the county park located in Lakeside. In late May there are also good opportunities to try your luck at catching trout and bass in the Tenmile Creek outlet. The lakes are located 12 miles north of Coos Bay on U.S. 101 at the community of Lakeside.

Bays, Rivers, and Streams

Chetco River

The Chetco River produces good runs of fall chinook that can be landed from September through December. Winter steelhead are another favorite catch on the Chetco River, with the peak season happening in January. The Chetco meets the ocean at Brookings, and several boat launches are present along the North Bank Chetco River Road, which follows the river east from Brookings. Camping is available at Alfred A. Loeb State Park, 7.5 miles east of Brookings off the North Bank Chetco River Road.

Coquille River

This river features spring chinook, fall chinook, and winter steelhead runs. Coho are also present in this river. Fall chinook begin running in September and coho begin running in October. Winter steelhead runs peak in January. Boat ramps are available at Bullards Beach State Park, located 2 miles north of Bandon off U.S. 101, and at the Bandon Boat Basin.

Coos Bay

Try catching lingcod, perch, and greenling off the south jetty in Coos Bay. You

Insiders' Tip

Fishing regulations vary depending on the region and species of fish. To help you sort through all the regulations, it is highly recommended that you pick up a copy of *Oregon Sport Fishing Regulations*, which is available at local outdoor stores or tackle shops where tags and licenses are sold. You can also view the regulations on-line at www.dfw.state.or.us or call (503) 872-5268.

can reach the south jetty by turning west from U.S. 101 in Coos Bay on to Newmark Street, which turns into the Cape Arago Highway. Follow the Cape Arago Highway southwest for approximately 8 miles to the community of Charleston. Drive through Charleston and in 2 miles watch for a sign indicating the turnoff to Bastendorff Beach Park located on the north side of the highway. Turn north and proceed to Bastendorff Beach Park. The south jetty can be accessed from this county park. Fishing for perch is also popular from the docks and bridges at downtown Charleston's waterfront.

Coos River

If you want to have some fun fishing for shad, you can try using small spinners or wobblers to catch these feisty fighting fish during May and June. Fair winter steelhead runs are also present on the Coos River during December and January. The Coos River empties into Coos Bay and only runs for 5 miles from its origin at the convergence of the South Fork of the Coos River and the Millacoma River.

Elk River

Fall chinook runs are popular on the Elk River and good bank access can be found by heading south on the beach from Cape Blanco State Park to the mouth of the river. Winter steelhead fishing is also present during January and February. You can reach Cape Blanco State Park by driving 46 miles south of Coos Bay or 4 miles north of Port Orford on U.S. 101 to the junction with Cape Blanco Road. Turn west and drive 5 miles on Cape Blanco Road to Cape Blanco State Park.

Rogue River

The Rogue is a very productive river with quality runs of spring and fall chinook and summer and winter steelhead. September through February are the prime months to fish for steelhead, and August and September are the peak months for chinook. The Rogue meets the ocean just north of Gold Beach. The Sand Spit offers good bank fishing for fall chinook July through September. The Sand Spit can be accessed via Gold Beach Airport Road in Gold Beach.

Sixes River

Wild trout can be landed in the Sixes River in the early spring, and steelhead and chinook runs hold their own in this 36-mile-long river. You can fish for steelhead from November through March and for fall chinook from October through December. Access the river via Cape Blanco State Park. To reach Cape Blanco State Park drive, 46 miles south of Coos Bay or 4 miles north of Port Orford on U.S. 101 to the junction with Cape Blanco Road. Turn west and drive 5 miles on Cape Blanco Road to Cape Blanco State Park.

Umpqua River

The Umpqua River provides bountiful fishing for spring chinook, coho, white and green sturgeon, winter and summer steelhead, and shad. Good shad fishing can be found at Sawyers Rapids, which can be reached by driving 27 miles east of Reedsport on Oregon Highway 38. Winter steel-head fishing is good at Scottsburg, located about 17 miles east of Reedsport on OR 38. During the winter and spring months, good sturgeon fishing can be found between Reedsport and Winchester Bay. Fair numbers of white and green sturgeon are usually caught using sand shrimp, smelt, anchovies, or herring. Striped bass are another likely catch on the river between Gardiner and Scottsburg, with the best season beginning in the late spring and lasting through the fall months. Good chinook fishing can be found in the river above Winchester Bay, with July and August being peak months. Good spots for bank fishing for chinook salmon include South Jetty, Half Moon Bay, Osprey Point, and Orca Point, which are located near the mouth of the Umpqua River south of Winchester Bay on Salmon Harbor Drive, which is accessed off U.S. 101.

Winchester Bay

Winchester Bay offers the best sturgeon fishing on the Oregon Coast. Striped bass, perch and spring and fall chinook are other prime catches in this productive bay. Peak times to catch white sturgeon are in mid-March and green sturgeon are present in midsummer. Winchester Bay is located 4 miles south of Reedsport via U.S. 101. See the Ocean Charter Services and River Outfitters section in this chapter for recommendations for finding a guide for Winchester Bay.

Clamming

You can clam anywhere on the Oregon Coast for free, and the only gear you need is a pair of rubber boots, a bucket, and a clam gun or shovel. You need to dig clams at a minus tide; tide tables are published in local newspapers and most tackle shops have yearly tide tables available for free. Razor clams are abundant on the sandy beaches starting at the mouth of Columbia River and stretching south to Seaside. Cockle, littleneck, butter, and gaper clams can be caught in Nehalem and Tillamook Bays. Netarts Bay is another excellent place to have fun clamming. Gaper, razor, and softshell clams can be harvested in Winchester Bay, and Umpqua Bay is thought to have the largest population of softshell clams on the Oregon Coast. Favorite places to clam in and around Winchester Bay are 1 mile upriver from Winchester Bay and approximately a mile north of Gardiner. You can also try the mud flats at the mouth of the Smith River. See the Boat and Equipment Rental section for places to rent clam guns.

North Coast

Columbia River

Dig for razor clams on the flat sandy beaches starting at the south jetty at the mouth of the Columbia River stretching south to Seaside.

Fort Stevens State Park

At low tide the beaches in Fort Stevens State Park are home to fast-digging razor clams. You can rent clam guns from many gas stations along U.S. 101. The park is located 10 miles west of Astoria off U.S. 101. Follow the signs to the park. For more information on Fort Stevens State Park see the Coastal Parks section of The Great Outdoors chapter.

Nehalem Bay

Try your luck at digging for softshell clams in the mud flats about 3 miles above the mouth of Nehalem Bay off Bayside Gardens Road. Nehalem Bay is located approximately 15 miles south of Cannon Beach off U.S. 101.

Netarts Bay

Netarts Bay is a prime clamming area, and you can find good numbers of butter, cockle, gaper, and littleneck clams via the spit at Cape Lookout State Park, on the north part of the bay near the mouth, Wilson Beach, and Whiskey Creek Flats. Smaller numbers of razor clams can also be found here. Netarts Bay is located approximately 5 miles south of Tillamook via the Netarts Highway.

Nestucca Bay

Nestucca Bay produces healthy numbers of softshell clams that can be found in the mud flats off of Brooten Road located approximately 2 miles south of Pacific City.

Siletz Bay

During a zero tide, Siletz Bay offers good softshell clam harvesting on the tidal flats between Cutler City and Kernville. Siletz Bay is located 5 miles south of Lincoln City via U.S. 101.

Tillamook Bay

This bay is one of the top-producing clamming spots on the coast. Cockles, gaper, softshells, and razor clams can be found in tidal flats along the perimeter of the bay. Butter clams and littleneck clams are more prevalent in the northern part of the bay. U.S. 101 skirts the east part of the bay at Bay City and Garibaldi, and Bayocean Road parallels the south and west sides of the bay.

Central Coast

Alsea Bay

Dig up some cockle clams on the south shore of Alsea Bay along Lower Bay Flats. Along the north shore Lower Bay Flats,

Insiders' Tip

Be sure to pack a large cooking pot to cook the crabs or clams you may catch, as well as a small ice chest packed with ice where you can store your clams and crabs before you cook them.

you'll discover cockles and gaper clams. Softshell clams can be found in the mud flats above Eckman Slough. Alsea Bay can be accessed via U.S. 101 at Waldport. Waldport is located 17 miles south of Newport and 8 miles north of Yachats on U.S. 101.

Siuslaw Bay

Softshell clams thrive in Siuslaw Bay. The mud flats on the east and west sides of the mouth of the bay are good digging sites. Siuslaw Bay is located at Florence.

Winchester Bay

Softshell clams can be found in many of the mud flats and coves surrounding Winchester Bay. Winchester Bay is located 4 miles south of Reedsport via U.S. 101

Crabbing

Crabbing season is open year-round on the lower Columbia River and no license is required. Boats, crab pots, and rings can be rented from local marinas. Tillamook Bay, Netarts Bay, Alsea Bay, Winchester Bay, and Coos Bay are excellent destinations to try your luck at catching tasty Dungeness crabs. Dungeness crabs are in peak quality in the winter months beginning in December. You should be aware that there are regulations on which crabs you can keep. You can only keep male crabs that are have a minimum shell width, between points, of 5.75 inches. You can identify male crabs by the elongated flap on their underside, while the female crabs have a rounded flap. For more information on where you can rent a boat or crab rings and purchase bait, see the Boat and Equipment Rental section in this chapter.

North Coast

Nehalem Bay

Nehalem Bay offers prime crabbing in the lower channel during the summer and fall. Nehalem Bay is located approximately 15 miles south of Cannon Beach off U.S. 101.

Netarts Bay

Netarts Bay is one of the most productive crabbing bays on the Oregon Coast. Peak months to catch tasty Dungeness and red rock crab are September through November. Netarts Bay is located 5 miles southwest of Tillamook via the Netarts Highway.

Siletz Bay

Excellent crabbing opportunities exist in Siletz Bay and popular crabbing spots are off the public fishing docks in the bay. Siletz Bay is located 5 miles south of Lincoln City via U.S. 101.

Tillamook Bay

Try your luck at catching some crabs from the refurbished wheelchair-accessible pier located west of Garibaldi off U.S. 101. If you have a boat, you can try your luck at Crab Harbor located east of Bayocean Peninsula.

Yaquina Bay

Dungeness crab can be taken year-round in Yaquina Bay. Crab pots are favored over crab rings in the bay due to hungry seals that will steal your bait. You can also try your luck from the shore on either side of the Yaquina Bay channel to the east of the Yaquina Bay Bridge. Yaquina Bay is located in the community of Newport.

Central Coast

Alsea Bay

A hot spot for crabbing in Alsea Bay is in the main channel below Lint Slough. You can rent boats and supplies in Waldport. Waldport is located 17 miles south of Newport and 8 miles north of Yachats on U.S. 101.

Siuslaw Bay

Prime crabbing sites in Siuslaw Bay are in the lower channel of the bay and at the "Rock Dock," a wheelchair-accessible pier located east of the south jetty. Siuslaw Bay is located at Florence.

Winchester Bay

You're more than likely to bag your limit of crabs in Winchester Bay. The best season to catch crabs in this productive bay is in the spring off Winchester Point. Winchester Bay is located 4 miles south of Reedsport via U.S. 101.

Boat and Equipment Rental

North Coast

Wheeler Marina
278 Marine Drive, Wheeler
(503) 368–5780

If you want to try catching some delicious Dungeness crab in Nehalem Bay, you can rent a boat from Wheeler Marina for $40.00 for three hours and $8.00 for each additional hour (up to a maximum of $70.00 per day). Crab rings rent for $3.00 each and bait is $2.00. If you want your crabs cooked, the charge is 25 cents per crab. Clam shovel rentals are a reasonable $4.00 per day. The marina also has a full line of fishing poles and tackle, life jackets, rain gear, rope, etc. The marina is open 6:30 A.M. to dark seven days a week during from May through mid-November. They are open from 7:00 A.M. to dark on the weekends from mid-November through May 1. Visa, MasterCard, and American Express are accepted.

Garibaldi Marina
302 Mooring Basin Road, Garibaldi
(503) 322–3312

You can rent boats to go crabbing in Tillamook Bay from Garibaldi Marina for $50 for three hours and $10 for each additional hour. Crab rings are $5.00 each and bait is $2.00. The marina also has a crab cooker and they will cook your crabs for free. The marina also stocks bait and tackle, rain gear, crabbing equipment, clam shovels, and other marine supplies. The marina is open from 6:00 A.M. to 6:00 P.M. seven days a week from March through November, and Friday, Saturday, and Sunday from 7:00 A.M. to 4:00 P.M.

December through February. Visa and MasterCard are accepted.

Bayshore RV Park and Marina
2260 Bilyeu Street, Tillamook
(503) 842–7774
www.netartsbay.com

If you want to go crabbing in Netarts Bay, Bayshore RV Park and Marina offers boat rentals, crab ring rentals, and bait for sale. A crabbing package is available that includes a boat and motor, bait, and three crab rings for three hours for $45. They also have crab cooking facilities and charge $5.00 a dozen to cook your crabs. The crabbing season in this area is late September through December. Visa and MasterCard are accepted.

Central Coast

Newport Marina Store & Charters
2122 Southeast Marine Science Drive, Newport
(541) 867–4470, (877) 867–4470
www.newportmarinacharters.com

Newport Marina Store & Charters has a diverse set of charters that are sure to please just about anyone. This outfitter's most popular charter is a six-hour trip that combines bottom fishing with crabbing. Other charters offered include a spring chinook salmon trip, silver salmon trip, and albacore tuna trips beginning in late July. Whale-watching trips are also offered. This outfit charges a basic rate of $10 per hour per person and the type of trips offered depend on season and availability of fish. If you want your catch filleted, the charge is 40 cents for small fish and $1.00 for large fish. To catch some tasty Dungeness crab, you can rent a boat with three crab rings for $55 for four hours and bait is $1.50. A crab cooker is also available and you can cook your crab catch for $5.00 per dozen with a $5.00 minimum. The recommended season for crabbing is December through February. This store also has groceries, ice, and other marine supplies. The marina is open from dawn to dusk May through October and from 8:00 A.M. to 5:00 P.M. November through April. Visa and Master-Card are accepted.

The Dock of the Bay Marina
1245 Mill Street, Waldport
(541) 563-2003

Discover the bounty of clamming and crabbing in Alsea Bay by renting a boat and crabbing or clamming gear from the Dock of the Bay Marina. This marina offers a crabbing special that includes a boat, crab rings, life jackets, and bait for $45 for three hours. The peak crabbing season in this area is August through November. Visa and MasterCard are accepted.

Reedsport Outdoor Store
2049 Winchester Avenue, Reedsport
(541) 271-2311

The Reedsport Outdoor Store offers a full line of fishing tackle, bait, and marine supplies. They also stock camping, crabbing, and clamming supplies and equipment. You can also obtain hunting and fishing licenses from this friendly outdoor store.

Winchester Bay Market
8th Street and U.S. Highway 101,
Winchester Bay
(541) 271-2632

Winchester Bay Market has a smorgasbord of supplies that will meet the needs of just about anyone who walks in their door, including bait and tackle supplies, crab ring sales and rental, groceries, espresso, video rental, and a post office.

South Coast

Sporthaven Marina
16374 Lower Harbor Road, Brookings
(541) 469-3301

Insiders' Tip

To find information on the statewide effort to restore salmon and trout in the watersheds, visit The Oregon Plan for Salmon and Watersheds home page at www.oregon-plan.org.

This full service marina offers tackle, licenses and bait, deep-sea fishing charters, local salmon and steelhead river guides, and other marine supplies. Call for rates and reservations.

Ocean Charter Services and River Outfitters

There are hundreds of ocean charter and river outfitters on the coastline and it would be impossible to list them all. In this section, we have listed ocean charter and river outfitters from some of the best ocean and river fishing hot spots along the Coast. If you don't see an outfitter listed in the area you are visiting, we recommend that you visit the local chamber of commerce and ask for a list of quality outfitters for you to contact.

North Coast

Charleton Deep Sea Charters
P.O. Box 637, Warrenton 97121
(503) 861-2429, (503) 338-0569

Charleton Deep Sea Charters offers full-day ocean charters for bottom fish (red snapper, lingcod, halibut, flounder) during May and June for $85 per person. They also offer day trip ocean charters for silver and chinook salmon in late July for $85 per person. During the month of May, river charters are available to catch sturgeon and salmon in the Columbia River for $85 per person. All bait and tackle is included with the one-day charge and the crew can also fillet your fish for you. Whale-watching trips are offered during late December and January for $40 per person.

Salmon Masters Guide Service
1135 Avenue F, Seaside
(503) 717-9901

Dennis Steward is a local expert guide who offers salmon and sturgeon guided trips on the Lower Columbia near Astoria and Nehalem Bay. He recommends fishing for chinook and coho salmon on the Lower Columbia from the beginning of August through mid-September. Dennis commented that "300,00 fish make their annual run up the Lower Columbia beginning in August making this one of the biggest salmon runs on the West Coast." Dennis charges $125 per day per person, and this includes bait and tackle and cleaning fish. He can take up to four people at a time in his boat. Dennis also mentioned that his busiest time of the year is March through August, and he asks for a $50 deposit when you make a reservation. He also recommends that you bring rain gear, sunglasses, sunscreen, and a sack lunch.

J.R. Amicks Guide Service
150 Vista Drive, Tillamook
(503) 842–3775
www.amicks.com

James Amick guides salmon and sturgeon fishing trips in Tillamook Bay, Nehalem Bay, and Nestucca Bay as well as the Wilson, Trask, Kilchis, Nestucca, and Columbia Rivers. You can fish for fall chinook salmon from August through December, and spring chinook trips can be taken in May and June. The catch limit for salmon is two fish per day. This outfitter charges $140 per person and can take up to four people in his 20-foot boat. This charge includes bait and tackle and fish cleaning. You need to purchase your own license from a local tackle shop or at Fred Meyer. Sturgeon fishing is year-round and the limit is one fish per day. This outfitter requests that you call ahead to make a reservation and also asks for a 50 percent deposit to reserve the boat.

Haystack Fishing Club, Inc.
P.O. Box 935, Pacific City 97135
(888) 965–7555
www.oregoncoast.com/haystack

Take a unique fishing charter in one of Pacific City's famous dory boats. These boats are launched from the beach right into the surf and can accommodate up to six people. This outfitter offers fishing trips for salmon, halibut, lingcod, sturgeon, and bottom fish. Bottom fishing trips are $130 per person, and halibut and salmon fishing trips are $145 per person. These rates are based on a four-person trip and bait and tackle are included with

this price. If you would like your fish cleaned, this outfitter will clean and vacuum seal your fish for an additional fee. The main ocean-fishing season is May through October and guided river trips are offered beginning in October for fall chinook. Exciting whale-watching tours are also offered as are guided river trips for chinook salmon and sturgeon. This outfitter recommends that you make a reservation at least a month ahead for summer weekends and one to two weeks in advance for summer weekday trips. Gift certificates are also offered.

Tradewinds Charters
U.S. Highway 101, Depoe Bay
(800) 445–8730
www.tradewindscharters.com

This outfitter has been in business since 1938 and offers five-hour bottom fishing trips for $55 per person, five-hour coho salmon trips for $60 per person, and halibut and tuna trips for $165 per person. They also offer one- to two-hour whale-watching tours.

Central Coast

Newport Tradewinds
653 Southwest Bay Boulevard, Newport
(800) 676–7819
www.newporttradewinds.com

This full-service ocean charter service offers bottom fishing, halibut and tuna fishing, crabbing, and whale-watching trips. Five-hour bottom fishing trips are $60 per person and this includes bait and tackle. The crew will clean your bottom fish for a charge of $1.00 per three fish. Halibut fishing begins in May and it usually last only six days; the charge is $150 per person. You can have your halibut filleted for 25 cents per pound. Tuna season is mid-August through October 1. A 33-hour trip runs $325 per person, a 20-hour trip is $225 per person, and a 12-hour trip is $150 per person. Group discounts are also offered. You can take a three-hour crabbing trip in Yaquina Bay for $35 per person that includes crab rings and bait. Have your crabs cleaned for $3.00 per dozen and cooked for $5.00 per dozen.

Peak whale-watching months are December and January and March and April. You can participate in a fun two-hour trip for $18.00 for adults and children 13 and under are $9.00.

Strike Zone Marine & Charters
465 Beach Boulevard, Winchester Bay
(800) 230–5350
www.strikezonecharters.com

This U.S. Coast Guard-approved charter service offers fun fishing charters for salmon, halibut, and bottom fish. They also offer scenic whale-watching tours and specialty trips to suit your needs. Call for rates and reservations.

South Coast

Betty Kay Charters
P.O. Box 5020, Charleston 97420
(800) 752–6303
www.bettykaycharters.com

Betty Kay Charters offers several different charter fishing trips where you may catch blue rockfish, black sea bass, cabezon, yellow tail, rose thorn, turkey rock, vermilion, or china rock. Six-hour trips are $60 per person, nine-hour trips are $100 per person, and twelve-hour tuna trips are $150 per person. Bait and tackle are included, and you also have the option of purchasing a one-day license from this outfitter. They also offer whale-watching trips for $30 per person. A 50 percent deposit is required with your reservation and group discounts are offered.

Tide Wind Sportfishing
16368 Lower Harbor Road, Brookings
(800) 799–0337
www.sportfishing-at-tidewinds-brookings-oregon.com

Owned by Jim and Jan Pearce, Tide Wind Sportfishing has three vessels in its charter fleet and offers charters for bottom fishing, salmon, and albacore tuna. Bottom fishing is $65 per person, salmon fishing is $90 per person, and albacore tuna fishing is $150 per person. Bait and tackle are included as well as coffee, hot chocolate, and tea. In addition to fishing charters, Tide Wind Sportfishing offers whale-watching trips,

day trips to view the historic St. George lighthouse, and other sightseeing trips. This outfitter recommends that you dress warmly and bring sunglasses, a camera, and snacks along with you.

Hiking

Hikes are listed geographically from north to south.

Cathedral Tree to Astoria Column, Astoria

The moderate 3-mile out-and-back route explores a unique coastal forest right in the heart of Astoria. On this tour you'll get to view a 300-year-old Sitka spruce and climb to the top of the historic, 125-foot Astoria Column. From the top of the column, you'll have gorgeous views of downtown Astoria and the Columbia River.

To get there from U.S. 101 in Astoria, turn south onto 16th Street toward the Astoria Column. Travel 0.3 mile and turn left on Irving Street. Continue 0.8 mile and park in a small, gravel parking area on the right side of the road. Start walking on the wide gravel path. At 0.4 mile turn right and begin walking on a wooden ramp. Turn left at the next trail junction and continue a short distance to the Cathedral Tree. After viewing this impressive tree, go back to the last trail junction and continue straight up a series of stairs. Watch for blue and white circular trail markers placed on trees marking the route. After 1.1 miles turn right and continue toward the signed Astoria Column. At 1.5 miles you'll arrive at the historic Astoria Column. Climb the narrow, spiral staircase to the top of the 125-foot tower. Enjoy the spectacular views from the top and then retrace the same route to your starting point.

For more information, contact Astoria/Warrenton Chamber of Commerce, (800) 875–6807.

Haystack Rock at Cannon Beach

Haystack Rock is a well-known landmark in the small, artsy coastal community of Cannon Beach. This 235-foot rock is situated 1.1 miles south of downtown on a scenic stretch on flat, sandy beach. Part of the Oregon Islands Wildlife Refuge, it is home to nesting pigeon guillemots, pelagic cormorants, tufted puffins, and western gulls. The rocky tide pools at the base of the landmark are filled with colorful creatures such as sea-green anemones, bright orange starfish, and prickly purple sea urchins. To explore this scenic landmark, take the easy 2.2-mile out-and-back beach walk from downtown Cannon Beach.

To get to Cannon Beach and Haystack Rock, drive 90 minutes west of Portland on U.S. Highway 26 to U.S. 101 South. Take the Ecola State Park/Cannon Beach exit off U.S. 101. Head into downtown Cannon Beach to the intersection with Second Street and park in the public parking area. From the parking area, head west on Second Street to the beach. Walk south along the beach about a mile to Haystack Rock. Before you head out be sure to grab lunch to go at Osburne's Grocery Store & Delicatessen on Hemlock Street just north of Second Street.

For more information, contact the Cannon Beach Chamber of Commerce and Information Center, (503) 436–2623; www. cannonbeach.org.

Neahkahnie Mountain, Cannon Beach

This difficult, 3.2-mile out-and-back trail climbs through forests of Sitka spruce and open meadows to the 1,631-foot summit of Neahkahnie Mountain, where you'll have far-reaching views of the scenic Oregon coastline. Start hiking on the single-track trail marked with a brown trail sign. You'll immediately begin climbing steeply. After 1.5 miles you'll round a sharp bend to the right (before emerging from the trees). Look for a rough trail that heads steeply uphill to the right. Turn right and ascend on this rough, rocky trail to the summit viewpoint. Return to the trailhead on the same route.

To get there from the junction of U.S. 26 and U.S. 101 (just north of Cannon Beach), travel 17.2 miles south on U.S. 101 (or 28 miles north of Tillamook) to the junction with gravel Road 38555 marked by a brown hiker sign (this turn is difficult to see). Turn left (east) and continue on Road 38555 for 0.6 mile and park in a pullout on the left.

For more information, contact Oregon State Parks and Recreation, (800) 551–6949; www.oregonstateparks.org.

Munson Creek Falls, Tillamook

This easy 0.6-mile out-and-back route takes you on a short stroll through spectacular old-growth red cedar and Sitka spruce to a viewpoint of Munson Falls—

Scenic views from the summit of Neahkahnie Mountain. PHOTO: LIZANN DUNEGAN

Take a Walk Through Time

Walking and viewing the geologic features on the Oregon Coast gives you a snapshot of the area's rich geologic history. Rocky headlands, sea stacks, and eroding high cliff walls all provide clues to a time long ago when hot lava rushed toward the sea. Here we've listed some locations you may want to visit to view some unique geologic formations.

Devil's Churn Parking Area at Cape Perpetua

The Devil's Churn parking area is located a few miles south of Yachats off U.S. 101. Note there is a $3.00 day use fee to park here. You can purchase a day use permit at the Cape Perpetua Visitor's Center located about a mile south of the Devil's Churn parking area off U.S. 101.

The Devil's Churn area is an exposed volcanic shoreline that is a slice in geologic time. Forty million years ago hot lava originating from a string of offshore volcanoes intruded the softer sedimentary rock. As the hot lava cooled, hot gases escaped into the atmosphere and formed air spaces in the rock, leaving behind the rough, porous texture that you see today. Over millions of years, waves crashing into the lava rock created a sea cave. Eventually, the roof of the cave collapsed, leaving the wide rocky channel of Devil's Churn open to the sky. As waves crash into this wide channel, you'll be able to see spectacular displays of frothy ocean spray shoot dozens of feet into the air.

Quarry Cove at Yaquina Head Outstanding Natural Scenic Area

From Newport drive 3 miles north on U.S. 101 and turn left at the Yaquina Head Outstanding Natural Scenic Area sign. Drive 0.5 mile to the Quarry Cove parking area. (You'll have to pay a $5.00 fee at the entrance station.)

The shape and texture of rocky headlands differs depending on how the lava cooled and solidified. The curved and creviced cliff walls in Quarry Cove are made of crystalline basalt, breccia basalt, and columnar basalt. Crystalline basalt has a felt-like surface and is made of fine-grained crystals of pyroxene, feldspar, and magnetite, mixed with a dash of volcanic glass. Breccia basalt is formed from an age-old recipe of volcanic glass, and the variously shaped pieces have a broken glass or fragmented appearance. As the name implies, the straight vertical columns

A young couple enjoys a stroll on Cobble Beach in the Yaquina Head Outstanding Natural Area.
PHOTO: LIZANN DUNEGAN

of basalt that form along the cliff walls can be recognized as columnar basalt. The symmetrical columns were created when the basalt cooled very slowly and cracks formed in the solidifying rock perpendicular to the cooling surfaces. Look at cliff faces in Quarry Cove and see if you can recognize any of these forms of basalt.

Sunset Bay to Cape Arago

From U.S. 101 in Coos Bay, follow the signs to Charleston Harbor and Ocean Beaches and drive on the Cape Arago Highway 12 miles southwest to Sunset Bay State Park. Park in the day use picnic area located on the west side of the highway. Look for the Oregon Coast Trail marker located on the right side of the rest rooms.

The Oregon Coast Trail takes you on a tour of the rocky coastline between Sunset Bay State Park and Cape Arago. The intricately carved cliffs are composed of sandstones that were deposited here over 45 million years ago when this area was a shallow sea. Over millions of years these sandstone layers have eroded away uncovering layer upon layer of gold-colored sandstone with detailed designs. Many of these layers are tilted and bent—while others are curvy where ancient ocean currents left their mark as soft swirls in the layers of sandstone.

Oregon's second-highest waterfall.

To get there from the intersection of the Three Capes Scenic Highway and U.S. 101 in Tillamook, travel 7.4 miles south on U.S. 101 to the signed Munson Creek Falls State Natural Site turnoff on the left side of the road. Turn left (east) on Munson Creek Road and go 1.5 miles to a circular parking lot and the trailhead.

Cascade Head, Lincoln City

This 4.2-mile moderate route takes you on a trek through the Cascade Head National Scenic Research Area that harbors rare wildflowers and one of the six remaining populations of the threatened Oregon silverspot butterfly. You'll take a journey through coastal forest where you may see Roosevelt elk or black-tailed deer and then arrive on the top of the open, windy summit of Cascade Head.

To get there from the junction of Oregon Highway 18 and U.S. 101, travel north on U.S. 101 for 1.3 miles to the junction with Three Rocks Road. Turn left and continue 2.5 miles to a parking area on the left side of the road at Knight County Park.

For more information, contact Cascade Head Scenic Research Area, The Nature Conservancy of Oregon, 821 Southeast 14th Avenue, Portland; (503) 230–1221; www.nature.org.

Drift Creek Falls, Lincoln City

This easy 3-mile out-and-back forest path descends 340 feet for a fun tour through a thick coastal forest and across a magnificent suspension bridge over Drift Creek. From the bridge you'll have a grand view of the shimmering cascade of Drift Creek Falls.

To get there from U.S. 101 just past milepost 119 in Lincoln City, turn left (east) on Drift Creek Road. Go 1.6 miles on Drift Creek Road to the junction with South Drift Creek Road and turn right. Go 0.4 mile and turn left onto Drift Creek Camp Road. Continue 0.9 mile to another road junction signed DRIFT CREEK FALLS TRAIL and turn left. Continue about 9.8 miles (following signs to the Drift Creek Falls Trail) to a parking area on the right side of the road. A $5.00 Northwest Forest Pass is required for this hike. You can purchase a pass on-line at www.fs.fed.us/r6/feedemo or by calling (800) 270–7504.

For more information, contact Siuslaw National Forest, Hebo Ranger District, P.O. Box 235, Hebo, OR 97122; (503) 392–3161; www.oregoncoast.com/hebord.

Mike Miller Educational Trail, Newport

This 1-mile interpretive trail explores a unique coastal forest ecosystem in the Mike Miller Educational Area. The tour takes you past old-growth Sitka spruce trees and huge rhododendrons and over a small creek where you may see blue herons, ducks, and geese feeding.

To get there from the junction of U.S. 101 and U.S. Highway 20, travel 2.8 miles south on U.S. 101 and turn left (east) at the Mike Miller Educational Area sign. Continue on a gravel road for 0.2 mile to the signed trailhead on the left side of the road.

For more information, contact the Lincoln County Public Works office, (541) 265-5747; www.co.lincoln.or.us/lcparks.

Alsea Falls and Green Peak Falls, Waldport

Waterfall lovers will enjoy this 5-mile out-and-back tour of Alsea Falls and Green Peak Falls in the Alsea Falls Recreation Area. The route travels next to the South Fork of the Alsea River to Alsea Falls and then leads you through a cool forest corridor along the banks of smooth-flowing Peak Creek to Green Peak Falls. There is a picnic area at the trailhead and the campground is just down the road if you want to stay overnight.

To get there from U.S. 101 in Waldport, turn east onto Oregon Highway 34 and travel 39.5 miles and enter the small town of Alsea. At an unnamed road turn right where a sign states LOBSTER VALLEY and cross the North Fork of the Alsea River. Continue to the junction with South Fork Road and turn left where a sign indicates ALSEA FALLS 9/MONROE. Go 8.7 miles (the pavement ends after 1.8 miles) and turn left at a sign for the Alsea Falls Recreation Area. Continue 0.2 mile and park in a large parking area adjacent to the trailhead.

For more information, contact the Bureau of Land Management, (503) 375-5646; www.or.blm.gov/salem.

Cape Perpetua Trails, Yachats

Take your pick of 10 trails that wind through the 2,700-acre Cape Perpetua Scenic Area. Depending on the trails you select, you can experience a botanical wonderland of coastal forest, rocky tide pools, and other ocean spectacles such as the geyserlike spouting horn and the narrow rock channel of Devil's churn. While you're here, plan on spending a few hours at the Cape Perpetua Interpretive Center.

The center provides a good introduction to the plants and animals that live here as well as a look into the area's rich history.

To get there from Yachats, travel 3 miles south (or 22 miles north of Florence) on U.S. 101 to the Cape Perpetua Interpretive Center located on the east side of the highway. A $3.00 day use fee is required to park here.

For more information, contact the Cape Perpetua Interpretive Center, (541) 547-3289; www.newportnet.com/capeperpetua.

Sweet Creek Falls, Florence

This easy 2.2-mile out-and-back route takes you along the banks of bouldery Sweet Creek to a viewpoint of Sweet Creek Falls.

To get there from Florence, head 15 miles east (or 46 miles west of Eugene) on Oregon Highway 126 to Mapleton and the junction with Sweet Creek Road. Turn south onto Sweet Creek Road and travel 10.2 miles to the Homestead Trailhead on the right. From the Homestead Trailhead, start walking upstream. You'll pass small waterfalls, and after 1.1 miles you'll reach 20-foot Sweet Creek Falls (your turnaround point). Head up a short side trail to a fantastic view of the upper falls. This trail requires a $5.00 Northwest Forest Pass.

For more information, contact Siuslaw National Forest, (541) 902-8526; www.fs.fed.us/r6/siuslaw.

Kentucky Falls, Reedsport

This moderate 4-mile out-and-back route descends 760 feet through a mossy forest of western hemlock and Douglas fir dotted with trillium, sword fern, and oxalis. After about 0.5 mile you'll arrive at the shimmering double cascade of Upper Kentucky Falls. Continue about another 1.5 miles to a viewpoint of Lower Kentucky Falls and North Fork Falls (your turnaround point).

To get there from Reedsport, head north on U.S. 101. cross a bridge over the Umpqua River, and turn right (northeast) onto Smith River Road (Forest Road 48). Go approximately 14.5 miles on Smith River Road and turn left (north) on North Fork Road. go about 10 miles on North Fork Road to its intersection with Forest

Road 23. Turn right onto Forest Road 23 and follow signs to Kentucky Falls. After another 9.8 miles you'll arrive at a T intersection. Turn left on Forest Road 919 and continue 2.6 miles to the trailhead.

For more information, contact the Mapleton Ranger District, (503) 268-4473; www.fs.fed.us/r6/siuslaw/mapleton.

North Fork Smith River, Reedsport

This difficult, 17.4-mile out-and-back route travels along the banks of the North Fork Smith River, which is filled with many great swimming spots. You'll hike through a jungly coastal forest where you can admire huge old-growth Douglas firs. You are treated at the trail's turnaround point with a great view of Kentucky Falls.

To get there from Reedsport, head north on U.S. 101, cross a bridge over the Umpqua River, and then turn right (northeast) on Smith River Road (Forest Road 48). After about 15 miles, turn left (north) onto North Fork Road 48A. Continue about 9.5 miles to a road junction and go right toward Mapleton. Go 0.5 mile to another road junction and turn right on Forest Road 23. Continue 4 miles to the trailhead parking area on the left side of the road.

For more information, contact the Mapleton Ranger District, (503) 268-4473 www.fs.fed.us/r6/siuslaw/mapleton.

South Slough Estuarine Preserve, Coos Bay

You can explore a series of trails through a wetland ecosystem at this 4,700-acre Coos Bay estuary. Paths lead through fresh and saltwater marshes, mudflats, and floodplains. The visitor center is open from 8:30 A.M. to 4:30 P.M. Monday through Friday during winter and from 8:30 A.M. to 4:30 P.M. daily during summer.

To get there from Coos Bay or North Bend, follow signs to Charleston, Shore Acres State Park, and Ocean Beaches. From Charleston, head west on Cape Arago Highway and in 0.1 mile turn left (south) onto Seven Devils Road. Follow signs to South Slough Sanctuary and Bandon. Drive 4.5 miles, turn left at the interpretive center, and continue to a parking area. The trailhead is past the interpretive

Insiders' Tip

You can buy an annual day use permit for $30 that is good for all Oregon state parks for a year. The permit is pasted to the inside of your windshield. If you don't have an annual pass, getting into a day use fee park costs $3.00 per vehicle per day (state park campers get in at no charge on the day they're camping). Most state parks that require a day use permit also have self-pay stations where you can purchase a permit.

center to the left of a panel entitled JOURNEY TO THE SEA.

For more information, contact South Slough National Estuarine Research Reserve, (541) 888-5558; www.south sloughestuary.com.

Golden and Silver Falls State Natural Area, Coos Bay

This spectacular trail takes you on a tour of the shimmering cascades of Golden Falls and Silver Falls.

To get there from U.S. 101 in Coos Bay, head east on the Coos River Highway, following signs to Allegany. Travel 13.5 miles east on the north side of the Coos River to the town of Allegany. From here, follow state park signs another 9.5 miles to the Golden and Silver Falls State Natural Area. Start by crossing a bridge over Silver Creek. At the junction, head left and enjoy the shady canopy of old-growth Douglas fir trees. At 0.4 mile turn left to view the billowing 160-foot cascade of Silver Falls. After viewing the falls, head back to the main trail and turn left. Continue uphill as the trail follows the edge of a steep cliff to the viewpoint of Golden Falls at 0.9 mile (your turnaround point). For a less precipitous view of Golden Falls, take the right fork at the beginning of the hike and walk 0.3 mile to the viewpoint.

For more information, contact Oregon State Parks and Recreation, (800) 551–6949; www.oregonstateparks.org/park_96.php.

New River, Coos Bay

Several different trails explore the New River area, which is haven to an abundance of wildlife including mallard ducks, northern pintails, green-winged teal, bufflehead, hooded mergansers, and tundra swans. Raptors you may see include peregrine falcons, northern harriers, and bald eagles. Trails lead through coastal forest and open meadows to viewpoints of the New River, which is an outlet stream of Floras Lake.

To get there from Bandon, travel 9 miles south (or 18 miles north of Port Orford) on U.S. 101 to the junction with Croft Lake Road. Turn west onto Croft Lake Road and go 1.5 miles to a road fork. Turn right and continue to the first trailhead adjacent to a small group of buildings.

For more information, contact Bureau of Land Management, (888) 809–0839; www.or.blm.gov/coosbay.

Horseback Riding

Riding on the beach or through a scenic coastal forest on horseback is a fun afternoon's adventure on the Oregon Coast. In this section, we've listed some outfitters that offer guided trips in geographical order from north to south.

Northwest Equine Outfitters
Manzanita
(503) 801–RIDE (801–7433)

This outfitter offers hourly and half-day rides for spectacular views of Nehalem Bay. Call for rates and times.

C&M Stables
90241 North Highway 101, Florence
(541) 997–7540

The experienced wranglers at C&M Stables will take you on guided trips through a scenic forest to the beach. Rides are scheduled at 12:30 P.M. and 3:30 P.M. daily. The facility is open from 10:00 A.M. to dusk daily.

Bandon Beach Riding Stables
2640 Beach Loop Drive, Bandon
(541) 347–3423

Have fun riding on the beach on your trusty steed from Bandon Beach Riding Stables. You can rent a horse by the hour or choose scenic sunset rides, buggy rides, or pack trips. All ages are welcome as well as handicapped riders. Call ahead for trip schedules and reservations.

Jet Boat Tours

Jerry's Rogue Jets
P.O. Box 1011, Gold Beach 97444
(800) 451–3645
www.roguejets.com

Jerry's Rogue Jets, gift shop, and museum, is located at the mouth of the Rogue River in Gold Beach. This guide service offers world-class educational river tours for all ages. On each tour you'll be able to view a variety of wildlife on this National Wild and Scenic River. You can take a 64-mile, 80-mile or 104-mile trip up the Rogue River, which varies between six and eight hours. The 64-mile round trip is $34 per adult and $14 for children ages 4 to 11. The 80-mile round trip is $49 for adults and $24 for children ages 4 to 11. The 104-mile round trip is $75 for adults and $35 for children ages 4 to 11. Overnight trip packages are also available. Call ahead to make reservations and for departure times.

Surfing Hot Spots

Surfing on the Coast is cold, clean fun. Huge and small breaks can be found along the entire Coast. Beware that the locals can sometimes be territorial and unfriendly to out-of-towners but don't let this deter your adventurous surfing spirit. There are plenty of waves and plenty of awesome rides for everyone. Note that when you surf off the Oregon Coast you'll need a full 5mm wet suit, booties, and gloves.

In this section we've listed some recommended surf spots from north to south. We've also included information about local surf shops so you can rent gear in case you don't have your own.

The Point

If you are an experienced surfer and don't mind braving the mad rush of a strong rip tide boulder-strewn beach, you can ride a huge left-handed break off The Point located off Sunset Avenue in Seaside. You can also surf the less radical cove that can be accessed off the sandy beach. Be forewarned—the locals are a tight-knit group that doesn't always appreciate outsiders. You can rent wet suits, surfboards, and boogie boards from Cleanline Surf Company, 719 1st Street, Seaside, (503) 738-7888.

Indian Beach and Haystack Rock

Indian Beach, a pretty little cobble beach located in Ecola State Park located off U.S. 101 2 miles north of Cannon Beach on Tillamook Head, has some great right-handed wave action. You'll have to pay a $3.00 day use fee to enter this state park. Another popular spot is "The Needles" break just south of Haystack Rock You can rent gear from Cleanline Surf Company, 171 Sunset Boulevard, Cannon Beach, (503) 436-9726.

Short Sands Beach

Short Sands Beach is thought to be one of the best surfing spots on the Coast. This secluded, scenic beach can be reached by driving to Oswald West State Park, located 10 miles south of Cannon Beach

Surfers test the waters at Cape Kiwanda in Pacific City. PHOTO: LIZANN DUNEGAN

off U.S. 101. You'll have to hike in about a mile to the beach through an old-growth Sitka spruce forest. This beach is also popular with kayakers and boogie boarders. Expect crowds during the summer months. You can rent gear from Cleanline Surf Company, 171 Sunset Boulevard, Cannon Beach, (503) 436-9726.

Cape Kiwanda Beach at Pacific City

Protected by Cape Kiwanda, Cape Kiwanda Beach in Pacific City is an ideal spot for catching a good break. Pacific City is located 25 miles south of Tillamook and 20 miles north of Lincoln City off U.S. 101 on the Three Capes Scenic Loop. You can rent gear from South County Surf, 33310 Cape Kiwanda Drive, Pacific City, (503) 965-7505.

Surf Spots around Newport

Some good waves can be found at **Beverly Beach** located 7 miles north of Newport off U.S. 101 and some good breaks can also be found at **Agate Beach** just south of Yaquina Head. Agate Beach is located 1 mile north of Newport off U.S. 101. **South Beach State Park** will also not disappoint you. Check out the waves around the south jetty. South Beach State Park is located 2 miles south of Newport. Get local advice and gear from Ocean Pulse Surfboards located at 429 Southwest Coast Highway, Newport, (541) 265-7745.

Golf

Sweeping dunes, spectacular ocean views, bubbling creeks, and coastal forest are the primary backdrop to the golf courses on the Oregon Coast that allow public play. All the courses in this chapter have their own set of unique and challenging holes that will give all levels of players a fun golfing experience. Along with spectacular scenery, you'll find that the majority of the courses have a pro shop, snack bar, and putting area, and offer lessons and club rentals. Most of the courses listed are open year-round but can close due to wet and windy conditions, and we recommend that you always call ahead to find out what the current weather conditions are.

We've listed the course descriptions for each course by region—North Coast, Central Coast, and South Coast—and then by city from north to south. The yardages given are for men's white tees, and we've listed cart rentals separately. All the courses listed accept Visa and MasterCard. If you would like to check out golf resort packages, you should contact Salishan Golf Links or Sandpines on the Central Coast or Bandon Dunes located on the South Coast. These premier resorts offer world-class courses, fine dining, and excellent accommodations.

North Coast

Gearhart

Gearhart Golf Links
1300 North Marion Avenue, Gearhart
(503) 738–3538
www.gearhartgolflinks.com

Wide fairways with a good mix of rolling hills, mounds, and bunkers will challenge you at the Gearhart Golf Links course. Established in 1892, this 5922-yard par 72 classic seaside links course is open year-round. Gearhart Golf Links is the only 18-hole course in Clatsop County and is geared toward all levels of players. This course has an excellent PGA staff steered by pro Jim Smith and assistant pro Zee Barbie. Greens fees from March 15 through October 31 are $45 Friday through Monday, and $35 Tuesday through Thursday. From November 1 through March 14, the rates are $35 Friday through Monday and $25 Tuesday through Thursday. If you need to rent clubs or fine-tune your game, rentals and lessons are offered. Other amenities include a driving range, snack bar, and the newly renovated Kelly House, which includes the First Tee Golf Shop, a restaurant and lounge, and meeting and banquet rooms. If you feel your game is especially good, see if you can beat the course record of 63. Soft spikes are required. Reservations are recommended starting in June.

The Highlands at Gearhart
1 Highlands Road, Gearhart
(503) 738–5248
www.oregongolf.com/highlands

If you like to golf nine holes with an ocean view, The Highlands at Gearhart may be the course for you. This 2000-yard par 30 course is built on sand dunes and stays in immaculate condition year-round. Spectacular ocean views and narrow rolling fairways that are well bunkered add to your golfing fun at this well-managed facility.

If you want to warm up before you play a round, you can do so in an area with a putting green and a chipping green with a sand bunker. The head PGA pro at the course is Dan Strite and Nicholas Mabry specializes in individual instruction. The pro shop boasts the lowest prices in the country on all major brands of equipment and offers free shipping anywhere in the U.S. The operating goal at this course is "Offering value for dollar every day" and the reasonable greens fees or $12 for nine holes and $22 for 18 holes reflect this goal. You'll get plenty of exercise when you play here because power carts are not available. However, you can rent a pull cart for $2.00.

Seaside

Seaside Golf Course
451 Avenue U, Seaside
(503) 738–5261
www.oregongolf.com/seaside

The scenic Necanicum River runs through the 2593-yard par 35 Seaside Golf Course, which is a popular nine-hole course in the Seaside area. Seaside is open year-round though it has a tendency to get wet during the winter months. Besides seeing other players on this course, you may also see some local wildlife such as blue herons, beavers, and elk. This 80-year-old course is an easy walking course and is a favorite for novice players. The top-rated No. 4, a 485-yard par 5, splashes widely to the left, bending with the turns of Necanicum River to a small, tree-lined green. The Necanicum River also comes into play on the No. 8 and No. 9 holes. Amenities at this course include a snack bar, restaurant and lounge, and pro shop. Greens fees for this course are $12 for nine holes and $22 for 18 holes. Power carts rent for $12 for nine holes and $22 for 18 holes. Reservations are not required.

Manzanita

Manzanita Golf Course
Lakeview Drive, Manzanita
(503) 368–5744
www.oregongolf.com/manzanita

The Manzanita Golf Course is a picture-perfect nine-hole course that has a fast driving range and a well-manicured putting green. This 2100-yard par 33 course is fairly flat and has a sprinkling of hills with narrow fairways. The highly rated No. 4, a 320-yard par 4, has some sweeping views of the Pacific Ocean and is characterized by its thin uphill sweep to a well-manicured green. The No. 9, a 225-yard par 3, has a challenging approach due to the pond that sits just to the right of the hole. This course is open year-round and metal spikes are permitted. Greens fees are $15 for nine holes and $28 for 18 holes. Pull carts rent for $2.00.

Manzanita does not have power carts. If you want to take a break from the sometimes damp and windy weather, check out the pro shop or grab a quick bite to eat in the snack bar. Be sure to call ahead for reservations during the summer.

Tillamook

Alderbrook Golf Course
7300 Alderbrook Road, Tillamook
(503) 842–6413, (503) 842–5611
www.oregongolf.com/alderbrook

The 18-hole Alderbrook Golf Course is a beautiful well-established 5692-yard par 69 course with rolling terrain, crowned greens, and nice views from the holes. This course is open year-round and challenges all levels of players with its short and long holes that dogleg left and right and its numerous bunkers, streams, and ponds. Bright evergreens accentuate this 100-acre facility, and deer, elk, rabbits, and a variety of birds can often be seen here. The No. 13, a 373-yard par 4, will test your skills, as a creek and thick trees line the left side of this shot. The No. 15, a 128-yard par 3, strikes a short, steep pitch that has earned respect from those who play here often. PGA pro Jon Kukula oversees day-to-day course activities and the pro shop offers lessons and carries signature apparel, gloves, hats, balls, shoes, bags, and clubs. Alderbrook also features a snack bar with a high-quality menu. The greens fees for this old-style course are $15 for nine holes and $27 for 18 holes. Carts are available for $15 for nine holes and $25 for 18 holes. Pull carts rent for $2.00. Reservations are not required.

Bay Breeze Golf and Driving Range
2325 Latimer Road, Tillamook
(503) 842–1166
www.oregongolf.com/bay-breeze

Built in 1993, this nine-hole course was designed and built by Bud Gienger and Mike Lehman. A creative water hazard named "Bud's Bay" will test your skills on the No. 6 and No. 7 holes. Bentgrass greens and sand are also present on this fun 1061-yard par 27 course. At the handy, covered driving range you can practice your power strokes, and a smooth putting green is

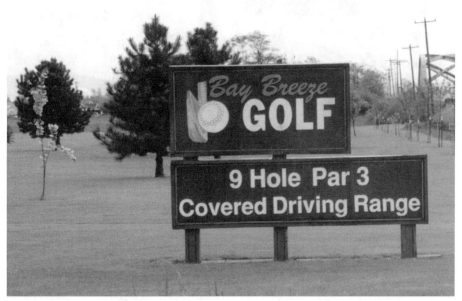

Public golf courses are geared toward all levels of players. PHOTO: LIZANN DUNEGAN

available where you can practice your softer strokes. Greens fees are $6.00 every day of the week and metal spikes are allowed. Power carts are not available but you can rent a pull cart for $1.00. Additional facilities at this course include a deli, clubhouse, and pro shop. Keep in mind that this course is closed from November through mid-February. Reservations are not required.

Neskowin

Neskowin Beach Golf Course
Hawk Creek Avenue, Neskowin
(503) 392-3377
www.oregongolf.com/neskowin

Kiwanda and Butte Creeks wind their way through the 2616-yard par 35 links style Neskowin Beach Golf Course. This pretty seaside nine-hole course is flat and easy to walk and is home to abundant wildlife, such as bald eagles, blue herons, swans, beavers, elk, and deer. Situated at sea level, Neskowin Beach can be wet during periods of high rain or high tides. An unusual approach has been used to combat this problem: Nicknamed "The Jewel," this course features 13 greens and has three

different course layouts (white, red, and green) sloped and rated by the Oregon Golf Association. This unique plan allows players to avoid wet areas and still provides an interesting and challenging golf experience. In early May, golfers play the white course and then transition to the red course as summer approaches. During July, August, and September, golfers can play the green course. When the wet fall weather begins, players switch back to the white course before the course is closed for the winter from November 1 through May 15. Good holes on this course are the No. 1, a 287-yard par 4 that wanders over rolling terrain to a smooth green, and the 311-yard, par 4 No. 5 that is intersected by Kiwanda and Butte creeks, offering a unique water-hazard challenge. Greens fees for the different courses range from $9.50 to $15.00 for nine holes and $15.50 to $25.00 for 18 holes. This golf course offers discounts to seniors and junior players during the week. Power carts are $18.00 for nine holes and $36.00 for 18 holes, and pull carts are $2.00 per day. A snack bar and pro shop are available when you want to take a break from playing.

Lincoln City

Lakeside Golf & Racquet Club
3245 Northeast 50th Street, Lincoln City
(541) 994–8442
www.oregongolf.com/lakeside

The 18-hole Lakeside course has a reputation of being tough and tricky. With some parts of the course situated on a hillside with narrow rolling fairways filled with bunkers and water hazards, this 4310-yard par 65 course will test your skills. Before you begin your round, you may want to practice on the well-maintained putting or chipping green. In addition to a pro shop and snack bar, this facility also has a health and fitness center, racquetball courts, and tennis courts. Greens fees at this challenging course are $20 for nine holes and $35 for 18 holes. Power carts rent for $15 for nine holes and $25 for 18 holes. It is highly recommended that you call ahead for tee times.

Gleneden Beach

Salishan Golf Links
7760 North U.S. Highway 101, Gleneden Beach
(800) 452–2300, Pro Shop (800) 890–0387
www.salishan.com

The Salishan Golf Links is a classic 18-hole Scottish Links–style course that was designed by Fred Federspiel and renovated in 1996 by Bill Robinson. Named by *Links* magazine in 1997 as one of the top 100 resort courses in the United States, this premier 6390-yard, par 73 course challenges you with water hazards, elevated greens, and steep slopes. The course weaves through a forest-strewn hillside and offers spectacular views of Siletz Bay and the Pacific Ocean. The course is open year-round but expect windy, wet weather in the winter months. This beautiful and well-designed course is designated as a Certified Audubon Cooperative Sanctuary and was the first Oregon course to receive this designation. The facilities at Salishan are hard to beat. The pro shop offers club rentals and lessons and hosts tournaments. There is also an 18-hole

Insiders' Tip

Bring your camera with you on the golf course to capture some of the most beautiful Oregon Coast scenery.

putting green and a driving range to practice your strokes. Greens fees for 18 holes are $75 in May, $95 June through October, $55 November through December, and a reduced price January through April. Greens fees include golf cart rental and a basket of balls for the driving range. These rates are discounted if you are a Salishan Lodge guest. It is recommended that you call two weeks in advance for tee times. When you're finished with your game, you catch a quick bite in the coffee shop or head to one of Salishan's three restaurants. If you want to stay a few days, you can stay in one of the lodge's 205 guest rooms that are fully equipped with a fireplace, balcony, and covered carport. Other activities you can enjoy at this resort are hiking, tennis, and walking on miles of sandy beach.

Newport

Agate Beach Golf Course
4100 North Coast Highway, Newport
(541) 265–7331
www.oregongolf.com/agate_beach

The 3000-yard par 36 Agate Beach Golf Course offers excellent year-round play and excellent ocean views. Located on an easy-sloping hill this nine-hole course has a wide track with some fun holes. The tree-lined No. 6, a 501-yard par 5, will test your swing and a water hazard comes into play on the No. 7. Equipped with a pro shop, restaurant, and clubhouse, this is a favorite nine-hole course for all levels of players. Greens fees are $15 for nine holes and $30 for 18 holes. Power carts are $12 for nine holes and $24 for 18 holes. Reservations are recommended.

Toledo

Olalla Valley Golf Course
1022 Olalla Road, Toledo
(541) 336–2121

The Olalla Valley Golf Course will challenge you with hilly, wooded terrain and water hazards on seven of its nine holes. Olalla Creek meanders through this challenging 3078-yard par 36 course and provides a pretty distraction as well as a water hazard. Kids can play for $8.00 for nine holes and adults play for $13.00 for nine holes and $24.00 for 18 holes all seasons of the year. If you want to play the course from the convenience of a cart, you'll pay a reasonable charge of $10 for nine holes and $18 for 18 holes. A driving range, pro shop, and full-service restaurant are some of the additional services offered at this fun course.

Waldport

Crestview Hills Golf Course
1680 Southwest Crestline Drive, Waldport
(541) 563–3020
www.oregongolf.com/crestview

The nine-hole Crestview Hills Golf Course is open year-round and is to many golfers a best-kept secret. This 50-acre, 2881-yard par 36 course is fairly flat and is host to a dual-tee track that offers a good round for intermediate players. Trees and a pond await you at the top-rated No. 5 and the same landscape hazards are present on the No. 6. Crestview Hills has a friendly, family atmosphere and has many tournaments during the summer months where they invite anyone passing through to stop by and join the fun. Discounts are offered to kids, who play for $8.00, and adults play for $14.00 for nine holes and $22.00 for 18 holes. Carts are reasonable at $10 per nine holes of play. Reservations are recommended up to a week in advance during the summer months.

Florence

Ocean Dunes Golf Links
3345 Munsel Lake Road, Florence
(541) 997–3232
www.oregongolf.com/ocean_dunes

The 5613-yard par 71 Ocean Dunes Golf Links is a sweeping 18-hole course that is located on rolling sand dunes and resembles a true links course. Wind, sand, and sun will challenge you on this carefully constructed course, which has narrow fairways and water hazards. One of the toughest holes on this course is the No. 16, which is surrounded by dunes on a sloping green. Every amenity you could ever want is offered at this course, including a pro shop, restaurant, driving range, putting green, club rentals, lessons, and banquet and tournament facilities. You can ride in a cart on this course for $26 and greens fees are $32 seven days a week. Discounts are offered to juniors and seniors. Call ahead for times and rates.

Sandpines
1201 35th Street, Florence
(800) 917–4653
www.sandpines.com

The award-winning Sand Pines 18-hole course captures the natural surroundings of dunes, forest, and lakes. Well-known golf course architect Rees Jones designed this 6085-yard par 72 course that tracks through wind-swept dunes on the inward nine and takes you among pine forest and small lakes on the outward nine. This course was rated by *Golf Magazine* as one of the top 50 courses for women in 1998, and the May 1999 edition of *Golf Digest* rated

Insiders' Tip

If you want to find out more about golfing in Oregon Coast and the rest of Oregon, you can request the free Official Golf Directory Oregon from the Oregon Tourism Commission, 775 Summer Street NE, Salem, OR 97310, (800) 547-7842, www.traveloregon.com.

Sandpines as a "4-star rated Places to Play in the USA." Living up to its award-winning reputation, the facilities at this course include a well-stocked pro shop, snack bar, a driving range, and a beautifully manicured putting green. Greens fees for 18 holes are $45 during May and June, $59 June through September, and $35 the rest of the year. Carts are $26 for 18 holes and $18 for nine holes. For the little ones there is a Wee Links Putting Course that is $5.00 for 18 holes. To find out about golf packages, contact Driftwood Shores Resort at (800) 422–5091. Driftwood Shores Resort has spectacular ocean-view rooms, fine dining at the Surfside restaurant, indoor pool and Jacuzzi, and 10 miles of sandy beach for you to explore.

Reedsport

Forest Hills Country Club
#1 Country Club Drive, Reedsport
(541) 271–2626
www.oregongolf.com/forest_hills

You can play nine challenging holes at the Forest Hills Country Club a 3086-yard par 36 course that is host to wide, flat fairways and fast, well-bunkered greens. This facility is semiprivate but allows unlimited public play. Forest Hills is host to different tournaments in the summer

Insiders' Tip
If you plan on spending a summer weekend playing golf on a scenic course, be sure to call ahead and ask if a tournament is being held on the weekend you are planning to visit. Tournaments are often fun to watch, but they can bring large crowds and close the course to public play.

and fall months that offer couples play, four-man team play, senior play, and ladies-only play. A fully stocked pro shop is also available, as well as a restaurant that is well known for its Peppered New York Steak. Other offerings include a driving range, clubhouse with storage, locker rooms, and club repair. Greens fees are $14 for nine holes and $25 for 18 holes. Power carts are always available for $12 for nine holes and $22 for 18 holes. If you prefer to walk the course, pull carts rent for $2.00 for nine holes and $3.00 for 18 holes and discounts are offered to students. During the summer months, it is recommended that you call two weeks in advance to reserve a tee time.

South Coast

North Bend

Kentuck Golf Course
680 Golf Course Road, North Bend
(541) 756–4464
www.oregongolf.com/kentuck

Water comes into play at almost every hole on the 18-hole Kentuck Golf Course. This easy-to-walk 5394-yard par 70 course is open all year long but has a reputation for being wet during the winter months because it lies in a flood plain. You can play a round for $24. Power carts rent for $20.00 and pull carts for $2.00. A pro shop, snack bar, and club rentals are added pluses at this course.

Coos Bay

Sunset Bay Golf Course
11001 Cape Arago Highway, Coos Bay
(541) 888–9301

Sunset Bay Golf Course is adjacent to Sunset Bay State Park and is a popular golfing destination for RVers who stay at the state park. This nine-hole course is in a picturesque setting of hemlock and spruce near the pounding Pacific Ocean. The 2609-yard par 36 course is impeccably maintained and is quite challenging due to Big Creek, which comes into play on eight out of nine holes. You can warm up on the putting or chipping green or have a refreshing drink at the snack bar. If you need balls or want to rent clubs, you should check out the pro shop. Greens fees for this architecturally sound course are $12 for nine holes and $22 for 18 holes on the weekdays, and $13 for nine holes and $23 for 18 holes on weekends. You can enjoy the view from a power cart for $14 for nine holes and $25 for 18 holes.

Bandon

Bandon Dunes
Round Lake Drive, Bandon
(888) 345–6008
www.bandondunesgolf.com

Opened in May 1999, the 6112-yard par 72 Bandon Dunes course designed by David McLay Kidd sits atop a scenic stretch of sand dunes 100 feet above the sandy shoreline. This 18-hole course is fairly flat with some hills and has sweeping ocean views from every hole. Greens fees for this world-class course are $200. A replay fee of $80 is charged if you want to play another round in the same day. Bandon Dunes is a walking only course and professional caddies are available. Single-rider carts are available for the physically challenged. A chipping area, putting green, and driving range are available for warming up. When you are finished with your round, the Clubhouse at Bandon Dunes offers every amenity under the sun, including a pro shop, spa and sauna, hot tub, exercise and locker rooms, a restaurant and bar, 15 single rooms, and two four-bedroom luxurious suites.

Bandon Face Rock Golf Course
3235 Beach Loop Drive, Bandon
(541) 347–3818
www.bandonbythesea.com/golf.htm

The Bandon Face Rock Golf Course sits right next to the frothy Pacific Ocean and is a great place to bring the family for a fun nine-hole round. Johnson Creek meanders through the 2096-yard par 32 course and serves as a water hazard for many holes. One such hole is the 351-yard par 4 No. 2, which traipses next to Johnson Creek and ends at a domed green.

Insiders' Tip

Plan to golf in the morning to avoid the often-windy conditions that are common in the afternoon.

Keep in mind that the conditions here can be very windy due to its location. This course is open year-round and lessons and club rentals are available. A covered driving range will let you try out your strokes even if the weather is wet. Bandon Face Rock Golf Course hosts four tournaments a year between June and October. You'll enjoy an ocean view from the new clubhouse as well as fine dining. The greens fees are $22 for 18 holes and $12 for nine holes. You can gaze at the course and the ocean from a cart, which rents for $12 for nine holes and $22 for 18 holes.

Gold Beach

Cedar Bend Golf Club
34391 Squaw Valley Road, Gold Beach
(541) 247–6911
www.oregongolf.com/cedar_bend

Cedar Bend Golf Course is a nine-hole course located in a quiet forested setting in Squaw Valley located 14 miles south of Port Orford and 12 miles north of Gold Beach. This 2872-yard par 36 course is open year-round and is a good walking course due to the mostly flat terrain. Fun holes are No. 8, a 320-yard par 4, which has a large pond as a water hazard, and the No. 9, a 405-yard par 4, that has a fast right hooking fairway that leads to a sloping green. An RV park and a driving range are added bonuses in addition to the clubhouse, lounge, snack bar, and pro shop. You'll appreciate the reasonable greens fees at this facility: $13 for nine holes and $18 for a second round. You can go on the fast track by renting a power cart for $13 for nine holes or $20 for 18 holes.

Day Trips

Nothing is more fun than taking off for a day or a weekend to a destination you've not visited before, and the fun of driving to a new place and stopping at different points along the way is just as much fun as arriving. While the scenery and activities on the Oregon Coast are hard to beat, you may want to try heading east and checking out some of Oregon's world class wineries; Portland, the largest city in Oregon; or the impressive cave formations at Oregon Caves National Monument located in the Siskiyou National Forest in southern Oregon.

Winery Tours

Oregon has three distinct appellations (winegrowing regions) that are accessible from the Oregon Coast: the Willamette Valley, Umpqua Valley, and Rogue Valley. The wineries listed below are in alphabetical order by region.

The **Willamette Valley** is an easy day trip from the North and Central Coast and is the largest source for wine grapes in the state, with Pinot Noir and Chardonnay being the most planted grape varieties. The Willamette Valley stretches approximately 100 miles from north to south from Portland to Eugene and is approximately 60 miles wide at its broadest point. You can access the Willamette Valley via U.S. Highway 26 just north of Cannon Beach; Oregon Highway 6 from Tillamook; Oregon Highway 18 just north of Lincoln City; U.S. Highway 20 at Newport; and Oregon Highway 126 at Florence. Most wineries in this region are located in the lower hills on the western edge of the Willamette Valley in distinct regions. These regions include the region west of Eugene close to the town of Veneta, the South Salem Hills, the Eola Hills located northwest of Salem, and the Red Hills of Dundee located southwest of Portland.

The **Umpqua Valley** is easily accessible from the Central and South Coast via Oregon Highway 38 at Reedsport or Oregon Highway 42 at Coos Bay and is located in the Coast Range between Roseburg and the coast. This region is higher and drier than the Willamette Valley and is host to a rich diversity of soils that produce excellent varieties of Chardonnay, Sauvignon Blanc, Cabernet Sauvignon, Pinot Noir, and Riesling.

The Rogue Valley located in southern Oregon stretches from Ashland westward to the Illinois Valley, and south to the wild, rugged Siskiyou Mountains. This appellation is at the highest elevation of all Oregon wine appellations and is the most accessible. You can get there by traveling east from Coos Bay on OR 42 toward Roseburg and then traveling south on Interstate 5 to Grants Pass, Medford, or Ashland. This appellation consists of three subregions: the Bear Creek Valley, Applegate Valley, and the Illinois Valley. The warmer eastern side of the Rogue appellation features Cabernet Sauvignon, Merlot, Cabernet Franc, Sauvignon Blanc, and Syrah; and the cooler, western side of this appellation produces Pinot Noir, Pinot Gris, Pinot Blanc, Chardonnay, and Gewürztraminer.

All three of these appellations have moderate temperatures and long growing cycles. Two significant geographic factors that affect the climatic conditions for winegrowers in the western half of Oregon are the Pacific Ocean and the north-south Cascade mountain range. Moist marine air flows in from the coast and the Cascade Mountains form a barrier that keeps most of the moisture on the west side of the mountains, creating rainfall that averages between 40 and 80 inches a year. This moisture results in a moderate tempera-

Oregon Grapes

The Reds

Cabernet Sauvignon takes on the flavors of berries and herbs when grown in cooler regions of Oregon and spicier flavors of mushroom and dark chocolate in warmer regions. When aged in oak barrels, these flavors blend into a more sophisticated, softer wine.

Merlot is a rich wine that has distinctive fruity flavors of cherry and plum. This wine is a favorite across the country and is grown mainly in the southern and eastern parts of the state. Over time, this wine combines flavors of mushroom, toasted nut, and tobacco.

Pinot Noir is the most common variety produced in Oregon and grows well in Oregon's cool climate. This variety is complex and when still young captures the flavors of black cherry, currants, and plum. As the wine ages and grows in complexity, flavors can become a mix of earth, leather, mushroom, spice, and tobacco.

Zinfandel is grown in warm regions and, when young, blends flavors of berry, cherry, and plum. This wine becomes very strong and can develop flavors that resemble roasted coffee.

Other Reds: Wineries throughout Oregon are beginning to produce other red varietals such as Dolcetto, Gamay Noir, Maréchal Foch, Nebbiolo, Syrah, and Tempranillo.

The Whites

Chardonnay is crisp and complex and comes in second behind Pinot Noir as the most-planted grape in the state. Chardonnays have an acidic profile and can range in flavor from green apple, banana, and citrus to caramel, herbs, and toasted hazelnuts.

Gewürztraminer is a pungent grape that produces flavors of cinnamon, ginger, and honey and is a good match for spicy cuisine.

Müller-Thurgau is mild and low in acidity and complements spicy dishes.

Pinot Blanc is a dry, crisp wine. It captures the essence of apples, pears, almonds, and a touch of lavender, with a buttery finish.

Pinot Gris is a crisp, fruity wine with floral aromas that is emerging as a popular varietal for Oregon growers.

Sauvignon Blanc can have traits of citrus or herbs with strong varietal aromas. These vibrant tastes and aromas soften as the wine ages.

White Riesling is produced in the cooler wine-growing regions in Oregon and can be made into a dry, crisp wine or a sweeter wine.

Other Whites: Wineries throughout Oregon are beginning to produce other white varietals such as Muscat, Viognier, and Semillon.

ture zone and when combined with warm sunlight and cool nights the perfect environment for grapes to ripen is created.

Oregon is home to many world-class wineries, and before you plan your winery tour, we thought it would be helpful to introduce you to the different varieties of wines produced in Oregon and also give you some wine tasting tips.

Willamette Valley Wineries

Amity Vineyards
18150 Amity Vineyards Road SE, Amity
(888) 264–8966
www.amityvineyards.com

Amity Vineyards is well known for its Pinot Noir. They also feature Gewürztraminer and Riesling, Gamay Noir, and Oregon

Winetasting Tips

Winetasting is a fun way to learn about different types of wine, and we thought we would help you in your winetasting tour by providing you with a few winetasting tips. When you are served a glass of wine, pay attention to the winery that produced the wine and the type of grape. Swirl the wine in your glass and notice its color and clarity. Wines that display brown characteristics have become oxidized or stale. The wine should be clear and not cloudy, although some older wines may leave sediment at the bottom of the glass. After you swirl the wine in the glass, hold the glass close to your nose and smell the aroma of the wine. Many wines have aromas that are very distinctive, and, with practice, you will learn the nuances of a fine wine's scents. Next, take a small sip of wine, slowly swallow, and concentrate on the different flavors of the wine as you swallow. Fine wines have a complex range of tastes that you'll learn to distinguish.

Blush. A newer addition to this winery's outstanding selections is Pinot Blanc. This vineyard is open from February 1 through December 23 from noon to 5:00 P.M. daily; they are closed from December 24 through January 31. Other locations where you can sample Amity's outstanding wines are The Oregon Wine Tasting Room and The Lawrence Gallery, located 9 miles southwest of McMinnville on OR 18, (503) 843–3787; and the Oregon Wine Tasting Room Too with the Nestucca Bay Trading Company, located in Pacific City (2.5 miles west of U.S. Highway 101), (503) 965-7369.

Archery Summit Winery
18599 Northeast Archery Summit Road, Dayton
(800) 732–8822
www.archerysummit.com

The Archery Summit Winery produces premium Pinot Noir wine that is harvested from more than 100 acres of vines and is aged in French oak barrels. You can taste current vintages by calling for an appointment for one of the following times: 11:00 A.M., 1:00 P.M., and 3:30 P.M. Thursday through Sunday.

Argyle Winery
691 Oregon Highway 99W, Dundee
(503) 538–8520
www.argylewinery.com

You can enjoy tasting Chardonnay, Pinot Noir, and Dry Riesling in a quaint Victorian farmhouse at Argyle Winery. Argyle produces grapes on more than 235 acres of premium vineyards and is well known for its New World sparkling wines. Visitors are welcome 11:00 A.M. to 5:00 P.M. daily. The winery is closed Easter, Thanksgiving, Christmas, and New Year's Day.

Chateau Benoit
6580 Northeast Mineral Springs Road, Carlton
(503) 864–2991
www.chateaubenoit.com

Chateau Benoit winery is located on a stunning hilltop and has sweeping views of the Yamhill County. Dry Riesling, Chardonnay, Sauvignon Blanc, Pinot Noir, dry Gewürztraminer, Sweet Marie (dessert wine), and Brut sparkling wine are this winery's specialities. Visitors are welcome at the winery 10:00 A.M. to 5:00 P.M. daily. The winery is closed Thanksgiving, Christmas, and New Year's Day. You can also find Chateau Benoit's wines at the Chateau Benoit Wine and Food Center located in the Factory Stores at Lincoln City, (503) 996-3981.

Duck Pond Cellars
23145 Oregon Highway 99W, Dundee
(503) 538–3199
www.duckpondcellars.com

Duck Pond Cellars in Dundee produces award-winning wines at affordable prices. Some featured varieties include golden, buttery Chardonnays; Pinot Noirs that have the rich essence of black cherries and cedar; and spicy, velvety Merlots. Another favorite is Semillon Ice Wine—a rich dessert wine that has splashes of apricot and pineapple. Visitors are welcome 10:00 A.M. to 5:00 P.M. daily (May through October) and 11:00 A.M. to 5:00 P.M. daily (November through April). The winery is closed New Year's Day, Easter, Thanksgiving, and Christmas Day.

Elk Cove
27751 Northwest Olson Road, Gaston
(503) 985–7760
www.elkcove.com

Elk Cove is well known for its dessert wines as well as Chardonnay, Cabernet Sauvignon, Pinot Gris, Pinot Noir, and Riesling. Visitors are welcome from 10:00 A.M. to 5:00 P.M. daily. Elk Cove is closed Thanksgiving, Christmas Eve, Christmas, and New Year's Day.

Eola Hills Wine Cellars
501 South Pacific Highway (99W), Rickreall
(503) 623–3405
www.eolahillswinery.com

Eola Hills has an award-winning late-harvest Gewürztraminer named "Vin d'Epice" that is part of its vast line of wines produced at four different vineyards that include Visconti, Rivenwood, Oak Grove, and Illahe Hills. Other surprises you'll find at this winery are luscious berry Cabernet and herby Sauvignon Blanc. Fabulous Sunday brunches are also featured at this winery. Visiting hours are 11:00 A.M. to 5:00 P.M. daily. Eola Hills is closed Thanksgiving, Christmas, and New Year's Day.

Erath Vineyards Winery
9409 Northeast Worden Hill Road, Dundee
(503) 538–3318
www.erath.com

Located in the picturesque Dundee Hills, Erath Vineyards produces excellent Pinot Gris, Pinot Noir, Pinot Blanc, Riesling, Gewürztraminer, and Dolcetto. More than two-thirds of the wine production at Erath Vineyards is dedicated to Pinot Noir. The red clay soil of the Dundee Hills is ideal for growing Pinot Noir and four different types of Pinot Noir are offered at the winery. The least expensive is the Vintage Pinot Noir, which displays fruity characteristics and is easy drinking. The Vintage Select Pinot Noir is rich and complex and is made from only select grapes. The Reserve Pinot Noir and Single Vineyard Pinot Noir are very special batches that are made in small quantities and

Insiders' Tip

Keep these thoughts in mind before you begin your wine tour:

Always call a winery ahead of time to verify the times they are open.

Make sure you have a designated driver.

Allow enough time for your planned route; the distances between some wineries can be deceiving.

If it's during dry weather, bring a blanket and pack a picnic lunch. Most wineries have picnic facilities.

Always be prepared for wet weather by packing an umbrella, rain gear, and warm clothing.

only come from the rare and special vineyard sites. Visiting hours for this winery are 11:00 A.M. to 5:00 P.M. daily.

King Estate Winery
80854 Territorial Road, Eugene
(800) 884–4441
www.kingestate.com

King Estate lives up to its name by producing top-quality Pinot Noir, Pinot Gris, and Chardonnay on more than 820 acres in the southern Willamette Valley. Everything about this winery breathes success, starting with its 110,000-square-foot European chateau wine-making facility to its carefully managed nursery and orchards. Visiting hours are noon to 5:00 P.M. daily Memorial Day through Labor Day; noon to 5:00 P.M. weekends only Labor Day to Memorial Day; closed Thanksgiving, Christmas Eve, Christmas, and New Year's Day.

Oak Knoll Winery
29700 Southwest Burkhalter Road, Hillsboro
(503) 648–8198
www.oakknollwinery.com

Oak Knoll Winery gained its early success from producing berry wines at an affordable price. Star varieties from this winery include Pinot Gris, Pinot Noir, Chardonnay, Riesling, and a scrumptious raspberry wine labeled as Frambrosia. Oak Knoll is also proud to sell Niagara, which is produced from a grape varietal called Niagara, a member of the Vitus Labrusca family of vines. This wine is the color of pale straw and has a slightly sweet grape flavor that is long lasting. Visiting hours

are 11:00 A.M. to 5:00 P.M. on the weekends and 11:00 A.M. to 4:00 P.M. Monday through Friday. The winery is closed major holidays.

Ponzi Vineyards
14665 Southwest Winery Lane, Beaverton
(503) 628–1227
www.ponziwines.com

Ponzi Vineyards is one of the oldest wineries in Oregon and has Pinot Noir, Chardonnay, Riesling, and Pinot Gris vines that were planted in the 1970s. This winery makes one of the most well loved Pinot Gris in Oregon. Another favorite is the Pinot Noir, which is smoky and complex. The tasting room for the winery is open 11:00 A.M. to 5:00 P.M. daily. Ponzi also runs the Dundee Bistro, (503) 554–1650, which serves delicious Northwest cuisine featuring local wines, and the Ponzi Wine Bar, located at the corner of 7th and OR 99 in Dundee, (503) 554–1500. The Ponzi Wine Bar is open 11:00 A.M. to 5:00 P.M. daily.

Redhawk Vineyard
2995 Michigan City Avenue NW, Salem
(503) 362–1596
www.redhawkwine.com

Redhawk Vineyard produces French oak-barrel-aged estate Pinot Noir, Pinot Gris, and Chardonnay. Cabernet Sauvignon and Merlot are also favorites from this winery. Redhawk's wines stand out from the crowd by their silly cartoon labels such as "Grateful Red" and "Chateau Mootom," which have won them "Worst Label Awards" by *Decanter* magazine.

While the label choices may be questioned, the wines are first class and worth tasting. Visiting hours are noon to 5:00 P.M. daily (April through November) and noon to 5:00 P.M. Monday through Friday (December through March).

Rex Hill Vineyards
30835 North Oregon Highway 99W, Newberg
(503) 538-0666
www.rexhill.com

Rex Hill Vineyards boasts a warmly furnished tasting room with a huge fireplace, antiques, and an interesting collection of modern art. Winemaker Lynn Penner-Ash produces wonderful Pinot Blanc, Pinot Noir, Pinot Gris, Chardonnay, Sauvignon Blanc, and White Riesling on more than 225 acres of vineyards. Visiting hours are from 11:00 A.M. to 5:00 P.M. daily and 10:00 A.M. to 5:00 P.M. daily during the summer months. The winery is closed Thanksgiving, Christmas Day, and New Year's Day.

Sokol Blosser Winery
5000 Sokol Blosser Lane, Dundee
(800) 582-6668
www.sokolblosser.com

Susan and Bill Blosser started Sokol Blosser Winery in 1971. The grapes at this winery are harvested by hand and Pinot Noir and Chardonnay are aged in French oak casks to produce full-flavored wines. In addition to a fine tasting room with grand views of the Willamette Valley, this winery also features a walk-through showcase vineyard that is designed as a self-guided tour where you can learn about the different grape varieties and seasons at the vineyard. Visiting hours are 11:00 A.M. to 5:00 P.M. daily. The winery is closed Thanksgiving, Christmas, and New Year's Day.

Tualatin Estate Vineyards
10850 Northwest Seavey Road, Forest Grove
(503) 357-5005

Tualatin Estate Vineyards produces Chardonnay, Gewürztraminer, Pinot Noir, Pinot Blanc, Riesling, and Semi-Sparkling Muscat on 145 acres of vineyards. Established in 1973, this winery is one of the oldest in the Willamette Valley. Visiting hours are noon to 5:00 P.M. Saturday and Sunday (March 1 through December 31). The winery is closed Thanksgiving, Christmas, New Year's Day, and Easter.

The Red Hills of Dundee produce some of Oregon's best Pinot Noir wines. PHOTO: LIZANN DUNEGAN

Umpqua Valley Wineries

Abacela Vineyards & Winery
12500 Lookingglass Road, Roseburg
(541) 679–6642
www.abacela.com

Abacela produces handcrafted Dolcetto, Grenache, Malbec, Syrah, and Tempranillo varietals that are aged in oak casks. You can visit the winetasting room 11:00 A.M. to 5:00 P.M. daily.

Callahan Ridge Winery
340 Busenbark Lane, Roseburg
(541) 673–7901, (888) WINE–4US
(946–3487)
www.callahanridge.com

The Callahan Ridge Estate produces Chardonnay, Cabernet Sauvignon, and Pinot Noir, as well as Zinfandel, Riesling, Chardonnay, Merlot, Grenache, and Syrah. The winetasting and production facility is housed in an historic 1878 restored hay barn. You can visit the tasting room from 11:00 A.M. to 6:00 P.M. daily. The winery is closed from November through March.

Girardet Wine Cellars
895 Reston Road, Roseburg
(541) 679–7252
www.girardetwine.com

Girardet Wine Cellars was established in 1971 by Philippe Girardet and is one of the few wineries in the West producing Baco Noir and Seyval Blanc. Wines pro-duced here are grown on 25 acres of care-fully cultivated vineyards. The winery also produces Cabernet Sauvignon, Chardonnay, Pinot Noir, Riesling, White Zinfandel, Country Rosé, Vin Rouge, and Maréchal Foch. Visitors are welcome 11:00 A.M. to 5:00 P.M. daily. The winery is closed major holidays.

Henry Estate Winery
687 Hubbard Creek Road, Umpqua
(541) 459–5120, tasting room:
(800) 782–2686
www.henryestate.com

Chardonnay, Pinot Noir, Pinot Gris, Gewürztraminer, Müller-Thurgau, and White Riesling are specialties of the Henry Estate Winery, which was established in 1972. Located next to the scenic Umpqua River, this winery has a pretty picnic area and flower gardens and welcomes visitors 11:00 A.M. to 5:00 P.M. daily. The winery is closed major holidays and Super Bowl Sunday.

La Garza Cellars & Gourmet Kitchen
491 Winery Lane, Roseburg
(541) 679–9654

Established in 1968, La Garza Cellars features Cabernet Sauvignon, Merlot, Dry Riesling, Pinot Gris, and a dry, white cabernet called "Rosado de la Casa." The Gourmet Kitchen serves lunch Sunday through Wednesday (May through September). Visiting hours for the winery are noon to 4:00 P.M. Sunday through Wednesday (February

Insiders' Tip

Turn your day trip wine tour into a weekend wine tour. Plan on enjoying the wine country longer by staying at a bed-and-breakfast. Wine Country Farm (800) 261-3446 near Dayton is at the center of several different wineries including Archery Summit, Erath Vineyards, and Sokol Blosser. Another wonderful bed-and-breakfast is the Baker Street Bed and Breakfast in McMinnville (800) 870-5575 that is conveniently located near Amity Vineyards and Chateau Benoit.

through May and October through mid-December); and daily 11:00 A.M. to 5:00 P.M. (June through September). The winery is closed late December through January.

Rogue Valley Wineries

The Academy
18200 Oregon Highway 238 (Applegate),
Grants Pass
(541) 846–6817

The Academy produces rich Cabernet Sauvignon, Merlot, Pinot Noir, and Chardonnay in the sunny Applegate Valley. Visitors by appointment and 2:00 to 5:00 P.M. most holiday weekends.

Ashland Vineyards
2775 East Main Street, Ashland
(541) 488–0088
www.winenet.com

Ashland Vineyards is located in the heart of Ashland and produces top-quality Cabernet, Merlot, Chardonnay, Sauvignon Blanc, Cabernet-Merlot Blend, Pinot Gris, and Müller-Thurgau. You can taste these fine wines in a friendly, country cottage tasting room. Visiting hours are: January and February by appointment only; 11:00 A.M. to 5:00 P.M. Tuesday through Saturday during November, December, and March; and 11:00 A.M. to 5:00 P.M. Tuesday through Sunday (April 1 through October 31); closed December 24 through January 1.

Bear Creek Winery
6220 Caves Highway, Cave Junction
(541) 592–3977

Bear Creek Winery makes Pinot Noir, Cabernet Sauvignon, Merlot, Sauvignon Blanc, and Gewürztraminer from some of the oldest vineyards in Oregon. The winery features a picnic area with grand views of the Siskiyou Mountains. Visiting hours are noon to 5:00 P.M. daily Memorial Day through Labor Day. By appointment only from September through March.

Bridgeview Vineyards
4210 Holland Loop Road, Cave Junction
(877) 273–4843
www.bridgeviewwine.com

Insiders' Tip

If you want to spend the weekend exploring the Rogue Valley wineries, you can stay at the Kerbyville Inn located at 24304 Redwood Highway, Kerby, (541) 592-4689.

Bridgeview is located in the sunny coastal mountains of Southern Oregon and produces award-winning Pinot Noir, Chardonnay, Merlot, Pinot Gris, Gewürztraminer, and Riesling. The winery has two vineyards covering 165 acres and boasts state-of-the-art equipment and a unique tasting room surrounded by beautiful landscaping and panoramic views. Visiting hours are 11:00 A.M. to 5:00 P.M. daily.

Foris Vineyards Winery
654 Kendall Road, Cave Junction
(800) 84–FORIS (843–6747)
www.foriswine.com

Foris Vineyards is located in the Siskiyou Mountains and is a leader in making Chardonnay, Gewürztraminer, Early Muscat, Pinot Blanc, Pinot Gris, Pinot Noir, and Ruby (Pinot Port)—a unique variety that exhibits juicy cherry character and earthy chocolate. Visiting hours are 11:00 A.M. to 5:00 P.M. seven days a week. Call ahead if you plan to visit on a holiday.

Valley View Winery
1000 Upper Applegate Road, Jacksonville
(541) 899–8468
Anna Maria's Tasting Room, Jacksonville
(541) 899–1001
www.valleyviewwinery.com

Valley View Winery makes Cabernet Sauvignon, Merlot, Chardonnay, Syrah, and Cabernet Franc, which thrive in the sunny, warm climate of the Applegate Valley. Valley View's premium wines are marketed under the "Anna Marie" label and their more affordable wines are labeled "Valley View."

Oregon wineries produce world-class wines that are just waiting to be tasted. PHOTO: LIZANN DUNEGAN

Visiting hours are 11:00 A.M. to 5:00 P.M. daily. Anna Maria's Tasting Room is open noon to 6:00 P.M. Wednesday through Sunday (January through April) and 11:00 A.M. to 6:00 P.M. daily (April through December).

Weisinger's of Ashland
3150 Siskiyou Boulevard, Ashland
(541) 488–5989
www.weisingers.com

Weisinger's is located just off Interstate 5 in Ashland and features a deli, gift shop, and tasting room. Weisinger's makes Chardonnay, Cabernet Blanc, Pinot Noir, Merlot, and Gewürztraminer. They also feature red and white blends such as 50 percent Chardonnay and 50 percent Semillon. The picnic area has outstanding views of the Rogue Valley. Visiting hours are 10:00 A.M. to 6:00 P.M. during

the spring and summer months and 11:00 A.M. to 5:00 P.M. during the fall and winter months.

Portland

Portland is a beautiful city that is only a couple hours drive from the Central and North Coast. Portland covers 130 square miles and is filled with over 37,000 acres of parks, historic bridges, unique shopping districts, art museums, funky bookstores, cream-of-the-crop coffeehouses, boisterous brewpubs, unique restaurants, and fun nightlife. Portland is separated into east and west sides by the Willamette River and U.S. 26 is the main arterial highway leading into downtown Portland from the west; Interstate 5 leads into the city from the south and north; and Interstate 84 comes in from the east. The city is separated into the Northwest, Southwest, Northeast, and Southeast districts by the east-west running Burnside Street and the Willamette.

A good place to start exploring Portland is the downtown core area, which is made up of the Southwest District and part of the Northwest District. Be sure to stop by the **Portland Visitors Association,** 26 Southwest Salmon Street, (503) 222–2223, where you can find a free copy of the *Official Visitors Guide, Portland, Oregon* that contains detailed maps and descriptions about Portland and the surrounding area. Or pick up a copy of the *Insiders' Guide to Portland* at local bookstores. If you look at a map of the downtown area, you'll see that Broadway and 6th Street run right through the heart of the downtown. Front Avenue runs north-south along the edge of the Willamette River and parallels **Tom McCall Waterfront Park,** which runs for 2 miles along Front Avenue. The vast lawns and jogging paths of this park are a favorite for walkers, joggers, and rollerbladers. RiverPlace is located on the south end of the park and features a hotel, restaurant, shops, and marina. **The Japanese-American Historical Plaza** is located on the north end of the grassy park and is a memorial to the Japanese-Americans who were interned by the U.S.

government during World War II. Another popular attraction along the waterfront is **Saturday Market,** 108 West Burnside Street, which is located under the Burnside Bridge and features arts and crafts from local artists and fabulous ethnic food from a wide assortment of vendors. Saturday Market is open on weekends from March 1 through Christmas Eve on Saturday 10:00 A.M. to 5:00 P.M. and Sunday 11:00 A.M. to 4:30 P.M.

Book lovers need to be sure to stop by **Powell's City of Books** located at 1005 West Burnside Street, (503) 228–4651. Powell's City of Books is a Portland landmark and is the largest independent bookstore in the United States. The one-of-a-kind bookstore covers an entire city block and features over a million new and used books. **Powell's Travel Store,** 701 Southwest 6th Avenue, (503) 228–1108, is another great bookstore where you can find numerous guidebooks on Oregon and the Northwest as well as other travel destinations. This bookstore is located in Pioneer Courthouse Square, a redbrick square that is host to numerous concerts, festivals, and exhibits throughout the year. Pioneer Courthouse Square is at the heart of downtown and is close to some of Portland's major shopping venues such as **Pioneer Place,** Southwest 5th Avenue and Morrison; **Nordstrom,** 701 Southwest Broadway; **Meier & Frank,** 621 Southwest 5th Avenue; and **Niketown,** 930 Southwest 6th Avenue. Another unique shopping district worth visiting is the **Pearl District,** which stretches from Northwest 10th to Northwest 14th Avenues between Everett and Glisan. This unique shopping district contains galleries, boutiques, and fun restaurants in an area of renovated industrial sites and hip new buildings. A fun event in this district is the first Thursday **art walk,** when galleries stay open late the first Thursday of each month and admission is free. If you are in the mood for more art, you should visit the **Portland Art Museum,** 1219 Southwest Park Avenue, (503) 226–2811, or catch a play or symphony concert at the **Portland Center for Performing Arts,** 1111 Southwest Broadway, (503) 248–4335. If you are a movie buff, visit the **Northwest Film**

Center, 1219 Southwest Park Avenue, (503) 221–1156.

From the downtown area you can catch a ride on **MAX** (Metropolitan Area Express) light rail that heads east toward Gresham crossing over the Steel Bridge and passing through the **Lloyd District.** The Lloyd District includes the massive **Rose Garden Arena,** home to the Portland Trail Blazers and the **Lloyd Center,** with more than 200 stores and a large ice rink that is a popular hang our for kids. MAX also heads west and stops right at the **Oregon Zoo,** (503) 226–1561, and **World Forestry Center,** (503) 228–1367, before continuing toward Beaverton and Hillsboro. You can also catch a ride on **Tri-Met** transit, (503) 238–RIDE (238-7433). Rides on Tri-Met and MAX are free in the 300-block downtown area known as "Fareless Square." To pick up schedules and find out more information, visit the **Tri-Met office** located on Southwest 6th Avenue between Morrison and Yamhill at Pioneer Courthouse Square.

If you want to check out scrumptious cuisine, stop by **Canita,** 503 West Burnside Street, which serves up rich Cuban dishes such as fried pork adobo; **Brasserie Montmartre,** 626 Southwest Park Avenue, which offers excellent French-style dishes and great cocktails; **The Heathman Hotel,** 1001 Southwest Broadway, a classy club that plays cool jazz with no cover. Good blues music can be enjoyed at the **Candlelight Cafe & Bar,** 2032 Southwest 5th Avenue, seven nights a week. If you just want to check out the Portland night scene, stop by **Hubers,** 411 Southwest 3rd Avenue, which is famous for its flaming Spanish coffees served with style and flair, or you can try blending into the hip, late-night scene at the trendy **Montage** located at 301 Southeast Morrison.

The **Southeast District** is filled with unique antiques shops, bookstores, second-hand stores, and brewpubs. It is also home to **Oregon Museum of Science and Industry** (OMSI), 1945 Southeast Water Avenue, which contains interesting exhibits on science and technology and also shows movies in its state-of-the-art Omnimax Theater. If you're in the mood for a movie and a brew, mosey on over to the **Bagdad**

Theatre and Pub, 3702 Southeast Hawthorne Boulevard, (503) 236-9234, where you can see a movie and taste some local McMenamin's brewed beers. Hammerhead and Terminator are two favorite brews at this pub. A favorite locals' hangout is **The Lucky Labrador Brew Pub,** 915 Southeast Hawthorne Boulevard, which serves great local brews and bentos (a bowl of rice topped with veggies or meat with a special sauce, such as curry sauce) in a warehouse-style atmosphere. Recommended brews are the Lucky Dog IPA or Hawthorne Bitter. If you don't mind hanging out in the outside eating area, you can bring your canine pal along to keep you company as you sip your brew. Unique restaurants are sprinkled throughout this district, such as **Esparza's Tex-Mex Cafe,** 2725 Southeast Ankeny Street, which serves dishes in true Texas tradition including fried cactus and buffalo briskets, outlandish ostrich dishes, and cheesy, jalapeno enchiladas; **Niki's,** 736 Southeast Grand Avenue, serves delicious Greek food, which should always be accompanied by nourishing hummus and fresh, hot pita bread; **Noho's Hawaiian Cafe,** 2525 Southeast Clinton Street, makes a mean bowl of yakisoba noodles and vegetables as well as other outlandish ethnic dishes that will tantalize your palate; **Caprial's Bistro,** 7015 Southeast Milwaukee Avenue, serves wonderful Northwest dishes such as salmon with white truffles. Great Mexican food can be found at the **Iron Horse Restaurant,** 6034 Southeast Milwaukee Avenue.

The trendy **Northwest District** has two popular avenues (Northwest 21st and Northwest 23rd) that are filled with trendy coffeehouses, treasure-filled shops, and unique restaurants. This area of Portland also has some magnificently restored Victorian houses gracing its side streets. Parking is tight and walking is the recommended method for getting around this area. If you are looking for a perfect cup coffee or some scrumptious ice cream, be sure to stop by **Coffee People** located at 533 Northwest 23rd Avenue. For a fun place to sip on a brew and eat some tasty Mexican food go to **Santa Fe Tacqueria,** 831 Northwest 23rd Avenue, where you can order a huge plateful of Chicken Mole nachos that won't break your pocketbook. Other notable restaurants in this district include **Wildwood,** 1221 Northwest 21st Avenue, which serves innovative Northwest cuisine; **Tapeo,** 2764 Northwest Thurman Street, a Spanish restaurant that serves a variety of small appetizers called tapas, such as roasted eggplant, marinated trout, or Serrano ham and cheese; **La Buca,** 2309 Northwest Kearney Street, which dishes up simple and healthy pasta dishes, Italian-style panini, and wine by the glass; and **Portland Brewing Company,** 2730 Northwest 31st Avenue, which serves delectable German sausages, delicious rosemary fries, and other German-style fare and homemade local brews. Artsy film flicks can be seen at **Cinema 21,** 616 Northwest 21st Avenue, (503) 223-4515. Northwest Portland is also the gateway into the green expanse of 5,000-acre **Forest Park.** A good place to start exploring this forest-filled park is at **Lower McCleay Park,** which can be accessed at the end of Northwest Upshur or via stairs at the Northwest Thurman Street Bridge. A well-maintained hiking trail leads you next to tumbling Balch Creek and eventually leads you to the **Audubon Society, Pittock Mansion,** and **Washington Park.** If you feel like cycling through the park, you can rent a mountain bike at **Fat Tire Farm,** 2714 Northwest Thurman Street, (503) 222-3276, and ride up to the end of Northwest Thurman and hook up with **Leif Erikson Drive** that winds through a forest landscape filled with big-leaf maple and evergreens. There are several fire lanes that also lead off Leif Erikson Drive where you can use up some calories on thigh-burning ascents. Be sure to pick up a free **Forest Park Trail map** at Fat Tire Farm to help you plan a route that will fit your mood and skills.

Oregon Caves National Monument

Established in 1909, the Oregon Caves National Monument is located in the rugged Siskiyou Mountains of southern

Oregon. The 480-acre monument is an easy two-hour drive from Brookings and can be accessed by driving 20 miles south on U.S. 101 to Crescent City, California. From Crescent City, drive 46 miles north on U.S. Highway 199 and then turn east on OR 46 at the town of Cave Junction and travel 20 miles east to the park entrance. (Note that the last 8 miles to the park entrance are narrow and windy and trailers are not recommended. You have to enter California to reach this Oregon site).

The main attraction at this national monument is a large, intricately carved cave that contains 3 miles of chambers and the fast flowing River Styx, which runs through the entire length of the cave. This cave began as limestone deposits in a shallow sea about 200 million years ago. As the continental crust shifted, the limestone layers were lifted up and molten lava protruded into rock faults and formed marble. As the Siskiyou Mountains continued to rumble and shake, the marble formations were exposed and water began to erode the soft rock, creating tunnels and caves. You can explore this magnificent cave by taking a 90-minute guided **cave tour** through more than a half mile of the gleaming marble passageways. Cave tours are given year-round except Thanksgiving and Christmas. Fees for the cave tour are $7.50 for adults, $5.00 for juniors age 16 and younger. Children under 42 inches tall are not allowed on standard cave tours but can participate in a five- to ten-minute free tour given by the park staff. Dress warmly for the tour because the cave has a constant temperature of 41 degrees Fahrenheit year-round and can be wet and slippery. The tour takes you through passages filled with stalactites, columns, cave popcorn, pearls, and moon milk. For more information, call Oregon Caves National Monument at (541) 592-2100; www.nps.gov/orca.

Other activities at the monument include 5 miles of trails that wind through a predominantly Douglas fir forest that is home to 80 species of birds, 35 species of mammals, and more than 110 unique species of plants. The **Cliff Nature Trail**

Insiders' Tip

If you want to taste some locally produced wines on the way to the Oregon Caves National Monument, be sure to stop by Bridgeview Vineyards, 4210 Holland Loop Road, and Foris Vineyards, 654 Kendall Road, both located off Oregon Highway 46. For more information about these two wineries, see the "Winery Tours" section of this chapter.

is a 0.75-mile loop with informative signs that describe the geology, plants, and trees of the wild and beautiful Siskiyou Mountains. **The Big Tree Trail** is a 3.3-mile loop that takes you on a tour of a magnificent old-growth forest whose shining star is a 1,200-year-old Douglas fir. Unfortunately, dogs are not allowed on any of the trails in the monument.

Another attraction that should not be missed is the **Oregon Caves Chateau,** (541) 592–3400. The chateau is an attractive six-story wooden lodge and restaurant that boasts a magnificent fireplace and numerous windows with a spectacular view. The lodge is open Memorial Day through the last weekend of September. A snack bar in the lower part of the lodge is open year-round. This is the only overnight accommodation in the monument. If you want to camp, you can drive to **Cave Creek Campground** located 4 miles from the monument or **Greyback Campground** located 8 miles from the monument. For more information on these campgrounds you can contact the **Siskiyou National Forest,** (541) 471–6500, www.fs.fed.us/r6/siskiyou.

Relocation

According to our unscientific survey, most people who move to the Oregon Coast are seduced by the beauty of the ocean. And when they arrive, they are thrilled to find charming towns that have robust cultural scenes, wonderful restaurants, and interesting museums; and they are enchanted to discover that the Coast also has lovely rivers and lush forests to explore. Then there are the hikes, bike trails, surfing, games of golf, and other outdoor activities that demand attention. And that is before they realize that there are so many absorbing classes at the local community college and opportunities to volunteer. They find themselves busier than ever, even before they find a job. Or maybe not. That's the wonderful thing about the Oregon Coast. You can be as busy or as idle as you wish.

However you choose to spend your time, your choices will be dominated by the terrain. Sometimes that's easy to forget. When you actually have to drive around the block twice to find a place to park on a sunny August afternoon, the coastal towns of Oregon seem like other swarming hubs of culture and commerce. But if you parked your car in the same spot in January, you would remember the central truth about the Oregon Coast: It is a remote area with an ocean on one side and a mountain range on the other. The land and the sea define the ways of life for all coastal residents: They define the region's weather, industries, prices, architecture, and every other fact of daily existence. We dwell in a land that is always changing. Not that we're complaining: We love the changes. They can slow us down, though. Roads wash out; the sands shift; we have to reroute.

Even so, modern life on the Oregon Coast is not that difficult to achieve—we have Web designers, cell phones, and telecommuting; espresso can be found in the unlikeliest places. Modern life just takes place at a gentler pace. This chapter, then, is devoted to helping you adjust to the coastal balance between the ancient rhythms of the earth and the modern rhythms of culture. We hope that the information provided in the following sections will help you find your own balance and free your time for walking on the beach.

Life at the Coast

Before moving to the Oregon Coast, you will have to decide where you want to live. Do you want the forests of the North Coast? Do you long for the dunes of the Central Coast? Or the windswept solitude of the South Coast? Not only must you choose a geographical area, but you must also choose whether you want to live in town or out, in a planned community or independently, in a golf course condominium or on a lonely bluff overlooking the ocean. Plan carefully: When U.S. Highway 101 washes out and you have to take a two-hour detour to the grocery store, the house on the bluff that seemed like the per-

fect antidote to civilization can feel pretty forlorn. You may wish you lived closer to town.

When deciding where to live, you should think about how you like to spend your time in the rain. Oregonians are used to the rain. We don't see it as a deterrent to many activities we wish to pursue; we'd never go anywhere or do anything if we waited for the sun. Some waterproof shoes and a Gore-Tex jacket or a couple of sweaters will see us through all but the very worst weather. We have other ways of managing the weather, too. In the winter months, when the Oregon Coast has the wettest and windiest weather in the state and a foot of rain in one month is no surprise, we entertain ourselves by watching the storms from comfortable indoor spots. And these theatrical storms leave behind them many beachcombing prizes. Of course, it is not all rain here on the Oregon Coast. We also have fog. But the sun shines too; typically, the driest months are July and August and the hottest is September. These months, with their splendid evening light and plentiful stars, are the due reward for all the months of rain.

Work may be another factor in your decision about where to live. If you don't have a job before you move and you're planning to get one, do some research before you decide. The cost of living can be a little higher here than in other parts of Oregon. Goods have to travel farther to get to the stores and so do you. Moreover, while renting houses or apartments can be less expensive than in the city, wages are also proportionately less. And although there are many jobs in this 400-mile stretch of country, unemployment rates on the coast of Oregon are uneven and vary wildly within the region. That's because many of the coastal towns rely on fishing, timber, and tourism, all seasonal and unpredictable.

Nevertheless, you can find good work on the Coast. In an effort to make economic life more stable, many communities have encouraged businesses that are less seasonal. The past 10 years have seen the development of new industries, resorts, research facilities, museums, an aquarium, and other cultural attractions, to list a few of the recent projects on the Coast.

Another option is to start a business. A useful Web site sponsored by the Oregon Secretary of State provides an excellent guide to important information for those who wish to start businesses in Oregon, and you can find it at www.filinginoregon. com. If you plan to start a small business, make use of the Small Business Development Centers that have been established in the coastal community colleges. They will provide research materials, seminars on management, different kinds of training, help with writing a business plan or finding a great site, counseling, and other services—many of which cost little or nothing. Check out their Web site at www.econ.state.or.us/lstsbdc.htm. You can contact Small Business Information Services in the office of the Secretary of State at (503) 986-2200 for more about small businesses in Oregon. Another tip: Take a look at the Department of Economic and Community Development Web page at www.econ.state.or.us. This fascinating site not only links you to all the Small Business Development Centers in Oregon and contains community profiles of all incorporated towns and cities in Oregon, but it also dispenses a staggering amount of information on the economic life of the state. You can also reach the Department of Economic and Community Development at (800) 233-3306.

Most people find that starting a small business on the Oregon Coast is not terribly complicated, but a note of caution is in order. Some business services are not as plentiful as they are in cities. While UPS, Federal Express, RPS, and other delivery companies do serve the Coast, you may have to set up special accounts, drive to drop-off boxes, or adjust to the U.S. Postal Service schedule. And high-speed Internet access is for the most part a dream for the future. It's a good idea to contact the local chamber of commerce before you make your move to get an accurate picture of the labor market, available services, utility costs, office space, and so forth. But the

Insiders' Tip

A few months before you move to a new community, subscribe to its local paper to get a clear picture of the cost of living, cultural events, and issues of local importance.

most important thing to have for your new small business is enough capital. The first winter can be tough, so you should have some money in reserve.

People move to the Oregon Coast for many reasons—to be closer to the ocean, to live a simpler life, to play more golf. Some seek solitude, others desire the intimacy of small-town life where everyone knows the neighbors. Sometimes work brings people; sometimes it's retirement.

With 400 miles of real estate to choose from, you are bound to find something to suit your taste. Following are brief descriptions of coastal towns to help you form an impression about where you'd like to live, and the overall real estate picture. The best way to find the perfect place to live, of course, is to go exploring for yourself (taking this book with you).

North Coast

Astoria/Warrenton

These unpretentious, hardworking towns near the camp of the Lewis and Clark Expedition have a relatively long history. They began as early settlements—Astoria gives 1811, when John Jacob Astor set up a trading post out here, as its official birth date, though it was held by the British for a few years after that. Still, it retained its pioneer spirit: It became the first post office west of the Rocky Mountains in 1847. And it preserves its historical air, with lovingly maintained Victorian houses and buildings adding appeal and character to the town. However, Astoria and Warrenton do not look back on a glorious past—the people here are too busy with the fishing fleet and the salmon charters and the tourists and with piloting huge oceangoing ships up and down the Columbia River. Warrenton has a big shopping center right on the highway; Astoria has an old-fashioned main street to explore. The Astoria/Warrenton area is one of the few on the Coast to have a comprehensive public transportation system. Houses here tend to top out at about $250,000, but many are priced much lower; you can get a lot of house for your money, especially compared with other North Coast locales.

Gearhart

Even though there is a resort here, many of the houses are actually owned by people who live in them. Gearhart is a peaceful little town with many weathered houses and a nice beach renowned for its clamming. Small shops and offices line the main street. It also has the second-oldest golf course in the west, built in 1892. (See the Golf chapter for more details.) Nice houses line the golf course in addition to those that overlook the sea. The resort, Gearhart by the Sea, is thriving. Houses here tend to be expensive. Condominiums in the resort complex can run more than $300,000 and beachfront houses can cost more than $600,000.

Seaside

Seaside was the favored resort community for Portlanders at the turn of the 19th century, and the beachfront houses built then can now fetch millions of dollars (though you can also buy a cute cabin a few blocks off the beach for less than $115,000 and a nice, quiet town house in the foothills of the Coast Range for $150,000). Between the houses and hotels and the beach grass is a long walkway called "the Prom"; residents and tourists alike love to amble along its 2-mile length. And there are many tourists: Seaside has a brand new convention center, an outlet mall, a number of large hotels, bumper cars, candy shops, gift stores, and a really big, popular, sandy beach filled with admirers.

Cannon Beach

What can we say about Cannon Beach? If you are a Microsoft executive with a suitcase full of cash, this is the town for you. The North Coast, especially the Cannon Beach area, is not only the hottest market on the Coast, it may be the hottest market in the state. In Clatsop County as a whole, the average price for a house was $143,000 in 2000. But according to the *Realty Times,* the average price of a house in Cannon Beach was $365,000 in 2002, which put it

Dear Paddy,

I can't wait to see you, hug y[ou]
play football with you and be your best

always listen to your mom and dad
about your grandpa because he will
you and how proud he is of you.

I love you now and will only love
as I get to hold you for the first t[ime]

I love

Gra

, kiss you, love you,

friend.

and always think

ways think about

you more as soon

me.

you so much,

l you

well beyond the average house price for Lake Oswego, a Portland suburb and one of the highest-priced communities in Oregon. Of course, these are only averages. You can still find nice houses in the Cannon Beach area for much less than $300,000; they just won't be right on the water. Property seekers in Cannon Beach usually start out wanting a house right on the beach, but now that beachfront properties sell in the $850,000 to $1 million range, they are looking around at other possibilities.

And why does everyone want to come to Cannon Beach? Besides the lovely beach with the visual interest of Haystack Rock; besides the cohesive feel of the community; besides the local ambiance of artist and intelligentsia and gallery and bookshop; besides the imaginative chamber of commerce that has developed interesting festivals, celebrations, and ceremonies throughout the year; besides all these, there is planning. Cannon Beach thus far has been careful and thoughtful about its building and architecture, so it has retained an attractive character. And in addition, it is right at the end of U.S. Highway 26, which is the principal route from the Coast to Portland.

Manzanita/Neah Kah Nie

Manzanita is a peaceful town off the highway that is mostly residential with some tourist business. We can't say enough good things about this friendly, quiet community. The beach stretches from the base of Neahkahnie Mountain to Nehalem Bay State Park to the south; if you walk all the way to the south end, you'll find a jetty where seals and sea lions like to play. Manzanita also has some excellent restaurants and shops, a fine bed-and-breakfast, and possibly the best periodical selection of the entire Oregon Coast. (See the appropriate chapters for more information.) Housing prices, predictably, have skyrocketed in the past few years. The Neah Kah Nie development, has brought many more houses onto the market, and the demand for them doesn't seem to be slowing. Prices are a little lower than at Cannon Beach, but not much lower.

Tillamook

Tillamook is a quaint hamlet with old-fashioned stores, a wonderful natural history museum, and, of course, a big cheese manufacturing plant just to the north of town. Though floods did a lot of damage a few years ago, this dairy farming community seems to be recovering. Tillamook, and the fishing towns to the north like Garibaldi, Wheeler, and Nehalem, are residential, working places; the properties here tend to be houses that people live in instead of simply visit. You can get some very good value for your money here. Riverfront properties are another option: All that water coming down from the mountains into the ocean makes for some enchanting real estate. While resort communities, such as Neskowin and Oceanside, are established on the coastline here, the area is a little more remote, and therefore less hectic, than some of the more northern communities. Prices vary; you can find everything from a $23,000 mobile home to a $500,000 oceanview property to a four-acre farm by a river with a greenhouse and an atrium for $125,000.

Central Coast

The Central Coast has a lot of great properties for sale; it's a popular weekend spot for people who live in Corvallis and Eugene. Realtors here say that compared with pricier communities farther north, you can get a lot of house for your money.

Lincoln City

Once this area was five independent towns; they joined together to form the "20 Miracle Miles," and the rest is development history. This congested bit of highway is busy all year long; that means, however, that the economy is relatively healthy. Lincoln City itself has about 7,500 people, employed mostly in tourism, with retirement-related industries and services rounding out the economic picture. Though the highway is

crowded, the area itself has some remarkable landscapes, and a beautiful 7.5-mile beach. The town is surrounded by water—not just the ocean, but also Devils Lake to the east, the Salmon River to the north, and Siletz Bay to the south. Like many places on the Coast, the median price of a house is about $160,000, reflecting the wide range of available properties from $75,000 to more than $500,000.

Newport

An active center on the Central Coast, Newport is an exemplar of farsighted planning. An economic development committee made up of local businesspersons realized in the mid-1980s that the economy of Newport had to diversify if the town was going to survive the continual crises in fishing, tourism, and timber. It is now a year-round destination, with attractions that include not only the Oregon Coast Aquarium but also a beautiful performing arts center, an active community theater, and a flourishing arts scene. Newport boasts one of the few real airports on the Coast, as well, so it is easier to get to than some places; moreover, it has a brand-new, modern instrument landing system to help navigate the marine air stew. This is all in addition to the busy fishing fleet that you can watch from the appealing waterfront on Yaquina Bay. Houses in Newport tend to fall a little below the national average; you can find a lot of properties for less than $200,000, and a lot of properties with dramatic views of the bay.

Florence

Florence is a charming city at the edge of the dunes; it is poised to take advantage of all the beauty and recreation activities therein. The landscape changes dramatically here—miles of sand between you and the ocean. The Siuslaw River lends its green grace to the area too, making it one of the most interesting spots on the Coast. Florence also has, however, a new events center and, nearby, a prosperous Old Town shopping district that draws both tourists and locals. Average house prices in Florence run a little less than those of Newport.

Also look at Florence's northern neighbors Yachats (that's ya-HOTS) and

Waldport. Both of these quiet communities offer great fishing, clamming, some charming hotels and restaurants, and great, if more expensive, real estate. You can find more luxury houses in these areas than in some of the surrounding ones; the average price for a house in Yachats is about $180,000.

Reedsport/Winchester Bay

Winchester Bay is a little fishing town built where the Umpqua River spills into the sea. Upstream, Reedsport is a quiet community that attracts retirees (see the Retirement section) with its temperate weather, its mix of activity and leisure, and its natural beauty. The headquarters for the Oregon Dunes National Recreational Area are here, and an elk preserve attracts drivers to the side of U.S. Highway 38. Many little cottages and mobile homes can be purchased here for less—much less—than $100,000 and properties don't seem to go much higher than $250,000.

South Coast

The South Coast has many good properties for sale—it's a buyers' market here. Its location—it takes awhile to get there—means that the property prices have not appreciated as fast as they have in the north. Sometimes you can find amazing bargains: fixers for $30,000, for instance. Keep in mind, though, that the economy is not quite as vigorous as it is in the north either.

Coos Bay/North Bend

Coos Bay has had it rough for a while as the timber market and fishing industries have morphed into tourism. Unemployment tends to be higher in Coos County than in other coastal areas. But development officials are making the best of it, emphasizing their assets—a rich history, one of the few airports on the Coast that connect to PDX in Portland, and the largest coastal harbor between Puget Sound and San Francisco, with a refurbished boardwalk that's nice for hanging out. You won't see them from U.S. 101, but Coos Bay has some beautiful old houses that are restored and well maintained. Go up the hill, away from the waterfront and you'll see what we mean. These houses are more expensive than the average. Average prices for a three-bedroom, two-bath house in the area are in the $115,000 range, though, like anywhere, you pay more for a good view.

Bandon

Bandon is an enchanting town—some folks say it actually is enchanted—with a handsome lighthouse (Coquille River Lighthouse), unusual rock formations, and an attractive Old Town district with art galleries and cafes. The town's key industries are dairy products and cranberries, and tourists and residents alike take advantage of excellent golf, fishing, windsurfing, and beachcombing. Contractors are being kept busy on Beach Loop Drive, with its dramatic views of Bandon's rock formations and its beach access. Overall, you may find many properties listed for under $100,000 and the most expensive and elegant beachfront houses can be had for under $500,000.

Gold Beach

The Rogue River meets the ocean here, and it makes for some dramatic scenery. If we say that Gold Beach offers the usual assortment of recreational activities associated with the Coast—beachcombing, fishing, horseback riding, golf, hiking,

Insiders' Tip
Owners of vacation properties sometimes look for long-term leasers and offer their houses at significantly cheaper prices per month than they would be if you were just renting the house for a week. Ask your vacation rental agency.

and so on—it is merely that we are suffering from an embarrassment of riches. And that's even before we get to talking about the recreational opportunities on the Rogue River. Housing prices in this area, about 40 miles north of the California border, tend to be similar to those found in Brookings or maybe a little less.

Brookings-Harbor

Practically as far south as you can get and still be in Oregon, the Brookings-Harbor area offers natural beauty, a busy harbor, and charm. The surrounding beaches are uncrowded and the surf pounds them smooth; spectacular bluffs with meadows of profuse wildflowers drop dramatically to the frothy blue-green water below. And that doesn't include the great fishing on the Chetco River or the redwood groves nearby. Brookings is a wonderful place that inspires great devotion in residents and visitors alike. Many of these are retirees attracted by the beauty of the area and the weather: It tends to be warmer here than anywhere else on the Coast. Brookings is a little larger than many of the boroughs on the Coast, with 6,000 residents. The real estate scene is varied; everything from manufactured homes for

under $100,000 to luxury houses at $500,000. The high-end houses are not as expensive as they are in, say, Cannon Beach; correspondingly, the average house price is lower—less than $200,000.

Real Estate

There are two strong markets for houses on the Coast: residential properties and vacation properties. The economic boom that urban areas like Seattle and Portland have enjoyed is trickling down to some communities on the Coast. The demand is strong for vacation properties and for middle-income year-round houses, but the money involved with the first group puts pressure on the second, especially in the North, where beachfront houses may now sell in the $850,000 to $1,000,000 range. All along the Coast, properties are selling well; they seem, however, to move faster and have appreciated more in the North. If you are a middle-income person thinking of relocating to the Oregon Coast, you might try some of the areas that have fewer vacation houses. And whatever your budget and location, expect to pay a lot more for houses that are on the water. These proper-

Cedar shake bungalows are popular vacation homes on the Oregon Coast. PHOTO: LIZANN DUNEGAN ties will occasionally skew the curve—an average house in a town might cost $180,000 but a fancy one on the beach could be four or five times that.

If you're interested in buying a vacation property, be sure to cover the same steps that you would if you were buying a residential property: Study the markets, comparison shop, hire an inspector, and so on. Some additional factors, however, will be important in your vacation house purchase. Consult property management companies in the area about vacancy and rental rates. Experts say that the most important factor in vacation house purchasing is the accessibility of recreational activities. So be sure that there are enough recreational activities in the area for the house to maintain its value. And develop an accurate picture of the expenses of maintaining a second house. Will you be maintaining it yourself, or will you hire someone to do it? If you're considering the purchase of a condominium in a resort complex, for example, find out the cost of fees and maintenance. Finally, make sure you understand the tax rules: If you rent out the house, you may not be able to take a mortgage-interest deduction on it. Ask your tax advisor.

Building a house is another alternative. Some developers will build to suit you or modify their designs. Whether you go it alone or go with a developer, make sure you fully comprehend any development restrictions. And you might consider hiring an engineer: Sands have been known to shift and threaten even expensive developments with irreparable erosion. The Oregon Coast has quite a few builders associations that can help you sort through the hundreds of contractors and subcontractors waiting to help you break ground. Most chambers of commerce can help you find the one for your area, or you can look at a list of a number of Oregon builders associations at www.contractor find.com/assoc/or.htm. The Oregon Building Industry Association can be reached at (503) 378–9066, www.obia.net; they can also provide information on Building Associations. Once you have a contractor, you should check that he has a current registration number with the State of Oregon; this registration can offer you some (but not comprehensive) financial protection if something goes wrong. The 24-hour contractor inquiry line is (503) 378–4610.

Building permits have held fairly steady in recent years after an upward trend early in the 1990s. As with other aspects of real estate on the Coast, the hot building spots vary from county to county, with the North Coast seeing the most activity.

Whether or not you are planning to purchase a house, renting can be a fine way to get to know an area. Realtors can often help you find rental houses; many of the companies listed below have property management divisions. Apartments on the Oregon Coast seem to all be in the $400 to $600 range, with occasional cheaper studios and more expensive condominiums. Some property management companies can help you find an apartment, and these companies can sometimes put you in touch with long-term leases of vacation properties too. And finding employment as an on-site property manager can procure rental rates that are excellently low, enabling you to move to the Oregon Coast sooner than you might have otherwise.

The beauty of the Oregon Coast brings people here and therefore, paradoxically, contains the seeds of its own destruction.

One of the most pressing difficulties facing coastal residents is to maintain the aesthetic quality of the Coast and to preserve the environment while at the same time encouraging business. The pace and manner of growth is a subject of much debate at town meetings all up and down the Coast, and you should be aware of this debate if you are planning to buy or build on the Coast.

Oregon Association of Realtors
P.O. Box 351, Salem 97308
(800) 252–9115
http://or.realtorplace.com

The Oregon Association of Realtors is the professional organization for Oregon Realtors and it tries to ensure its members follow strict ethical practices. While they won't recommend a particular realtor, they can give you comprehensive information about locating realtors in the areas where you want to look for property or about simply finding properties. And they can give you information about local Associations of Realtors. Their Web site is useful for information about legislation that affects real estate and for obtaining publications that can help make your real estate transactions simpler.

North Coast

Pete Anderson Realty Inc. Better Homes and Gardens
Main office: 2480 South Holladay Drive, Seaside
(503) 738–9531, (800) 800–2988
www.homesnorthwest.com

Eight offices on the Coast from Astoria to Newport, and more in Portland, make this large company a leader in North and Central Coast realty. With about 60 agents on the Oregon Coast, they live up to their motto, "We move the most on the Oregon Coast," and the agents are among the top producers each year.

Coldwell Banker Kent Price Realty Inc.
Seaside: 2367 South Roosevelt
(503) 738–5558, (800) 829–0419
Cannon Beach: (503) 436–1171
Manzanita: (503) 368–5179
www.coldwellbanker.com

In business since 1941, this company has 20 agents and three offices. The Realtors in this firm handle every type of property in Tillamook and Clatsop Counties, and their long history in the area makes them extremely knowledgeable.

Duane Johnson Real Estate
296 North Spruce, Cannon Beach
(503) 436–0451, (800) 453–3167
www.duanejohnson.com

This firm sells more real estate in the Cannon Beach area than anyone else. Duane Johnson has been in the real estate business for over 20 years himself, and his firm has been in operation for more than 10 years. Johnson attributes their success to their low-key approach and complete devotion to the area—they handle properties that are in Cannon Beach and Arch Cape, and that's it.

Windermere/Manzanita
467 Laneda Avenue, P.O. Box 820, Manzanita 97130
(503) 368–6609, (888) 741–9329
www.manzanitarealestate.com,
www.windermere.com

Kay and Walt Covert affiliated with Windermere in the mid-1990s. Their office, with five agents total, specializes in the Manzanita, Wheeler, and Nehalem Valley regions and also has many listings at the Neah Kah Nie and Pine Ridge developments. Their love for the area makes them good matchmakers for prospective buyers and properties.

Central Coast

Coldwell Banker Gesik Realty, Inc.
1815 Northwest U.S. Highway 101, Lincoln City
(541) 994-7760, (800) 959-7760
www.newport.net/cbg

A big player in the resort market on the Central Coast, Gesik lists properties for Salishan, Searidge, Waters Edge, and other condominium communities. And that doesn't even count the beachfront properties: This firm has excellent resources for finding you a vacation house. Bernice Gesik, the Designated Broker-Owner, has agents who specialize not just in resort properties but also in lakefront and other exotically located houses.

Coldwell Banker 1st Newport Realty
306 East Olive (U.S. 20), Newport
(541) 265-2345, (800) 866-2988
www.jonlynchrealtor.com

Over 25 years of experience make this firm one of the top sellers in the area. Broker-owner Jon Lynch's expertise extends from beach property to commercial property, and his agents list everything from cute condominiums to spectacular view lots. They know Newport like nobody knows Newport.

Oregon Coast Properties, Inc.
905 Southwest Coast Highway, Newport
(541) 265-8531, (800) 234-7485
www.newportnet.com/ocp

This eclectic firm is the source for a number of lower-priced properties, including fixers. But they don't stop there—they list a number of commercial and multiunit investment properties, as well as view lots, development sites, and coastal retreats. Oregon Coast Properties is an independently run office.

Prudential All Coast Properties
285 Southwest U.S. Highway 101, Waldport
(541) 563-7000, (888) 884-8456
348 North U.S. Highway 101, Yachats
(541) 547-5000, (888) 345-8456
www.allcoastproperties.com

This firm dedicates itself to coastal property and undertakes as part of its mission the education of the client. Customers here get a crash course on owning coastal property and living in the area—the relocation services are a specialty. Eleven agents in two offices give the firm an edge when it comes to covering the region between Newport and Florence, and they handle residential, commercial, and investment properties.

Pam Zielinski
Prudential Northwest Properties
6125 Northeast Cornell Road, Suite 200, Hillsboro
(503) 842-3046
http://pru-nw.com

Though her office is just outside Portland, Pam Zielinski spends most of her time at the Central Oregon Coast where she is a devotee of luxury properties. She has been handling coastal vacation, investment, and retirement properties for over 20 years. The fact that she has to come into town to check in with the office means that she also has great contacts in Portland. This could be useful for urbanites or visitors to Portland who are thinking of buying property out west.

Insiders' Tip

The cost of living, the cost of housing, taxes, education, and the weather: These quality-of-life issues are critical for those who are moving to a new community. Relocation expert Patrice Kuchulis, of the Hasson Company in Portland, advises to find out as much about these as possible before you buy a new house.

South Coast

Pistol River and have behind them the considerable resources of the Century 21 network.

David L. Davis Real Estate
1110 Alabama Street, Bandon
(541) 347–9444, (800) 835–9444
www.bandonhomes.com

Want to buy a cranberry farm? David Davis can find one for you. In business since 1970, this firm lists an impressive array of commercial properties in the Bandon area from picturesque farms to multiplex dwellings to sites on U.S. 101 ready to be transformed into your dream business. The firm also handles residential properties including beachfront mansions and cute little cabins, and everything in between.

Gold Coast Properties, Inc.
55980 Oregon Avenue, Bandon
(541) 347–4533
www.coastproperties.com

While this company has been in business only since April 1999, it has already established an impressive reputation for itself by listing a number of million-dollar properties. The firm consists of three brokers, Designated Broker-Owners Chris and Debbie Lewellyn, and their associate broker Brian Winters. They have a combined experience of almost 30 years in real estate; what's more, they are making use of the latest technology in order to move their properties, including digital photos, detailed property information, plat maps, floor plans and so on, all available on-line. They cover the entire area of Coos and Curry Counties.

Century 21 Agate Realty
29642 Ellensburg Avenue, Gold Beach
(541) 247–6612, (800) 421–8553
Brookings: (800) 637–4682

Century 21 Agate Realty has been in business since 1978 with two offices in Brookings and one in Gold Beach. Agate Realty was awarded a "Top Company" designation by the 1999 Power Book. The Gold Beach office has seven full-time agents whose combined experience totals over 50 years. The agents in these offices handle every kind of property in the areas of Brookings, Carpenterville, Gold Beach, Harbor, Hunter Creek, Nesika Beach, and

Blue Pacific Realty
16340 Lower Harbor Road, Suite 102, Brookings
(541) 412–8424, (888) 412–8424
www.blupac.com

Though she opened her own agency only in 1999, owner Jeanette McVay and her team already list an impressive number of quality residential properties in the Brookings-Harbor area. The staff has had an average of 20 years of experience selling real estate, and they commit themselves to the area they know best, from the California border north to Pistol River and no farther. The hardworking team of six will not rest until they find the right house for you. They also have a very active Web site, meticulously updated every single day.

Coldwell Banker Oregon Coast Realty
703 Chetco Avenue (U.S. 101), Brookings
(541) 469–7755, (800) 342–9405
www.oregoncoastrealty.com

Locals say that this big firm knows its stuff: They are experts in the area from Gold Beach south, and they have been here a long time. With 10 agents, the firm's goal is to pass on its educated decision making to the customer. Owner Eldon Gossett's motto is that "you have the right to expect the best, especially when it comes to making the biggest investment decision of your life." The company's main Brookings office is downtown in the Central Building, convenient to resident and tourist alike.

Education and Child Care

Education is a number one priority for parents, and the Oregon Coast is lucky to have 15 school districts and 4 community colleges that offer state-of-the-art technology and a variety of educational opportunities for children and adults. In the 21st century, Oregon is faced with developing higher standards of education for its children. Known for its innovative, pioneering spirit Oregon has embarked on a mission to require higher educational standards for its children. This mission has come to fruition with the passage of the Oregon Educational Act for the 21st Century in 1991. This act dictates that Oregon students must not only master reading, writing, and arithmetic, but should also become proficient at advanced studies in mathematics and science and be able to apply academic knowledge in meaningful and practical ways.

As part of this legislation, graduating high school students are awarded a Certificate of Initial Mastery (CIM) if they achieve academic standards in the arts, a second language, English, civics, economics, geography, history, mathematics, and science. In order for students to receive the CIM, they must pass state tests that are given in grades 3, 5, 8, 10, and 12. The first Certificates of Initial Mastery in coastal school districts will be awarded during the 2002–2003 school year. In addition to the CIM, a Certificate of Advanced Mastery (CAM) program is also being phased into coastal schools. By the 2004–05 school year, students will earn a Certificate of Advanced Mastery if they meet the grade 12 benchmarks in all academic subjects as well as become involved in community projects and enterprises and participate in career-related learning experiences. Each school district develops its own plan for meeting the requirements of the Oregon Educational Act for the 21st Century. To find out the specific requirements, we recommend that you contact the school district in the area where you live. For easy reference, we have included the contact information and a brief summary for all the school districts on the Oregon Coast.

Four community colleges, Clatsop, Tillamook Bay, Oregon Coast, and Southwestern, offer a variety of programs that will meet the needs of those who want to obtain a one-year certificate, a two-year associate degree, a four-year bachelor's degree, or even a master's degree in a variety of disciplines. In addition, all four community colleges offer courses that are transferable to four-year colleges and universities, and they also offer distance education classes that are given via the Internet or a two-way interactive video conferencing system. See the Colleges section in this chapter for more detailed information on each of these community colleges.

Another difficult challenge parents must face is finding affordable, safe, and stimulating child care for their children. In the state of Oregon, there are generally three types of certified child care providers that are available to you: a group child care home that is located in a single family dwelling, has a certified provider who can care for up to 12 children, and can hire additional employees; family child care where one person is certified and responsible for caring for up to 10 children in the home without additional help; and child care centers that are located in a commercial building, are inspected and certified by the state, and have a number of employees. Child care providers that are certified by the state are inspected and must abide by a comprehensive list of regulations that are designed to provide a safe environment for your child. In addition, there are babysitters who are not certified who can be hired to work evenings, weekends, and odd hours on a short-term basis. In this chapter, we've listed child care referral services for each county on the Oregon Coast. If you are new to an area and looking for a child care provider or traveling and need short-term care, the referral services listed in this section can help you find a provider that will fit your unique needs and also provide resource materials that will help you select the best child care provider in your area.

North Coast

Public Schools

Astoria School District
3196 Marine Drive, Astoria
(503) 325–6441
www.astoriaschools.org

The Astoria School District has an enrollment of more than 2,300 students and represents Astor Elementary, Gray Elementary, Lewis & Clark Elementary, Olney Elementary, Astoria Middle School, and Astoria High School. All elementary schools in this district enroll students in grades K through 5. Astoria Middle School teaches grades 6 through 8 with the high school handling 9 through 12.

Knappa School District
Route 6, Box 226, Astoria 97103
(503) 458–6166

Represented by Knappa High and Hilda Lahti Elementary, Knappa School District has an enrollment of more than 600 students. Hilda Lahti Elementary enrolls students in kindergarten through 8th grade and Knappa High serves grades 9 through 12.

Warrenton/Hammond School District
820 Southwest Cedar Street, Warrenton
(503) 861–2281

The Warrenton/Hammond School District serves 950 students who live in Warrenton, Hammond, Sunset Beach, and outlying areas. The district has a high-quality staff of more than 50 teachers and 60 support staff. Bus transportation is available for more than 90 percent of the students who attend Warrenton Grade School and Warrenton High School. The goals of the district are to educate and prepare students to attend college, enter a professional technical program, or to enter the workforce. The district currently has a plan in place to prepare students to obtain the Certificate of Initial Mastery (CIM). The curriculum has been redesigned to meet the challenges of the CIM requirements. In order to obtain the CIM, students must master skills and pass standards and benchmarks required by the CIM program. Special classes are offered for students with special needs. The district works in collaboration with Clatsop County to offer classes that include resources and classroom instruction for students with disabilities based on the needs of the individual. Students identified as talented and gifted (TAG) are given the opportunity to attend advanced classes in courses that fit their needs.

Warrenton Grade School teaches classes in computer technology, math, music, physical education, science, and social studies. Electives offered to middle school students include band, choir, computer technology, publications, Spanish, sports, and visual arts. More than 300 students attend Warrenton High School and have multiple electives from which to choose to prepare them for jobs or for college once they graduate. The high school has two state-of-the-art computer labs that have Internet access. Computers that give students additional access to the Internet and other research media are also available in the science labs and library. All classes are geared toward preparing students for college. Courses offered include biology, English, geology, marine biology, chemistry, physics, and natural resource management. Students can attend the Area Vocational Center, which offers applied science and technology courses. Students are also involved in several community projects, such as repopulating fish to streams and lakes, returning wildlife to the bay, and assisted in planting trees and cleaning up after floods. Students also have the opportunity to further challenge themselves by participating in extracurricular sports, chorus, drama, and instrumental music.

Jewell School District
83874 Oregon Highway 103, Seaside
(503) 755–2451
www.orednet.org/~jewell

Jewell School District has an enrollment of 147 students serving kindergarten through 12th grade. To graduate, high school students must complete a Certificate of Initial Mastery (CIM) as well as 24 total credits in Language Arts, Written Composition, Mathematics, Science, Health Education, Physical Education, Current Events, Global Studies, U.S. History, American Government, Computer Education, Economics, Fine Arts, and Languages.

Seaside School District
1801 South Franklin Street, Seaside
(503) 738–5591
www.seaside.k12.or.us

The Seaside School District has a healthy enrollment of more than 1,760 students and serves the educational needs of Cannon Beach, Gearhart, Seaside, and rural Clatsop County. The students in this school district in grades K through 5 attend one of three elementary schools depending on where they live: Cannon Beach Elementary, Gearhart Elementary, or Seaside Heights Elementary. Students in grades 6 through 8 attend Broadway Middle School in Seaside and those in grades 9 through 12 go to Seaside High School also located in Seaside. According to Dr. Doug Dougherty, Superintendent, the students in the Seaside School District have some of the best assessment scores in the state. More than 70 percent of the 115-member staff in the district hold a master's degree and this contributes to the success of the students.

Neah-Kah-Nie School District
504 North 3rd Avenue, Rockaway Beach
(503) 355-2222
www.neahkahnie.k12.or.us

With one combined junior and senior high school and two elementary schools, the Neah-Kah-Nie School District serves more than 800 students with a staff of 58. The Neah-Kah-Nie Junior/Senior High School offers classes to about 385 students in grades 7 through 12. Garibaldi Elementary School serves 215 children in kindergarten through 6th grade who live in the Garibaldi area. Approximately 212 children living in the Nehalem area attend Nehalem Elementary School, which also offers classes to children attending kindergarten through 6th grade.

Tillamook School District
6825 Officers' Row, Tillamook
(503) 842-4414
www.tillamook.k12.or.us

Covering 404 square miles, the Tillamook School District has four elementary schools, a junior high school, and a senior high school that serve more than 2,250 students with a staff of 275. Elementary and junior high students are exposed to classes that focus on basic subjects, social skills, and becoming lifelong learners. The district offers a Title 1 Family Resource Center (located at the Liberty School Media Center, 1700 Ninth Street, Tillamook) where students and families living in the district can check out computers and software, parenting books and videos,

children's books, and pamphlets and other information about community resources. Tillamook High School offers courses in agriculture, art, business, English, family/consumer studies, foreign languages (Spanish, French, Russian), math, music, physical education and health, science (astronomy, aquaculture, biology, chemistry, coastal ecology, marine biology, physics), technology (automotive, digital electronics, electronic technician, mechanical technician, woodworking technician). Opportunities also exist for students to participate in extracurricular sports and clubs (Future Farmers of America, Key Club, Foreign Language Club, Pep Club, Speech Team, and Student Council).

Nestucca Valley School District
31565 Oregon Highway 22, Hebo
(503) 392-4892
www.nestucca.k12.or.us

Nestucca Valley School District is made up of Nestucca High School (located in Cloverdale), which serves more than 250 kids attending grades 9 through 12; Nestucca Middle School (located in Beaver) offers classes to more than 152 children in grades 6 through 8; and Nestucca Elementary School (located in Beaver) gives instruction to more than 280 children in grades K through 5.

Child Care Referral Services

Caring Options
#10 6th Street, Suite 108, Astoria
(503) 325-1053

Caring Options is a tri-county child care referral service for Clatsop, Columbia, and Tillamook Counties that serves the community under the umbrella organization of Community Action Resource Enterprises, Inc. (CARE). The Caring Options staff will listen to your child care needs and then provide you with a list of child care options including state registered in-home day-care providers and day-care centers. For short-term care, the staff can put you in touch with evening and weekend babysitters who can come to your home or hotel fully prepared to provide high-quality care to your child.

Child Care Resource & Referral
2211 11th Street, Tillamook
(503) 842-5261

Child Care Resource and Referral provides child care options for family child care, group home child care, and child care centers in Tillamook County. The staff will assess your child's needs and provide you with a list of certified or registered providers over the phone, and they will also mail you a list. This office also has a list of short-term babysitters who can watch your child during evenings, weekends, or weekdays. They cannot give you the list of babysitters' names over the phone but they are happy to let you look at the list if you visit their office.

Central Coast

Public Schools

Lincoln County School District
P.O. Box 1110, Newport 97365
(541) 265-4407
www.lincoln.k12.or.us

Lincoln County School District is the largest district on the Oregon Coast and serves 6,165 students living in the following communities: Newport, Lincoln City, Waldport, Eddyville, Siletz, and Toledo. The schools in the Newport area are made up of two elementary schools (grades K through 5), one middle school (grades 6 through 8), an Arts, Sciences & Technology School (grades 6 through 8), and a high school (grades 9 through 12). Newport schools are striving to prepare their students for the 21st century. For example, Newport Middle School has a program called STRUT (STudents Recycling Used Technology) which is an after-school program where students refurbish, rebuild, and upgrade computer systems that are donated by the community. This program allows students to gain valuable hands-on computer technology experience and gives their school a free computer for other students and staff to use.

There are three elementary schools (grades K through 5), a middle school (grades 6 through 8) and a high school (grades 9 through 12) that serve students in the Lincoln City community. Lincoln City schools are also keeping up with technology by having access to the Internet via NERO, a very fast data communications network that works in conjunction with the Oregon State System of Higher Education. Using this system, students can set up e-mail accounts and create their own Web pages under the supervision of their teachers.

Waldport schools include a grade school

(grades K through 5), middle school (grades 6 through 8), and a high school (grades 9 through 12). Two schools serve students in the Eddyville and Siletz areas: Eddyville School serves grades K-12 and Siletz Elementary and Middle Schools enroll students in grades K through 8. Schools in the Toledo Area include two elementary schools (grades K through 5), a middle school (grades 6 through 8), and a high school (grades 9 through 12).

Mapleton School District
10870 East Mapleton Road, Mapleton
(541) 268-4312
www.mapleton.k12.or.us

The Mapleton School District serves just over 275 students who live in the communities of Deadwood, Mapleton, and Swisshome, and is made up of an elementary school (grades K through 5), middle school (grades 6 through 8), and high school (grades 9 through 12). The district is one of five in the state of Oregon that has been recognized by the Oregon Department of Education as a High Performance Learning Center. The district has earned this recognition by meeting all the Oregon education standards; having the high school accredited by the Northwest Accreditation Association; students having achieved high scores on the Oregon Mathematics Assessment, Oregon Writing Assessment, and Statewide Assessment tests; teachers having high expectations for superior achievement by the students.

In addition to these achievements, the school district also has ensured that there is a computer lab with Internet access in each school in the district. Each computer lab has at least three leading-edge computers with updated software. The district also offers a free breakfast to all its students and a free or reduced-cost lunch to those students who qualify. Students can also learn to swim at the school district's pool, which was donated by the community.

Siuslaw School District
21111 Oak Street, Florence
(541) 997-2651
www.siuslaw.k12.or.us

The Siuslaw School District is composed of Siuslaw High School, Siuslaw Middle School, Rhododendron Elementary School, and Rhododendron Primary School. More than 1,675 students live in the district, which encompasses 210 square miles of the city of Florence and surrounding areas. The district has a staff of 115 and a student-to-teacher ratio of about 24 to 1. Siuslaw High School has a student body of more than 520 students who attend grades 9 through 12. Siuslaw Middle School offers classes to more than 410 students attending grades 6 through 8. Rhododendron Elementary teaches more than 450 children in grades 3 through 5 and Rhododendron Primary serves more than 380 children attending grades K through 2.

Child Care Referral Services
Lane Family Connections
Lane Community College 4000 East 30th, Eugene
(800) 222-3290
www.lanecc.edu/lfc/index.htm

The staff at Lane Family Connections can provide you with resources and referrals for registered and exempt family care providers, group home providers, and registered child care centers in the Florence and Mapleton areas. Registered family care providers are registered with the Oregon Child Care Division to provide child care at their residence. The state requires that family child care providers be registered if they are caring for three or more children or children from more than one family (other than their own children) at any given time. If these conditions do not apply, then the family care provider is not required to registered with the state and is exempt. The center can also provide you with short-term care referrals and support materials in to answer your child care questions. This service is provided on a sliding scale basis based on income. The maximum amount you would pay is $25. If you are traveling through the Florence or Mapleton area and need to find out about short-term care you can also call the center and the staff can provide you with a list of short-term care providers. They accept payment in the form of Visa or MasterCard, so you can obtain the information over the phone.

South Coast

Public Schools

Coos Bay Public School District
1330 Teakwood Avenue, Coos Bay
(541) 267-3104
www.coos-bay.k12.or.us

The Coos Bay Public School District enrolls more than 4,100 students who live in Coos Bay and surrounding unincorporated areas. The district has six elementary schools that teach grades K through 5 and range in size from 250 to more than 500 students. Middle school students (grades 6 through 8) attend one of two middle schools in the district: Millacoma (440 students) and Sunset (530 students). More than 1,250 high school students in grades 9 through 12 attend Marshfield High School, which is the largest high school on the Oregon Coast. An integrated curriculum is used in the elementary schools in the district and instruction is offered in traditional classrooms as well as classrooms that have children of different ages. Students are tested for academic progress in grades 3, 5, 8, and 10. Middle school students are on a trimester schedule so they can take advantage of taking a wide variety of elective courses. High school students have the opportunity to choose from a number of upper division courses in math, science, language arts, social studies, and language. Students can earn college-level credit for attending courses at Southwestern Oregon Community College.

Bandon School District
455 9th Street SW, Bandon
(541) 347-4411
www.coos.k12.or.us/~bandonsd

The Bandon School District is composed of Ocean Crest Elementary, Harbor Lights Middle School, and Bandon Senior High School, which enroll just over 900 students. Ocean Crest Elementary School enrolls students in grades K through 4 and maintains a staff of about 13 certified staff members. All students attending grades 1 through 4 are offered music education and there are also opportunities for students to participate in after-school activities such as basketball, drama, dance, baseball, and soccer. Students also have the opportunity to participate in the Gross Creek Wildlife Project, where they will build a nature trail parallels Gross Creek and extend it to the Coquille River. As the nature trail and other miniature outdoor gardens are built, students will learn about life science, outdoor ecosystems, soil and water conservation, and the community benefits from restoring riparian areas.

Central Curry School District
29516 Ellensburg Avenue, Gold Beach
(541) 247-2003
www.ccsd.k12.or.us

More than 850 students who live in Gold Beach and the surrounding areas are enrolled in the Central Curry School District. This school district is made up of Riley Creek Elementary, Agness Elementary, and Gold Beach High School. Riley Creek Elementary enrolls more than 570 students in grades K through 8; Agness Elementary has a very small enrollment of students in grades K through 6; and about 260 students attend Gold Beach High School in grades 9 through 12. Students who attend Gold Beach High School are required to take courses in English, mathematics, science, health, fine/applied arts, foreign language, social studies, physical education, economics, career development, technical applications, and electives. In order to receive their Certificate of Advanced Mastery (CAM), students in their junior year must select an academic area to study from one of six areas: arts and communications, business and management, health services, human resources, industrial and engineering systems, or natural resource systems.

Brookings-Harbor School District
564 Fern Avenue, Brookings
(541) 469-7443
www.brookings.k12.or.us

More than 1,925 students make up the Brookings-Harbor School District, which is composed of two elementary schools, one middle school, and one high school. Kalmiopsis Elementary School offers classes to students in grades K through 4 and has a student enrollment of just over

Insiders' Tip

Visit the Oregon
Department of Education
Web site at
www.ode.state.or.us
for comprehensive
information on school
performance reports,
performance require-
ments, and school
listings and Web sites.

632 students with a teacher-to-student ration of 1 to 21. Upper Chetco Elementary School enrolls about 80 students in grades 2 through 5. Azalea Middle School has a teacher-to-student ratio of 1 to 21 and enrolls more than 590 students in grades 5 through 8. Brookings High School has an enrollment of more than 625 students in grades 9 through 12 and has a teacher-to-student ratio of 1 to 19. The Brookings-Harbor School District prides itself on its excellent programs in special education, music, art, and computer technology, and district students consistently earn national recognition in art competitions.

Child Care Referral Services

Coos/Curry Resource & Referral Agency
Southwestern Oregon Community College,
1988 Newmark, Coos Bay
(541) 888–7096
www.socc.edu

This agency provides child care referrals for exempt and registered providers in Coos and Curry Counties. Parents can call in and explain their short- or long-term child care needs, and the staff at this friendly agency will provide the parents with a list of providers that should fit their needs. Brochures and other literature are also available that educate parents on what to look for when seeking child care. The agency also has a lending library for registered providers that contains brochures and books on state regu-

lations, child education programs, and tips for running a child care facility, etc.

Colleges

Clatsop Community College
1653 Jerome Avenue, Astoria
(503) 325–0910
www.clatsopcollege.com

Established in 1958, Clatsop Community College's main campus is located in the hills above downtown Astoria and enrolls about 7,500 students who live in Clatsop County, the Long Beach Peninsula, and other surrounding areas. Clatsop Community College offers three types of two-year degree programs in more than 30 disciplines: Associate in Arts—Oregon Transfer, Associate of Applied Science, and Associate in General Studies. Students can also earn a bachelor's degree without ever leaving town by signing up for four-year degree programs that are given in association with Linfield College, Oregon State University, and Oregon Health Sciences University. Linfield College offers a bachelor's degree in social and behavioral sciences through weekend and evening upper-division courses at the Clatsop campus. You can complete a four-year liberal arts degree through Oregon State University's directed learning program that offers 50 undergraduate and graduate courses given via the Oregon-EDNET system. You can also earn a bachelor's degree and obtain a registered nurse certification at the Clatsop campus by attending distance-learning classes that are given via a two-way interactive video system from Oregon Health Sciences University. If you are interested in taking courses in maritime science, coastal resources, or environmental studies, you may want to check out programs offered by the Marine and Environmental Research and Training Station located 4 miles east of Astoria on South Tongue Point.

Tillamook Bay Community College
2510 1st Street, Tillamook
(503) 842–8222
www.tbcc.cc.or.us

Tillamook Bay Community College offers a variety of courses to more than 3,500

Tillamook County residents. Degree programs include two-year Oregon Transfer Associate of Arts, Associate of General Studies, and Associate of Science Transfer. Students can also earn one-year certificates or a two-year Associate of Science degree in multiple disciplines. The college also offers classes in adult basic education, English as a second language, high school equivalency (GED), and personal enrichment. Distance-learning courses, such as drawing, modern art history, anatomy and physiology, microbiology, accounting, and many others, are also available.

Oregon Coast Community College
332 Southwest Coast Highway, Newport
(541) 265-2283
www.occc.cc.or.us
North County Center
Lighthouse Square, 4157 West U.S. Highway
101, Suite 123, Lincoln City
(541) 996-4919
South County Center
285 Cedar Street, Waldport
(541) 563-4502

Established in 1987, Oregon Coast Community College has three centers located in Newport, Lincoln City, and Waldport and offers courses to more than 3,000 students living in Lincoln County. Programs offered include adult basic education, community education, college transfer, profession/technical, and small business assistance. The college is accredited with the Northwest Association of Schools and Colleges and has a close partnership with Chemeketa Community College in Salem. Students also have the opportunity to take distance courses via the Internet or videotape in a wide variety of subject areas.

Southwestern Oregon Community College
1988 Newmark, Coos Bay
(800) 962-2838
www.socc.edu

Formed in 1961, Southwestern Oregon Community College is accredited by the Northwest Association of Schools and Colleges and by the Commission on Colleges and offers a variety of programs to meet the needs of more than 11,000 students in Coos and Curry Counties. The college offers two-year associate degree programs in the arts and sciences, two-year associate transfer programs, certificate programs, a high school diploma program, and adult education and enrichment courses. The college also offers upper division and master's degree classes through its partnership with Oregon Health Sciences University, Linfield College, Oregon Institute of Technology, Portland State University, Southern Oregon University, and Oregon State University. The college also offers a variety of teleconferences and telecourses that can be taken via satellite and also via interactive conferencing through the Oregon-EDNET system.

Health Care

There are hospitals and dozens of medical clinics spanning the coastline that provide high-quality health care to the coastal communities. Many hospitals offer a wide variety of services such as emergency and surgical care, obstetrics, radiology, rehabilitation, community education classes, home health, and hospice services. If you have an emergency, all hospitals offer 24-hour emergency care and can be reached by dialing 911. Following is a listing of other emergency numbers and hot lines in case you are faced with an emergency situation and need help or support. In the Clinics section, you will find a listing of medical clinics that see minor emergencies on a walk-in basis as well as other clinics that see patients by appointment only. We are fortunate to have access to a broad range of alternative health care and in the Alternative Health Care section in this chapter we have included information about the different types of alternative health care available and tips on how to find a licensed provider in your area as well as a listing of recommended alternative health care providers.

North Coast

Hospitals

Columbia Memorial Hospital
2111 Exchange Street, Astoria
(503) 325-4321
www.columbiamemorial.org

Established in 1870, Columbia Memorial Hospital is an independent, nonprofit 49-bed hospital that offers a comprehensive list of health care services to the residents of Clatsop County and the Lower Columbia River region of western Washington. This hospital has a level-three trauma center and offers high-quality emergency services from physicians and nurses who are ACLS (Advanced Cardiac Life Support) certified.

This hospital is the second-largest employer in Clatsop County and has a staff of physicians and health professionals who offer services in allergy/dermatology; ear/nose/throat; family/general practice;

gerontology; internal medicine; midwifery; nephrology; primary care; obstetrics; orthopedics; pediatrics; plastic surgery; psychiatry; radiology; and urology. The hospital has a high-quality rehabilitation department staffed by licensed physical therapists and physical therapy assistants who provide services in speech therapy, pediatric therapy, and occupational therapy.

The hospital has a state-of-the-art imaging center that CT scanning, an accredited mammography facility, ultrasound (including noninvasive vascular ultrasound), nuclear medicine imaging, and clinical radiographic and fluoroscopy studies and is staffed by board-certified radiologists and registered technologists.

Columbia Memorial offers monthly health insurance assistance classes to seniors and diabetes education classes. They also have a monthly newsletter called *Vital Signs* that features articles on health and wellness and keeps residents up to date on services offered by the hospital.

Providence Seaside Hospital
725 South Wahanna Road, Seaside
(503) 717-7000
www.providence.org/northcoast

Providence Seaside Hospital is a 32-bed acute-care facility serving the residents and visitors in the Seaside area. As part of the Providence Health System, this hospital offers a variety health care services including a birthing center, chemotherapy, echocardiography, day surgery, emergency services, imaging services, intensive care, coronary care, mammography, ultrasound, physical therapy, occupational therapy, and home health.

A 22-bed Extended Care facility located in the hospital helps elderly patients transition from the hospital setting back to their home. Additional programs and services include a low-cost community health clinic staffed by volunteers, the Health and Lifestyle Center, a diabetes education program, and occupational health services that provide safety education, vaccinations, and health screenings for local businesses.

Providence Seaside Hospital has an informative web site where you can view the most up-to-date class schedule for the Health and Lifestyle Center. Classes offered cover a wide variety of health issues such as childbirth and infant care, how to stop smoking, grief management, nutrition, and weight management. Classes are open to Providence members at a discounted price and also to the general public.

Other helpful links on this Web site make it easy for you to find the nearest medical clinic and information on home health care, extended care, and health plans.

Tillamook County General Hospital
1000 3rd Street, Tillamook
(503) 842-4444
www.tcgh.com

Tillamook County General Hospital is part of the Adventist Health System, which includes 70 hospitals nationwide. It features a modern birthing center, emergency, surgery, recovery, and laboratory facility.

Tillamook County General Hospital's Emergency Department is a level-three trauma center and is staffed 24-hours a day. The Medical/Surgical unit offers services that include immunization evaluation, diabetic management, spiritual care, social services, and rehabilitation. This facility also has hospice care for assistance with patients in their home and at the hospital. A unique service the hospital oversees is called Lifeline. Those who sign up for this service receive a small communication device that is placed in their home. At the press of a button there is someone available to help them 24 hours a day, seven days a week. This service allows patients with special needs to live in their own home but also have the assurance that there is someone there if they need help.

Classes offered to the community may include diabetes education, wellness screening, and CPR and first aid. The hospital has an informative Web site that allows you to find a doctor on-line. Physicians affiliated with the hospital specialize in general surgery, occupational health, radiology, family practice, podiatry, internal medicine, obstetrics, and midwifery.

A patient library is available on-line that has information on topics such as nutrition, parenting and child health, asthma, allergies and respiratory conditions, medications and drugs, cancer, and dieting and weight loss.

Clinics

Providence North Coast Clinic
727 South Wahanna Road, Seaside
(503) 717-7556
www.providence.org/northcoast

This clinic is affiliated with Providence Seaside Hospital and has seven physicians and a nurse practitioner on staff. Office hours for this clinic are Monday through Friday 8:30 A.M. to 5:00 P.M. Insurance plans accepted includes Providence Health Plan, Providence PPO, ODS, Blue Cross—Indemnity and PPO, QualMed (formerly PACC), and other insurance plans.

The O'Donovan Minor Emergency Clinic
580 U Avenue, Seaside
(503) 738-5571

The O'Donovan clinic has a staff of physicians specializing in family practice, gastroenterology, internal medicine, neurology, orthopedic surgery, pulmonary medicine, urology, and vascular surgery. This clinic has a doctor on call 24-hours a day, seven days a week. The clinic accepts walk-in patients and minor emergencies. The clinic is open 9:00 A.M. to 5:00 P.M. Monday through Friday and accepts most major insurance plans.

Insiders' Tip

If you are relocating to a coastal city, many hospitals with a Web site have a physician referral page where they list the name, location, and contact information for physicians who have been accredited by the participating hospital.

Providence North Coast Clinic
171 North Larch, Suite 16 (Sandpiper
Square), Cannon Beach
(503) 717-7556
www.providence.org/northcoast

This clinic has a family practice physician and a family nurse practitioner on staff. The clinic accepts walk-in appointments. Office hours are Tuesday through Friday 8:30 A.M. to 5:00 P.M. Insurance coverage accepted includes Providence Health Plan, Providence PPO, ODS, Blue Cross—Indemnity and PPO, QualMed (formerly PACC), and other insurance plans.

Tillamook County General Hospital Physicians
1000 3rd Street, Tillamook
(503) 842-4444
www.tcgh.com

Tillamook County General Hospital has a group of family practice physicians and other specialists who have received credentials from the hospital. Most major medical insurance is accepted.

Central Coast

Hospitals

Samaritan North Lincoln Hospital
3100 Northeast 28th Street, Lincoln City
(541) 994-3661
www.samhealth.org/snlh

Samaritan North Lincoln Hospital offers inpatient and outpatient services to the residents of Lincoln City. The hospital features an emergency department that is level-four certified; surgery; diagnostic imaging including CT scans, MRI, nuclear medicine, mammography, and ultrasound; dialysis; respiratory therapy; laboratory; nutrition services; rehabilitation therapy; and home health care.

The rehabilitation department uses conventional and holistic approaches to help patients who need physical therapy, occupational therapy, or speech therapy. A Lifeline service is offered to those patients who want to live at home but have someone to call if they need help. Social services, a wellness program, and hospice care are also offered.

Samaritan North Lincoln Hospital has a family-centered approach to childbirth.

Using this philosophy, family members are part of the birth experience and new mothers can experience the joy of motherhood in a private birth suite. The birth suite is a fully equipped birthing room that gives the new mother privacy but has the resources the staff may need to ensure mothers have a safe and comfortable childbirth. Birth suites are also available for women who need to have a cesarean. The hospital teaches classes designed especially for new parents on topics such as "Overview of Birth and Delivery," "The Labor Process," "Comfort Measures," "Medications and Anesthesia," "Breathing Techniques," and "Birth Plans and Options."

Samaritan Pacific Communities Hospital
930 Southwest Abbey Street, Newport
(541) 265-2244
www.samhealth.org/pch

Serving the Newport community, Samaritan Pacific Communities Hospital is a 48-bed hospital that was established in 1946 as a privately owned health care facility called Pacific View Hospital. Over the years, several expansion projects have occurred at the hospital. In 1964 20 more beds were added, and in 1968 intensive care, laboratory, and radiology departments were added. The hospital has a Clinical Services Center. Other services include a birthing center, diagnostic imaging, critical and intensive care, in-home care, and hospice care.

Peace Harbor Hospital
400 9th Street, Florence
(541) 997-8412

Peace Harbor Hospital is an acute-care hospital with a staff of 60 physicians and more than 300 employees who provide care to more than 17,000 patients a year. Peace Harbor Hospital is part of a large health care system that encompasses home health, hospice services, and counseling services and is also affiliated with Health Associates of Peace Harbor, a multispecialty medical group. The hospital offers services in labor and delivery care; emergency medicine; intensive care and post-cardiac care; inpatient medical and surgical services; and diagnostic and therapeutic services.

Lower Umpqua Hospital
600 Ranch Road, Reedsport
(541) 271–2171
www.lowerumpquahospital.com

Lower Umpqua Hospital is a full-service hospital serving the Reedsport community. This hospital has 24-hour emergency service that includes ambulance service and acute care, a family birthing center, rehabilitation therapy, imaging services (CT scan, MRI, mammography), general surgery, day surgery, hospice services, and a long-term nursing facility.

Clinics

The following clinics all have licensed family practice physicians who have obtained their credentials from Samaritan Pacific Communities Hospital in Newport:

Depoe Bay Clinic
Mall 101, Suite A, Depoe Bay
(541) 765–3265

The Depoe Bay Clinic is staffed with one family practice physician and a physician's assistant. This clinic is open for appointments 9:00 A.M. to 3:00 P.M. Monday through Friday and accepts most major medical plans.

John Lehrer, M.D.
775 Southwest 9th Street, Suite G, Newport
(541) 265–3772

This is a single-doctor family practice staffed by John Lehrer, M.D. The office is open 8:30 A.M. to 4:30 P.M. Monday, Tuesday, Thursday and Friday and 8:30 A.M. to 11:30 A.M. on Wednesday. This medical office accepts most major medical plans.

Toledo Clinic
1744 Northwest Business Highway 20, Toledo
(541) 336–5181

Two family practice physicians staff the Toledo Clinic. The clinic is open 8:30 A.M. to 4:30 P.M. Monday through Friday and accepts most major medical plans.

Waldport Clinic
150 Southwest Arrow, Waldport
(541) 563–3197

The Waldport clinic is staffed with two family practice physicians. Open 8:30 A.M. to 5:00 P.M. Monday through Friday and accepts most major medical plans.

South Coast

Hospitals

Bay Area Hospital
1775 Thompson Road, Coos Bay
(541) 269–8111
www.bayareahospital.org

Bay Area Hospital is the largest publicly owned acute-care facility on the Oregon Coast and provides high-quality health care to Coos County residents. This 172-bed facility was built in 1970 at a cost of $6.75 million. Diagnostic and therapeutic inpatient and outpatient services include critical care, home health, oncology, obstetrical, pediatric, psychiatric, surgical, and other specialties. Patients at Bay Area Hospital can also take advantage of imaging services that include MRI, CT scan, and mammography.

The hospital is well known for its accredited cancer program, where cancer patients receive treatment in a modern radiation therapy center that was opened in 1990. The hospital also has a housing facility for the families of cancer patients so they can be close by to offer much-needed support. This facility also teaches patient and community health care classes.

Coquille Valley Hospital
940 East 5th, Coquille
(541) 396–3101
www.cvhospital.org

Coquille Valley Hospital is a 30-bed hospital that serves the community of Coquille. This community hospital offers a fully staffed 24-hour emergency department and services in respiratory therapy, radiology, general and orthopedic surgery, laboratory services, and a birthing suite. In addition, this hospital offers diabetes and childbirth education classes and home health services and has a physician's referral line.

Southern Coos Hospital and Health Center
900 Southeast 11th Street, Bandon
(541) 347–2426

The community of Bandon has a new full-service 20-bed general, acute-care hospital. This hospital features a 24-hour staffed emergency department and imaging services including CT scan, mammography, and MRI. The hospital also owns and manages the Ocean View Care Center that offers long-term care for elderly patients.

Curry General Hospital
94220 4th Street, Gold Beach
(541) 247–6621
www.currygeneralhospital.com

Curry General Hospital is a full-service hospital offering quality health care to Gold Beach residents. This hospital offers emergency, surgery, imaging, laboratory, and other community health care services.

Clinics

North Bend Medical Center
1900 Woodland Drive, Coos Bay
(541) 267–5151
www.nbmc-inc.com/coosbay.html

This clinic is fully staffed with physicians who specialize in audiology, family practice, gynecology, hematology, internal medicine, occupational medicine, oncology, orthopaedic surgery, pediatrics, plastic reconstructive surgery, radiology, surgery, and urology. This clinic also has a licensed nurse practitioner on staff and a licensed acupuncturist. The clinic has a health resource center, gives vaccinations for those

traveling abroad, and has a licensed midwife on staff. This medical center has affiliated clinics in the following cities:
Bandon (541) 347–2313
Coquille (541) 396–3111
Gold Beach (541) 247–7047

Alternative Care

Many coastal communities offer alternative health care options including acupuncture, herbal medicine, homeopathy, massage, and aromatherapy. Health food stores are an excellent resource for finding alternative care providers. Ask for referrals from the owner or other workers in the store and be sure to check to see if they have a bulletin board where business cards and flyers are often posted. *Hipfish,* a monthly alternative publication (see the Media chapter), also contains a business listing for alternative health care providers for the North Coast.

Columbia River Day Spa
1215 Duane Street, Astoria
(503) 325–7721
www.columbiariverdayspa.com

The friendly day spa offers massage therapy, hydrotherapy and sauna, body wraps, facials, aromatherapy, and hand and foot treatments.

Seaside Spa & Wellness Center
2647 U.S. Highway 101 N., Seaside
(503) 717–1770
www.shopseaside.com/spa

The Seaside Spa & Wellness Center offers acupuncture, massage, facials, pedicures, and hair-care services from a staff of licensed professionals. This full-care spa also has a licensed naturopathic physician who specializes in women's and children's health care. The spa stocks massage oils, bath products, and other self-care products. The spa is open 9:00 A.M. to 5:00 P.M. Monday through Saturday.

Rejuvenation Massage & Spa
4783 Southwest Highway 101, Lincoln City
(541) 994–1819
www.rejuvenationmassageandspa.com

Rejuvenation Massage & Spa is owned by Carol Ritzert and Donna King and has

Before you choose to see a naturopathic physician or other alternative health care provider, ask for references, learn how many years they have been practicing, and make sure they are licensed.

licensed massage therapists on staff. This spa offers several different services that will relax the mind and spirit including body treatments, facials, massage, hydrotherapy, aromatherapy, and reflexology (the zones of the feet are massaged). This spa also has a small retail shop that stocks scented candles, natural soaps, skin products, massage tools, and much more. The spa is open 10:00 A.M. to 5:00 P.M. Monday through Saturday and it is recommended that you call ahead to schedule an appointment.

Wellness Massage Center
530 Northwest 3rd Street, Suite B, Newport
(541) 265–8468

The Wellness Massage Center has a staff of four licensed massage therapists and is open Monday through Saturday from 10:00 A.M. to 7:00 P.M. by appointment only. Techniques offered at this facility include Swedish massage, lymphatic drainage, and deep tissue massage.

Bandon Massage
190 2nd Street, Bandon
(541) 347–9877

This office offers a full range of massage services.

Retirement

Many people retire to the Oregon Coast, drawn by its temperate climate and low-key style of life. Some of those people spend the sunny seasons here on the Coast and flee the winter gloom. Others stay year-round, especially at the South Coast, which tends to be warmer than the rest of Oregon during the winter. Brookings and Gold Beach are particularly popular; there, seniors make up a large sector of the economy and the services for seniors are relatively plentiful. But all counties can provide some kind of advice and assistance, notably in the population centers of Astoria, Seaside, Tillamook, Lincoln City, Newport, Florence, Coos Bay, and North Bend. Furthermore, senior centers, community colleges, houses of worship, arts guilds, historical societies, and many other organizations supply fellowship, education, and entertainment. Wherever you decide to go, retiring to the Oregon Coast will put you in good company.

Oregon Senior & Disabled Services Division
500 Summer Street NE, Salem
(503) 945–5733
www.dhs.state.or.us/seniors

The Senior & Disabled Services Division (SDSD), part of the Oregon Department of Human Services, is the state agency that provides assistance to older adults, persons with disabilities, and caregivers, and they are dedicated to helping people live dignified and independent lives.

The following numbers are for branch offices of SDSD and related agencies on the Coast. The staff at these offices will help you find local options for transportation, meal services, shopping, housekeeping, medical care and supplies, employment or volunteer opportunities, and many other services and possibilities in which you may be interested. They will do whatever they can to help you stay in your own house. They can also help you evaluate whether residential or nursing home care is appropriate and help you find the right facility.

Astoria Area Agency on Aging
800 Exchange Street, Astoria
(503) 325–4543

North Coast Senior Services
278 Rowe Street, Wheeler
(503) 368–4200

Senior Centers

Seniors centers on the Coast often provide the central locations for the outreach services arranged by SDSD; they may coordinate the dial-a-ride service; they may provide meals there or in your home; they may help you with Medicare and taxes; and that's just the beginning. In addition, they usually sponsor a smorgasbord of special events and social activities, from bingo to samba lessons and everything in between. Even if you're just traveling through, many senior centers will welcome your participation.

Astoria Senior Center, 1111 Exchange, Astoria; (503) 325–3231
Seaside Senior Center, 1225 Avenue A, Seaside; (503) 738–7393
Senior Center Drop-in Center, 316 Stillwell, Tillamook; (503) 842–9660
Newport Senior Center, 20 Southeast 2nd, Newport; (541) 265–9617
Florence Boosters Senior Center, 1424 West 15th, Florence; (541) 997–8844
Lower Umpqua Senior Center, 460 Winchester Avenue, Reedsport; (541) 271–4884
Bay Area Senior Activity Center, 886 South 4th, Coos Bay; (541) 269–2626
North Bend Senior Recreation and Activity Center, 1470 Outpost Lane, North Bend; (541) 756–7622
Bandon Senior Activity Center, 1100 Southwest 10th, Bandon; (541) 347–4131
Port Orford Senior Center, 1536 Jackson, Port Orford; (541) 332–5771
Gold Beach Senior Center, 29841 Airport Way, Gold Beach; (541) 247–7506
Chetco Senior Center, 550 Chetco Lane, Brookings; (541) 469–6822

Tillamook Area Agency on Aging
1800 Front Street, Suite B, Tillamook
(503) 842–4221, (800) 584–9712

Newport Area Agency on Aging
111 Southeast Douglas, Suite F, Newport
(541) 265–7719

Florence Area Agency on Aging
3180 U.S. Highway 101, Florence
(541) 997–8251

Reedsport Area Agency on Aging
680 Fir Avenue, Reedsport
(541) 271–4835

Area Agency on Aging
93781 Newport Lane, Coos Bay
(541) 269–2013, (800) 858–5777

Gold Beach Multiple Services Office
(including SDSD)
94145 5th Place, Gold Beach
(541) 247–4515, (800) 257–1385

Brookings/Harbor Multiple Services Office
(including SDSD)
97829 Shopping Center Avenue, Suite F, Brookings
(541) 469–0481, (541) 469–9299

Residential Care and Nursing Homes

Astor House
999 Klaskanine Avenue, Astoria
(503) 325–6970
Hillside House
1400 Southeast 19th Street, Lincoln City
(541) 994–8028

Part of the Assisted Living Concepts network of facilities, which specializes in rural senior care, Astor House and Hillside House are dedicated to providing their residents with an atmosphere that is as uninstitutional as possible. Hence, apartments have small kitchens; residents can bring their pets and cars with them;

there are plenty of social activities and ample, pleasant common spaces; and homecooked meals are served. But in addition to the comforts of home, Astor House and Hillside House provide the extra services that their clients need: assistance with the administration of medication; with bathing, dressing, or grooming; with medical or physical conditions such as incontinence or dementia. Best of all, services are adaptable as a resident's needs change.

Neawanna by the Sea
20 North Wahanna Road, Seaside
(503) 738-5526

Neawanna by the Sea has nearly 60 units, 40 of them assisted-living units and the remainder duplexes for those who are more independent. The tidy facility was built in 1990 within walking distance of the ocean and overlooking Neawanna Creek in Seaside. The duplexes each have two bedrooms and two baths, full kitchens, washers, and dryers; moreover, they offer yard care, housekeeping and building maintenance, and a 24-hour emergency call system. Plus, those living in duplexes have access to the amenities of the main building, which include a dining room, a beauty salon, transportation services, and social activities. The assisted-living apartments in the main building, which are private apartments of one or two bedrooms or studios, include all the same amenities. In addition, they provide kitchenettes, housekeeping and linen services, three daily meals, and the security of an emergency call system, a 24-hour staff, and people trained to look out for the well-being and health of their clients.

Suzanne Elise Assisted Living
101 Forest Drive, Seaside
(503) 738-0307, (800) 652-0750

Suzanne Elise Assisted Living is a large, immaculate facility in Seaside with well-trimmed grounds and a large, sunny patio. Residents live in private apartments with attentive housekeeping, laundry, and linen services; transportation is provided or coordinated for clients (including a luxurious bus with a wheelchair lift); and a 24-hour emergency alert system is also offered. Three meals a day are included. Suzanne Elise's philosophy is to keep residents in their homes as long as possible, and it's a close community with many activities featured and a lot of interactivity with the larger community. Schoolchildren trick or treat; the high school students might put on a play; local artists visit. It's also a good place just to hang out. The library is especially nice.

Nehalem Valley Care Center
280 Rowe Street, Wheeler
(503) 368-5171

Insiders' Tip

The Web site for the Senior and Disabled Services Division, www.sdsd.hr.state.or.us, is worth a special trip into cyberspace. The agency's Web site is user friendly and comprehensive, seemingly designed for those of us who are tourists on the information superhighway. In addition to its own well-organized material about programs and services for seniors in the state of Oregon, it features many links to local, state, and national organizations that can give you material on everything from how to look for residential care to legal advocacy for seniors. This excellent resource should not be missed.

Right next to the noted Rinehart Clinic in the charming village of Wheeler, you'll find the Nehalem Valley Care Center. This Medicare-contracted nursing facility offers both ongoing nursing care and rehabilitative services. In addition to a special Alzheimer's and dementia program, the 50-bed center provides teams of caregivers in order to give the most comprehensive care possible—their goal is always to get the patient back home and, once there, to enable him or her to live as independently as possible. Rooms are private. The Agency on Aging office is next door so social service outreach programs are coordinated here—especially useful after a person is discharged.

The Dorchester House
2701 Northwest U.S. Highway 101 , Lincoln City
(541) 994-7175

The Dorchester House offers studio or one-bedroom apartments in an old-fashioned house with a big stone fireplace in the living room and other lovely common room areas like a library and garden. This spot is for the relatively independent—there's not a medical staff. But there are services to make life more comfortable and easy. In addition to housekeeping and linen service, two meals are served each day, a security and emergency alert system gives you peace of mind, and a management staff will be there to keep an eye on you and your place.

Ocean Crest Retirement
192 Norman Avenue, Coos Bay
(541) 888-2255

An attractive building with nicely landscaped grounds, Ocean Crest is both a retirement home and a licensed assisted-living facility with several levels of personal care. They'll develop a plan to fit your own assistance requirements. Their basic plan provides three daily meals and scheduled transportation, as well as cleaning and maintenance of your apartment, laundry areas, and beauty and barber shops on the premises. They'll help plan the social calendar too, with a number of recreational activities scheduled weekly.

Ocean View Care Center of Bandon
2790 Beach Loop Road, Bandon
(541) 347-4402

A newly built nursing home overlooking the sea in Bandon, the setting of the Ocean View Care Center is an exquisite place in which to receive nursing care. For those clients who can manage to tear themselves away from the window, there are four scheduled activities each day, including such activities as visits with pets, Golden Age Radio, and trivia games. At least one outing is scheduled per week; this may be a scenic drive, a bus tour, or a special shopping trip.

Elder Home Adult Foster Care
903 Lakeshore Drive, Port Orford
(541) 332-1007

For some people, a small homelike care facility is best and that's just what Elder Home provides. This licensed facility in a nice house has just five bedrooms. They'll provide either short- or long-term care. They can also help you set up a program for day care or respite care.

Chetco Inn Residential Care Facility
417 Fern Street, Brookings
(541) 469-5347

Brookings is a favorite with retirees and so is the Chetco Inn, which sits on a hill above town. The building used to be a hotel; it was built in 1915 and retains many of its lovely original furnishings and features, including the fireplace in the living room and a staircase that sweeps up to the second floor (there's also an elevator). The Chetco Inn has 35 private or partially private units; they will provide you housekeeping and linen services, three meals each day, emergency phones by the bed and in the bathroom, and private telephones. You will also receive 24-hour medical supervision, with a medical director, two RNs, and a LVN on staff. The backyard is a favorite gathering place for horseshoes and croquet or just for chatting peacefully in the sun.

Macklyn House
755 Elk Drive, Brookings
(541) 469-7182

The maintenance of independence is the mission of the folks at Macklyn House, a licensed assisted-living facility. Macklyn house provides basic assisted-living services, but it also has a 24-hour staff trained to provide nursing, personal, and other care for more complex problems such as confusion. The studio and one-bedroom apartments are private (you can lock the doors), but they have emergency call systems for extra security. Three meals are served each day; laundry facilities are provided; and transportation can be arranged. Pets are welcomed, too.

Worship

The first two-legged inhabitants of the Oregon Coast worshipped in ways that have been lost to history but evidence suggests that they turned to their medicine men and women who not only danced as healing shamans but who were also in care of the tribe's spiritual health. To aid in all of this, Raven, Coyote, and Salmon were called upon to insure wisdom, cleverness, and abundance.

After the arrival of the Europeans in the early 19th century, the incantations toward heaven were of a different and more organized nature. Although gold miners, fur trappers, and loggers were not widely known as worshipping folk, the settling and civilizing of the Coast brought the usual assemblage of denominations. Finns who came to Astoria to work in the salmon canneries brought the Lutheran Church; the Chinese, who also worked in the canneries, met to express their faith in the principles of Confucius or the rules of Taoism. And, of course, there were thousands of pioneers who rolled up sleeves to build Baptist, Methodist, Presbyterian, and other houses of worship. Now there are choices for all faiths in most coastal cities. There are no mosques or synagogues along the Coast but there are Jewish Sabbath and Havurah affinity groups in Astoria, Florence, and Coos Bay. Also, for those who embrace what is generically referred to as "New Age Thought," there are a few places to gather with others interested in "the heart of the soul."

Here are a few anecdotal histories to offer a flavor of how the coastal people have come together to share spiritual growth.

The first church built in Yachats was finished in 1930 on land donated by Sir Robert Perks of England. This log building was originally an Evangelical Church but now the "Little Log Church" is home to a Presbyterian congregation.

The present North Bend Church of Christ grew from two smaller congregations, one in North Bend, the other in Coos Bay. The Coos Bay church first met in June 1950 at the home of Arley and Happy Moore on Flannagan Street, the only Church of Christ congregation on the Coast from Eureka, California, to Aberdeen, Washington. Mr. Moore put an

The coastline is dotted with historic churches that serve many different faiths. PHOTO: LIZANN DUNEGAN

ad in the paper calling for members, and the congregation soon outgrew the Moores' home. For some time it met in the old American Legion Hall at 4th and Curtis. Brother George Button (still a member, at North Bend now, and an elder) remembers coming into the Hall early Sunday morning to clean up the mess—spilt drinks and full ashtrays—left over from Saturday night's Legion meetings.

In 1952 the congregation purchased the old Episcopal Church building at Fourth and Market for $5,000. Historian Ginger Andrews remembers freezing in this big, beautiful old building when she was a little kid: "It cost a fortune to heat—we never really did get it warm." It served as a meeting place until the Coos Bay congregation dissolved in 1969 to join with the North Bend congregation on the present site—which was a house with the front room converted into a small auditorium. In 1969 a loan was secured for the new church building.

In the 1940s the Christian folks in Charleston decided that they needed to get together for a worship service. At first they met above the store—Davey Jones Locker—then grew larger and began meeting at the elementary school in Charleston. They wanted to build a church building but had no money for the materials. When the George Olson lumber ship wrecked on the North Spit, the congregation obtained salvage rights that enabled them to haul in enough lumber to build their church. The women of the congregation did most of the actual building of the church, because most of the men were off fighting in World War II.

The First United Methodist Church of Coos Bay had its beginning in the 1850s when white settlers had just started making their homes in the area. White men had apparently arrived in the area during the winter of 1851 when the U.S. troop ship Captain Lincoln wrecked north of the Coos Bay bar. The 35 or 40 soldiers from the ship were aided by the friendly Indians of the area and lived near the beach for several months. The first record of Methodist work in this area was found in the Oregon Conference Journal for 1854, showing Coos Bay and Port Orford "To be supplied" on the list of appointments and apportioned $175 for missionary work. Christopher Alderson, converted in 1855 while mining gold at Jacksonville, was appointed to Coos Bay and Port Orford in 1857. On September 10, he preached at the meeting hall over Foley's Drug Store in Empire City (now Coos Bay). In 1871 when the Rev. S. H. Todd was pastor, W. W. Luce, owner of an Empire City sawmill, donated two 50- by 100-foot lots in Block 31 to the congregation. This paved the way for the construction of the first church building in southwestern Oregon.

Tillamook Head, a looming, basalt headland, juts out from the land and separates Seaside from Cannon Beach. Here the Tillamook Head Lighthouse stands alone on an island. You can't get near it now because it's privately owned. Currently, the lighthouse houses urns of ashes—for those who've purchased the space ahead of time in this columbarium called Eternity At Sea.

At Lincoln City in 1837, the notable missionary Jason Lee, who established a Methodist mission near Salem, camped nearby for a week with his new bride. According to legend, the honeymooners cured themselves of malaria and evangelized the Salmon River Indians. They were the first known vacationers on the Oregon Coast.

Eighteen Protestant churches and one Catholic church serve the 12,000 mostly conservative folk in the Brookings area. Of these, 14 are evangelical in focus. All are small churches of less than 300 members. Anchor Chapels, located in a RV Park, spreads its message via television. Three newly built churches, Church of Nazarene, Assembly of God, and Star of the Sea Catholic Church suggest the vitality of coastal congregations.

Media

The media scene on the Oregon Coast reflects the rich history of the area, has a commitment to providing news coverage that informs residents of local issues, and celebrates the individuality of the people that live in coastal communities. The majority of these communities have a weekly or biweekly paper that has kept residents well informed for more than half a century. Two daily papers, the *Daily Astorian* and the *World*, provide local as well as international news. A large majority of the newspapers also have Web sites that provide easy access for those who like to read about local news and events on-line.

Monthly and bimonthly publications also focus on different aspects of Oregon Coast life. The monthly *Lower Columbia Business* focuses on business issues on the North Coast and includes stories on new businesses, prominent business leaders, and updates on the retail industry, the hospitality industry, and coastal construction news. *Oregon Coast* is a glossy, bimonthly magazine filled with colorful pictures that has a rich offering of stories on coastal communities, history, activities, attractions, and flora and fauna. *Hipfish* is a monthly alternative publication that focuses on the arts and entertainment scene, cultural events, alternative health care, and social and economic issues.

Many television viewers on the Oregon Coast choose to purchase cable service due to the Coast Range of mountains, which blocks television signals in many areas. Viewers on the South Coast with good antennas may be able to pick up four channels aired out of Medford: KOBI Channel 5 (NBC), KDRV Channel 12 (ABC), KTVL Channel 10 (CBS), and KSYS Channel 8 (PBS). In addition, five channels broadcast from Eureka, California, may also be received: KIEM Channel 3 (NBC), KAEF Channel 23 (ABC), KVIQ Channel 6 (CBS), KEET Channel 13 (PBS), and KBVU Channel 29 (Fox). When viewers purchase cable they receive better reception of local television stations and also have a wide variety of programming to choose from. In the Television section, we've provided you with a listing of the local TV channels available.

The Oregon Coast also has a rich variety of radio stations that play a broad range of music with Adult Contemporary and Country-Western dominating the radio airwaves. While you won't find much alternative music to listen to—you will find a wide collection of tunes to fit your musical mood. In the Radio section, we've listed the type of music, the call letters, number on your radio dial, and the coastal city where the music is broadcast to help you quickly find your favorite kind of music.

Newspapers

North Coast

Dailies

The Daily Astorian
949 Exchange Street, Astoria
(503) 325-3211, (800) 781-3210 ext. 233
www.dailyastorian.info

Established in 1873 by DeWitt Clinton Ireland, the *Daily Astorian* keeps over 9,100 readers up to date on the local happenings in Astoria and surrounding areas. At the time the paper was started it was called the *Tri-Weekly Astorian*. In 1903, the paper was sold to John S. Dellinger who owned the paper until 1930 when it was sold to E.B. Aldrich, Fred Lampkin, Lee D. Drake, and Merle Chessman. These new owners changed the name of the paper to the *Evening-Astorian Budget*. Another name change took place in 1960 when the paper was called the *Daily Astorian*.

According to Laura Sellers-Earl, managing editor, the main features of the paper include "strong local news, in-depth packages, and award-winning writing and photography including general excellence awards in 1997 and 1999." She adds, "While a small, community paper, the *Daily Astorian* strives to tackle issues full bore, providing in-depth coverage and analysis to help our readers understand the world around them. We have a unique location that is bursting with news both hard-edged and pleasingly soft. Our staff of passionate journalists seeks out the uncommon story in 'common' people."

In addition to local news, weather, sports, and opinions, this paper also contains local columns for seniors, restaurant and movie reviews, fitness, and gardening, and a "South County Slice of Life" column. Other highlights in the paper are syndicated columns from Ann Landers and the *New York Times*.

This paper also has an on-line version that was started in 1997. The on-line paper includes a handy "Visitors Guide" that will help you explore Astoria and the surrounding areas of Warrenton, Tillamook, Cannon Beach, Seaside, the Long Beach Peninsula, Naselle, and Grays River. The "Market Place" section has information on finding a home, classified ads, and a business directory that will help you find anything from antiques and collectibles to flea markets, golf courses, museums, and galleries. You can use the searchable databases to find arts and entertainment events and activities.

The *Daily Astorian* is published five days a week Monday through Friday. Subscription rates are $10 per month for a local subscription and $13 a month for a mail subscription. The paper's circulation area includes Clatsop County, northern Tillamook County, and Washington's Pacific and Wahkiakum Counties.

Weeklies and Biweeklies

The Columbia Press
926 East Harbor, Warrenton
(503) 861-3331

Established in 1922, the *Columbia Press* was originally published in Finnish and switched to English when the paper moved to an Astoria location in the 1940s. It moved to Warrenton in 1978. This community publication is distributed every Friday and provides news on local events for 1,500 paid subscribers. An annual subscription is $25.

The Seaside Signal
730 Broadway, Seaside
(503) 738-5561
www.seasidesignal.com

The *Seaside Signal* is published every Thursday and serves the communities of Seaside, Gearhart, Cannon Beach, and South Clatsop County. Inside the pages of this community paper you'll find accurate reports on the following topics: sports, community, business, opinions/public forum, classifieds, leisure, and property profiles. Established in 1905, this informative publication has more than 3,800 paid subscribers and offers the same news on-line. Subscriptions rates are $24 per year for residents of Clatsop County and $36 per year for subscribers living outside Clatsop County. A single issue is 50 cents.

Cannon Beach Gazette
115 North Hemlock Street, #3, Cannon Beach
(503) 436-2812
www.cannonbeachgazette.com

Published every Thursday, the *Cannon Beach Gazette* is a strictly community newspaper that has more than 3,000 paid subscribers.

Insiders' Tip

Be sure to visit the Web sites listed for each newspaper. Many of these Web sites provide links to local businesses, weather and tide information, activities, arts and entertainment, cultural events, and real estate.

The paper is distributed to subscribers who live in Cannon Beach, Tolovana, and Arch Cape. Published by Tom and Cat Mauldin, this paper features local news, sports, education, human-interest stories, classifieds, and tide reports. It also has an informative Web site for those readers who prefer to read their local news on-line. Subscription rates are $20 per year for residents of Clatsop County, $28 for subscribers who live outside Clatsop County, and $32 for readers who live outside of Oregon. A single copy is 50 cents.

Headlight-Herald
1908 2nd Street, Tillamook
(800) 275-7799
www.tillamookheadlightherald.com

The *Headlight-Herald* is a community newspaper that was established in 1888. This publication spotlights news, sports, community issues, and classified ads. Examples of feature stories include coverage of art festivals, the latest team scores for the high school football team, and farm tours that are available to the public. This paper is also available on-line and has links to The State of Oregon, Tillamook County, and local weather. This weekly paper is published every Wednesday and has 7,164 paid subscribers. An annual subscription for residents living inside Tillamook County is $28. For those living outside Tillamook County, an annual subscription is $36. A single issue is 50 cents.

Central Coast

Weeklies and Biweeklies

The News Guard
930 Southeast U.S. Highway 101, Lincoln City
(541) 994-2178
www.thenewsguard.com

The reporters of the *News Guard* cover the Lincoln City news beat for over 5,800 paid subscribers. This insightful paper is published every Wednesday and features news, announcements, beach life, business, legal notices, obituaries, classifieds, weather, sports, tide charts, and letters/opinions. "The Beach Life" section features stories on local residents as well as stories on local organizations and happenings. The on-line version of the paper contains a sample of the regular news and features found in the printed version as well as links to businesses, government, and fun things to see and do around Lincoln City. A restaurant guide and theater listings are also included to help you pick out a good place to try some local cuisine and the best place to watch a good movie. A one-year subscription for Lincoln County residents is $24 and $36 for those living outside Lincoln County. A single copy is 50 cents.

News-Times
831 Northeast Avery, Newport
(541) 265-8571
www.newportnewstimes.com

Established in 1882, the *News-Times* keeps over 10,500 paid subscribers in touch with local issues in Newport and surrounding areas every Wednesday and Friday. Regular features include local, regional, and world news; crime; sports; opinion; obituaries; weather; and classifieds. A "Lifestyles" section covers everything from gardening and household tips to helping your child plan for college. This paper also features an "Entertainment and the Arts" section that gives you the scoop on local art festivals, writing classes, plays, music events, and much more. The "Travel & Leisure" section gives you ideas for your next weekend getaway as well as other outdoor and travel-related topics. Many of this paper's features are also available on-line. The on-line paper has links to The Associated Press Web site, and also includes a link to an informative "Parents Guide" that has articles focusing on children's health, monitoring your child's progress in school, and fun family activities. The subscription rate for Lincoln County residents is $49 for one year. Out-of-county rates are $98 for one year.

The Siuslaw News
148 Maple Street, Florence
(541) 997-3441

Every Wednesday 4,355 subscribers look forward to reading the *Siuslaw News*. Established in 1890, this paper highlights local news, weather, sports, tides, court reports, opinions, and classifieds. The weekly insert "Soundings" covers the local arts and entertainment scene, contains TV and movie listings, and has a restaurant directory. Lane County residents pay $43.20 for a one-year subscription and those living outside the county pay $70.

The Umpqua Post
495 Fir Avenue, Reedsport
(541) 271-7474

Nancie Hammond and Elizabeth Adamo, owners of the *Umpqua Post*, started the paper from scratch in October of 1996. Nancie Hammond says, "We started the *Umpqua Post* because we believed this town needed a positive voice and we have been very well supported. We try to be 'solutions oriented' in our reporting, try to keep things generally positive, and strive to be supportive of our community." This community paper provides an active voice on school board issues, port happenings, city council meetings, police incidents, and generally includes one or two stories on local events or residents. Regular features in the paper include a "What's Up!" column that describes volunteer opportunities as well as community events and an "Outdoors and More" column that has articles covering topics like habitat improvement projects and fishing reports. Monthly features include a "Recollections" story that is an interview with a longtime resident and a

"What's Cooking'" page that is filled with world-class recipes. This local paper is published every Wednesday and is generally about 12 pages in length. The paper's circulation is 1,650 and the coverage area includes Reedsport, Winchester Bay, Scottsburg, Gardiner, and Lakeside. A one-year subscription for Douglas County residents is $22 and $35 for out-of-county residents. A single copy is 50 cents.

South Coast

Dailies
The World
350 Commercial Avenue, Coos Bay
(541) 269-1222
www.theworldlink.com

Established in 1878, the *World* is the largest daily paper on the South Oregon Coast. The paper has more than 14,000 subscribers for the Monday-through-Friday edition and more than 17,000 for the Saturday edition. This paper is distributed to readers in Coos County, Curry County, and selected areas in Douglas and Lane Counties. It offers a robust coverage of local and international news, weather, and sports, as well as a food page, classified ads, an opinions page, comics, police reports, and fire calls. Additional features that highlight the local community include a "Milestones" section with stories of local residents over the age of 50 and an "Out and About" section that lists local events and activities. In May and August of each year, the paper publishes a special section geared toward tourists called "Let's Go!" that features stories and information on local attractions, accommodations, and things to do. the *World* also has a comprehensive Web site that includes local news and events as well as access to archived stories and other information. The Web site also allows local businesses to link their Web sites to the paper's main site. Subscription rates are $9.00 per month for rural delivery and $9.25 per month for carrier delivery. Subscribers who receive the paper by mail pay $11.50. The cover price for the Monday-through-Friday edition is 50 cents and the Saturday edition is $1.00.

Weeklies and Biweeklies

The Coquille Valley Sentinel
#1 Barton's Alley, Coquille
(541) 396-3191

Over 2,100 paid subscribers look forward to reading the *Coquille Valley Sentinel* every Wednesday. The paper dates back to September 9, 1882, when J. A. "Doc" Dean fired up the presses and published the first edition of the *Coquille Herald*. In 1906, Orvil Dodge, a former editor of the *West Oregonian of Myrtle Point*, started another paper called the *Coquille Sentinel*. In 1914, H. W. Young purchased both papers and kept them both running until 1917 when he decided to combine them to form the *Coquille Valley Sentinel*. Currently, the paper is published by Fred Taylor and is produced in a historic bank building located in downtown Coquille. This paper covers local news, viewpoints, police reports, sports, classifieds, and includes a church directory. Subscription rates are $24 per year for residents of Coos County and $30 per year for those living out of the county. Seniors pay $18 per year. A single copy is 50 cents.

Western World
1185 Baltimore Avenue, Bandon
(541) 347-242
www.bandonbythesea.com/westernworld/westernw1.htm

Western World Enterprises, owned by Greg and Mary McNair, distribute the *Western World* to more than 2,500 subscribers in the Bandon vicinity every Wednesday. Solid reporting focusing on community issues makes this award-winning paper a local favorite. This paper is also available on-line and features daily events in and around Bandon, job listings, stories on the local arts scene, and a message board where Bandon readers can communicate their opinions in cyberspace. Subscription rates are $20 per year for Coos County residents and $24 per for those living outside Coos County.

Myrtle Point Herald
408 Spruce Street, Myrtle Point
(541) 572-2717

Started in 1889, the *Myrtle Point Herald* is printed every Wednesday and distributed every Thursday. This paper provides over 2,100 subscribers in south Coos County with coverage of local agricultural issues, events, sports, schools, editorials, business, and social news. Subscriptions are $20 per year for Coos County residents and $18 for seniors. Out-of-county subscriptions are $25. A single newsstand copy is 50 cents.

Port Orford News
519 West 10th, Port Orford
(541) 332-2361
www.portorfordnews.com

Published every Wednesday, the *Port Orford News* keeps more than 960 paid subscribers up to date on area happenings. A one-year subscription for residents of Curry County is $18 per year and for those living out of the county it is $25.

Curry County Reporter
29835 Ellensburg Avenue, Gold Beach
(541) 247-6643
http://currycountyreporter.com

A weekly community newspaper published every Wednesday, the *Curry County Reporter* has a paid circulation of 3,150 subscribers. General manager and owner Molly Walker describes the paper as a "true community paper" that focuses on the issues and events in the local area. For those readers who enjoy reading news on-line, this paper has a Web site that contains news briefs, a calendar of upcoming events, and classified ads. Subscription rates are $20 per year for Curry County residents and $27 for out-of-county residents. A single issue is 50 cents.

Curry Coastal Pilot
507 Chetco Avenue, Brookings
(541) 469-3123
www.currypilot.com

Established in 1946 by Dewey Akers and Dave Homan, the *Curry Coastal Pilot* is published every Wednesday and Saturday morning and focuses solely on community news. This paper is distributed to about 3,300 customers in the Brookings-Harbor area and Curry County. This paper averages 2,750 single copy sales and has about 800 out-of-county subscribers. Subscription rates are $38 per year for residents of Curry County and $48 per year for out-of-county subscribers.

The *Curry County Pilot* also has a Web site that provides highlights of the paper edition as well as 24-hour weather, tides, events and road conditions; computerized searching for all classified ads for the past month; links to Web sites concerning Brookings-Harbor and Curry County including public agencies and weather records, and business listings.

Magazines and Other Print Media

Hipfish
365 35th Street, Astoria
(503) 325–0661
www.hipfish.com

Started in 1997 by Dinah Urell and Ramey Holsman, *Hipfish* is a monthly alternative paper that is distributed in the Lower Columbia Pacific region that includes the lower Washington State peninsula, Astoria, and coastal communities as far south as Newport. This colorful publication is also distributed in the Portland and Seattle metropolitan areas. Dinah Urell says she and her copublisher started *Hipfish* because there was a need to cover the "rapid growth of the art, music, and cultural scene, social and community issues, as well as alternative health care in the Lower Columbia Pacific region." This lively and off-beat publication features local commentary on social and community issues, a monthly calendar of cultural events, a guide to gallery openings, "North Coast Eatery Guide," and classifieds for local businesses. The current distribution

Insiders' Tip
You can pick up a copy of *Hipfish* for free in many coffeehouses in the larger coastal cities from Astoria to Newport.

for this publication is 8,000. The subscription rate is $29.95 per year.

Lower Columbia Business
P.O. Box 1088, Seaside 97138
(503) 738–3398
www.lcbiz.com

Lesle Palmeri, owner and publisher of *Lower Columbia Business,* describes her publication as "the only business-to-business publication dedicated solely to Columbia, Clatsop, and Tillamook Counties in Oregon and the Long Beach Peninsula in Washington. *Lower Columbia Business* is distributed free of charge to licensed business owners and community leaders in our readership counties, as well as to selected individuals in Portland, Salem, and Washington, D.C." Lesle and her husband, Jack Palmeri, are the only staff for this publication. "Our publication provides information on new and changing businesses within our readership areas, as well as a business calendar listing, city council meetings, and other meetings, such as Kiwanis or Rotary International, for the convenience of our readers," she says. "We also print information on legislation and updates on the business environment, as well as occasional guest articles from professionals in an area of expertise, such as tax-related articles that would benefit small business owners. We also have rotating special sections highlighting construction along the Coast and retail and hospitality businesses, as well as what is happening with the Lower Columbia lifestyle." An annual subscription is $15. Single issues are $3.00.

Oregon Coast
4969 U.S. Highway 101 N., Florence
(541) 997–8401
www.northwestmagazines.com

This regional bimonthly magazine includes feature articles about the many things to see and do on the Oregon Coast. This photo-packed publication includes feature stories on subjects such as exploring the Coast with your kids, whale-watching spots, music festivals, and favorite hiking trails. A sample of some of the main departments in this glossy publication include

"Bed & Breakfasts," "Calendar of Events," "Coastal Gardening," "Galleries," "Theater on the Coast," "Travel Planner," and "Wildflowers." This regional publication has been in circulation for more than 18 years and can be found in major grocery stores, bookstores, and other large retailers on the Oregon Coast and throughout Oregon. A one-year subscription is $18.95 and a two-year subscription is $29.95. The cover price for a single issue is $3.50.

Television

KCBY-TV Channel 11 (CBS)
3451 Broadway, North Bend
(541) 269–1111
www.kcby.com

KCBY-TV is a CBS affiliate and offers a full lineup of programming from the CBS network. The coverage area for this 20-year-old station is Gold Beach, Reedsport, Coquille, and Myrtle Point. The station produces its own local newscast. It also has a Web site where you can view detailed information about prime-time shows, soaps, specials, children's shows, and late-night shows that feature long-running favorites like David Letterman.

KBSC-TV Channel 49
Oregon Coast Television Network, Inc.
613 "A" Chetco Avenue, Brookings
(541) 469–4999
www.kbsctv.com

KBSC-TV opened its doors in 1992 and is owned by the Oregon Coast Television Network, Inc. This flagship station serves over 50,000 viewers who live in the coastal areas of northern California and southern Oregon on UHF channel 49 and cable channel 9. Daniel Nelson, President of the Oregon Coast Network, Inc., explains that "although KBSC-TV is located in the Medford, Oregon, area of dominant influence (ADI), Medford television is only available in these areas on cable or microwave-fed translators because of distance and the interference of the coastal mountains. 'The Coastal Strip'—longtime center of logging and fishing—is now fast becoming a hub of tourism, retail, and service industries." He adds, "Brookings has been described as becoming 'the Monterey of Oregon' and only KBSC Television completely serves this growing 'sub-market' making it truly 'the heart of the Oregon Coast.'"

KBSC-TV broadcasts a full lineup of local programming, which includes shows produced entirely by the local high school media department on subjects such as cooking, karaoke, bingo, local sports, and much more. In addition, KBSC-TV produces and airs special event programs such as Brooking's Azalea Parade and Crescent City's Fourth of July Parade as well as fundraising auctions for the local chambers of commerce. Viewers on boats up to 57 miles offshore can watch their favorite programming from a special antenna set up by the station. In the near future, the Oregon Coast Network, Inc. plans to extend KBSC-TV's coverage area to include the entire Oregon Coast by delivering its broadcast signal to other coastal cities in Oregon and northern California.

Radio

Adult Contemporary

KACW 107.3 FM, Coos Bay/North Bend
KAST 92.9 FM, Astoria
KCBZ 96.5 FM, Cannon Beach
KDEP 105.5 FM, Newport
KGBR 92.7 FM, Gold Beach

KJMX 99.5 FM, Reedsport
KORC 820 AM, Waldport
KSND 95.1 FM, Newport
KTIL 104.1 FM, Tillamook
KYTE 102.7 FM, Newport

Christian

KYTT 98.7 FM, Coos Bay/North Bend

Country-Western

KCST 1250 AM, Florence
KCST 106.9 FM, Florence
KCYS 98.1 FM, Seaside
KDUN 1030 AM, Reedsport
KOOS 94.9 FM Coos Bay
KSHL 97.5 FM, Newport
KSHR 97.3 FM, Coquille
KVAS 1230 AM, Astoria

News, Talk, Sports

KAST 1370 AM, Astoria
KBBR 1340 AM, Coos Bay/North Bend
KMBD 1590 AM, Tillamook

KNPT 1310 AM, Newport
KTBR 94.1 FM, Myrtle Point
KURY 95.3 FM, Brookings
KWRO 630 AM, Coquille

Nostalgia/Oldies

KBCH 1400 AM, Lincoln City
KCRF 96.7 and 98.3, Lincoln City
KDCQ 93.5 FM, Coos Bay/North Bend
KHSN 1230 AM, Coos Bay
KKEE 94.3 FM, Astoria
KPPT 1230 AM, Newport
KRBZ 99.5 FM, Reedsport
KSWB 840 AM, Astoria

Public Radio Stations

KLCO 90.5, Newport
KMUN 91.9 FM, Astoria
KSYD 92.1 FM, Reedsport

Rock

KBDN 96.5 FM Bandon
KPPT 100.7 FM Newport

Index

A

Abacela Vineyards & Winery, 220
Academy, The, 221
accommodations. *See* bed-and-breakfast inns; hotels and motels
Adidas, 92
Adobe Resort, 32–33, 78
adult contemporary radio, 262–63
Adventure Kayak, 183
Agate Beach, 206
Agate Beach Golf Course, 210
Agate Beach State Recreation Site, 168–69
airports, 23–24. *See also* transportation
Alderbrook Golf Course, 208
Alder Dune, 66–67
Alder House II, 112, 125
Alder Lake, 187
Alder SmokeHouse, 80
Alfred A. Loeb State Park, 70–71, 146, 156–57, 179
Alsea Bay, 188, 193–94, 194
Alsea Bay Bridge Historical Interpretive Center, 115, 171
Alsea Falls, 202
Alsean tribe, 12–13
Alsea River, 188, 190
alternative health care, 249–50. *See also* health care
American Shadows, 125
Amity Vineyards, 215–16
Animal Crackers Toys and Gifts, 92–93
annual events and festivals, 147–53
Antique Week/Lincoln Days, 148
Arbors Bed and Breakfast, The, 45
Arcadia Beach State Recreation Site, 164
Arch Cape bed-and-breakfast inn, 44
Archery Summit Winery, 216
Area Agency on Aging, 251
area overview, 3–11
    Astoria, 4
    Bandon, 9–10
    Cannon Beach, 4–5
    Coos Bay, 8–9
    Depot Bay, 6
    Florence, 7–8
    Gold Beach and Brookings, 11
    Langlois to the Elk River, 10–11
    Lincoln City, 6
    Neskowin, 6
    Newport, 6–7
    Oregon Dunes National Recreation Area, 8
    Oysterville, 7
    Reedsport, 8
    Seaside, 4
    Tillamook, 5–6
    Waldport, 7
    Yachats, 7
Argonauta Inn/The Waves Motel, 27
Argyle Winery, 216
Art Center Gallery, 121
Art Faire, 135
art festivals and events, 134–35. *See also* arts
art galleries, 121–30. *See also* arts
    Central Coast, 125–28
    North Coast, 121–25
    South Coast, 128–30
Artists Gallerie, 121
art museums, 120
arts, 120–35
    art festivals and events, 134–35
    art galleries, 121–30
    art museums, 120
    music, 132
    music festivals and events, 134
    organizations, 135
    theater, 132–34
    writing events/retreats, 130–32
Art & Sign, 130
arts organizations, 135
ArtSpace Gallery Cafe, 75
ArtSpace Gallery & Cafe, 124
art walk, 223
Ashland Vineyards, 221
Astor House, 251–52
Astoria. *See also* North Coast
    area overview, 4
    attractions, 105–7
    bed-and-breakfast inns, 41–43
    hotels and motels, 25
    kidstuff, 137–38
    map, x
    nightlife, 84–85
    relocation, 228
    restaurants, 72–73
    shopping, 91–92

Astoria Area Agency on Aging, 250
Astoria Column, 105
Astoria Inn, 41–42
Astoria School District, 237–38
Astoria's Riverfront, 137
Astoria-Warrenton Crab & Seafood
    Festival, 149
Astor Street Opry Company, 84, 132
At Home . . . by the Sea, 102–3
attractions, 105–19
    Astoria, 105–7
    Bandon, 119
    Brookings, 119
    Cannon Beach, 107
    Central Coast, 112–15, 118
    Coos Bay, 119
    Florence, 115
    Gold Beach, 119
    Grand Ronde, 113
    Lighthouses, 110–12
    Lincoln City, 112–13
    Newport, 113–15
    North Bend, 118–19
    North Coast, 105–9
    Otter Rock, 113
    Pacific City, 108–9
    Port Orford, 119
    Reedsport, 118
    Seaside, 107
    South Coast, 118–19
    Tillamook, 107–8
    Waldport, 115
    Yachats, 115
ATV and dune buggy rentals and tours,
    180. See also sports and activities
Audubon Society, 224
Azalea Festival, 149
Azalea Festival Art Show, 135

B

Backroom Bookstore, 91
Baghdad Theatre and Pub, 223–24
Bailey's Cedar House Bed and Breakfast, 56
bait shops, 189
Ballantyne & Douglass Fine Art, 121–22
Banana Belt Trading Company, 103
Bandon
    area overview, 9–10
    attractions, 119
    bed-and-breakfast inns, 56–57
    camping, 69
    golf, 213
    history, 17–18
    hotels and motels, 35–37

kidstuff, 145–46
map, xviii
nightlife, 89–90
relocation, 231
restaurants, 81–83
shopping, 100–102
Bandon Beach Riding Stables, 204
Bandon Bill's Steak & Seafood, 81
Bandon Cranberry Festival, 151
Bandon Dunes, 35–36, 82
Bandon Dunes Golf Course, 213
Bandon Face Rock Golf Course, 213
Bandon Glass Art Studio and Gallery, 129
Bandon Marsh National Wildlife
    Refuge, 158
Bandon Massage, 250
Bandon Mercantile Company, 100
Bandon Playhouse, 89, 133–34
Bandon School District, 242
Bandon State Natural Area, 175
Bank Brewing Company, 88
Bay Area Hospital, 248
Bay Breeze Golf and Driving Range, 208–9
Bay City restaurant, 75
Bay Haven Tavern, 87
Bay House, 76
Bay Moss Studio, 129
Bayocean Peninsula, 158
bays, rivers, and streams, 185–87, 188,
    190, 191–92
Bayshore RV Park and Marina, 195
Beachcomber Days, 150
Beachfront Gifts, 103
Beach Junction Market & Deli, 83
Beachside State Park, 66, 171
Bear Creek Winery, 221
bed-and-breakfast inns, 40–51, 55–59, 61.
    See also hotels and motels
    Arch Cape, 44
    Astoria, 41–43
    Bandon, 56–57
    Brookings, 59, 61
    Central Coast, 46–55
    Coos Bay, 55–56
    Depoe Bay, 46
    Florence, 51, 55
    Gold Beach, 58–59
    Hammond, 40–41
    Langlois, 57–58
    Manzanita, 45
    Newport, 46–48
    North Coast, 40–46
    Oceanside, 45
    Pacific City, 44–46

Port Orford, 58
Seaside, 43–44
South Beach, 48–49
South Coast, 55–59, 61
Yachats, 49–51
Beech Street Bed and Breakfast, 56–57
beeswax shipwreck, 19
Benjamin Young Inn Bed and Breakfast, 42
Beppu Gallery, 124
Best Western Beachfront Inn, 39
Best Western Inn at Face Rock, 36
Best Western Salbasgeon Inn, 35
Betty Kay Charters, 198
Beverly Beach, 206
Beverly Beach State Park, 65, 168
Bicycles 101, 181
bicycling, 180–83. *See also* sports and
    activities
Big Guy's Diner, 77
Big Nestucca River, The, 187
Big Tree Trail, The, 225
Big Wheel General Store, 101
Bike Shop, The, 181
bike shops, 181
Bill's Tavern, 85
Bistro, The, 74
BJ's, 99
Blackberry Arts Festival, 151
Black & Decker, 92
Blossom Gulch Nature Trail, 143–44
Blue Hen, The, 79
Blue Heron Bistro, 80
Blue Heron Cheese Company, 107, 139
Blue Heron Gallery, 128
Blue Heron Landing, 183
Blue Moon Restaurant and Lounge, 88
Blue Pacific Realty, 236
Blue Sky Cafe, 74–75
boat and equipment rental, 195–96. *See
    also* sports and activities
Boice Cope County Park, 175–76
Boiler Bay State Scenic Viewpoint, 168
Bolon Island Tideways State Scenic
    Corridor, 173
bombs, fire, 17
bonfire of the sentries, 18
Book Dock, 103
Book End Books, 96
Bookworm, The, 102
Brandy Peak Distillery, 119
Brasserie Montmartre, 223
Brian McEneny Woodcarving Gallery, 127
Bridgeview Vineyards, 221

Bridgewater Seafood Restaurant and
    Oyster Bar, The, 79
Bronze Coast Gallery, 122
Brookings. *See also* South Coast
    area overview, 11
    attractions, 119
    bed-and-breakfast inns, 59, 61
    camping, 70–71
    hotels and motels, 39
    kidstuff, 146
    map, xix
    nightlife, 90
    relocation, 232
    restaurants, 83
    shopping, 102–4
Brookings/Harbor Multiple Services
    Office, 251
Brookings-Harbor School District,
    242–43
Brookings South Coast Inn, 59, 61
Bruce's Candy Kitchen, 93
Bullards Beach State Park, 69, 175
Burd's Nest Inn Bed and Breakfast, 49–50
Burke Gallery, 121
bus services, 22–23. *See also*
    transportation

C
Cafe Uniontown, 84–85
Callahan Ridge Winery, 220
camping, 62–71
    Bandon, 69
    Brookings, 70–71
    Cannon Beach, 63
    Central Coast, 65–68
    Coos Bay, 68–69
    Florence, 65–68, 66
    Hammond, 62–63
    Lincoln City, 65
    Manzanita, 63
    Nehalem, 63–64
    Newport, 65
    North Coast, 62–64
    Port Orford, 69–70
    Reedsport, 68
    South Beach, 65
    South Coast, 68–71
    Tillamook, 64
    Waldport, 66
Candlelight Cafe & Bar, 223
Canita, 223
canneries, salmon, 17
Cannery Cafe, 72–73

Cannon Beach. *See also* North Coast
  area overview, 4–5
  attractions, 107
  camping, 63
  hotels and motels, 27–28
  map, xii
  nightlife, 85
  relocation, 228–29
  restaurants, 74
  shopping, 92–94
Cannon Beach Arts Association
  Gallery, 122
Cannon Beach Gazette, 257–58
Cannon Beach Hotel, 27
Cannon Beach Sandcastle Contest, 150
canoeing and kayaking, 183. *See also*
sports and activities
Canyon Beach Book Company, 93
Canyon Way Bookstore and Restaurant,
  77, 97–98
Cape Arago Lighthouse, 111
Cape Arago State Park, 175
Cape Blanco Lighthouse, 112
Cape Blanco State Park, 69–70, 176–77
Cape Cod Cottages, 32
Cape Kiwanda, 108–9
Cape Kiwanda Beach, 206
Cape Kiwanda State Natural Area, 166
Cape Lookout State Park, 64, 162, 166
Cape Meares Lake, 184
Cape Meares Lighthouse, 110
Cape Meares State Park, 162
Cape Meares State Scenic Viewpoint,
  165–66
Cape Perpetua Interpretive Center, 115
Cape Perpetua Scenic Area, 66
Cape Perpetua Trails, 202
Cape Perpetua Visitors Center, 171
Cape Sebastian State Scenic Corridor, 178
Caprial's Bistro, 224
Caravan Airport Transportation, 23
Caring Options, 239
Carl G. Washburne Memorial State Park,
  66, 172
car rentals, 22. *See also* transportation
Carter Lake, 68
Carter's, 96
car travel, 20–22
Carvers & Designers, 124
Cascade Head, 157, 201
Cascade Head Chamber Music Festival, 86
Cascade Head Music Festival, 134, 150
Castaway-by-the-Sea, 37
Catch the Wind Kite Shop, 99, 167

Cathedral Tree to Astoria Column
  hike, 198
Cat House, 97
Cave Creek Campground, 225
cave tour, 225
Cedar Bay Restaurant, 132
Cedar Bend Golf Club, 213
Cedar Tree at Westin Salishan Resort,
  The, 76
Center Diamond, 93
Central Coast. *See also specific towns*
  airports, 24
  art galleries, 125–28
  attractions, 112–15, 118
  bed-and-breakfast inns, 46–55
  boat and equipment rental, 195–96
  camping, 65–68
  child care referral services, 241
  clamming, 193–94
  clinics, 248
  coastal parks, 167–74
  crabbing, 194–95
  education and childcare, 240–41
  fishing, 187–88, 190
  golf, 210–12
  health care, 247–48
  hospitals, 247–48
  hotels and motels, 30–35
  kidstuff, 139–43
  map, viii
  newspapers, 258–59
  nightlife, 86–87
  ocean charter services and river
    outfitters, 197–98
  public schools, 240–41
  real estate, 235
  relocation, 230–31
  restaurants, 76–80
  shopping, 96–99
  theater, 133
Central Coast Water Sports, 183
Central Curry School District, 242
Century 21 Agate Realty, 236
Chainsaw Sculpture Championships, 150
chambers of commerce, 116–17
Channel House Bed and Breakfast, 46
Charisma Gifts, 97
Charleston. *See also* South Coast
  kidstuff, 144–45
  restaurants, 81
Charleston Merchant's Annual Crab
  Feed, 148
Charleton Deep Sea Charters, 196
Chateau Benoit, 216

Cheap Frills, 98
Cheri's at Sea Towne, 126
Chetco Inn Residential Care Facility, 253
Chetco River, 191
Chetco River Inn, 39
Chetco Valley Historical Society, 119
child care referral services
    Central Coast, 241
    North Coast, 239–40
    South Coast, 243
Child Care Resource & Referral, 240
children's activities. *See* kidstuff
Chinook Winds Casino, 86, 112–13
Chives, 83
Chowder Blues and Brews Festival, 151
Christian radio, 263
Cinema 21, 224
clamming, 192–94. *See also* sports and
    activities
Clatsop Community College, 243
Clawson's Windward Inn, 79
Cleanline Surf Shop, 92, 164
Clear Lake, 190
Cleawox Lake, 187
Clementine's Bed and Breakfast, 42–43
Cliff Nature Trail, 225
climate, 155–56
clinics
    Central Coast, 248
    North Coast, 246–47
    South Coast, 249
Clock Tower Gallery, 129
C&M Stables, 204
coastal landscape, 156–63
coastal parks. *See* parks, coastal
Coaster Theater, 85, 132
Coast Range roads, 21
Coast Roast Coffee Company, 97
Cobbler's Bench, The, 101
Coffee People, 224
Coffinbury Lake, 184
Coldwater Creek, 92
Coldwell Banker Gesik Realty, Inc., 235
Coldwell Banker Kent Price Realty Inc., 234
Coldwell Banker Oregon Coast Realty, 236
Coldwell Banker 1st Newport Realty, 235
colleges, 243–44
Collide, 122
Columbia Chocolates, 91
Columbia Memorial Hospital, 245
Columbian Cafe, 73
Columbia Press, The, 257
Columbia River, 184, 193
Columbia River Day Spa, 249

Columbia River Maritime Museum,
    91–92, 105, 137
Columbia Sportswear, 96
Cook Gallery, 129
Coos Art Museum, 120
Coos Bay. *See also* South Coast
    area overview, 8–9
    attractions, 119
    bed-and-breakfast inns, 55–56
    camping, 68–69
    fishing, 191
    golf, 212–13
    hotels and motels, 35
    kidstuff, 143–44
    map, xvii
    nightlife, 88–89
    relocation, 231
    shopping, 100
Coos Bay Public School District, 242
Coos County Historical Museum, 118–19
Coos/Curry Resource & Referral
    Agency, 243
Coos River, 191–92
Coquille nightlife, 89
Coquille River, 191
Coquille River Lighthouse, 112
Coquille tribe, 13–14
Coquille Valley Hospital, 249
Coquille Valley Sentinel, The, 260
Cosmos Gallery, 126
Cottage Gardenware at Nye Beach, 98
country-Western radio, 263
crabbing, 194–95. *See also* sports and
    activities
Craft Warehouse & Antique Mall, 98
Cranberry Festival, 135
Cranberry Sweets, 101
"Creatures of the Night" Halloween
    Party, 152
Crest Motel, 25
Crestview Hills Golf Course, 211
Crustacean Classics Crab Festival, 147
Crystal Dolphin Gallery, 128
Cullaby Lake, 184–85
Cummins Creek Loop, 181, 183
Curry Coastal Pilot, 260–61
Curry County Museum, 119
Curry County Reporter, 260
Curry General Hospital, 249
Custom Threads, 91

D
Daily Astorian, The, 256–57
Darlingtonia State Natural Site, 173

Darlingtonia Wayside, 142
David L. Davis Real Estate, 236
day trips, 214–25
    Oregon Caves National Monument,
        224–25
    Portland, 222–24
    Rogue Valley wineries, 214–15, 221–22
    Umpqua Valley wineries, 214, 220–21
    Willamette Valley wineries, 214,
        215–19
    winery tours, 214–22
Dean Creek Elk Viewing Area, 118, 157
Del Ray Beach State Recreation Site, 163
Depoe Bay. *See also* Central Coast
    area overview, 6
    bed-and-breakfast inns, 46
    fishing, 185–86
    restaurants, 77
Depoe Bay Clinic, 248
Devil's Elbow State Park, 162
Devils Lake, 187
Devils Lake State Park, 65, 167
Devils Punch Bowl State Natural Area, 168
Dining Room at Westin Salishan Resort,
    The, 77
Divine Decadence, 99
Dock of the Bay Marina, The, 196
Dockside, 97
Dog Show at the Beach, 152
Dolly Ware's Doll Museum, 142–43
Dooger's, 73–74
Dorchester House, The, 253
Dory Cove, 76
Dragonfire Interactive Studio and
    Gallery, 122
Dress Barn, 92, 96
Drift Creek Falls, 201
Driftwood Beach State Recreation Site, 170
D River State Recreation Site, 167
Duane Johnson Real Estate, 234
Duck Pond Cellars, 216–17
dune buggy rentals and tours, 180. *See
    also* sports and activities
dunes, sand, 158
Dusty Saw Theatre, The, 133

E
Eagle's View Bed and Breakfast, 45–46
Earthworks, 125–26
Earthworks Gallery, 128
Ecola Creek, 186
Ecola Square, 93
Ecola State Park, 162, 163–64
Eddie Bauer, 96

Edgewater Cottages, 32
Edgewater Inn, 26
Edgewater Inn on the Pacific Coast, 35
education and childcare, 236–44
    Central Coast, 240–41
    colleges, 243–44
    North Coast, 237–40
    South Coast, 242–43
Edwin K Bed and Breakfast, 51
Eel Lake, 190
Elbow Lake, 187–88
Elder Home Adult Foster Care, 253
Elk Cove, 217
Elk River, 10–11, 192
El Mundo for Men, 93
Embarcadero, 77–78
Endicott Gardens Bed and Breakfast, 58
End of the Trail Trading Post, 99
Eola Hills Wine Cellars, 217
Erath Vineyards Winery, 217–18
Erhart Lake, 188
Ernest Bloch Music Festival, 134
Ernst & Ernst Collectors Gallery, 122
Esparza's Tex-Mex Cafe, 224
estuaries, 157–58
European settlement, 16–18
explorers, 14–16
ExposureArt Gallery, 121

F
Face Rock State Scenic Viewpoint, 175
Factory Stores at Lincoln City, The, 96
Fall Kite Festival, 151–52
Fat Tire Farm, 224
festivals and annual events, 147–53
Fine Art Gallery, 121
Finn Ware, 91
fire bombs, 17
Fireside Motel, The, 33
Fisherman's Wharf Restaurant & Lounge,
    The, 87
Fisher Poets Gathering, 130
fishing, 183–92. *See also* sports and
    activities
    Central Coast, 187–88, 190
    North Coast, 184–87
    South Coast, 190–92
fishing guides and bait shops, 189
Flavel House, 105–6
Flora Pacifica, 103
Floras Lake, 190
Floras Lake House by the Sea Bed and
    Breakfast, 57–58, 176
Floras Lake State Park, 176

Floras Lake Windsurfing, 176
Florence. *See also* Central Coast
    area overview, 7–8
    attractions, 115
    bed-and-breakfast inns, 51, 55
    camping, 65–68, 66
    golf, 210–12
    hotels and motels, 35
    kidstuff, 142–43
    map, xvi
    nightlife, 87
    relocation, 230–31
    restaurants, 79–80
    shopping, 99
Florence Area Agency on Aging, 251
Florence Events Center, 87, 132, 133
Florence Events Center Gallery, 128
Flying Dutchman Winery, 113
Fogarty Creek, 186
Fogarty Creek State Recreation Area, 168
Forest Hills Country Club, 212
Forest Park, 224
forests, 156–57
Forget Me Knots Quilting &
    Needlework, 101
Forinash Gallery, 126–27
Foris Vineyards Winery, 221
Fort Clatsop National Memorial, 106,
    137–38
Fort Stevens State Park, 62–63, 138,
    163, 193
Fourth of July Celebration, 150
Frame Cellar & Gallery, 126
Frames of Florence—Gallery, 101, 128
Franklin Street Station Bed and
    Breakfast, 43
Fraser's Restaurant and Quarterdeck
    Lounge, 89
Freed Gallery, 126
freshwater lakes, 184–85, 187–88, 190–91
Frogblossom Studio & Gallery, 128–29

G
G. H. Bass, 96
Gales Bar & Grill, 85
Gallery at Salishan, 126
Gallery 101 at the Bookworm
    Bookstore, 130
Gap Kids, 96
Gap Outlet, 96
Garibaldi Marina, 195
Garrison Lake, 190
Gearhart. *See also* North Coast
    golf, 207–8

hotels and motels, 26
map, xi
relocation, 228
restaurants, 73
Gearhart by the Sea, 26
Gearhart Golf Links, 207
Gearhart Ocean Inn, 26
Geisel Monument State Heritage Site, 178
geology, 155
Geppetto's Toy Shoppe, 93–94
Gilbert Inn and Vacation Rentals, 26–27
Girardet Wine Cellars, 220
Girtle's Restaurant & Lounge, 85
Glastonbury Renaissance Faire, 134
Gleneden Beach. *See also* Central Coast
    golf, 210
    hotels and motels, 30–31
    restaurants, 76–77
    shopping, 97
Gleneden Beach State Recreation Site, 167
Godfather's Books and Espresso, 91
Gold Beach. *See also* South Coast
    area overview, 11
    attractions, 119
    bed-and-breakfast inns, 58–59
    golf, 213
    hotels and motels, 37–39
    relocation, 231–32
    shopping, 102
Gold Beach Multiple Services Office, 251
Gold Beach Resort, 37–38
Gold Coast Properties, Inc., 236
Golden and Silver Falls State Natural
    Area, 203–4
golf, 207–13. *See also* sports and activities
    Bandon, 213
    Central Coast, 210–12
    Coos Bay, 212–13
    Florence, 210–12
    Gearhart, 207–8
    Gleneden, 210
    Gold Beach, 213
    Lincoln City, 210
    Manzanita, 208
    Neskowin, 209
    Newport, 210
    North Bend, 212
    North Coast, 207–10
    Reedsport, 212
    Seaside, 208
    South Coast, 212–13
    Tillamook, 208–9
    Toledo, 211
    Waldport, 211

Good for You!, 103
Gooney's Sports Bar & Grill, 88
Gourmet Coastal Coffees, 80–81
Governor Patterson Memorial State
    Recreation Site, 170–71
Gracie's Sea Hag Restaurant and
    Lounge, 77
Grand Central Pizza, 78
Grandma & Me, 98
Grand Ronde attractions, 113
Grandview Bed and Breakfast, 43
Grantland Mayfield Gallery, 129–30
Grape Leaf, 99
Grateful Bread Bakery, 75
Grayback Campground, 225
Gray Whales Gallery, The, 130
Great Oregon Beach Cleanup, 149
Greaver Gallery, 122
Green Gables Bed and Breakfast &
    Bookstore, 46–47, 97
Green Peak Falls, 202
Greyhound Lines, 22
Gussie's, 89

H
Hammond. *See also* North Coast
    bed-and-breakfast inns, 40–41
    camping, 62–63
Harbor, 232. *See also* South Coast
Harbor Lights Books, 101
Harbor Theater, 99
Harp's Restaurant and the Hideaway
    Lounge, 82
Harris Beach State Park, 70, 179
Harvest Book Shoppe and The Coffee
    Corner, 100
Hatfield Marine Science Center, 113–14,
    141–42, 169
Hawk Creek Gallery, 125
Haystack Fishing Club, Inc., 166, 197
Haystack Gallery, 122
Haystack Program in the Arts &
    Sciences, 131
Haystack Rock, 107, 198–99
Headland's Country Mercantile, The, 100
Headlight-Herald, 258
health care, 245–50
    alternative care, 249–50
    Central Coast, 247–48
    North Coast, 245–47
    South Coast, 248–49
Heathman Hotel, The, 223
Hebo Lake, 185
Heceta Head Lighthouse, 111

Heceta Head Lighthouse Bed and
    Breakfast, 50
Heceta Head Lighthouse State Scenic
    Viewpoint, 172–73
Henry Estate Winery, 220
Heritage Center Museum, 106
Highlands at Gearhart, The, 207–8
hiking, 198–204. *See also* sports and
    activities
Hipfish, 261
Historical Tours of Astoria, 106
history, 12–19
Hog Wild Cafe, 83
Home by the Sea Bed and Breakfast, 58
horseback riding, 204. *See also* sports and
activities
hospitals
    Central Coast, 247–48
    North Coast, 245–46
    South Coast, 248–49
hotels and motels, 20–39. *See also* bed-
    and-breakfast inns
    Astoria, 25
    Bandon, 35–37
    Brookings, 39
    Cannon Beach, 27–28
    Central Coast, 30–35
    Coos Bay, 35
    Florence, 35
    Gearhart, 26
    Gleneden Beach, 30–31
    Gold Beach, 37–39
    Lincoln City, 30
    Nehalem, 28–29
    Neskowin, 30
    Newport, 31–32
    North Coast, 20–30
    Otter Rock, 31
    Pacific City, 29–30
    Port Orford, 37
    Reedsport, 35
    Seaside, 25–27
    South Coast, 35–39
    Tolovana Park, 28
    Waldport, 32
    Wheeler, 29
    Yachats, 32–35
Hot Pots, 97
House of the Potter, 122
Hubers, 223
Hughes House, 119
Hug Point State Recreation Site, 164
Humbug Mountain State Park, 70, 177–78
Hume's salmon canneries, 17

I

Icefire Glassworks, 123
Indian Beach and Haystack Rock, 205
Indian Style Salmon Bake, 152
Inn at Cape Kiwanda, 29–30
Inn at Nesika Beach, 58–59
Inn at Otter Crest, 31
Inn at the Shore, 27
Ireland's Rustic Lodges, 38
Iron Horse Restaurant, 224

J

J. Ader Gallery, 130
Japanese-American Historical Plaza,
    222–23
Jeffrey Hull Gallery, The, 122–23
Jerry's Rogue Jets, 204
Jessie M. Honeyman State Park, 67–68,
    143, 173
jet boat tours, 204. *See also* sports and
    activities
Jewell Meadows Wildlife Area, 157
Jewell School District, 238
Johnson House Bed and Breakfast, The,
    51, 55
Jot's Resort on the Rogue River, 38
J.R. Amicks Guide Service, 197
Judith Anne Antiques, 96–97
Judy's Corner Frame Shop, 130
Jupiter's Rare and Used Books, 94

K

Kalypso, 74
kayaking, 183. *See also* sports and
    activities
Kentuck Golf Course, 212
Kentucky Falls, 202–3
kidstuff, 137–46
    Astoria, 137–38
    Bandon, 145–46
    Brookings, 146
    Central Coast, 139–43
    Charleston, 144–45
    Coos Bay, 143–44
    Florence, 142–43
    Newport, 139–42
    North Coast, 137–39
    Port Orford, 146
    Seaside, 138
    South Coast, 143–46
    Tillamook, 139
Kilchis River, 186
King Estate Winery, 218
Kitchen Collection, 92, 96

Kittiwake Bed and Breakfast, The, 50–51
Knappa School District, 238
Kum-Yon's, 81
Kusan tribe, 13

L

La Buca, 224
La Garza Cellars & Gourmet Kitchen,
    220–21
Lakeport, 16
lakes, freshwater, 184–85, 187–88, 190–91
Lakeshore Lodge, 80
Lakeside Golf & Racquet Club, 210
Lakeside restaurant, 80
Landmark Inn, The, 35
landscape, coastal, 156–63
Lane Family Connections, 241
Langlois. *See also* South Coast
    area overview, 10–11
    bed-and-breakfast inns, 57–58
La Serre, 78–79
Latimer Center Gift Shop, 95
Latimer Quilt and Textile Center, 107–8
Lazy Susan Cafe, 74
Le Domaine, 97
Lehrer, John, 248
Leif Erikson Drive, 224
Leroy's Blue Whale, 78
Let It Rain, 91
Lighthouse Bed and Breakfast, 57
lighthouses, 110–12
lily bulbs, 17
Lincoln City. *See also* Central Coast
    area overview, 6
    attractions, 112–13
    camping, 65
    golf, 210
    hotels and motels, 30
    map, xiv
    nightlife, 86
    relocation, 230
    restaurants, 76
    shopping, 96–97
Lincoln County Historical Society
    Museums, 114
Lincoln County School District, 240–41
Lincoln Days, 148
Little Theater on the Bay, 87–88, 133
Lloyd Center, 223
Lloyd District, 223
Lloyd's, 89–90
Lord Bennett's, 82
Lost Creek State Recreation Site, 170
Lotus, The, 87

Lovejoy's Imports, 99
Lowden's Beachfront Bed and
    Breakfast, 59
Lower Columbia Business, 261
Lower McCleay Park, 224
Lower Umpqua Hospital, 248
Lucky Labrador Brew Pub, The, 224
Lucy's Books, 91, 92
Luna Sea Products, 98

M
M. Sellin, 94
Macklyn House, 254
magazines and other print media,
    261–62. *See also* media
Maggie's Guestrooms, 29
Manhattan Beach State Recreation
    Site, 165
Manzanita. *See also* North Coast
    bed-and-breakfast inns, 45
    camping, 63
    golf, 208
    nightlife, 85
    relocation, 229
    restaurants, 74–75
    shopping, 94–95
Manzanita Golf Course, 208
Manzanita News and Espresso, 94
Mapleton School District, 241
maps
    Astoria, x
    Bandon, xviii
    Brookings, xix
    Cannon Beach, xii
    Central Coast, viii
    Coos Bay, xvii
    Florence, xvi
    Gearhart, xi
    Lincoln City, xiv
    Newport, xv
    North Coast, vii
    Seaside, xi
    South Coast, ix
    Tillamook, xiii
Marketplace at Salishan, The, 97
Mary Anna's $12 Store, 92
MAX (Metropolitan Area Express), 223
McBee Motel, 27
media, 256–63
    magazines and other print media,
        261–62
    newspapers, 256–61
    radio, 262–63
    television, 262

Meier & Frank, 223
Mercer Lake, 188
meteorite, Port Orford, 19
Metropolitan Area Express (MAX), 223
Michael Gibbons Gallery: The
    Vicarage, 127
Migrations, 95
Mikasa, 96
Mike Miller Educational Trail, 201–2
Mike's Bike Shop, 164
Mill Casino, The, 80, 88
Mindpower Gallery, 128
Montage, 223
Mory's Mini Gallery, 130
Mo's, 78, 79, 99
Mossy Creek Pottery, 126
Mostly Hats, 92
motels. *See* hotels and motels
Mother Nature's Natural Foods, 94–95
mountain bike trails, 181–83. *See also*
    sports and activities
municipal airports, 23, 24. *See also*
    transportation
municipal buses, 22–23. *See also*
    transportation
Munsel Lake, 188
Munson Creek Falls, 199, 201
Muriel O. Ponsler Memorial State Scenic
    Viewpoint, 172
music, 132. *See also* arts
music festivals and events, 134. *See
    also* arts
Myrtle Point Herald, 260
Myrtlewood Gallery, 128

N
natural world, 154–55
Nature Art & Sounds, 123
Neah Kah Nie, 229
Neahkahnie Institute, 131
Neahkahnie Mountain, 19, 181, 199
Neah-Kah-Nie School District, 239
Neawanna by the Sea, 252
Necanicum Gallery & Picture Framing, 121
Necanicum River, 186
Nehalem
    camping, 63–64
    hotels and motels, 28–29
Nehalem Bay, 186, 193, 194
Nehalem Bay Kayak Company, 183
Nehalem Bay State Park, 63–64, 165
Nehalem River, 186–87
Nehalem River Inn Lodge, Restaurant &
    Wine Cellar, 28–29

Nehalem Valley Care Center, 252–53
Neptune State Scenic Viewpoint, 172
Neskowin. *See also* North Coast
    area overview, 6
    golf, 209
    hotels and motels, 30
Neskowin Beach Golf Course, 209
Neskowin Beach State Recreation Site, 167
Nestucca Bay, 187, 193
Nestucca Valley School District, 239
Netarts Bay, 158, 193, 194
New Carissa, 18
Newport. *See also* Central Coast
    area overview, 6–7
    attractions, 113–15
    bed-and-breakfast inns, 46–48
    camping, 65
    golf, 210
    history, 16–17
    hotels and motels, 31–32
    kidstuff, 139–42
    map, xv
    nightlife, 86–87
    relocation, 230
    restaurants, 77–78
    shopping, 97–98
    surfing, 206
Newport Area Agency on Aging, 251
Newport Belle Bed and Breakfast, 48–49
Newport Lighted Boat Parade, 153
Newport Marina Store & Charters, 195
Newport Municipal Airport, 24
Newport Performing Arts Center, 86–87,
    97, 132, 133
Newport Seafood & Wine Festival, 148
Newport Tradewinds, 197–98
Newport Visual Arts Center, 120
New River, 204
News Guard, The, 258
newspapers, 256–61. *See also* media
news radio, 263
News-Times, 258–59
nightlife, 84–90
    Astoria, 84–85
    Bandon, 89–90
    Brookings, 90
    Cannon Beach, 85
    Central Coast, 86–87
    Coos Bay, 88–89
    Coquille, 89
    Florence, 87
    Lincoln City, 86
    Manzanita, 85
    Newport, 86–87

North Bend, 87–88
North Coast, 84–86
Otis, 86
Pacific City, 85–86
Pistol River, 90
Seaside, 85
South Coast, 87–90
Yachats, 87
Nike, 92
Niketown, 223
Niki's, 224
Nine West, 92
Noho's Hawaiian Cafe, 224
Nordstrom, 223
Norm Thompson, 96
North Bend. *See also* South Coast
    attractions, 118–19
    golf, 212
    nightlife, 87–88
    relocation, 231
    restaurants, 80–81
North Bend Lanes Bowling Center, 87
North Bend Medical Center, 249
North Bend Municipal Airport, 24
North Coast. *See also specific towns*
    airports, 23–24
    art galleries, 121–25
    attractions, 105–9
    bed-and-breakfast inns, 40–46
    boat and equipment rental, 195
    camping, 62–64
    child care referral services, 239–40
    clamming, 193
    clinics, 246–47
    coastal parks, 163–67
    crabbing, 194
    education and childcare, 237–40
    fishing, 184–87
    golf, 207–10
    health care, 245–47
    hospitals, 245–46
    hotels and motels, 20–30
    kidstuff, 137–39
    map, vii
    newspapers, 256–58
    nightlife, 84–86
    ocean charter services and river
        outfitters, 196–97
    public schools, 237–39
    real estate, 234
    relocation, 228–30
    restaurants, 72–76
    shopping, 91–95
    theater, 132–33

North Coast Senior Services, 250
North Fork Smith River, 203
North Lincoln County Museum, 113
Northwest by Northwest Gallery, 123
Northwest District, 224
Northwest Equine Outfitters, 165, 204
Northwest Film Center, 223
Northwest Kitchens, 97
Northwest Passage, 99
nostalgia/oldies radio, 263
nursing homes, 251–54
Nye Beach Gallery, 127
Nye Beach Hotel and Cafe, 31

O

Oak Knoll Winery, 218
Oar House Bed and Breakfast, 47–48
OCCA (Oregon Coast Council for the Arts), 135
ocean charter services, 196–98. *See also* sports and activities
Ocean Crest Retirement, 253
Ocean Dunes Golf Links, 211
Ocean Festival, 151
Ocean Haven, 33
Oceanic Arts, 127
OCEAN (Oregon Coast Extended Arts Network), 135
Ocean Pulse Surfboards, 169
Oceanside. *See also* North Coast
bed-and-breakfast inns, 45
restaurants, 75
Oceanside Beach State Recreation Site, 166
Oceanside State Park, 162
Ocean View Care Center of Bandon, 253
O'Donovan Minor Emergency Clinic, The, 246
O'dysius, The, 30
Officers' Inn Bed and Breakfast, 40–41
Olalla Valley Golf Course, 211
Old City Hall Grand Ballroom, 88
Old Tower House Bed and Breakfast, The, 56
Old Town Florence shopping, 99
OMSI (Oregon Museum of Science and Industry), 223
Ona Beach State Park, 170
On Broadway Theater, 89, 133
Onion Peak Reading Series, 131
Oregon Arts Commission, 135
Oregon Association of Realtors, 234
Oregon Caves Chateau, 225
Oregon Caves National Monument, 224–25

Oregon Coast, 261–62
Oregon Coast Aquarium, 114–15, 141, 162–63, 169
Oregon Coast Aquarium's "Creatures of the Night" Halloween Party, 152
Oregon Coast Aquarium's "Sea of Lights," 153
Oregon Coast Bike Route, The, 180–81
Oregon Coast Community College, 244
Oregon Coast Council for the Arts (OCCA), 135
Oregon Coast Extended Arts Network (OCEAN), 135
Oregon Coast Jams, 102
Oregon Coast Music Festival, 134
Oregon Coast Properties, Inc., 235
Oregon Connection House of Myrtlewood, 119
Oregon Dixieland Jubilee, 134
Oregon Dune Mushers Mail Run, 148
Oregon Dunes National Recreation Area, 8
Oregon Dunes Visitor Center, 118
Oregon Gallery, 123
Oregon House, The, 33
Oregon Islands National Wildlife Refuge, 162
Oregon Museum of Science and Industry (OMSI), 223
Oregon Senior & Disabled Services Division, 250
Oregon Shorebird Festival, 152
Oregon Writer's Colony, 131
Oregon Zoo, 223
Original Bard, 127
Osborne Studio & Gallery, 124
Oshkosh B'Gosh, 92
Oswald West State Park, 63, 157, 164–65
Otis Cafe, 75–76
Otis Junction restaurant, 75–76
Otis nightlife, 86
Otter Crest State Scenic Viewpoint, 168
Otter Point State Recreation Site, 178
Otter Rock. *See also* Central Coast
attractions, 113
hotels and motels, 31
outdoors, 154–79
climate, 155–56
coastal landscape, 156–63
coastal parks, 163–79
geology, 155
natural world, 154–55
Overleaf Lodge, 33–34
Oysterville area overview, 7

P

Pacific City. *See also* North Coast
  attractions, 108–9
  bed-and-breakfast inns, 44–46
  hotels and motels, 29–30
  nightlife, 85–86
  restaurants, 75
  shopping, 95
Pacific City Gallery, 125
Pacific Moon Gallery, 124
Pacific Rim Gallery, 121
Pacific Sands Resort, 30
Pacific View Bed and Breakfast, 61
Pacific Way Bakery and Cafe, 73
Pam Zielinski Prudential Northwest
  Properties, 235
Pancake Breakfast & Parade, 151
Paper Moon Rubber Stamps, 91
parks, coastal, 163–79
  Central Coast, 167–74
  North Coast, 163–67
  South Coast, 174–79
Peace Harbor Hospital, 247
Pearl District, 223
Pelican Bay Arts Association, 130
Pelican Pub & Brewery, 109
Pendleton Woolen Mills, 96
Pete Anderson Realty Inc. Better Homes
  and Gardens, 234
Pioneer Place, 223
pirates and explorers, 14–16
Pistol River Friendship Hall, 90
Pistol River nightlife, 90
Pistol River State Scenic View Point, 178
Pittock Mansion, 224
Pizza 'a fetta, 74
Planet Yachats, 98–99
Point, The, 205
Ponzi Vineyards, 218
Port Dock One, 87
Portland Art Museum, 223
Portland Brewing Company, 224
Portland Center for Performing Arts, 223
Portland day trips, 222–24
Portland International Airport, 23–24
Portland Visitors Association, 222
Port Orford. *See also* South Coast
  attractions, 119
  bed-and-breakfast inns, 58
  camping, 69–70
  hotels and motels, 37
  kidstuff, 146
  shopping, 102
Port Orford Heads State Park, 177

Port Orford meteorite, 19
Port Orford News, 260
Portside, 81
Powell's City of Books, 223
Powell's Travel Store, 223
Prehistoric Gardens, 146
Premiere Pasta, 73
Prom Bike Shop, 181
Promenade, The, 107
Providence North Coast Clinic, 246, 247
Providence Seaside Hospital, 245–46
Prudential All Coast Properties, 235
public radio stations, 263
public schools
  Central Coast, 240–41
  North Coast, 237–39
  South Coast, 242–43
Purple Pelican, The, 121, 123

Q

Queen Anne Vacation Suites, 36–37
Queen of Hearts, 98

R

radio, 262–63. *See also* media
Radmacher Gallery, The, 123
Raindrop Factory, 99
Rare Discovery, 123
Raz Transportation Company, 22
real estate, 232–36
  Central Coast, 235
  North Coast, 234
  South Coast, 236
Redhawk Vineyard, 218–19
Redwood Theater, 90
Reedsport. *See also* Central Coast
  area overview, 8
  attractions, 118
  camping, 68
  golf, 212
  hotels and motels, 35
  relocation, 231
Reedsport Area Agency on Aging, 251
Reedsport Outdoor Store, 196
Rejuvenation Massage & Spa, 249–50
relocation, 226–55
  Astoria/Warrenton, 228
  Bandon, 231
  Brookings-Harbor, 232
  Cannon Beach, 228–29
  Central Coast, 230–31
  Coos Bay/North Bend, 231
  education and childcare, 236–44
  Florence, 230–31

Gearhart, 228
Gold Beach, 231–32
health care, 245–50
life at the Coast, 226–32
Lincoln City, 230
Manzanita/Neah Kah Hie, 229
Newport, 230
North Coast, 228–30
real estate, 232–36
Reedsport/Winchester Bay, 231
residential care and nursing homes,
   251–54
retirement, 250–51
Seaside, 228
South Coast, 231–32
Tillamook, 229–30
worship, 254–55
residential care and nursing homes, 251–54
restaurants, 72–83
   Astoria, 72–73
   Bandon, 81–83
   Bay City, 75
   Brookings, 83
   Cannon Beach, 74
   Central Coast, 76–80
   Charleston, 81
   Depoe Bay, 77
   Florence, 79–80
   Gearhart, 73
   Gleneden Beach, 76–77
   Lakeside, 80
   Lincoln City, 76
   Manzanita, 74–75
   Newport, 77–78
   North Bend, 80–81
   North Coast, 72–76
   Oceanside, 75
   Otis Junction, 75–76
   Pacific City, 75
   Seaside, 73–74
   South Coast, 80–83
   Waldport, 78
   Wedderburn, 83
   Yachats, 78–79
retirement, 250–51
Rex Hill Vineyards, 219
Rhododendron Festival, 149
Rickert Gallery, 127
Ripley's Believe It Or Not!, 142
River Gallery, 124
River House Motel, 35
Riverhouse Restaurant, 75
river outfitters, 196–98. See also sports
   and activities

rivers. See bays, rivers, and streams
RiverSea Gallery, 121
roads, 20–22. See also transportation
Roads End State Recreation Area, 167
Robert ("Bob") Straub State Park, 166
Rockport, 96
rock radio, 263
Rod 'n' Reel, 83
Roger's Zoo, 88
Rogue Ales Public House, 78
Rogue River, 192
Rogue Valley wineries, 214–15, 221–22.
   See also Umpqua Valley wineries;
   Willamette Valley wineries
Roseanna's Oceanside Cafe, 75
Rosebriar Hotel, 25
Rose Garden Arena, 223
Rubio's Mexican Restaurant, 83
Ryan Gallery, 126

S
Saddle Mountain State Natural Area and
   Campground, 63, 163
Saddle Mountain State Park, 157
Safari Town Surf Shop, 167
Salishan Golf Links, 210
Salish tribe, 12
salmon canneries, 17
Salmon Masters Guide Service, 196–97
Salmon River, 187
Salmon River Cafe, 76
Saltworks, The, 138
Samaritan North Lincoln Hospital, 247
Samaritan Pacific Communities
   Hospital, 247
Samuel H. Boardman State Scenic
   Corridor, 178–79
Sandcastle Contest, 151
sand dunes, 158
Sand Dunes Frontier and Theme Park, 143
Sand Lake, 185
Sandland Adventures, 143, 180
Sandpines Golf Course, 211–12
Sandy's Kitchen and Gift Shop, 103–4
Santa Fe Tacqueria, 224
Saturday Market, 223
Saunders Lake, 190–91
Sawdust Theatre, 89
Schooners Cove Inn, 27–28
Scribbles, 97
Sea Dreamer Inn Bed and Breakfast, 61
Sea Lion Caves, 115, 142
Seal Rock State Recreation Site, 170
"Sea of Lights," 153

Sea Rose—A Bed and Breakfast, 45
Seaside. *See also* North Coast
    area overview, 4
    attractions, 107
    bed-and-breakfast inns, 43–44
    golf, 208
    history, 17
    hotels and motels, 25–27
    kidstuff, 138
    map, xi
    nightlife, 85
    relocation, 228
    restaurants, 73–74
    shopping, 92
Seaside Antique Mall, 92
Seaside Aquarium, 138
Seaside Carousel Mall, 92
Seaside Chocolate Festival and Bridal
  Show, 148
Seaside Factory Outlet Center, 92
Seaside Golf Course, 208
Seaside Historical Museum, 107
Seaside School District, 238–39
Seaside Signal, The, 257
Seaside Spa & Wellness Center, 249
Sea Sprite, The, 28
Sea Star Bistro, 82
Sea Towne Books, 98
Sea Towne Courtyards, 98
Second Street Gallery, 129
Senior Centers, 251
sentries, bonfire of the, 18
Seven Devils State Recreation Site, 175
Shamrock Lodgettes Resort and Spa, 34
Shepherd Gallery, 124
Sheri's at Sea Towne, 98
shopping, 91–104
    Astoria, 91–92
    Bandon, 100–102
    Brookings, 102–4
    Cannon Beach, 92–94
    Central Coast, 96–99
    Coos Bay, 100
    Gleneden Beach, 97
    Gold Beach, 102
    Lincoln City, 96–97
    Manzanita, 94–95
    Newport, 97–98
    North Coast, 91–95
    Old Town Florence, 99
    Pacific City, 95
    Port Orford, 102
    Seaside, 92
    South Coast, 100–104

Tillamook, 95
    Yachats, 98–99
shore, rocky, 158–59, 162–63
Shore Acres State Park, 174
Short Sands Beach, 205–6
shuttle service, 23. *See also* transportation
Signature Imports, 92
Siletz Bay, 190, 193, 194
Siletz Bay Park, 158
Siletz River, 190
Siletz tribe, 12
Siltcoos Lake, 188
Siltcoos Lake Trail, 183
Siskiyou National Forest, 225
Sitka Center for Art and Ecology, 131–32
Siuslaw Bay, 194
Siuslaw News, The, 259
Siuslaw Pioneer Museum, 115
Siuslaw River, 190
Siuslaw School District, 241
Siuslaw tribe, 12–13
Sixes River, 192
Smelt Sands State Recreation Area, 171
Smith Lake (Clatsop County), 185
Smith Lake (Tillamook County), 185
Soaring Crane Gallery, 125
Sokol Blosser Winery, 219
Solace By the Sea Bed and Breakfast, 48
South Beach
    bed-and-breakfast inns, 48–49
    camping, 65
South Beach State Park, 65, 170, 206
South Coast. *See also specific towns*
    airports, 24
    art galleries, 128–30
    attractions, 118–19
    bed-and-breakfast inns, 55–59, 61
    boat and equipment rental, 196
    camping, 68–71
    child care referral services, 243
    clinics, 249
    coastal parks, 174–79
    education and childcare, 242–43
    fishing, 190–92
    golf, 212–13
    health care, 248–49
    hospitals, 248–49
    hotels and motels, 35–39
    kidstuff, 143–46
    map, ix
    newspapers, 259–61
    nightlife, 87–90
    ocean charter services and river
      outfitters, 198

public schools, 242–43
real estate, 236
relocation, 231–32
restaurants, 80–83
shopping, 100–104
theater, 133–34
South County Surf, 166
Southeast District (Portland), 223
Southern Coos Hospital and Health
Center, 249
South Slough Estuarine Preserve, 203
South Slough Estuary Interpretive
Center, 118
South Slough National Estuarine
Reserve, 144–45, 158
Southwestern Oregon Community
College, 244
Spicy Bambu, 94
Spinreel Dunebuggy Rentals, Inc., 180
Spirit Mountain Casino, 113
Spirit of Oregon, 129
Sporthaven Marina, 196
sports and activities, 180–206
    ATV and dune buggy rentals and
        tours, 180
    bicycling, 180–83
    boat and equipment rental, 195–96
    canoeing and kayaking, 183
    clamming, 192–94
    crabbing, 194–95
    fishing, 183–92
    hiking, 198–204
    horseback riding, 204
    jet boat tours, 204
    ocean charter services and river
        outfitters, 196–98
    surfing, 204–6
sports radio, 263
Spring Lake, 185
Spring Whale Watch Week, 149
St. Bernard's Bed and Breakfast, 44
Stand, The, 73
Steidel's Art/S. Clay's Designs, 123
Stephanie Inn, The, 28
Stonefield Beach State Recreation Site, 172
Stormy Weather Arts Festival, 152
streams. See bays, rivers, and streams
Strike Zone Marine & Charters, 198
Stuff for Guys, 104
Sumin's, 81
Summer House Bed and Breakfast, 43–44
Sunset Bay Golf Course, 212–13
Sunset Bay State Park, 68–69, 174
Sunset Lake, 185

Sunset Oceanfront Accommodations, 37
surfing, 204–6. See also sports and
    activities
Sutton Creek, 67
Sutton Lake, 188
Suzanne Elise Assisted Living, 252
Sweet Creek Falls, 202
Sweet Delights, 97
Sylvia Beach Hotel, 31–32, 97

T
Table Rock Motel, 36
Table Rock Vacation Suites, 36–37
Takenitch Lake, 188
talk radio, 263
Tapeo, 224
Tea and Tomes, 97
television, 262. See also media
Tenmile Creek, 66
Tenmile Lakes (North and South), 191
theater, 132–34. See also arts
Theater West, 133
This Olde House, 55–56
Threads That Bind, 100
Three Village Gallery, 124
Thrifty Threads Consignment Shop, 99
Tidal Raves, 77
Tidewaters, 85–86
Tide Wind Sportfishing, 198
Tillamook. See also North Coast
    area overview, 5–6
    attractions, 107–8
    camping, 64
    golf, 208–9
    kidstuff, 139
    map, xiii
    relocation, 229–30
    shopping, 95
Tillamook Air Museum, 108
Tillamook Area Agency on Aging, 251
Tillamook Bay, 193, 194
Tillamook Bay Community College,
    132–33, 243–44
Tillamook Cheese Factory, 108, 139
Tillamook County General Hospital, 246
Tillamook County General Hospital
    Physicians, 247
Tillamook County Rodeo, 150
Tillamook Pioneer Museum, 108
Tillamook Rock Lighthouse, 110
Tillamook School District, 239
Tillamook tribe, 12
Timeworn Treasures, 102
Toledo Clinic, 248

Toledo golf, 211
Toledo Summer Festival, 151
Tolovana Beach State Recreation Site, 164
Tolovana Inn, 28
Tolovana Park hotel, 28
Tom McCall Waterfront Park, 222
Touchstone Gallery, 128
Toujours Boutique, 97
Town Center Carousel, 138
Tradewinds Charters, 197
transportation, 20–24
Traveler's Cove, 79–80
Treasures by the Bay, 99
Triad Gallery, 127
Tri-Met transit, 223
Tsunami Ceramics, 97
Tualatin Estate Vineyards, 219
Tu Tu' Tun Lodge, 38–39

U

Umpqua Discover Center Museum, 118
Umpqua Lighthouse State Park, 68,
    173–74
Umpqua Post, The, 259
Umpqua River, 192
Umpqua River Lighthouse, 111
Umpqua Valley wineries, 214, 220–21. *See
    also* Rogue Valley wineries; Willamette
    Valley wineries
Under the Big Top Toys, 92
Uppertown Firefighters Museum,
    106–7, 137
U.S. Highway 30, 20–21
U.S. Highway 101, 20
U.S. Highway 199, 21–22

V

vacation rentals, 60. *See also* bed-and-
    breakfast inns; hotels and motels
Valley Bronze of Oregon, Inc., 123–24
Valley View Winery, 221–22
Viking's Cottages and Condos, The, 32
visitor centers, 116–17

W

Waldport. *See also* Central Coast
    area overview, 7
    attractions, 115
    camping, 66
    golf, 211
    hotels and motels, 32
    restaurants, 78
Waldport Clinic, 248

Wanda's, 89
Warm Coverings, 97
Warrenton, 228. *See also* North Coast
Warrenton/Hammond School
    District, 238
Washington Park, 224
Waves Motel, The, 27
Wax Works—A Living Museum, The, 142
Wedderburn restaurant, 83
Weisinger's of Ashland, 222
Wellness Massage Center, 250
West Coast Game Park Safari, 145–46
Western World, 260
Westin Salishan, 30–31, 76, 77
Westlight Gallery, 127
Westwind Gallery, 125
Wet Dog Cafe, The, 85
whale, exploding, 19
Whale's Tale, 78
Wheeler hotel, 29
Wheeler Marina, 195
Wheelhouse Restaurant & Crow's Nest
    Lounge, 82
White Bird Gallery, 124
Wild River Pizza, 83
Wildwood, 224
Willamette Valley Chateau Benoit, 96
Willamette Valley wineries, 214, 215–19.
    See also Rogue Valley wineries;
    Umpqua Valley wineries
William M. Tugman State Park, 68, 174
Wilson River, 187
Winchester Bay, 192, 194, 195, 231. *See
    also* Central Coast
Winchester Bay Market, 196
Windermere/Manzanita, 234
Windermere on the Beach Motel, 37
Windjammer Windborne & Nautical
    Gifts, 104
Windridge Gallery, 124
Wine Haus, The, 92
winery tours, 214–22
Winter River Books, 102
Winter Whale Watch Week, 147
Woahink Lake, 188
Wooden Duck, 97
Wood Gallery, Inc., 127
Wool Company, The, 119
Words and Pictures, 104, 130
World, The, 259
World Forestry Center, 223
worship, 254–55
writing events/retreats, 130–32. *See also* arts

Y

Yachats. *See also* Central Coast
  area overview, 7
  attractions, 115
  bed-and-breakfast inns, 49–51
  hotels and motels, 32–35
  nightlife, 87
  restaurants, 78–79
  shopping, 98–99
Yachats Arts & Crafts Fair, 149
Yachats Commons, 87
Yachats Crab and Chowder House, 79
Yachats Inn, 34
Yachats Leroy's Blue Whale, 79
Yachats Ocean Road State Natural
  Site, 172
Yachats Original Arts and Crafts
  Fair, 134–35

Yachats State Recreation Area, 171
Yakonan tribe, 12–13
Yankee Clipper, 79
Yaquina Art Center, 97, 127
Yaquina Bay, 158, 190, 194
Yaquina Bay Lighthouse and
  Museum, 111
Yaquina Bay State Recreation Site,
  169–70
Yaquina Head Lighthouse, Interpretive
  Center, and Tidal Basin, 110–11,
  139–41, 169
Yaquina Head Outstanding Natural Area,
  162, 169–70

Z
Ziggurat, 34–35

About the Authors

Lizann Dunegan

Lizann Dunegan has spent the last 25 years living in and exploring Oregon, and the Oregon Coast is one of her favorite destinations. She grew up on a cattle ranch in Central Oregon—where she developed her love of the Oregon outdoors. In 1983, she moved to Portland to attend Portland State University. Since that time, Lizann has worked as a freelance writer and photographer and has published several outdoor and travel guidebooks about Oregon including: *Canine Oregon, Trail Running Oregon, Road Biking Oregon, Hiking Oregon, Mountain Biking Oregon,* and *Hiking the Oregon Coast.*

When Lizann isn't busy writing, she spends almost all of her free time in the outdoors hiking, camping, mountain biking, trail running, and cross-country skiing. She is often accompanied by her two fun-loving Border Collies, Levi and Sage, and her equally energetic and enthusiastic partner, Ken Skeen. Lizann currently resides in Portland and spends many weekends exploring the beaches, forests, and communities on the Oregon Coast.

Rachel Dresbeck

Rachel Dresbeck grew up in Bellingham, Washington, and spent most family vacations wandering the coasts of Oregon and northern California. During graduate school at the University of Oregon she moved to Portland, where she taught writing and literature at Portland Community College and wrote cultural commentary for a variety of publications. Rachel is also the coauthor of *Insiders' Guide to Portland.* Currently a writer and editor, Rachel Dresbeck lives with her husband and daughters in Portland.

Dave Johnson

Dave Johnson is a native Oregonian who has worked as a journalist and freelance writer for more than 30 years at newspapers and magazines in the Pacific Northwest. An avid traveler and outdoor adventurer, he is also the coauthor of the *Insiders' Guide to Portland.*

He served two years as the director/curator of the Bandon Historical Society Museum and one year as an instructor at the Oregon State School for the Blind. His interests included hiking, fishing, cycling, visiting historic sites, and collecting old postcards. He is married to poet Josephine Bridges and lives in a 1912 bungalow in the historic Brooklyn neighborhood of Southeast Portland.